Stations on the Journey of Inquiry

ALSO BY DAVID B. BURRELL

Books:

Analogy and Philosophical Language (1973)
Exercises in Religious Understanding (1974)
Aquinas: God and Action (1979)
Knowing the Unknowable God: Ibn-Sina, Maimonides, Aquinas (1986)
Freedom and Creation in Three Traditions (1993)
Original Peace: Restoring God's Creation (with Elena Malits) (1997)
Friendship and Ways to Truth (2000)
Faith and Freedom: An Interfaith Perspective (2004)
Deconstructing Theodicy: A Philosophical Commentary on Job (2008)
When Faith and Reason Meet: The Legacy of John Zahm, CSC (2009)
Learning to Trust in Freedom: Signs from Jewish, Christian, and Muslim Traditions (2010)
Towards a Jewish-Christian-Muslim Theology (2011)
Questing for Understanding: Persons, Places, Passions (2012)

Editions:

Verbum: Word and Idea in Aquinas, by Bernard J. Lonergan (1967)
Evangelization in the American Context (with Franzita Kane) (1977)
God and Creation: An Ecumenical Symposium (with Bernard McGinn) (1990)
Voices from Jerusalem: Jews and Christians Reflect on the Holy Land (with Yehezkel Landau) (1991)
The Muslim World, special issue of *Islamic Philosophy* 94 (January 2004)
Creation and the God of Abraham (with Carlo Cogliati, Janet M. Soskice, and William R. Stoeger) (2010)

Translations:

The Ninety-Nine Beautiful Names of God (al-Maqsad al-asnā fī sharh asmā' Allāh al-husnā), by Al-Ghazali (with Nazih Daher) (1992)
Three Messengers for One God, by Roger Arnaldez (with Mary Louise Gudé and Gerald Schlabach) (1998)
Faith in Divine Unity and Trust in Divine Providence (Kitāb al-Tawhīd wa'l-Tawakkul), by Al-Ghazali. Translation of Book XXXV of *The Revival of the Religious Sciences (Ihyā' 'ulūm al-dīn)* (2001)
Al-Ghazali, Averroes and the Interpretation of the Qur'an: Common Sense and Philosophy in Islam, by Avital Wohlman (2009)

Stations on the Journey of Inquiry

Formative Writings of David B. Burrell, 1962–72

Edited by
Mary Budde Ragan

Foreword by
John Milbank

Introduction by
Stanley Hauerwas

Critical Response by
Stephen Mulhall

 CASCADE *Books* · Eugene, Oregon

STATIONS ON THE JOURNEY OF INQUIRY
Formative Writings of David B. Burrell, 1962–72

Copyright © 2017 David B. Burrell. All rights reserved. Except for brief quotations in critical publications or reviews, no part of this book may be reproduced in any manner without prior written permission from the publisher. Write: Permissions, Wipf and Stock Publishers, 199 W. 8th Ave., Suite 3, Eugene, OR 97401.

Cascade Books
An Imprint of Wipf and Stock Publishers
199 W. 8th Ave., Suite 3
Eugene, OR 97401

www.wipfandstock.com

PAPERBACK ISBN: 978-1-4982-2176-4
HARDCOVER ISBN: 978-1-4982-2178-8
EBOOK ISBN: 978-1-4982-2177-1

Cataloguing-in-Publication data:

Names: Burrell, David B. | Ragan, Mary Budde, editor. | Hauerwas, Stanley, 1940–, introduction. | Milbank, John, foreword. | Mulhall, Stephen, critical response.

Title: Stations on the journey of inquiry : formative writings of David B. Burrell, 1962–72 / edited by Mary Budde Ragan ; foreword by John Milbank ; introduction by Stanley Hauerwas ; critical response by Stephen Mulhall.

Description: Eugene, OR : Cascade Books, 2017 | Includes bibliographical references and index.

Identifiers: ISBN 978-1-4982-2176-4 (paperback) | ISBN 978-1-4982-2178-8 (hardcover) | ISBN 978-1-4982-2177-1 (ebook)

Subjects: LCSH: Philosophical theology. | Analytic philosophy.

Classification: BT40 .B87 2017 (paperback) | BT40 .B87 (ebook)

Manufactured in the U.S.A. 03/22/17

The portrait on the book cover is reproduced with permission from Austin Zucchini-Fowler and is based upon an original photograph of David B. Burrell taken by Eileen Klee Sweeney in January 2014.

To a wise woman,
Nina Burrell Klee,
whose reception of others shows what this is all about

Knowing is knowing how to go on, or when to stop.

(Adapted from Wittgenstein)

Contents

Acknowledgments | ix
Editorial Note | xi
Aquinas Abbreviations | xiv
Foreword by John Milbank | xv
Preface by David B. Burrell | xxiii
Introduction by Stanley Hauerwas | xxvii
Critical Response by Stephen Mulhall | xxxiii

Chapter 1
Substance: A Performatory Account | 1

Chapter 2
Aristotle and "Future Contingencies": Another Interpretation | 26

Chapter 3
Entailment: "E" and Aristotle | 43

Chapter 4
How God Achieves His Ends according to Saint Thomas Aquinas | 60

Chapter 5
What the Dialogues Show about Inquiry | 75

Chapter 6
C. S. Peirce: Pragmatism as a Theory of Judgment | 96

Chapter 7
Classification, Mathematics, and Metaphysics: A Commentary on St. Thomas Aquinas's Exposition of Boethius's *On the Trinity* | 114

Chapter 8
How Complete Can Intelligibility Be? A Commentary on *Insight*: Chapter XIX | 136

Chapter 9
Truth and Historicity: Certitude and Judgment | 142

Chapter 10
**Religious Language and the Logic of Analogy:
Apropos of McInerny's Book and Ross's Review | 154**

Chapter 11
Beyond a Theory of Analogy | 170

Chapter 12
**Reading *The Confessions* of Augustine:
An Exercise in Theological Understanding | 179**

Chapter 13
Religious Life and Understanding | 203

Bibliography | 225
Index | 235

Acknowledgments

ALL OF BURRELL'S ESSAYS in this collection have been published elsewhere. The original versions have been preserved with only minor alterations in spelling (e.g., American for British) and punctuation (e.g., double quotation marks in place of single) according to publication guidelines. Of note, revisions of abbreviations for Aquinas's works have been made for the sake of consistency and are detailed below. We are grateful to the following publishers for granting permission to reproduce these works here. Publication details follow.

"Substance: A Performatory Account." *Philosophical Studies* (Maynooth) 21 (1972) 137–60. Reprinted in *Substances and Things: Aristotle's Doctrine of Physical Substance in Recent Essays*, edited by M. L. O'Hara, 224–49. Washington, DC: University Press of America, 1982.

"Aristotle and 'Future Contingencies': Another Interpretation." *Philosophical Studies* (Maynooth) 13 (1964) 37–52.

"Entailment: 'E' and Aristotle." *Logique et Analyse* 7 (1964) 111–29.

"What the Dialogues Show about Inquiry." *Philosophical Forum* 3 (1972) 104–25.

"C. S. Peirce: Pragmatism as a Theory of Judgment." *International Philosophical Quarterly* 5 (1965) 521–40.

"Classification, Mathematics, and Metaphysics: A Commentary on St. Thomas Aquinas's Exposition of Boethius's *On the Trinity*." *Modern Schoolman* 44 (1966) 13–34.

"How Complete Can Intelligibility Be? A Commentary on *Insight*: Chapter XIX." *Proceedings of American Catholic Philosophical Association* 41 (1967) 250–53.

"Truth and Historicity: Certitude and Judgment." *Proceedings of American Catholic Philosophical Association* 43 (1969) 44–55.

"Religious Language and the Logic of Analogy: Apropos of McInerny's Book and Ross' Review." *International Philosophical Quarterly* 2 (1962) 643–58.

"Beyond a Theory of Analogy." *Proceedings of American Catholic Philosophical Association* 46 (1972) 114–22.

"Reading *The Confessions* of Augustine: An Exercise in Theological Understanding." *Journal of Religion* 50 (1970) 327–51. Reprinted in *Exercises in Religious Understanding: Jung, Anselm, Aquinas, Augustine, Kierkegaard*, 11–41. Notre Dame: University of Notre Dame Press, 1974.

"Religious Life and Understanding." *Review of Metaphysics* 22 (1969) 676–99.
Copyright to the following article was not renewed during its 28th year, thereby falling into the public domain. It appears here under the doctrine of fair use.
"How God Achieves His Ends according to Saint Thomas Aquinas." *Sciences ecclésiastiques* 14 (1962) 461–75.

Editorial Note

FOR AQUINAS, WE HAVE adopted Burrell's particular style of abbreviation, which he refined during the past fifty years in an effort to simplify references for other Thomists. Special attention has been given to this suggested format found in his prefaces and notes for *Aquinas: God and Action* (1979) and *Faith and Freedom* (2004).[1] Care has been taken to trace this development through his other books as well as his numerous articles, especially those contained in this volume.

References to Aquinas's works are as follows. The *Summa Theologiae* is abbreviated using Arabic numerals while retaining the title: *ST* 1.13.1.4, which means Part I, question 13, article 1, response to fourth query. Translations after 1964 are from the Blackfriars edition; those prior are from the Leonine edition. *Summa Contra Gentiles* is abbreviated: *CG* 2.24.3, indicating Part II, chapter 24, paragraph 3. References to *Quaestiones Disputatae* follow this style of reference as well; for example, *de Ver.* 3.2.6 means question 3, article 2, response to objection 6. Note these abbreviations: *de Pot.*, *de Ver.*, *de Subst Sep.*, *de Malo*, and so forth. The Latin titles of Aquinas's philosophical commentaries follow Burrell's preferred translation, while abbreviations refer to Marietti editions unless otherwise noted—for example, *In 3 Meta.* 4.385 indicates book 3, chapter [*lectio*] 4, paragraph 385. For Aquinas's commentary on Lombard, *Scriptum super Libros Sententiarum*, book, distinction, question, article, solution, reply is referenced as *In 3 Sent.* 25.2.3.2.3.

Regarding Aristotle and Plato: Stephanus pagination is used to reference works of Plato, also using full titles. References to Aristotle's works give the Bekker annotation with full titles. Roman numerals indicate the appropriate book with Arabic numerals and letters for all else. For the most part, in-text citations are the preferred mode.

---

1. See Burrell, *Aquinas: God and Action*, xiv–xv, as well as *Faith and Freedom*, ix–xi.

For Augustine, references to the *Confessions* are noted in books and chapters, hence 1.13 indicates book I, chapter 13. Again, in-text citations are employed for ease of reading.

For the works of Albertus Magnus, references include full title yet follow a similar style of abbreviation for *librum* (if relevant), *tractus*, and *capitulus* (if relevant) using Arabic numbers—for example, *Commentarium in Priorum Analyticorum* 4.6.

All other abbreviations and referencing changes, for Peirce especially, are explained in the notes of the particular essay.

Every effort was made to include Burrell's own corrections penciled within the margins on the original copies of these articles. Changes in phrasing of key passages may be of interest and show Burrell's own reflection on his way of proceeding. While there are few such emendations, they are included as editorial remarks within the notes. For any remaining inadequacies and oversights in editing, I take full responsibility.

Lastly, I am profoundly grateful to David Burrell for inviting me to seek truth along with him through this endeavor. This journey of editing his early works has been a spiritual exercise. For studying his text and footnotes, tracking down his sources, wrestling with his preferred manner of referencing Aquinas, trying to better understand *his own* understanding, and increasing my awareness of what he is *doing* more than what he is *saying* has proven to be an immensely formative *discipline* for me. To engage Burrell's writing exacts more from the reader than merely a cognitive approach, an intellectual foray, a linguistic or logical analysis. Rather, I have found that to grasp what Burrell is up to, we must invest our entire selves in the activity of reading closely, risking a complete turnabout, not merely in our interpretation of Aristotle or Plato or Augustine or Aquinas or Wittgenstein or Lonergan, but in our way of living. These writings remind us over and over again that metaphysics is neither passé nor reserved for the erudite, but is inescapable for each of us. Through these stations of inquiry, Burrell shows us how this is best realized within our community and tradition.

I deeply appreciate the unwavering support and encouragement of Stanley Hauerwas, who not only directed me to Cascade Books but has followed this project through to fruition. His longstanding friendship and Wittgensteinian kinship with Burrell are evident in his insightful introduction. The genius of Stephen Mulhall, as evident in his 2014 Stanton Lectures as well as his lecture for the 2012 Aquinas Colloquium at Blackfriars Hall, has revived our interest in Burrell's early work on analogy and inquiry. Many thanks to him for his incisive and thought-provoking critical response to these formative writings. Only someone of John Milbank's intellectual breadth and depth could pen the foreword to this collection of

Burrell's early philosophical theology. We are indebted to him for the care he has taken to orient the reader to the rigorous essays that follow.

During graduate studies, my professor, Ted Vial, read several of Burrell's writings with me and encouraged my undertaking of this project. For the gift of his time, I am most grateful. Thanks must also be extended to Carole Baker for the grace with which she responded to my numerous requests as well as her invaluable feedback along the way.

Projects such as this one bring together individuals whose paths might never have crossed otherwise but whose encounter brings forth remarkable results—as we see displayed in the cover portrait of David Burrell created by Denver artist Austin Zucchini-Fowler in collaboration with South Bend photographer Eileen Klee Sweeney. For their joint interpretation, we are thankful.

I am grateful to the editors and staff at Cascade Books for welcoming the publication of these essays. Charlie Collier, Jim Tedrick, Christian Admondson, Matthew Wimer, Ian Creeger, Jacob Martin, and Shannon Carter have been more than patient with my questions as well as exceedingly generous with their time. Their attention to detail and respect for the development of this project has surpassed all expectations.

Thank you to the assistant rectress of Farley Hall in 1986, Michele Thomas (Wornhoff), whose recommendation that I take one of her Uncle David's classes at Notre Dame led to a long-lasting friendship across the years and miles. Much gratitude to Michele's mother and David's sister, Nina Burrell Klee, to whom this collection has been dedicated, whose clarity of purpose and quiet strength have sustained us all.

As this project has been three years in the making, I wish to acknowledge my husband, Dave, and my four children, Emily, Kate, Sarah, and Ben, whose collective perseverance and creativity helped me find the necessary time and space in which to work and whose loving presence helps me carry on.

M. B. R.
Denver, Colorado

Aquinas Abbreviations

CG	*Summa Contra Gentiles*
de An.	*Quaestiones Disputatae de Anima*
de Ente	*de Ente et Essentia*
de Malo	*Quaestiones Disputatae de Malo*
de Pot.	*Quaestiones Disputatae de Potentia*
de Spir Creat.	*Quaestiones Disputatae de Spiritualibus Creaturis*
de Subst Sep.	*Tractatus de Substantiis Separatis*
de Ver.	*Quaestiones Disputatae de Veritate*
In de An.	*In Aristotelis Librum de Anima Commentarium*
In de Caelo	*In Aristotelis Libros de Caelo et Mundo Expositio*
In de Causis	*In Librum de Causis Expositio*
In de Divin Nom.	*In Librum Beati Dionysii de Divinis Nominibus Expositio*
In de Gen et Corr.	*In Aristotelis Libros de Generatione et Corruptione Expositio*
In de Meteor.	*In Aristotelis Libros Meteorologicorum Expositio*
In de Sensu.	*In Aristotelis Libros de Sensu et Sensato Commentarium*
In de Trin.	*Expositio super Librum Boethii de Trinitate*
In Ethic.	*In decem Libros Ethicorum Aristotelis ad Nicomachum Expositio*
In Meta.	*In duodecim Libros Metaphysicorum Aristotelis Expositio*
In Peri Herm.	*In Aristotelis Libros Peri Hermeneias Expositio*
In Phys.	*In octo Libros Physicorum Aristotelis Expositio*
In Post Anal.	*In Aristotelis Libros Posteriorum Analyticorum Expositio*
In Sent.	*Scriptum super Libros Sententiarum*
Quodl.	*Quaestiones Quodlibetales*
ST	*Summa Theologiae*

Foreword

IT IS AN IMMENSE pleasure and honor for me to be able to write this foreword to a collection of the early writings of David Burrell. I first encountered his work when I read *Aquinas: God and Action* while a student at theological college, on the double recommendation of Donald MacKinnon and Rowan Williams. I was immediately captivated by two arguments of the book. First, that action was not primarily about change and transformation (against the process theologians); and second, that analogy in Aquinas had much to do with his understanding of the inherently open, indeterminate though not anarchic character of the words that we use. The book also led me for the first time into complex issues of the relationship between Thomism and post-Kantian, so-called "transcendental" modes of philosophical inquiry.

Later I had the immense good fortune to get to know David and to realize that he was a man who lived up to all the rigors and charitable demands of his calling to the religious life. What struck me at first was his remarkable generosity toward younger scholars and patience even with their critiques of his own approach, however callow those might be in some respects. Later I came to see that he was also a person of heroic stature and almost superhuman energy, whose innovative work as a thinker was only one part of a life also devoted to mission, pedagogy, sojourns in difficult places, and demanding religious dialogue. Later still in retrospect I am beginning to understand how the thought and practice are all of one piece.

As a thinker David Burrell occupies a very significant place among the names of those Anglo-Saxon thinkers who have contributed to the rescue of Thomas Aquinas from neoscholastic misunderstandings—a work that now, lamentably, threatens to be undone by writers whose engagement with the analytic legacy is much more superficial than his own. His contribution can be thought of as typically Anglo-Saxon and even American insofar as it has been focused both on linguistic usage and on practical, existential commitment as fundamental even for theoretical thought. More specifically, one can think of his work as the most decisive in taking aspects of so-called "transcendental Thomism" in a linguistic direction, heavily influenced by Wittgenstein, but also somewhat by Peirce.

However, to think of Burrell as operating as a philosopher mainly within a "transcendental" space would be highly misleading. Rather, as in the case of the key transcendental Thomist with whom he initially engaged, Bernard Lonergan, his thought seeks to work through all the problems of contrast between pre-Kantian metaphysical approaches and so-called "post-critical" ones which either disallow metaphysics or pursue it in a much more chastened manner.

The question that most arises here is whether it is valid for any Christian thought that wishes to remain metaphysical to commence with a modern "subjective" starting point—that is, to begin philosophy with a reflexive examination of how it is that we know and the genuine possibilities of understanding. Quite apart from any theological concern here, one can also wonder both whether any such inquiry can advance beyond skepticism to some sort of ontologically realist affirmation, and whether a critique of one's own cognitive perspective is seriously viable, given that we have none other from which to obtain any vantage.

But Burrell was fully aware of these difficulties and just for this reason arguably did not remain with a purely transcendental inquiry, since in the end he speaks in emphatically metaphysical tones of God, Being and the fundamental modes that being takes, after Aristotle. The question in his case is rather one of whether one can genuinely advance to the objectively realist from a subjective starting point, focused initially on the transcendental forms that our understanding is bound to observe, if it is to remain coherent and verifiable.

To approach this question, perhaps the most important thing to be said is that the post-Socratic approach to philosophy, with which Christian thought was always primarily engaged, already included a "half-turn" to the subject. Pre-Socratic thought had been largely focused on the physical or abstractions from the physical. But with Socrates philosophy starts to be also a reflexive inquiry about human knowledge, the goals of human life, and the nature of human existence in terms of love, artistry, and citizenship. But it is only a half-turn because Plato's thinking is tensionally poised between the primacy of the human and the primacy of the cosmos.

And one might claim that just this "poise" remains somewhat true of Lonergan and much more so of Burrell. The latter in this volume is not, I think, saying (as Lonergan might be taken to say) that the notion of substance is really a matter of how we are to classify the world, but rather that how we do so gives important clues to the structure of reality. Thus in his essay on substance in Aristotle he argues that substance is more "like a statement" than it is like a name—in other words like a complex sentential judgment rather than the sticking on of a label. It is like a statement because substance in Aristotle's usage hovers between common "essence," on the one hand, and the "holding together" that makes a particular thing a thing at all, on the other. Thus when we state something we *judge* that a certain essential condition pertains in a particular instance. Neither the perception of an essence nor the process of predication is like a "thing" in the ordinary sense. But in realizing that our cognitive access to things lies via this meta-thingly detour, both Aristotle and Burrell are also saying that the meta-thingly lies out there in the world, besides being in the structure of our understanding. It is, as Burrell realizes, the analogy *between* the composition of being and the composition of thought/discourse that fascinates Aristotle. This pre-Kantian aspect is natural to the latter because he assumes, without question, that reality has a divinely orientated, intelligible structure. And once the biblically derived faiths had embraced a doctrine of creation, then this notion of a meaningful reality is much reinforced. Thus for Aquinas there is indeed a parallel between the order of being and the order of knowing, just because the world is the product of the divine mind.

For this reason, to interpose a "transcendental" approach is not wholly invalid. As Stanislas Breton has noted, there is for Aquinas a homology between the way the mind reaches a judgment—something not wholly unlike Kant's "transcendental deduction"—and his neoplatonized understanding of the emanative generation of Aristotle's categories in a series. So one might say that belief that the world is the work of divine intelligence justifies commencing one's philosophy *either* with being *or* with understanding. Or perhaps it somehow requires both at once, in the way that the Platonic dialogues try to sustain.

And perhaps this "both at once" is really pursued by the early Burrell if one thinks of his focus on "judgment" as being much more Newmanesque than it is Kantian (whereas with Lonergan the situation is possibly more ambiguous). For Kant (at least before the *Opus Postumum*), judgment only regards an ineradicable aesthetic illusion, or the "as if" of equally unavoidable teleological attribution to nature. But for Burrell in these essays, in violation of any Kantian "limits of pure reason," the exercise of judgment is a valid portal to the metaphysical. Like Lonergan, he deploys the transcendental approach against the tendency of neoscholasticism to think in a thoroughly modern way, at once positivist and rationalist, such that God and spiritual realities are thought of as being much like other "things" and reality is held to be deducible from rational first principles. Instead, for Burrell (and essentially in keeping with Aquinas if one agrees with

Olivier Boulnois's sophisticated and scholarly reading of his understanding of metaphysics) to think metaphysically is to engage in a kind of cautious conjecture about the non-material, formal dimension to finite things suggested by the resonance between them and the structures of our thought/language, and about the reality of spiritual form and mind existing outside matter, space, and time altogether.

The distance here from Kant and from any pure transcendentalism is given not just by this manifest transgression of Kantian strictures but also by Burrell's insistence (perhaps departing from Lonergan's dynamized apriorism and refusal of any notion of knowledge as vision) that the act of assertion or of affirmation by which a substance as essence is ascribed to *this* substance as a thing always exceeds any transcendentalist application of pre-given cognitive categories to clearly manifest empirical evidence. It rather involves an unpredictable exercise of something like *phronesis*, existential commitment, adjustment of spiritual attitude—and all this through the application of language which has been both corporeally and socially formed. Here one can say that while the "linguistification" of transcendental Thomism may arguably (as with Wittgenstein) still too much treat language as an epistemological framework when it is also always already ontological engagement, nevertheless a linguistic and an affective, corporeal, and collective *a priori* has become a very impure sort of *a priori* indeed. To inflect the *a priori* in this way is not at all to take it yet further in the direction of the sheerly formal and away from things, but rather to half-concede that, while thinking and categorial being are by no means "things" in the usual sense, they are also not completely *outside* any sense of *res* which, for Aquinas, as also with the term "something" (*aliquid*), was a fully fledged transcendental. If, for the scholastics, as for Burrell, not just thought but all other real things always fall under being, the one, goodness, truth, beauty, thing, and something, then the division between the formal and the substantive has been somewhat violated—as one would expect if the world in its aspects of both existing and thinking and in both its content and its modes is the work of one *simple* God, in whom these realities coincide. An emphasis on divine simplicity runs through all of Burrell's *oeuvre* and allows him to explode many impertinent rationalist questions about future contingencies, etc. as evidenced in this volume.

One can see this positive violation silently at work in two respects in these essays. First, if theoretical judgment is mostly imprescriptible, then, while substantive essence and substantive instance, or sense and reference, etc. are indeed distinguished, they cannot be unproblematically divided. For if there is no algorithm or observational procedure that will infallibly tell us when "this thing" is an instance of x, then it follows that our sense of an essence is somewhat inflected by our judgment as to when it is instanced, while inversely our certainty as to the existence of a thing at all somewhat depends upon our being able to characterize it as to essential properties. By the same token Burrell cannot ascribe to the usual analytic view that truth is a function of propositions (which might be computerized) but must believe that it is rather a quality of soul as mind: in other words, truth for him, in contrast to any simplistic "anti-psychologism," requires a "truth-maker."

In support of this perspective on the tangled mutual implication between definition and assertion, recent scholarship shows clearly that Aquinas *rejected* any supposedly "Avicennian" version of the real distinction of *essentia* and *esse* that would see them as absolutely and atomically sundered even within finite realities. Along with Aquinas, one should surely refuse here any phantom of an essence existing only as essence (too extreme a realism about universals, combined with a priority of possibility over act) and equally any Gilsonian phantom of an essence of the purely existential, bereft of any characterizing features. And it seems to me that to insist like Burrell on the primacy of a pragmatic, assertoric judgment for our insight into reality is to be committed to the primacy of an undoable entanglement of sense with reference, for all the evident difference between them.

This is surely as unFregean as it is unKantian. Just because category and evidence, the *a priori* and the *aposteriori*, are from the outset mixed up with each other—in language, for our body, for social apprehension—committed subjective judgment is primary, as an act of "assent" for which there is no rulebook, after John Henry Newman. But this means that, short of skepticism, the presumption must run in favor of realism rather than either empiricism or idealism—or the view that in reality also, *logos* and forceful circumstance, or perhaps even thinking and life, are always bound up with each other, as both Spinoza and Leibniz claimed, though in over-rationalist ways.

This point leads to the second aspect of transgression of transcendental bounds in these essays. It has to do with the problem, mentioned at the outset, of the coherence of the notion of self-critique, of the very possibility of rounding critically upon an instrument—thought—whose usage one can never evade. Such critical rounding is only possible at all if one embraces a dualism—whether of cognitive category and empirical content, sense and reference, or material reality and language, because then critique amounts (perhaps rather banally) to a checking as to whether the protocols of such a presumed division are being observed. Similarly, this Kantian mode of critique can only establish a boundary around the finite circle of possible understanding, because a closed circularity is achieved in terms of the supposed mutual destiny of organizational category and empirical information for each other. If these two components of knowledge do not derive from ascertainably different sources (as an anti-foundationalist metacritique is bound to conclude) then no circle of epistemological finitude is after all inscribed and so no circular boundary remains to forbid trespass into the domain of the infinite, which may rather be always speculatively entered upon in any human symbolic performance. In sheerly immanentist terms, neither a polishing of the instrument of understanding is possible, nor a confinement of its legitimate operation within ascertainable bounds.

But I have indicated ways in which the early Burrell does not, or at least does not consistently ascribe to any of these dualities which might inscribe such a circle. Thus if he nonetheless claimed to be able to criticize the basic human instrument which is thought, then this is for quite another, basically Platonic and non-secular reason, which also uncouples critique from a banishing of any metaphysical speculation. Thought can indeed otherwise criticize itself by reference to its participation in a higher divine thought by which it is illumined. And just this Augustinian approach is fundamental to Burrell—witnessed by his essay on the *Confessions* in this collection. To judge rightly in criticizing one's own capacity for thought is not just for him an act of self-reflection, spinning in a mirrored, virtual circle—rather the circle is constantly broken into and reconstituted by illumination from above. Of course that is not received in an alien "ontologist" fashion; we must judge also for ourselves as to authentic divine prompting, but that we can so judge involves a belief in and a certain experience of the guidance of God. To be guided by God is, for Aquinas, to be guided by his *ideas* and though these are not of course in any way ontic things (since God who simply *is* his ideas, as *esse ipsum* is himself not a defined thing in the ordinary sense), nevertheless the ideas are infinitely more "thingy" and concrete than any of our thoughts or abstractions, or even our bodies. The point being that in God the contrast of thought and thing, and of form and content, is *absolutely overcome.*

Of course Burrell, like any other author, is not perfectly consistent. If judgment is an encounter with being as well as a self-reflection, then how can the exercise of analogy which all imprescriptible judgment must constantly involve—the way things are paradoxically like and yet unlike other things and supremely created things are like and unlike God—apply mainly to the usage of words *rather than to* the apprehension of things? Instead, as with Burrell's account of substance, one should surely rather say that there is an *ontological* parallel between the analogous order of knowing and the analogous order of being. In Burrell's more recent writings he appears to move much more in this direction and implicitly to agree with the conclusion of Alain de Libera that analogy in Aquinas (as evidenced by several terminological usages) is *at once* a matter of grammar, of logic, and of ontology. All these usages being themselves analogically related, in a way that Burrell's theoretical practice has always attested, and all of them giving priority to analogy of "attribution"—"one thing referred to another"—in the way insisted upon by Burrell in these early essays.

In summary we can say that the early Burrell half-took the modern path of transcendental philosophy in order rightly to question the still early modern rationalism and empiricism of the neoscholastic reading of Aquinas. But already the linguistic version of this which he espoused led him in the direction of also questioning the newer metaphysical dogmatism of epistemological primacy after Kant, which we now know (from the work of Honnefelder, de Muralt, etc.) has ultimate roots in Scotus and Ockham, thinkers of whom Burrell has always been extremely wary. At the other side of this second questioning lies a renewal of metaphysical speculation, but in a different mode that tends to blend the subjective and objective (which duality Burrell explicitly refuses) in terms of our negotiation of the real world through judgment. These essays show that early on Burrell had arrived at that other side, even if his later engagement in religious dialogue (that inescapably involves the contrast of world views) has now helped lead him in a more obviously metaphysical direction. Thus these essays remain current and relevant in the new twenty-first-century climate of "speculative realism" that is gradually displacing both phenomenology and analytic philosophy, and is happy to question the hitherto sacrosanct notion of Kant as an inescapable watershed, in turning once more from the primacy of the subject to the primacy of things. Yet the very mark of its realism rather than materialism or empiricism is the lingering question of the subject as a "very odd sort of thing" indeed and as a higher manifestation of the nature of the real. We are back then, as Alain Badiou suggests, to the Platonic issue of the place of thought, art, love, and the city within the cosmos. Burrell then and now would surely persuade us to see that all these aspects of the real can only be kept in play through a theological vision. Indeed, as he repeats after Lonergan, the intelligibility of the world—the rational, civic, erotic, and aesthetic character of the cosmos itself if you like—is the best argument for the existence of God.

John Milbank
University of Nottingham

Preface

To RETRACE THE PATH discovered during that time of my life (1962–72) offers an opportunity for profound thanksgiving for the panoply of mentors whose serendipitous confluence made all this possible: an undergraduate "great books" program at University of Notre Dame (1950–54), studying theology with Bernard Lonergan in Rome (1956–60), and philosophy with Wilfrid Sellars at Yale (1961–65). Yet as is often the case, it was a "Wittgenstein reading group" among young faculty at Notre Dame in the early sixties that made the signal difference. Lonergan's exploration of Aquinas assured my theology had to be "negative" while the enquiring challenge of Wittgenstein inspired my attempt to explicate Aquinas in linguistic terms, and a studied grasp of his actual context confirmed that approach—one utterly foreign to a modernist "Thomist" agenda.

At this point, an invitation to serve our religious community of Holy Cross in East Bengal introduced me to a benign face of Islam, which I was able to pursue with a genial Egyptian Dominican, Georges Anawati, in Cairo, who showed me how beholden Aquinas had been to Jewish and Islamic scholars, notably Maimonides and Avicenna.[1] So I began to translate some of them, notably al-Ghazali, to discover yet more "negative" theology.[2] But it was Wittgenstein who showed me how to parse the term "negative" to align within other Abraham traditions, as they helped one another to offer a coherent way to characterize the "creator of all." Such comparative work confirmed the theological perspective I had come to appreciate in Aquinas, with his careful attention to language, as displayed by the work of Olivier-Thomas Vénard, OP, currently working at the École Biblique in Jerusalem.[3]

1. By way of introduction, see my "Aquinas and Islamic and Jewish Thinkers," yet for a more rigorous treatment, see my *Knowing the Unknowable God* as well as *Freedom and Creation in Three Traditions*.

2. See these translations: *Ninety-Nine Beautiful Names of God* and *Faith in Divine Unity and Trust in Divine Providence*.

3. See my essay "A Postmodern Aquinas: The *oeuvre* of Olivier-Thomas Vénard, OP."

It is truly amazing how well he can explicate cognate moves in Aquinas, as I have also found with a Persian philosopher, Mulla Sadra.[4] No obvious connection, but intelligence moves in recognizably similar ways, the desire for understanding displays the way of truth.

As these essays hope to show, what would it be to proclaim the truth? Would it be to make an assertion and then to insist that it was true; or as one wag put it: to stamp one's foot? In fact, of course, any properly formed assertion, actually stated, intends what is the case. Grammar is inherently ethical, which is why lying—deliberately stating what is not the case—is inherently wrong. Yet we know that our acceptance of what another says is often conditioned by the moral probity or veracity of the speaker. So "proclaiming the truth" of one's faith is better done than said, as the Amish community in Pennsylvania demonstrated to America by forgiving their children's killer. Merely stating one's faith convictions cannot in fact count as proclamation. What counts is witness; and while the fact of dialogue may give telling witness in certain situations, like Israel/Palestine, the intellectual endeavor of dialogue can at best be a means of sorting out awkward from promising ways of stating what we believe. But this is hardly a deficiency; it is simply what any conversation tries to do. Authentic proclamation is quite another thing, as the gospels remind us again and again.

John Henry Newman, Bernard Lonergan, and Nicholas Lash can each be invoked as witnesses to this crucial distinction. Newman reminds us in *Grammar of Assent* how sinuous is the path to arriving at truth, and how delicate are the balancing judgments involved. Bernard Lonergan professedly acknowledges Newman's reflections when he parses Aquinas's insistence that truth can only be ascertained by way of judgment. And Nicholas Lash's recent *Theology for Pilgrims*[5] deftly exhibits the quality of dialectical reasoning which must attend reliable judgment. In the spirit of Wittgenstein, the witness Lash's writing gives to constructive and critical dialogue offers a healthy antidote to current TV confrontations which leave listeners to "make up their own minds." One can almost hear Wittgenstein query, "I know how to make up my bed, but how might I make up my mind?" So whatever effective proclamation might be, it cannot be had without probing discussion and the conceptual clarification that dialogue can bring. Reduced to forthright assertion or downright insistence, it can neither be authentic nor effective. So there is no substitute for attending to meanings, as we attempt to minimize infelicitous expression in matters "pertaining to

---

4. See in particular these two works of mine: "Autonomous Reason versus Tradition-Directed Inquiry: Mulla Sadra, Lonergan, MacIntyre, and Taylor" and "Mulla Sadra on 'Substantial Motion': A Clarification and a Comparison with Thomas Aquinas."

5. Lash, *Theology for Pilgrims*.

God and the things of God" (as Aquinas views theology). For that same thinker reminds us that our language *at best* can but "imperfectly signify God."[6]

Yet precisely because of this slack which inevitably attends human language in speaking of the divine, thinkers operating within a tradition have often found space to interact with another tradition, so as to enrich their own. For the past thirty years, I have probed the ways Thomas Aquinas utilized the Jewish scholar Moses Maimonides, as they both adapted the Islamic metaphysics of Avicenna, in an effort to offer a coherent account of free creation—a teaching shared among Jews, Christians, and Muslims in the face of formidable philosophical alternatives.[7] Recall Aquinas's simple recommendations: should an apparent contradiction emerge between faith and reason, first determine whether the relevant interpretation of scripture is a faithful one, then look to see whether the reasoning in question has been carried out responsibly. Points of conflict become points of contact in responsible encounters. Proclamations of truth must be displayed in a way of life. Indeed, ethical humility and intellectual humility are intimately related, as proclamation is to witness, as we have seen in the Amish example.

From Bangladesh, I put together these preliminary remarks, reflecting not only on this collection and the fine contributions of my friends Stan Hauerwas, John Milbank, and Stephen Mulhall, whose responses have helped me better understand myself and what I have been doing all these years, but also giving thanks for the past six years spent in East Africa and Southeast Asia, during which time I have focused on "inner work." Anyone who has been privileged to undertake this special kind of "work" knows how it can reveal what we have managed to keep hidden, with the resulting illumination energizing a new life. Through distance and darkness, we can celebrate new life. So the work continues, with immense gratitude to the Holy Cross Congregation which makes it all possible and to a local community who have received me gracefully. In the process a memoir (in the making for nearly a decade) saw the light of day. I shall close with this excerpt.

> I have been blessed from birth, it seems, by a propensity to love whatever I am engaged in. So whatever others may have called accomplishments were less goals sought than emergent passions forged by each engagement. In the narrative that follows I try to give due expression to this extraordinary gift. For such a propensity may be regarded as purely temperamental, which

---

6. *ST* 1.13.1.

7. See my most recent work, *Towards a Jewish-Christian-Muslim Theology*, as a culmination of this journey with my friends.

Aristotle called "natural virtue" since it requires little or no effort. In that vein, some have dubbed it "pathological optimism," but there is more to it: a gifted sense to discern what is worthy of love from what is not. Probably the fruit of a healthy family formation, it can hardly be that "natural" after all. Yet this discerning sense is quite spontaneous, reflected in persons and endeavors to which I have been attracted. So we can only be grateful for something eluding explanation yet which has never ceased to keep me from self-destructing. For as little as this can be accounted for, we might as well speak of a "guardian angel," as examples of caring cumulate, in circumstances small and great. I have learned from Arab friends—Christian or Muslim—to simply exclaim "al-hamd-il-Ullah!"—"may God be praised!"; what else is there to say?[8]

David B. Burrell
Dhaka, Bangladesh

---

8. See my *Questing for Understanding*, 2.

Introduction

How did he do it? Anyone reading these early essays by David Burrell cannot help thinking, how did he do it? How did he negotiate the wilderness of modern philosophy, the sterility of scholastic Thomism, and a rather limited introduction to theological reflection? Somehow Burrell managed to write these extraordinary articles in which he began to develop a position we are only now beginning to appreciate. "A position," of course, is a misleading description of Burrell's accomplishment as these articles make evident. As the title of this collection indicates, and as David has always emphasized, he does not so much represent a position, but rather his work is an ongoing inquiry best understood as a journey that he invites us to join.

My hunch is that David cannot remember writing some of these articles. My hunch is that when he was asked to read them for this collection he could not help thinking, "That is pretty good. I did not remember I was that philosophically sophisticated." To be sure some of these early articles have the feel of a young man showing to his elders that he has mastered the philosophical canon, but the humanity that is David Burrell always trumps his attempt to show what he can do philosophically.

When I have the occasion to read something I wrote at the beginning of my work I often think that I did not know I thought x or y so early or had expressed myself in a manner I thought only came later. As a result I often better understand why I am now saying what I am. I suspect Burrell has similar reactions when reading these essays. Hopefully readers of Burrell will in a similar fashion discover that reading this book helps them better understand Burrell and why his work is so important.

I do not want to keep anyone in suspense. Readers of Burrell or readers of me will not be surprised that I am not going to try to answer the question, how did he do it? What I will do is try to provide some of the background that made Burrell such an extraordinary reader of texts. I certainly will make no effort to discuss or synthesize the interconnection between these essays. I could not do that even if I wanted to do so. Burrell is a philosopher and I am not. Burrell has what I can only describe as a naturally metaphysical mind. My eyes tend to glaze over when metaphysics is mentioned. He is, moreover, very smart. I just get by. However, we have been friends for many years. I will try to draw on what I have learned from our friendship to make a few observations that may help readers understand why it is not easy to say that what he has done in these articles is so significant or how he did it.

Of course friendship will turn out to be the heart of the matter. Though Burrell says little in these early essays about friendship, there is a deep connection between what he does here and his later book *Friendship and Ways to Truth*. Readers of *Stations on the Journey of Inquiry* will see how *Friendship and Ways to Truth* was, so to speak, waiting to be written, given Burrell's way of working in these essays. For if, as Burrell contends in the chapter on "Truth and Historicity: Certitude and Judgment," that logic is governed by ethics then the epistemological significance of friendship is undeniable. Thus Burrell's observation in *Friendship and Ways to Truth*:

> Friendship is a gift we have learned to receive and be immediately grateful for, so we learn through it—and through its ostensible loss—that life itself is a gift, whose loss leaves a space as ample, or as restricted, as our capacity to have received it. Indeed *capacity* becomes the clue we shall be following: friendship, death, and grieving all effect capacities in us; it is out of those spaces that we learn how to live.[1]

Our friendship began in 1970. I had been hired to teach in the theology department at Notre Dame. Burrell was, of course, in the department of philosophy, but because all faculty offices were in the basement of the library it just happened our offices were close to one another. As a result we were often in conversation, and it was obvious we shared some common intellectual passions. In particular we had both been deeply influenced by Wittgenstein. Burrell made it possible for me to meet his colleagues in the philosophy department. I soon was attending the philosophical discussion group that would spend a year reading the *Investigations*.

I had been hired to teach at Notre Dame by Jim Burtchaell, CSC, who was the head of the department of theology. However, just as I was arriving, Burtchaell was appointed provost. Charlie Sheedy was made chair for a year, but it soon became evident to everyone that David was destined to become chair of theology. It seems as if our lives were destined to be intertwined as we were joined in the common effort to understand what it might mean

---

1. Burrell, *Friendship and Ways to Truth*, 10.

to be a theology department that was at once Catholic but did not exclude Protestants or Jews.

Most of the essays in this book were written before Burrell and I got to know one another. I do not remember reading any of these essays other than the chapters on the *Confessions* and the last chapter on "Religious Life and Understanding" until I was asked to write this introduction. But I did read *Analogy and Philosophical Language* when it came out in 1973.[2] I think it fair to say that the essays in this book build on and develop what David had done in his dissertation and subsequent book. But if we are to understand Burrell well it turns out that these essays are crucial.

Burrell is often criticized for being "vague." I think anyone attending to the care that went into these articles will find it hard to sustain that criticism. I suspect critics of Burrell's alleged lack of clarity have in mind essays such as his account of Thomas's metaphysics. His suggestion, that for Thomas metaphysical objects do not "turn up" because we only know of them by what they are not, may seem to some hard to understand, but in fact that way of putting the matter turns out to be crucial if we are to understand Thomas's way of working. I encourage the reader to explore what Burrell is about in the article on the dialogues of Plato and his account of Thomas's metaphysics.

As I got to know and work closely with Burrell it became obvious to me what an extraordinarily astute reader he was. I think anyone reading these essays cannot help but confirm that judgment. By suggesting he is an astute reader I mean that he is able to read overly theorized texts without letting past readings determine how he now reads. He readily acknowledges, for example, that Augustine's world view is not ours, but drawing on Wittgenstein's reminder that to share a language is to share in judgments, he helps us see that Augustine, as well as ourselves reading Augustine, must struggle with questions involving the genuineness of our faith.

Burrell is not only an astute reader, but his reading habits are wide-ranging and surprising. That he could at once write articles on substance in Aristotle, a highly technical article on Aristotle's account of "future contingencies," on Platonic dialogues, C. S. Peirce, and Augustine is for one so young remarkable. He is a voracious reader. I suspect that he is so may have been learned as an undergraduate at Notre Dame. In his memoir, *Questing for Understanding: Persons, Places, Passions*, he reminds us he majored in Liberal Studies when he was a student.[3] Liberal Studies was the program that took as its task to introduce students to the most important books and

2. Burrell, *Analogy and Philosophical Language*.
3. Burrell, *Questing for Understanding*, 35–37.

developments in Western civilization. Burrell obviously took full advantage of that reading regime.

As important as his gregarious reading habits are it is perhaps even more significant that he is an extraordinarily sympathetic reader. He seems to have the attitude that there is no one or nothing that he cannot learn from. In his memoir he tells us he is a lover, and that he surely is. He is not "just" a lover of other persons, but he is a lover of the world of ideas. His first reaction to a text is never how do I disagree with what is being said. Rather, his first move is to see how what is being said helps him say what he is trying to say. That does not mean that he does not often find himself in disagreement with this position or person, but he usually seeks out areas that will allow him and his adversary to find a way to go on.

I think his reading habits may reflect his commitment to avoid what he describes as "the neurotic desire to find certitude where none will be forthcoming." He had studied with John Smith at Yale, which, I suspect, meant he had read his Dewey. Like Dewey, David had and continues to have little use for the "quest for certainty." But I think David's willingness to entertain positions that at first may seem antithetical to his deepest convictions is based in those very convictions. In short, David Burrell is so deeply immersed in the Catholic faith any defensive or protective stance would be inconsistent with that faith.

It is not insignificant that the essays in this book were written by a priest. Burrell would never use his priesthood to try to compel agreement from someone. To do so would be against everything it means to be a priest. But in so far as the priesthood is constitutive of his religious life his being a priest surely makes a difference for how he does philosophy. One must be very careful in making this kind of judgment, but I think it is surely the case that Burrell's reading of Aquinas and Augustine as inquirers reflects his own practice as a priest who is also a philosopher. That does not mean that either Burrell or I can say what difference it makes to how he does philosophy that he is a priest.

Then there is, of course, the importance of Wittgenstein for Burrell. I do not know when or where Burrell first read Wittgenstein, but the essays in this book obviously reflect Wittgenstein's pervasive influence. Burrell's reading of Wittgenstein is very significant because it is so easy to get Wittgenstein wrong. Many who count themselves followers of Wittgenstein hunger for Wittgenstein to have a position. They want Wittgenstein to have a theory about "meaning." Thus we are told over and over again that the meaning of a word is its use. Or Wittgenstein's private language argument is said to mean we cannot have thoughts that are peculiarly ours. Those are the kinds of mistakes that Burrell avoids.

Wittgenstein for Burrell does not give you a better theory about the meaning of words or of how we mean what we say. Rather, Wittgenstein for Burrell became a form of therapy to free us from the presumption that we have to have a theory to know what we say. Burrell's reading of Aristotle on substance obviously draws on Wittgenstein's understanding that we often can only show what is the case. To know, however, what such a showing entails is crucial for recognizing what cannot be said. So language for Burrell became a testimony for why our talk of God cannot help being displayed through analogy.

That, of course, is a crucial point if we are right to understand why the assumption that we can understand God only if we have a theory of analogy is so wrongheaded. Accordingly, Burrell made the great discovery, a discovery of considerable scholarly significance, that contrary to scholastic philosophy and theology Aquinas did not have theory of analogy. Rather, like Aristotle on substance, Aquinas's account of analogy is a performance. Rather than a theory of analogy what must be recognized, Burrell argued, is for Aquinas the analogous "sense of a word is always proportioned to a proper usage which is quite ordinary, and turns as well on the distinction of understanding and judgment." Burrell's life and work can be understood as the attempt to direct attention to properly proportioned words for our knowledge of God.

Burrell's understanding of analogy reflects his deepest conviction, a conviction that is at the heart of his engagement with Judaism and Islam, that creation does not necessitate that there be a creature. I have often thought how interesting Karl Barth might have found Burrell's account of Aquinas on analogy. Burrell's account of the relation between creation and creator, how we talk of God as well as how we must talk of God, indicates the kind of God that we worship and is a set of associations Barth might have found extremely interesting.

I have attributed Burrell's reading of Aquinas to the influence of Wittgenstein, but Burrell is surely right in his article "Religious Language and the Logic of Analogy" to call attention to the importance of Ralph McInerny's book *Logic of Analogy*. Over the years David and Ralph would find themselves on different sides of some of the issues confronting the Catholic Church, but David never failed to give Ralph credit for doing work that was crucial for David's reading of Thomas. Not to be missed in that article is David's account of logic as "the science of the argumentation whereby one proceeds from what is known to what is unknown. As such it includes the study of words and their meanings as preliminaries to reasoning, as well as formal deductive procedures."

No doubt Lonergan also played a decisive role in Burrell's intellectual formation, but not in the way Lonergan later became so influential. Burrell was never a "Lonerganian." Lonergan did have a decisive effect on Burrell, but it was not to give Burrell a "position." The significance of Lonergan for Burrell was to free him from neo-scholasticism. Recently neo-scholasticism seems to be attractive to many, making the publication of these essays all the more important. The quest for certitude never dies.

It is surely appropriate that in the last chapter of this collection Burrell suggests that his own understanding of what it means to "understand" has been informed by Kierkegaard and given shape by Wittgenstein. Burrell then defends an account of Kierkegaard as a thinker of "powerful philosophical acumen." He observes that Kierkegaard's supple intellect was at the service of a longing, a quest that was nothing less than a love affair. Interestingly enough, during my time at Yale, a time just after Burrell had finished his PhD, I was taught a similar view of Kierkegaard and Wittgenstein by Paul Holmer. I mention this only as a way to indicate how important it was for Burrell (and for me) that certain people were there at the right time and the right place. Our lives are made up of contingencies. For me David is one of those contingencies, and for that I will always be grateful.

I have said nothing about Burrell's linguistic ability or his extraordinary erudition. I always observed that David's idea of a good time, namely, the opportunity to learn another language, was my idea of hell. But David has never called attention to his scholarly achievements. Rather, he has always called attention to the One alone that has given us the gift of life. He has always been too busy celebrating the world and the people God has drawn into his life to call attention to himself. His is a life of gratitude that can only elicit in those who know him a wonder at his sheer vitality—a vitality, I think, properly called love. As promised I am sure I have not explained "how he did it," but these articles are clear evidence he did something quite remarkable.

As far as gratitude is concerned, however, we must all be extremely grateful to Mary Budde Ragan for bringing these articles together in this book. They are gems that would no doubt have been lost without her attention. Again it is by such acts of attention that our understanding of what we believe is enhanced, and hopefully we are enabled to avoid to some degree our penchant for self-deception.

Stanley Hauerwas
Duke University, Durham, North Carolina

Critical Response

SINCE THE PAPERS COLLECTED in this volume amount to preparatory studies for (or preliminary fruits of the work that resulted in) David Burrell's first book *Analogy and Philosophical Language*,[1] their publication is to be welcomed, here and now, because it will remind readers that a theologian probably best known to them as a scholar of Aquinas involved in sustained conversations with Judaism and Islam began his intellectual career with an equal interest in philosophy—in its origins, its nature, and its significance. It is not just that individual papers in this collection develop rigorous and fascinating readings of specific figures in the history of philosophy such as Plato, Aristotle, and Peirce—valuable as those local interventions are. It is also that those readings articulate a sophisticated and provocative conception of what makes the work of such different figures genuinely philosophical, and thereby allows us to comprehend them as participants in a continuous conversation about what is involved in doing something that might be worth calling a manifestation of the love of wisdom. Since everything else I want to say in response to Burrell's papers is responsive to that underlying conception of what philosophy is and might be, I must begin by summarizing my understanding of it.

On Burrell's conception, human beings are inquiring animals: we understand the world we encounter, and naturally develop methods for systematically extending, questioning, and refining that pre-theoretical comprehension of things—for example, in the form of the natural sciences, the social sciences, or the more humanistic disciplines. Within each domain of knowledge or discursive field, we seek accurately to apprehend each particular object, and to unify the resulting, initially plural or various concrete knowledge-claims within more systematic bodies of knowledge about objects of that kind. But that same inquiring impulse will naturally turn upon these modes of knowledge-acquisition themselves: sooner or later we ask

---

1. Burrell, *Analogy and Philosophical Language*. Hereafter: APL.

ourselves whether, why, and how each of them gives us access to how things are—we seek an explanation of our explanatory practices, an intelligible account of our ways of giving intelligible accounts of things. Kant would call it the point at which reason becomes self-critical; Heidegger would talk of a shift from ontic to ontological modes of questioning; Wittgenstein would speak of beginning a grammatical investigation. It is the moment of reflection, the philosophical moment.

To reject this kind of reflective inquiry would amount to accepting that all human modes of making sense of things themselves lack sense, which would mean regarding both human understanding and the reality it apprehends as devoid of substance, mere show. But if instead we take on the task, and attempt to make sense of our ways of sense-making, the beginning of wisdom—as Plato sees from the outset (of his own work, and so of philosophy itself: see "What the Dialogues Show about Inquiry")—lies in the recognition that any account we might attain of our modes of comprehending the world will necessarily differ from the kinds of accounts of concrete things that each such mode provides.

Not entirely, of course: for the task amounts to attempting to apprehend the distinctive nature of these various modes of comprehension, which will involve appreciating both how they differ from and resemble one another; and this is just the basic (reality-oriented, truth-seeking, unifying) character of our pre-reflective understanding manifesting itself at the reflective level—seeking order within or between these apparently plural or heterogeneous phenomena, attempting to make sense of them as one and all modes of comprehension without occluding their individuality (and so the distinctiveness of their objects). So our basic orientation as understanding animals does not entirely desert us; but the first step it requires us to take is to acknowledge that that which makes it possible to grasp a certain kind of object is not just one more such kind of object—indeed, is not obviously any kind of object, except in the thinnest sense (that of being an object of inquiry, a subject-matter). Hence, modes of explanation that are specifically suited for comprehending things will ipso facto not be suited for comprehending themselves.

This initial, essentially negative appraisal of our prospects is, however, also the means by which we can establish a more positive grasp of our reflective context. For first, if we are thus deprived of the more familiar, impersonal and methodical ways through which explanatory accounts are legitimately generated at the non-reflective level, we are necessarily thrown back to an unprecedented degree on our fundamental capacity for right judgment, which plays an ineliminable but more recessive and clearly demarcated role in such knowledge-acquisition. This is because we now have to attune that capacity to a context in which the frameworks that usually inform it are themselves the object of judgment, and hence no framing assumption or principle can be exempt from interrogation. So we must fall back on our basic ability to discriminate genuine understanding from its counterfeits, and real progress in understanding—however incremental—from its mere appearance; and that entails sincerely committing ourselves to acquiring and deploying whatever qualities of character the right exercise of such abilities relies upon.

Those qualities include courage and honesty, and in particular the honesty to acknowledge the limits of our own unaided ability to criticize our individual judgment as radically and unremittingly as this task requires: we might call this an acknowledgment of inquiry as a communal or social enterprise. Hence, we must cultivate a willingness to take seriously any seriously offered contribution to the task of enhancing our understanding, including any seriously offered criticism of our own best attempts to make progress; and a willingness to recognize that no resting point on this journey is or could be final (so that we best express our commitment to knowing by declaring how little we know). We must, in short, cultivate the spirit of Socrates—the spirit that informs the individual of that name in Plato's writings, is manifest in his way of participating in Athenian life, and is exhibited in the dialogic form through which his attempts to embody that spirit into a fully reflective mode of existence are conveyed to Plato's readers (thereby showing Plato's ability to incorporate that spirit into his own form of life as a writer and thinker).

In this way, Burrell connects the business of pursuing reflective understanding with that of acquiring self-understanding, and displays the internal relation between acquiring that understanding, acquiring a certain character, and living a certain kind of life (one in which self-reliance and reliance on others become mutually supporting rather than mutually exclusive ideals). But this set of connections does not simply underline the salience of the inquirer in the enterprise of reflective inquiry; it also indicates that reflective inquiries are ones in which form and content are not only internally related, but in which the former has a certain kind of priority—that the distinctive nature of such inquiries is such that its subject-matter must be properly reflected in or into its form. For what Plato's work (as Burrell lays it out in "What the Dialogues Show about Inquiry") reminds us is that reflective inquiry is primarily concerned with form rather than content—with that which frames or shapes or informs any concrete knowledge-claims (true descriptions, characterizations of essence, hypotheses, or theorems) advanced in any non-reflective cognitive domain, and which accordingly cannot be appropriately articulated by knowledge-claims of that kind (which are precisely formed so as to convey truths about objects).

The first paper in this collection ("Substance: A Performatory Account") gives us an illuminating example of how this general Platonic insight might be applied in the pivotal case of our understanding of substances. For it presents Aristotle as someone whose reflective inquiry into substance is guided by our ordinary ways of talking about such things and our most successful ways of working up that initial grasp into a genuinely scientific understanding of what substances are, and more specifically by attending to the formal "features" or aspects of those modes of discourse and inquiry (that which orders or organizes sentences and inquiries as linguistic and intellectual wholes, hence as comprising functionally interrelated parts).

But if Aristotle is sensitive to the fact that grasping the nature of anything is a matter of grasping it as a formal unity (a whole composed of parts), he is equally aware that this grasp is context-sensitive—amounting to something rather different depending on what kind of object is at issue, and so on the perspective through which we are judging and appraising it as a single, unified thing. Moreover, his guiding assumption in this specific inquiry (that the unity of substance and the unity of a sentence might cast light on one another) exploits and so is shaped by the recognition that true sentences (or at least a subset of those sentences that can be truly asserted of a substance—those defining sentences through which all that must be said of it can be derived) can articulate what it is to be a substance of that kind. Putting these claims together, Burrell's account of Aristotle's account of substance and fact-stating speech shows that it assigns a central role in both domains to four concepts: "one," "true," "being," and "good." And of course, these are the concepts with which philosophers have centrally concerned themselves ever since Plato under the label of "the transcendentals."

Aristotle's account displays their centrality to two categorically distinct discursive contexts; but he and his teacher agree that these terms are not in fact restricted to any given range of such contexts. They function trans-categorically, and so constitute a species of what Aristotle would call analogous terms: we find ourselves inclined, even compelled, to employ them in an open-ended diversity of contexts, in each of which their meaning is differently realized, but not to the point of equivocality. In his first book, Burrell specifies their distinctive role as follows:

> If . . . I want to say something is the case, I need to be able to fix the subject-matter into an object ("unity"). And since the effort may or may not be successful, I should be able to appraise it ("good") [and] to indicate whether or not I am stating what is

> the case ("true"). . . . . [S]uccessful reference includes both the
> "... exists" scheme and the "p is true" scheme, for we refer with
> expressions having a sense, and we successfully refer in the
> event such expressions are true. (APL, 224)

Each specific discursive domain will manifest some version of these schemas, because they appear to signify functions of language that are presupposed by anything else one would want to do with it; but each will flesh them out in its own way, and indeed must do so if it is to constitute a distinct, genuinely substantial kind of world-referring discourse.

> "Being" (x is a . . .) reflects no answer in particular but simply
> notes that the *question* "What is (the nature of) x?" is a question
> that will not down. To assert that "p is true" is simply gratuitous
> unless the context supplies some clues to the method of verifica-
> tion, to the kinds of statement that could count as evidence. And
> to say of anything that it is *one* (a unity, an individual) suggests
> little more than the viewpoint from which someone is regarding
> it and the general character of his intellectual concern about it.
> (APL, 223)

In the papers collected in this volume, Burrell offers no such explicit general account relating the demands of reflection to the role of the transcendentals; and although the papers on Aquinas make the case for a particular understanding of the nature and significance of analogical uses of words, in general and specifically for theology, the connection between this matter and the proper subject-matter and conduct of reflective inquiry—that is, philosophy—is not, as far as I can see, properly made out (that is, seen or shown) here either, at least not in the way that the books he published in the 1970s do. Nevertheless, the interpretation of Aristotle offered in the first paper shows that even in this early work the transcendentals are implicitly privileged terms; they indicate the presence of order in any domain about which we are in a position to make judgments or appraisals, while acknowledging the diversity of its specific manifestations, and so the elusiveness of its essence.

They will therefore particularly preoccupy anyone looking for an initial foothold in the project of reflective inquiry; but as we have already seen, the basic orientation that our capacity for non-reflective understanding bequeaths to us in this reflective context is similarly informed by these transcendentals, insofar as it directs us to attend both to the individuality of each mode of comprehending things and to that which makes them all modes of comprehension. For this directedness thereby shows that reflective understanding is one more domain within which we aspire to articulate the truth about how things are by appraising the relevant phenomena as unified (both as particulars, and as part of an ordered or organized field of knowledge). In other words, we find our footing in reflection analogically—by adapting the forms of non-reflective understanding to another new context.

This is another way of saying that reflecting on the transcendental structure or order of judgment is itself an exercise of judgment—an appraisal of our practices of appraisal; so we should expect that philosophical reflection on the order of things, thought and speech will itself have a transcendental structure, constituting one more context in which the categories of "being," "unity," "truth," and "goodness" will be put to use. At the same time, however, the way in which those terms apply in philosophical appraisal can be expected to differ just as much from the way in which they apply in straightforwardly categorical modes of appraisal as their application in any one such domain differs from their application in any other.

Properly self-aware reflective accounts of the human capacity to understand the world will therefore apprehend it as having three fundamental and interrelated formal aspects or "features." First, attending to the categorical diversity of our primary modes of discursive understanding (their distinctive modes of individuation, methods of verification, protocols of contestation, etc.) will disclose any trans-categorical structures that hold them together; so such reflection must (second) recognize the unity-in-diversity of such structures—the fact that what is presupposed by any category-specific mode of discourse is itself variously realized according to context (and so cannot be given the same kind of account as that of terms limited to a specific categorical domain, or set of domains). How, then, are philosophers to articulate these insights in a manner formally consonant with their nature? Since analogous terms are the ones best suited to expressing such unified diversity, we will find ourselves driven to make use of such discursive forms in our reflective account of their peculiar role in the accounts we give of things; and we thereby ensure (third) that they become not only the object but also the medium of this reflective enterprise.

In short, analogous terms are perfectly qualified for the task of articulating that which all cross-categorical expressions such as themselves presuppose and exploit—the diverse unity of all category-specific modes of discourse. But their amenability to projection into that new reflexive context—just like their primary ability to make themselves at home in diverse categorical contexts—depends upon their capacity to accommodate themselves to its highly distinctive character. Philosophers who truly comprehend the kind of reflective accounting in which they are engaged must therefore find a way of using analogous terms that neither simply reiterates nor flatly negates the more familiar forms of analogous usage that they aspire to account for. Analogous form and analogous content must here reflect one another in the only way possible—analogously.

It follows that any philosopher with the necessary self-understanding will manifest it in ways which, while bearing an affinity with the work of her peers, will nonetheless distinguish her from them—partly in her choice of terms to employ analogously in bringing out the significance of the transcendentals for judgment in general and philosophical judgment in particular, and partly in her ways of employing them. Burrell's early essays explicitly aspire to identify these signature terms or concepts and to exhibit the analogous uses to which they are put in the writings of Plato and Aristotle, Aquinas and Peirce; and his attempts to do so are informed by an implicit understanding of the analogous signature concepts of Wittgenstein and Heidegger. If he is to do this in an appropriately reflective way, however, he has to forge an account of each that simultaneously acknowledges their individuality while making salient their commonality as practitioners of genuine reflection. He must, in other words, relate them analogically to one another; and we might think of the terms "inquiry," "judgment," "reflection," and "appraisal" as the Burrellian signature concepts whose context-sensitive analogous employment across these papers exhibits the diverse unity that he perceives among his chosen thinkers, thereby inviting us to appraise his claims in the same Socratic, truth-seeking spirit in which he advances them.

This brings us to yet another aspect of reflective inquiry as Burrell understands it, and one whose identification in the work of Aristotle seems particularly dependent on Burrell's formative engagements with Wittgenstein. For Burrell's interpretation of Aristotle on substance depends upon aligning two distinctions: the first is between grasping the unity of a substance and grasping its individuality, and the second is between entertaining a sentence and asserting it. The unity of a substance is a matter of its having a particular intelligible nature, its being a certain kind of thing as opposed to another kind; its individuality is its being this particular substance, the existing individual presently confronting us, its being (here-now) as opposed to its not being (here-now or there-then). Heidegger marks the same distinction by talking of what-being as opposed to that-being; others might talk instead of essence as opposed to existence. Burrell's performatory interpretation of Aristotle culminates in the critical claim that, although Aristotle rightly affirmed that unity and individuality coincide in the substantial particulars that are the primary object of our inquiries, he was unable to show why they do. And according to Burrell, this is because—despite his general tendency to use our ways of talking as a means of access to the nature of the things talked about—Aristotle failed properly to appreciate the formal "feature" of fact-stating discourse that reflects both this distinction and its coincidence: the distinction between entertaining or articulating the possibility that things are a certain way (which amounts to entertaining the possibility that a given substance has a particular nature, and so an intelligible unity) and asserting that things are that way (with respect to a particular, individual substance confronting us here and now).

What this formal distinction brings out is the fact that we are not only surrounded by individual substances, we are confronted by them: they loom up in front of me, block my progress or alter my direction (something that is even more evident when the relevant individual is a person, as Simone Weil also appreciated[2]). And in being confronted by an individual substance, I am recalled to my own nature as a rational animal: I am challenged to respond, to take a position with respect to this thing, to actively judge it—to assert that this thing here has a certain kind of unity. And when I do, I thereby display or enact my concrete individuality: I make a certain active stance or posture in relation to the world my own, take responsibility for a specific appraisal of this object by declaring myself willing to justify that appraisal, to respond appropriately to criticism of it by other appraisers, to remain open to revising my appraisal in the light of further disclosures of and by the object, and so on.

In short, the coincidence of unity and individuality in the object of my inquiry is matched by the coincidence of unity and individuality in the inquirer. To judge that an object is thus-and-so is always to judge it as an object of a certain kind (to make a judgment informed by a particular evaluative framework, an intelligible unity of a kind comprehensible to any judging creature); but to judge that this particular object *is* thus-and-so is to respond to its concrete individuality over against me, and thereby to realize (to make concrete) my nature as an inquirer—to individuate myself as one willing to stand behind this knowledge-claim, made here and now for specific reasons.

This returns us to the Platonic idea of inquiry as both dialogical—a realm in which individual inquirers converse—and demanding; it is a praxis, a way of living that places existential claims on those who succumb to its invitation. And of course, one implication of Burrell's wide range of historical reference in this volume of papers is that this dialogical praxis might be used as an analogical model for how the history of philosophy is to be understood, or more precisely for how the relation between philosophy and its history must be managed if genuinely philosophical work is to be done by attending to it. For if Burrell's emphasis on the priority of assertion

2. See Weil, "The *Iliad*, Poem of Might."

over articulation in the context of inquiry is well placed, then it will not be enough simply to view the great figures who populate the landscape of philosophy's past as potential conversation partners, with one another and with us: we must not merely entertain that possibility, we must assert it. And that means not simply reporting their way of saying things but finding a way of saying them for ourselves: it means taking responsibility for their signature concepts by finding a way in which we can put them to use in the same spirit as that in which their originators forged and worked with them. After all, this kind of inquiry is into inquirers, so the individual substances with whom it confronts us are persons, and so historically (hence socially and culturally) positioned; and since we too are persons, that confrontation will simultaneously force us to declare our own historical position. So our claims to have understood them must reflect as fully as possible an acknowledgment of the historical individuality of both parties—a serious attempt to ensure that our reflections on their reflections are properly informed by a grasp of the relation of their concepts to their discursive contexts and the relation of ours to ours.

If we were to ask which elements of Burrell's discursive contexts most deeply inform his readings of past philosophers, and so his vision of philosophy, it is clear that any answer would have to acknowledge his membership of a religious order (The Congregation of Holy Cross), which must have helped him see the internal relation between speech and inquiry, on the one hand, and existential commitment to a disciplined form of life, on the other. As I have already noted, another obvious informing framework is the work of Wittgenstein, both early and late, which shaped what Burrell learned in his time at Yale (if not before). After all, the *Tractatus* helped found analytic philosophy as a tradition; and in the 1950s and 1960s, the later Wittgenstein's influence (together with that of Austin) deeply influenced philosophical practice in the English-speaking world under the banner of "ordinary language philosophy." But it is not just that Burrell's reading of Wittgenstein informed his work on Plato, Aristotle, and Aquinas; it is equally true that his work on the latter figures informed his way of making sense of Wittgenstein both early and late, giving it a very distinctive physiognomy.

With respect to the *Tractatus*, which Burrell cites as orienting his treatment of Aristotle on substance, he follows the familiar view that the early Wittgenstein emphasized that philosophical reflection must focus on the formal rather than the material features of language (and so of thought and reality), which can only be shown rather than given direct, articulate expression. But that familiar view is usually conjoined with the further assumption that what is thereby shown are unfortunately ineffable but undeniably substantial metaphysical truths—that, if we could (impossibly) state what can only be shown, then we would be stating truths of a particularly fundamental kind. Burrell's citations of the *Tractatus* never attribute any such view to Wittgenstein; and I strongly suspect that his Plato- and Aristotle-influenced awareness of the distinctive nature of formal objects of inquiry, and in particular their resistance being treated as properties or attributes of any kind (even ineffable ones), is what ensures this reticence. Initiated almost single-handedly by the work of an American philosopher named Cora Diamond,[3] recent Tractarian scholarship has been riven by a long-running debate between those who interpret its author as a believer in ineffable truths and those (known as resolute readers) who interpret him as aspiring to overcome even that minimal commitment to a picture of metaphysics as oriented to a subject-matter in just the way physics is.[4] The way in which these early papers refrain from endorsing the orthodox metaphysical reading of the early Wittgenstein, and recontextualize his saying-showing distinction in an emphatically effable interpretation of ancient Greek reflective inquiry, suggests to me at least that Burrell would find resolute readers to be kindred spirits in his enterprise.

What about the later Wittgenstein? Positioned as I am in relation to these essays as someone whose own formation by Wittgenstein's example was reshaped by an early encounter with the American philosopher Stanley Cavell, it is striking how precisely what Burrell takes from the later Wittgenstein echoes what Cavell took from his own encounters with Austin and Wittgenstein in roughly the same historical period.

Cavell's first book is a collection of essays titled *Must We Mean What We Say?*[5] which sounds exactly the note with which Burrell begins the introduction to *Analogy and Philosophical Language*:

> Being attentive to what we say becomes, before long, an unrelenting ideal. It is difficult to say what it exacts from us, for there seem to be no set tasks involved. What must I do to ensure that I say what I mean? What sort of accomplishment is it to mean what I say? (APL, 1)

Suppose we take this as a Wittgensteinian inflection of the task of reflective inquiry; then Cavell's Burrellian emphasis on meaning what we say and saying what we mean contests the all-too-familiar assumption that when Wittgensteinians claim to have found someone (another or themselves) speaking nonsense, they mean to say that the words in that utterance lack

---

3. See the essays collected in Diamond's *Realistic Spirit*.
4. For a good introduction to the debate, see Crary and Read, *New Wittgenstein*.
5. Cavell, *Must We Mean What We Say?*

meaning (for example, because they have somehow been cast out from their everyday housing in a language-game). Cavell invites us to consider an alternative possibility: that the words, taken in or as themselves, mean what they always mean, but the speaker cannot mean what she takes herself to mean in or by saying them. In short, he wants us to shift our reflective attention from the words or sentences to the utterance that the person employing them intends to perform, to the putative speech-act, and so to the speaker—to the relation to herself and her world that her commitment to that speech-act exhibits (or fails to).

This way of understanding Wittgenstein's signature term of criticism plainly acknowledges and exploits the distinction Burrell marks between entertaining or articulating and stating or asserting, which he correlates with the distinction between unity and individuality, and deploys to emphasize judgment as an action or activity—a move in a complex dialogical praxis. Cavell's long, involved discussion of skepticism in his major work *The Claim of Reason*[6]—which is a version of the PhD thesis he began during the 1960s, and which treats skepticism about other minds as an allegorical expression of skepticism about the external world (thereby echoing Aristotle's treatment of persons as exemplary substances)—is organized around the same distinction upon which his early essays pivot; but in this later text that distinction takes up a position in a field of concepts, distinctions, and emphases that is strikingly analogous to that of Burrell.

So, for example, in his diagnosis of other-minds skepticism (and what he takes to be misfiring Wittgensteinian responses to it), when investigating the grammatical schematism of our concept of pain, Cavell points out that grammatical criteria are criteria of identity rather than of existence (they articulate what it is for something to be *such-and-such*, not what it is for it to *be* such-and-such [CR, 45]). Then he emphasizes that no matter how good our grasp of the relevant criteria, there is always the further, qualitatively distinct question of whether we are willing to apply or employ them, to use them in our confrontations with particular individual creatures in the world (CR, 83). And he traces back both points to Wittgenstein's acknowledgment of the primary role of judgment in the life of a speaker.

> Judgement . . . in Wittgensteinian appeals to criteria comes up twice. [There is] the judgement's *predication*, its saying something *about* something . . . [and] the judgement's *proclamation*, its saying it out. . . . In Wittgensteinian . . . cases, *whether* to say it is as much a problem as what there is to be said.

---

6. Cavell, *Claim of Reason*. Hereafter: CR.

> Whether to speak has two aspects: determining whether you are willing to count something as something; and determining when, if ever, you wish, or can, enter your accounting into a particular occasion. Take . . . "He is in pain" . . . To proclaim it here and now you must be willing to call out . . . just that predicate on the basis of what you have so far gathered (. . . count that behavior as a wince); and you must find it called for on just this occasion, *i.e.* find yourself willing to come before . . . those to whom you speak it (e.g., declare yourself in a position to inform or advise or alert someone of something . . .). (CR, 35)

Here we see Cavell employing the Burrellian signature concept of judgment to emphasize the distinction between unity and individuality, or what-being and that-being, and in such a way as to emphasize the way the proclamatory aspect of judgment exposes the judger, requiring him to take a position and to take responsibility for it—for "our separate counts and outcalls of phenomena, which after all are hardly more than our interpretations of what occurs" (CR, 36). And since these judgments are as fundamental to Wittgensteinian grammatical investigations as they are to everyday speech, that sense of exposure, and so of an ineliminable moment of self-reliance and privacy (fragile and intimate, with no assurance of criteria on which to slough responsibility), carries over to the business of philosophical inquiry itself.

Underlying this account is Cavell's primary hermeneutic assumption that Wittgenstein's signature concept of a criterion is a version of the ordinary one; in Burrellian terms, he presents it as a concept Wittgenstein employs analogously in a reflective context. According to Cavell, criteria in the everyday sense are specifications on the basis of which some group judges whether something (a dive, a government, a university applicant) has a particular status or value: in other words, criterion-based judgments are ordinarily explicitly evaluative. At first sight, Wittgenstein's reflective employment of that concept reorients it to cases where no explicitly evaluative issue seems to arise. He asks for the criteria of someone's sitting on a chair, having an opinion, reading, and so on; and such cases seem quite unspecial, involving just the ordinary concepts and objects of our world, and so going proxy for any and every application of words to that world. And yet, for Cavell, the evaluative dimension of the everyday concept of a criterion remains active in Wittgenstein's analogous use of it, and so in his conception of human judgment:

> Wittgenstein's insight . . . seems to be something like this: that all our knowledge, everything we assert or question . . . is governed

> ... by criteria. Without the control of criteria in applying concepts, we would not know what counts as evidence for any claim, nor for what claims evidence is needed. And that suggests ... that every surmise and each tested conviction depend upon the same structure or background of necessities and agreements that judgements of value do. I do not say that, according to Wittgenstein, statements of fact *are* judgements of value.... The case is rather that ... both statements of fact and judgements of value rest upon the same capacities of human nature; that, so to speak, only a creature that can judge of value *can* state a fact.
>
> But doesn't that just come to saying that only a creature that has speech can make judgements and statements? And that is hardly surprising.... [Not] if what it means is that only a creature that can say something can say something in particular. But what motivates Wittgenstein to philosophize, what surprises him, is the plain fact that certain creatures have speech at all, that they can say things at all.... It is like being surprised by the fact that there is such a thing as the world. (CR, 14–15)

Should we be surprised by the fact that two philosophers attempting to find ways of meaning what Wittgenstein says and saying what he means in and for 1960s America should develop essentially the same field of concepts and insights concerning our condition as human knowers, a field in which the primacy of judgment not only activates the traditional array of transcendental terms (unity or oneness, being, truth, and goodness) and thereby relates the supposedly anti-metaphysical Wittgenstein to the metaphysical tradition originating with Plato, but also opens out onto the kind of experience of ourselves and our world that the early Wittgenstein would have called "mystical," and that Burrell's Aquinas would have seen as the hallmark of our origin and end in God's creative love? If we are willing to take these reflective conjunctions seriously, then—given Burrell's sustained early interest in Peirce as a worthy companion to Plato, Aristotle, and Aquinas (see "C. S. Peirce: Pragmatism as a Theory of Judgment" in this volume)—we might be struck by the further fact that Cavell and Burrell (as well as Diamond) are American thinkers. We might then feel inclined or even compelled to consider more generally whether there is something distinctively American about Burrell's Wittgensteinian way of exhibiting in contemporary terms his classical vision of what philosophy can and should be.

Within such a consideration, one point of specific difference between Cavell and Burrell would quickly become salient: for whereas Burrell's work takes Peirce as exemplary of American philosophy, Cavell gives that status to the Transcendentalism of Emerson (and Thoreau), and has often written relatively disparagingly about the pragmatist strand in American thought (although Dewey is usually his primary representative of it).[7] One might then be prompted to ask whether Burrell's work on Peirce would give Cavell reason to see an internal relation between Emerson and Peircean pragmatism, and whether Cavell's work on Emerson might lead Burrell to see American Transcendentalism as a prior inheritor of Platonic concerns in America.

Of course, my appraisal of these two thinkers as unified at such a fundamental level, both as readers of Wittgenstein and as inheritors of philosophy more generally, might instead be judged to be ultimately an artefact of their joint influence on my own way of thinking—about Wittgenstein, philosophy, and religion, and about America's ways of expressing itself philosophically. But as we have seen, reflective inquiry demands that its participants not merely entertain the possibility of such intelligible analogical unities in its objects, but assert their reality if they judge it to be responsive to what confronts them; for only then can that claim be properly appraised and consequently discarded, qualified, or built on. As Emerson, that canonical advocate of self-reliance, once said, after drawing an analogy between his own essays and the act of writing "Whim" on the lintels of his door post (and thereby relating his philosophizing to the life-preserving praxis underlying the Passover), "I hope it is something better than whim at last, but we cannot spend the day in explanation."[8]

Stephen Mulhall
New College, Oxford

---

7. See, for example, Cavell's essay "What's the Use of Calling Emerson a Pragmatist?"
8. See Emerson's essay "Self-Reliance."

Chapter 1

Substance
A Performatory Account

THIS ESSAY OFFERS AN interpretation of Aristotle. My aim in so interpreting him is to show how useful a guide he can be in unraveling issues surrounding meaning and reference, and in displaying the role which language plays in our understanding the world. More specifically, the manner in which we lay language out bespeaks our way of laying out the world. I shall focus on substance and argue against a misunderstanding, showing how it is linked to a misconception of the structure and function of the statement-making sentence. Getting back to Aristotle in this fashion has the purpose of getting down to issues. One test of success will be the extent to which I can also clarify disputed questions in Aristotle. Many of the arguments will have to be designed to help us see through some of our pet predilections to get ahold of the issues in a fresh way. The following preliminary distinctions serve that end.

SOME PRELIMINARY REMARKS

An element is an element of a whole. Hence the sense of "one" at work in discriminating *an* element will depend on that sense of "one" which picked out one of the wholes of which this item is said to be a component. Lead, for example, is a component of the steel used for automobile bodies, but steel is a component of the bodies; carbon is a component of the plastics used to construct a car, but specific plastics in definite shapes are components of the car. The units, the definite shapes, are shaped to the design of the car. And while plastic is not infinitely malleable, whatever constraints its use would have on the design of the car itself would be due not to any predetermined shapes, but to its consistency. Those constraints would stem from its being plastic, not from its being a unit—more from the components of plastic than from plastic used as a component.

Most of us are schooled to respect this shifting sense of "unit" (or of "object"). Yet we are tempted to resist its penetrating to affect our use of "element" (or of "component") as well. We cannot accept the shifting character of "unit," however, and fail to recognize that same shiftiness in any identifying phrase using the particle "a" or "an." This amounts, of course, to the venerable reminder that "one" is an analogous term. It is one of those four or five peculiarly pervasive notions that is present in every categorical division and appears indispensable to any language we might want to use. But all that reminder need come to for us at this point is a warning: be sure to specify the context when speaking of *an* anything. And the context of an element is the unit-whole of which it is an element.

What seems to work against our logical good sense here is some demand to locate units that are more *basic* than others. Or perhaps on closer examination we can detect such a demand already at work in the very way we use expressions so utterly analogous as "one," so that understanding that very demand would form part of our logical good sense.[1] We can look more closely at this as we proceed. One feature of logical good sense shows up already, however. That is that it will prove fruitless to look for *the* most basic (or elementary) unit, for we would have to locate something without elements. For the elements of a particular kind of unit would of course have to be considered more elementary than the unit itself, yet all the while owing the fact that they were elements to the unit. The language which picks out elements, however, is one shaped to the wholes of which they are elements, and it is a language fashioned to things composed of elements. Hence even what is most basic must be in some fashion composed if we are to be able to talk about it. What is without any composition whatsoever could not even be expressed.

It is these ambiguities in "one," "basic," and "elementary" which Aristotle was forced to negotiate in asserting *substance* to be primary. For all the difficulties he left us, however, he saw clearly what I have outlined so far, and did not flinch from taking on the seeming paradoxes involved. I want to look again at his accounts with this reciprocal sense of part/whole in hand, showing how the shifting sense of unit can prove a powerful key

---

1. This is Owen's contention in "Logic and Metaphysics."

in interpreting the role *substance* played for him. And delineating that role more clearly can have a cleansing effect on some contemporary discussions of ontology.²

Aristotle on Substance

It is no secret that Aristotle's presentation of substance derives from logico-grammatical reflections on the statement-making sentence. So understanding Aristotle's account of the sentence will go a long way towards our grasping what he intended by *substance*, and why it plays the role it does for him. My contention will be that substance is primary just as a statement-making sentence is primary. Neither is primary because it is without elements, but each displays its respective claim to be the basic unit (of the world or of discourse) in its manner of composition. The elements pertaining to these units are not themselves units of this most basic type, hence it becomes more proper to speak of matter/form and name/verb as principles rather than elements.³

This interpretation apparently contradicts some straightforward statements of Aristotle about the significant parts of a sentence, and certainly runs counter to a fairly common predilection for names as the basic units of discourse. I shall show that the contradiction is only apparent by noting how the context of the statements in question fixes an appropriate meaning of "unit" without claiming any further extension.

The accumulating arguments in favor of this interpretation should display a battery of relevant reasons for preferring sentence to name as the basic unit of discourse. The advantages lie not only in a more coherent understanding of Aristotle, but in exposing misleading uses of "substance" (Locke) as well as definitively avoiding metaphysical embarrassments like bare particulars.

---

2. For a clear contrast, compare the "classical" statement of Copi, "Objects, Properties, and Relations," with Ishiguro, "Use and Reference of Names." Copi is certainly correct in observing that "Wittgenstein's objects . . . correspond more closely to Aristotle's prime matter than to his primary substances" (185), yet he fails to remark any tension between that comparison and his identifying "objects as bare particulars" (184).

3. The distinction between *principle* and *element* is finally articulated at *Metaphysics* VII. 17, 1041a26–b32 after seven chapters of careful discussion. Passages from the *Metaphysics* are taken from Richard Hope's translation. I shall use "name" to translate ονομα in agreement with the reasons offered by Ackrill, *Aristotle's Categories and De Interpretatione*, 115.

This interpretation was inspired by a remark of Aquinas likening the noun to matter and the verb to form in the unit which is a sentence.[4] It has been guided by that medieval spirit which took logical grammar so seriously: whatever cannot be said should be able to be displayed from the structure of the statement itself. What sets off metaphysicians from dialecticians, Aquinas remarked, is neither intuition nor method, but simply the power of showing something forth.[5]

Plan of Exposition and of Argument

Substance forms the focus of many issues in Aristotle, notably of a theory of inquiry, and by implication, a metaphysics. I shall try to show how the issues which arise in the *Metaphysics* are rooted in the *de Interpretatione* and can be illuminated effectively from the *Posterior Analytics,* Aristotle's methodology. I shall show how the treatment of substance is itself an elaboration of the subject-predicate form of the sentence, but not in the ways that we might expect. Furthermore, the individuality of substance cannot be elucidated in any formal way, so something else is required. I shall argue that the "something else" is strictly correlative to that act whereby we assert what we have articulated, where we state what we have considered to be the case. Among the results should be a more sophisticated appreciation of Aristotle as well as a somewhat keener sense of our investment in the language which we speak, especially of the subtleties of the "subject-predicate" form of discourse, and of the indispensability of the speaker as an agent and user of language.

PHILOSOPHY AS ELUCIDATION: ELEMENTS OF DISCOURSE

We have in Ackrill's translation of the *Categories* and the *Peri Hermeneias* (*de Interpretatione*) an exquisite guide into this early attempt to do philosophy by elucidating logical grammar. Ackrill duly notes how often Aristotle failed to distinguish logical from grammatical form and kinds of sentences from kinds of speech-acts (120, 128).[6] Yet the very simplicity of his translation shows how useful were Aristotle's failures to distinguish. We are presented

---

4. *In 1 Peri Herm.* 5.54.
5. *In 4 Meta.* 4.573-74.
6. Ackrill, *Aristotle's Categories and De Interpretatione.* [Ed. note: For reference to Ackrill's notes in this essay, see in-text citations as given in parentheses.]

with a simple and direct example of elucidation. Beginning with the fact of speech, Aristotle searches for those patterns which allow it to do its job.

Speech is a significant sound. The *de Interpretatione* begins where Socrates did. The elements of speech are many: names, verbs, negations, affirmations, statements (αποφανσις), and sentences (λογος). Besides saying something about each of them it behooves us to order them, for much will depend on that. Aristotle is not explicit about ordering the elements, but he is clear about how to do it. He is interested here in one of the jobs that speech does: the statement-making job (17a5). The operative element here is the *sentence*, for it alone can be used to *affirm* or *deny*, that is, to *state* that something is or is not the case. *Names* and *verbs*, on this ordering, would qualify as elements of speech—become significant sounds—only insofar as they are constitutive parts of sentences.

The ordering so far is clear and thoroughly Aristotelian: as it is the purpose embodied in living, growing things which is the key to discovering the order in their make-up, so the stated aim of an inquiry orders what it perceives to be the relevant factors or elements that must be discussed. The aim of the *de Interpretatione* is at once universal and pointed: to elucidate some invariant structures of significant sound with special attention to what makes a statement work. What is significant is speech. Socrates provides the background here: what is significant is what a man says and does. Aristotle focuses on what we say and specifically what is done when we say something of something.

The analysis at this point is formal . . . by way of elucidation. The text refers to *de Anima* (III. 3–8) for what could be called an operational or causal analysis. The focus here is rather on the form of the sentence (λογος) and especially that kind of sentence most appropriate for making statements (αποφανσις) or for saying something of something. Sentences have many other roles. They can be used to invoke, command, cajole, commend, condemn, etc. All of these activities are significant because they belong to human speech. Aristotle does not single out one sort of speech activity—statement-making—as though it were a paradigm of significant sound, but rather takes it up because of its role in inquiry.

The pressure to isolate statement-making comes from the basic question form: What is it? Any answer to the question will have to say something about *that*. Coming to know what anything is involves learning a number of things *about* it, and these items are held fast in statements which purpose to assert or deny something of the thing in question (17a20). Although Aristotle did not use this language, what is known about the object in question is just that: a knowing-about it, or a fact. And what states the fact is a statement-making sentence, asserting something about the object or state of affairs in which we are interested.

A Standard Interpretation

All this sounds clear enough—even obvious—until we realize that it glides over some major difficulties, textual and philosophical. The textual problem arises when Aristotle muddies the nicely organic ordering I have suggested to assert that names and verbs are significant in their own right, in separation from the sentence. The philosophical issues arise when we ask how it is that names and verbs might signify. Aristotle does not supply us with a theory of reference; in fact, *semainein* incorporates in one expression two functions we have come to consider distinct: sense and reference. If we take his statements about names and verbs signifying in separation to fix them as basic units of discourse, then we are tempted to regard *referring* as the most basic feature in any expression's signifying something.

The way in which a sentence functions in stating something to be the case will be explicated, then, from the ways in which its unit-parts function. And since names signify by referring to something, perhaps verbs do too. If they did, we could explicate signifying from referring and be home free. An analysis of this sort would clear up the mysteries surrounding substance as well: the noun-subject refers to the substance and the verb to the modification we wish to assert of it. Was not that Aristotle's genius: to have modeled his basic ontological categories on the invariant structures of factual language?

This skeleton interpretation has been fleshed out too often to occupy us further now. We are certainly less confident than our immediate predecessors that we know what *referring* comes to, so we are less tempted by that promise of economy. Furthermore, the remarks of Aristotle on which this doctrine is based offer something less than a foundation. Their initial and sketchy character certainly allows for the neat picture: noun:substance:: verb:modification of substance. Yet those same remarks, scrutinized in their original context and tested against other relevant statements of Aristotle, may be rendered in a fashion which leads to a quite different version of substance.

The fact that Aristotle himself proposes not a doctrine but a few preliminary, schematic remarks betrays his canny philosophic wit. For one result of the doctrine mentioned has been to upset the proper ordering of the elements of speech and to land the methodical analyst in an ontological desert of bare particulars. The doctrine inverts the order of the elements by aligning name with substance. Since substance, however, represents what is ontologically first for Aristotle, we would expect to correlate it with the primary semantic unit: the statement-making sentence. If we follow the suggestion offered by the lines of a statement-making sentence then knowing is conveniently construed as knowing-about: to know anything is to know something about something. If we go on to identify the subject with what Aristotle featured as substance, then we must conclude that we cannot know what anything is. For whatever is known is carried by the verbal expression: it is known *about* the subject, which must remain radically unknowable itself. Yet substance, for Aristotle, was precisely what we seek after in asking the question: what is it?[7]

Something has gone awry. I shall try to show that the neat correlation of noun with substance and verb with modifications of substance is in no way necessitated by the text of Aristotle, and that another relation between grammar and ontology offers itself in its place. The *substance* which emerges from this interpretation can succeed in playing the role which Aristotle intended for it.[8]

Aristotle's Account

What exactly does Aristotle say about *names* and *verbs*? Interestingly enough, less about names than about verbs. "A name is a spoken sound significant by convention, without time, none of whose parts is significant in separation" (16a19). The last qualification silences any "rat" in "Socrates," the second last distinguishes noun from verb, and the remark about convention sets names apart from natural noises by gesturing towards the linguistic context which supplies this sound with a role. In Aristotle's words: "I say 'by convention' because no name is a name naturally but only when it has become a symbol" (16a26).

But what makes a noise (or an inscription) a symbol? An initial response would have to acknowledge context, specifically the sentence, and the sentence spoken. Since a name is part of a sentence, and Aristotle always defines parts by reference to the whole of which they are a part, this response seems the most natural one to offer. It is also the least committal

---

7. Cf. Lonergan, *Verbum*, 11–35.

8. Searle reminds us "the traditional road to substance is taken as soon as one construes facts as always in some sense *about* objects.... Thus, the traditional metaphysical notion of an irreducible distinction between facts and objects seems confused. *To have the notion of a* particular object is just to be in possession of a true uniquely existential proposition, i.e., a fact of a certain kind" (*Speech Acts*, 93). I shall be arguing that the notion which Searle is after is in fact the authentically Aristotelian one.

response one might make, for all we have done is to call attention to the way in which signifying is linked with something encompassing called "context." Innocent though such a response may be, however, it will serve as a leading principle for my interpretation of Aristotle. Fitting so naturally as it does into an Aristotelian *context*, a mere assent to this response lets us question the dogma which would link significance with a "referring relation."

In further support of the sentence as the defining context, little more is said about the verb than about names, but what is said is illuminating. "A *verb* is what additionally signifies time, no part of it being significant separately; and it is a sign of things said of something else" (16b6). Ackrill notes that the original meaning of the word translated "verb" is simply "what is said" (118). If it is the sentence, and specifically the statement-making sentence which we use to say something of something (or to state that such and such is the case), then the verb functions as the formal constituent of a sentence, making of it the peculiarly apt instrument that it is.[9] The temporal aspect of its role is an essential qualification "because it additionally signifies something's holding *now*" (16b9).

Aristotle's predilection for the present tense presages the puzzle over future contingents in chapter nine. It seems a quite natural feeling if we harken to the sentence as apt for stating what *is* the case. Aquinas introduces a helpful subtlety by suggesting it would be more proper to speak of a verb "consignifying time," recalling that time provides the background for whatever is said, and that the present situation is normally assumed unless otherwise indicated.[10] Aquinas also recommends that we treat compound expressions like "is white" as the verb, rather than consider the verbal expressions to be a "copula" linking two names. As innocent as this looks, it effectively shortstops an analysis of Aristotelian logic as a "logic of terms" in the usual sense in which this description grants primacy to *names*. Aristotle himself is not clear on this point, but Ackrill notes that he does insist that saying that a man walks is no different from saying that a man is walking (119–20, cf. 21b9). Relational expressions like "John hit Thomas" would certainly require a more sophisticated account, yet the rudimentary one given here will come in handy for an analysis of action and responsibility in ethics.

To return to the main line of the present inquiry, it is germane to comparing the brief accounts of name and of verb to note what Aristotle

---

9. *In* 1 *Peri Herm.* 5.54.

10. Ibid., 5.63. By "background" I mean a context which envelopes both speaker and what is spoken about: I said/say/will say that something was/is/will be the case. By "consignifies" Aquinas notes that my saying it requires a reflexive activity and expression if I wish to advert to it.

does *not* say about a name. He does not introduce a name as signifying the something else of which "things are said" when we make an assertion using a sentence. He does say that the verb functions as "a sign of things said of something else." Hence the verb signifies precisely as the formal aspect of the primary element of signification, the sentence. For we use a sentence when we want to assert that something is the case. The name is merely said to signify "by convention," which underscores the context of language and the immediate linguistic form of the sentence. Names, in other words, do not signify in their own right, but only as part of a sentence. And unlike verbs, no mention whatsoever is made of their role. This I take it, is what Aquinas is suggesting by calling their function a "material" one by contrast to the verb's formal or constitutive role.

Some Objections to So Interpreting Aristotle

One might retort: what you make much of Aristotle passes over because it is obvious. Names just refer to something, that's all. Their role is the elemental one of referring. An objection like this one reminds us how basic are the paradigms at work here. My response must call attention to the pseudo-clarity of referring, challenge the status of a referring relation as the basic constituent of meaning, and remind us of the primacy Aristotle accords to statement-making sentences. If sentences of this sort are the basic unit of discourse, then nouns (like verbs), as parts of them, do what they do in virtue of their role *in* the role played by the statement-making sentence. If that role is to refer, referring would then be explicated as part of what such sentences succeed in doing. And since the other paradigm has not been able to offer a clear view of the referring it takes to be basic, it would seem worth our while to explore another route.

So far I have relied heavily on a part/whole scheme when speaking of noun and verb in relation to the sentence. Parts are related to wholes, however, in more than one way, and the relation of parts of the sentence to the sentence is especially difficult to clarify. It is worth exploring before we go any farther—first to acknowledge the plausibility of the paradigm which I am opposing, and then to pinpoint more accurately the facts of which a new paradigm must attend.

The relevant statements are the following:

> A *sentence* is a significant spoken sound some part of which is significant in separation—as an expression (φασις), not as an affirmation (Καταφασις). (16b26)

> A single statement-making sentence is either one that reveals a single thing or one that is single in virtue of a connective. There are more than one if more things than one are revealed or if connectives are lacking. (Let us call a name or a verb simply an expression [φασις], since by saying it one cannot reveal anything by one's utterance, in such a way as to be making a statement, whether one is answering a question or speaking spontaneously.). (17a15–17)
>
> When uttered just by itself a verb is a name and signifies something—the speaker arrests his thought and the hearer pauses—but it does not yet signify whether it is or not. (16b19)

The first definition intends to distinguish *sentence* from *name* precisely from the character of their parts, for "none of the parts [of a name] is significant in separation" (16a20). The point is clear if its formulation appears too stringent: whatever significant expressions one might extract from the term "measure"—"me," "a," "sure"—their significance separately plays no role whatever in the meaning of "measure."[11] Nor is their meaning in any way a function of the meaning of the whole of which they are parts.

Perhaps the sense of Aristotle's formulation may be a little more apparent now: "me," "a," and "sure" are no more *parts* of "measure" than are "m," "eas," and "ure." It is not *qua* significant sounds that the first set appears, but by a double accident: the peculiar collection of letters in "measure" and an equally fortuitous partitioning of that string. The parts of a term are more properly the single letters (or phonemes) which make up the token, and these need have no significance apart from the term for the term itself to be significant.

The parts of a sentence, however, must be significant in separation. How, then, are they parts, and parts of a significant whole? More precisely, how can their significance be said to be a function of the significance of the whole of which they are parts? For that is what the new paradigm contends. The clue Aristotle offers in support of this contention is his distinction between expression (φασις) and affirmation (Καταφασις). It is one thing to signify (or to reveal) something, and quite another to affirm whether what is signified is or is not, i.e., to state what is the case.

The parts of a sentence signify, then, in their own right. What they cannot do separately is state that what they mean is in fact the case. Yet Aristotle expressly selects statement-making sentences as the focal instance of sentence for this inquiry into meaning and interpretation (17a5). This

---

11. Ackrill discusses the various possible ways of talking "in separation" (*Aristotle's Categories and De Interpretatione*, 116–17).

deliberate focus suggests that Aristotle considers the statement-making function of discourse to be more important than any other point discourse may have when it comes to considering how language does its job as a *significant* tool. In these terms, then, the linguistic unit designed to make statements becomes functionally the basic unit of discourse.

The fact that its parts are themselves significant units would not prohibit Aristotle's designating the sentence as the basic unit of significant speech. All that is required is that the way in which the parts signify must be in function of their role in a sentence, since the whole is contained in the definition of a part. This requirement would be satisfied were the sentence normally to supply the minimal context necessary for settling disputes regarding the meaning of a term. For invoking a sentence could only succeed in settling ambiguities if the sentence were the normal place wherein meaning could be said to be definite. In this originative and normative sense, then the *parts* of speech—notably nouns and verbs—could be said to signify separately, but only if the immediate context were able to exhibit their respective roles in a statement-making sentence, the focal unit of speech.

The question-form offers a handy example. "What was Paul doing today?" calls for an action term, so the response "walking" would be unequivocal even if Walking were a nearby suburb. Anyone who responded "walking" in this setting to the less definite question "where was Paul today?" could expect a further query: "*out* walking?" or "*in* Walking?" The single-term response "walking" will succeed in signifying "separately" only if this ambiguity is settled, and the question aims to settle it by determining in colloquial fashion what *part* of speech "walking" was in the initial response. The gestures of pointing or of moving one's first two fingers across a surface could serve the same purpose, of course. But they would do so by accomplishing the same end of fixing "walking" in the role of place-name or of action-term. And since the parts are parts of a sentence, and the roles are roles in a statement-making sentence, we may conclude that single terms may signify "in separation" only if their separate use manages to preserve enough of their sentential role to enable us to place them as parts of speech. In short, parts succeed in signifying separately only when they are not separated from their intrinsic role as a part.

The key requirement for a term's referring unequivocally is not that we manage to establish its connection with a definite object or characteristic, then, but that we succeed in locating its role in a sentence whose meaning is definite enough to meet the needs of the situation. In fact, "the situation" itself cannot be picked out without a set of descriptions which manage to circumscribe it. And those same descriptions will determine what are to count as objects within or characteristics of that situation. Aristotle's practice confirms this language-centered approach. He settles ambiguities by offering sample expressions employing the disputed terms. The presumption seems to be that language users are themselves in the world and have learned to make their way about in it by observing and employing the distinctions embodied in language to clarify and make definite what they intend to mean or to do.

In summary, I have developed a case for the primacy of the statement-making sentence as the basic unit of discourse for Aristotle, and then tried to be faithful to the implications of that position. By showing how it is possible to interpret his statements about parts of the sentence signifying separately in a manner which in no way disturbs the focus on the sentence, I have considerably weakened the plausibility of that view which links *substance* with *name*. In the process I also called attention to another way of handling the question of *reference*, namely by showing how in practice we work for more definite and unambiguous meaning by fixing the context of an expression in sentences. These textual and philosophical observations should prepare the way for another view of substance in Aristotle.

APPROACH TO SUBSTANCE

I shall begin gathering remarks about substance from the *Categories* (using Ackrill's translation) and then consider the relevant passages from the *Metaphysics*. The reason is a hermeneutical one: the *Categories* are closer to the *de Interpretatione* in spirit and in time of composition, and such a manner of proceeding defers to those who must distinguish logical from ontological considerations in Aristotle. If part of my aim is to render that distinction useless, it seems only fair to allow it to function while it can. The consideration about elements of speech has prepared us to notice carefully how Aristotle introduces key elements. Specifically, just as the naming or subject-role in the sentence was not defined in terms of substance, so substance is not defined by that role.

"Substance" in the *Categories*

"A *substance*—that which is called a substance most strictly, primarily, and most of all—is that which is neither said of a subject nor in a subject, e.g. the individual man or the individual horse" (2a11). The two characteristic ways of predicting—classifying or modifying—are covered by the "of a subject" or "in a subject" phrases, and adequately distinguished by their logical grammar. (Thus, if Socrates is a man and a man is an animal, then Socrates is an animal; but if Socrates is white and white is a color, then what?) So *substance* is what is *not* predicated, and the best examples are living individuals. Aristotle does not say what we might expect him to: that substance is the subject of what is said—however it is said to be, i.e., *of* or *in* the subject. By defining substance over against predication and by offering the examples he does, Aristotle seems intent upon accenting the individual existing thing, the manner in which substance is a *this* (το δετι).

Yet he does go on to speak less hesitantly of substance as subject: "all other things are either said of the primary substances as subjects or in them as subjects" (2b4–5). This remark is better taken as an observation than as a definition. Taken by itself, it can hardly be construed to be defining *substance* as that to which the subject refers, and hence as that thing of which something else is said. What the statement does is to locate whatever *functions* as subject in the domain of substance. The next sentence articulates what this linguistic fact exhibits: "If the primary substances did not exist it would be impossible for any of the other things to exist" (2b5–6). What exists is an individual, a this: "Every substance seems to signify a certain 'this'" (3b10).[12]

Hence Aristotle culminates this sketchy yet studied treatment by observing that "it seems most distinctive of substance that what is numerically one and the same is able to receive contraries" (4a10). That is, what makes substance so central yet so bothersome is that it is presupposed to the entire activity of saying things but cannot itself be said. Yet *it*, "for example, an individual man—one and the same—becomes pale at one time and dark at another, and hot and cold, and bad and good" (4a20). Notice that Aristotle does not find it remarkable that these different things can *be said of* substance, but that the same thing can *be* "pale at one time and dark at another." That is, what is said of the subject—when we use a sentence to say what we know of an individual thing—constitutes or enters into the make up of that substance about which we are speaking. In spite of the fact that whatever is said is said *of* substance, nevertheless what is known thereby *is* the substance.

It is in the sense that the modifications (signified by the verb) must be thought of as "received" into the thing in question. This fact is remarkable

---

12. A similar interpretation can be offered for *Categories* 2b15: "Further it is because the primary substances are subjects for all the other things and all the other things are predicated of them or are in them, that they are called substances most of all." (Contrast Edgehill's translation: "... that they are the entities which underlie everything else.") The linguistic role of subject exhibits a prime characteristic of primary substance, but does not exhaust its meaning. Thus the name cannot be said to signify the substance, but at best to indicate that something is at issue which cannot be subsumed into a predicative function—viz. an individual man.

enough, but it stands out even more sharply when the modifications are contraries: the sorts of things which, when said, exclude one another. If substance were to be linked directly and exclusively with the subject role in the sentence, then what Aristotle considers most distinctive of substance would not stand out for the remarkable fact that it is. For the modifications (signified by the verb) would appear still external to the substance (signified by the noun), however much one insisted that they were modifications *of* it. In fact, as history has shown, the ambiguities latent in the proposition "of" allow it to represent both internal and external relatedness.[13] The fact is however, that the man *is* pale. "Pale" is not said of him as though he (the substance) were neutral. What is said of him is that he is pale.

This final observation suggests that if anything signifies substance, it is not the name alone nor the name in a subject role, but the sentence itself. Substances are the usual sort of thing we talk about, and so much so that whatever we talk about we cannot help but construe as a substance. And we talk in sentences. Aristotle does not say this in so many words. But he does refrain from identifying substance with subject-role in every case where the parallel constructions call for it. (This care certainly challenges a reader to do something a little more skillful than simply assert the obvious identification which Aristotle avoided. Furthermore, the history of that identification has proven futile. A look at *Metaphysics* Z and H, where as Ackrill remarks, "the discussion of substance ... goes a good deal deeper than does this chapter of the *Categories*" [81], should provide some more positive indications.)

"Substance" in the *Metaphysics*

What we might call "features" of substance are not modifications in the usual sense. Otherwise substance could not function as "primary being." Of the two characteristics adduced in the *Metaphysics*, both were adumbrated in the *Categories*, and neither is strictly speaking characterizable: "'primary being' means something that is one and is a 'this-something'" (1037b27). What singles it out as "primary being" and hence axial to Aristotle's way of understanding is to identify *this* with *what-is-understood*—the intelligible object of an inquiry which must find unity to achieve understanding: "in the case of being primarily and essentially substance, the being is one and the same with its 'what' or intelligible constitution" (1032a5).

But the "what" here harkens to the question form: *what is x?*, not to the statement form and its verb part which signifies what is said. For what can be said of something is a "such" and not a "this" (1033b22). Hence the

---

13. Cf. Lieb, Review of *Word and Object*, with most relevant observations at 106–8.

verb portion of the statement-making sentence signifies not the substance but the form. The substance is signified better in the "definition which states what it is to be; and 'what it is to be' (το τι ην ειναι) belongs to primary being, either solely or especially, primarily and simply" (1031a12). Hence the sentence—specifically the statement-making sentence and notably a definition—best exhibits the unity or intelligibility which is substance.

It remains to be shown why the definition is so central to intelligibility for Aristotle by recalling how it functions. Then we have to wonder about identifying the *what* with *this*. Can anything more be said here, or are we reduced to a hard, substantial kick? Before undertaking these tasks, however, it is worth noting that Aristotle himself was aware of the muddles involved if one insists upon the "obvious" interpretation of *Categories* 4:

> We have now briefly stated what one sense of "primary being" is; namely being not what is said of a subject, but being the subject for whatever is said. However, we must not stop here; for this is not enough. The statement is itself not clear; and, besides, it implies that primary being is really the material. . . . If all attributes are removed, nothing but material appears to remain. . . . By "material" I mean that which is in itself not a particular thing or a quantity or anything else by which things are defined. . . . Hence, in the last analysis a subject is itself not a particular something or quantity or anything of the sort; not even their negations, for the negations, too, would belong to it only accidentally. It follows from these considerations that primary being is material. But this is incompatible with what we said about primary being as "a something"—something in particular. (1029a6–28)

ROLE OF DEFINITION

The unity or intelligible *what* which makes substance to be primary being, then, is displayed by the form of a statement-making sentence rather than by the name in its subject-place. And of these sentences, definitions are privileged: "the definition states 'what a thing is'" (1029b20). The Aristotelian legacy illustrates well enough how this contention about definition has been misunderstood. The results include another sort of unknowable status for substance. For we can never adequately define anything except our own intellectual constructions. Furthermore, preoccupation with definition encourages a search for formulae upon which we can all rely by rote. To understand Aristotle's point properly, however, and to grasp its implications for an understanding of substance, we must examine the *role* definition plays for him.

The appropriate source is his general theory of inquiry (or methodology) as elaborated in the *Posterior Analytics*. I need only present the main lines of the scheme. The aim of scientific inquiry is to attain a grasp of one's object in its essentials. Ideally, to know what a cucumber is would be to be able to list all of the context-invariant descriptions of which cucumbers obtain, and to be able to state as well why they are context-invariant. The first requirement is difficult enough, for it represents a formal as well as descriptive component: one must know that these and only these statements always obtain. The second requirement is explanatory and demands a causal analysis. The result would be a grasp of one's object in its essentials, for he would know all that must be said of the object and why it must be said.

Although investigation will be involved in formulating descriptions, we can understand what is essential only when we have demonstrated why it is essential. This aspect of scientific knowing is inevitably deductive—as in its analogue in the hypothetico-deductive account of contemporary science. In Aristotle's account, the proper principles of the deductive phase are supplied by the relevant definition. The general rules of inference come from logic, of course, but the formulae which shape an inquiry and provide it with a proper object and appropriate method are the definitions. For one effect of definitions is that a set of terms has been shown to be inter-related by being implicitly defined. The definitions which arise result from asking certain questions rather than others. In this sense, Newton's Laws would function quite analogously to the way Aristotle envisaged definitions working. That is not to say, of course, that they would meet all of the requirements which Aristotle laid down for definitions, nor is it to minimize the distance which separates the *Posterior Analytics* from hypothetical inquiry. I have only noted the similarities to accent the formal function of definitions in Aristotle's theory of inquiry.

In this idealized picture, *the* definition becomes the single formula through which everything which must be said about the subject can be deduced and hence demonstrated of it. I say "through which" to distinguish this premise from the others which will be present, since every inquiry presupposes a wider context. The definition acts like a differentiating factor, then, to mark off a specific domain within a larger region. In this role the definition becomes that conception which unifies one particular type of inquiry. All the relevant facts about the object in question will be derivable through the definition and, on the strength of this derivation, proclaimed to be the relevant or essential characteristics.

To be able to state whatever *must* be said about an object is to have attained a grasp of it in its essentials. There is nothing more one need to know about it; he can claim to know all about it, to know it. Now, if there were a single statement which, in conjunction with other more general theorems, allowed one to deduce those characteristics and only those characteristics—hence to *show* their necessity by the purely logical manner in which they were derived—such a statement would play a unique role. We could certainly say that it stated the most important, most relevant, indeed the central fact about the object concerned. We would probably even be tempted to say that this statement articulated what it is to be such an object. For everything that we need to know about the object in question can be derived through this single statement in the execution of an orderly process of inquiry. In this precise sense, then, the definition functions as a unifying conception, implicitly stating all the relevant facts about an object or situation, and hence articulating whatever it is that makes the thing what it is.

All this is quite ideal, of course. There is no guarantee that we can come up with such a statement. Aristotle's own discussion assumed that it would be one statement, but there would seem to be no difficulty with conjoining two or three such statements if that many were needed to specify an inquiry. More seriously, proper definition and properties (= relevant or essential characteristics) are mutually defined so as to produce a classic hermeneutic circle. The only way out would be a far more hypothetical and dialectical working procedure than Aristotle envisaged. In fact, Aquinas remarked that the *Posterior Analytics* demanded that the inquiry be so thoroughly circumscribed by intelligence that nothing could possibly qualify except a frankly constructed enterprise like geometry.[14] Yet interesting as these observations and reservations may be, they are not particularly germane to our present inquiry. Ours is frankly interested in exposing the ideal: why is the definition so central to intelligibility for Aristotle? How does it relate so closely to substance?

These questions have been met by showing the systematic role Aristotle requires of definition. The model for inquiry offered by the *Posterior Analytics* is certainly excessively restrictive, but that is not relevant to our inquiry. What is relevant is to have shown how definition articulates substance in the context of inquiry. For inquiry links us with the earliest inklings of the notion of substance in the basic question form: *what* is it? Substance, or *what-is*, becomes a shorthand way of referring to any object of inquiry—in the inescapable fashion that (a) everything which we ask about becomes in that capacity an object and hence a kind of substance, and (b)

---

14. *In 2 Post Anal.* 12.525.

we feel an inquiry resolved when it returns to explicate some facts about the world of this's and that's. Most specifically, however, we have seen what makes a definition unique: the role it plays in inquiry. The statement which articulates the essence of a thing—what it is to be that thing—can be said to do so because every relevant fact about the object can be derived through that statement. The status of the definition is materially no different from any other fact about x; it is its role that sets it off.

The model provides a clear vantage point from which to dispose of the mysterious claims for essences, definitions, substances, and the rest. Needless to say, a good deal of insight is required to come up with a good hypothesis, but what shows that the hypothesis is a good one is the role it plays in subsequent inquiry. The same holds for definition in Aristotle: if we intuit essences (what it is to be such a thing), our intuitions can never succeed in showing that we have hold of the essence in question. It is certainly mysterious how someone ascertains the relevant features of a situation; experience reminds us how rare it is. But that goes for *any* relevant fact. To go to order them in an explanatory or elucidatory fashion requires skill as well as insight. Yet it is this ordered process of inquiry, not some special cognitive power, which unveils for us what it is for something to be what it is. Such at least is the way Aristotle saw and taught it.

To return to our initial discussion of substance and the statement-making sentence, the applications should be clear. Were substance—the *what* of *what is it?*—linked with the subject of the sentence, and facts about substance—accidents and classes—linked with the verb, then it might seem plausible to look for some special access to substance, while observation and description would serve to hand over the facts. But if, on the other hand, the quest for substance is reflected by the sentence and not by any of its parts, since it is what is spoken of in every descriptive statement, then the same sentence form which articulates facts will articulate substance. A definition is in this respect a statement like any other factual statement. What sets it off is the role it plays in inquiry. So the statement which articulates what something is—a definition—enjoys that distinction bestowed by a privileged position in a framework of inquiry. In this precise way the definition displays the first feature of substance, an intelligible unity, by unifying whatever must be said—all the relevant facts—in an orderly manner.

A "THIS-SOMETHING"

Aristotle not only remarks that substance also has the character of a "this-something" but also insists that the this-something is an intelligible unity

(1032a5, 1037b27). Here we have an assertion which has managed to raise more issues than it settled. He claims that substance draws together what he recognizes elsewhere to be quite disparate: the existing individual and intelligible generality. The discussion so far furnishes us with enough material and skills to elucidate what Aristotle is claiming here, and to assess how much of a problem—if any—remains.

The original account of *substance* in the *Categories* was thoroughly negative: "that which is neither said of a subject nor in a subject," and capped off with two examples: "the individual man or the individual horse" (2a11). A living, growing individual is always taken as the paradigm for *substance*; often enough it is Socrates: this distinctive man. Not that Aristotle is attached to uniqueness. He keeps after his goal: to attain a grasp of his object in its essentials. Yet he is confronted not with essentials but with individuals, and the most confronting examples of these are the distinctive and unique ones.

So living, growing things—and especially unique human persons—are most notably individuals and hence naturally offer the best examples of substances. They might be said to possess their individuality to a greater degree, but however we try to put it, the simple fact is that persons are more present to us than any-thing or any-fact else. We must do violence to ourselves to deflect their being here in front of me—an inescapable "this-someone." For nothing confronts me so effectively as another person. Hence it was natural for Aristotle to offer Socrates as an example of substance, and the very naturalness with which he is offered provides a vantage point from which to grasp the essentials of Aristotle's use of "this-something." That same standpoint will help us see why Aristotle could make an easy identification of "this-something" with what-it-is-to-be that something.

"This" as Ostensive

"This here now" has not proven to be a transparent expression whose meaning is open for all to see, but clearly it is not a request for an explanation. That request stems from the other facet of substance: that it is one or an intelligible unity. Hence those projected inquiries into a "principle of individuation" manifest an elementary misunderstanding. The role of "principles"—matter/form, potency/act—is an intelligible one: to show the manner in which substance is (intelligibly) one, not to explain individuality (1045a20-b25). For individuality—the this-here-now feature of substance— is not what is up for investigation but what confronts us. Hence the abstract noun "individuality" is especially misleading here, for it immediately poses *this-here-now* as a *what* to be asked about, described, and presumed to have an intelligible unity. But is there another way to get some purchase on it?

A now classic attempt was to locate "this-here-now" as a logically unique expression: a logically proper name. This is clearly the proper tack, and to recommend it is to exhibit how the substance issue pervades inquiry. We have just noticed it is speaking of "individuality." If we want to get hold of one of the constitutive "features" of the central analytic and methodological notion of substance—a *feature* which is then *not* itself a substance—we will have to succeed in exhibiting something which cannot be said. For whatever can be said is said of a substance, so that a formal feature of substance must be displayed some other way.[15] How we construe this displaying poses our difficulty, and the failure of the ostensive model is illustrative. "This-here-now" cannot function in a straightforward ostensive way because nothing can. When these words couple with a gesture to point to something, they succeed exactly in the measure that the something is a *unity* for both speakers. A unity, not an individual—for *that* "feature," interestingly enough, is obvious—and therefore an intelligible unity reflecting a focus of concerns.[16] So construing "this-here-now" as ostensive does not succeed in exhibiting its logical uniqueness, but lands us back into the logic of substance: a *what* that is both one and a this-something.

"This" as Positioning

I would like to suggest as an alternative way of construing the logical peculiarity of "this-here-now" to say that it is a *positioning* expression. In this way I hope to catch both the obvious sense in which we are surrounded by individuals and also the manner in which we are confronted by them as individuals. The failure of the ostensive model illustrates how *individuality* and *unity* differ. "This-here-now"—even coupled with a gesture—does not succeed in picking out an object (= a substance) because an object is at once a unity as well as an individual: was it the surface or the table that you were interested in? In fact, unity seems more important than being a this-something. For whatever we talk about becomes an object by the fact that we attend to it, and hence assumes the guise of substance. Yet we are

---

15. I am adopting the expression "formal feature" in the sense in which Wittgenstein speaks of *formal* or *internal* properties of facts; cf. Zemach, "Wittgenstein's Philosophy of the Mystical," 362. Beginnings of this discussion can be found in Aristotle's reflections on the parts of the definition in *Metaphysics* VII.10.

16. Hence in learning a foreign language children are our best guides, for they seem bent on the same functional concerns as the beginner who simply needs to find his way around in the new world.

concerned with situations and states of affairs more often than we are with individuals. (In this sense, unity could be called the more *formal* feature of substance; and its being a this-something, its *material* side.) Yet there is something compelling about an individual, and that is not so much *what* it is but that it looms up in front of me, blocks my progress or alters my direction—in short, confronts me.

It is not the knowing-me but the making- or acting-me which is confronted. And in such a confrontation I am recalled to my making or acting self, and hence challenged or invited to respond. In being so recalled, I am immediately "positioned" over against the this-here-now; and my own response as an inquiring subject must be to "take a position" in regard to this thing. The latter activity will of course be of an articulate sort and hence carried out in the full-blown language of unities, not in the truncated aspect-language of "this-here-now." But the effect of a this-something has been to trigger this articulate response, and to do so by confronting me.[17]

Articulating and Asserting

I occupy a position as an individual. Hence the possibility of another individual thing's blocking my way. But I *take* a position by articulating and asserting something about the object confronting me. (In fact, the semantic charges on the terms "block" or "confront" already anticipate someone's responding by *taking* a position). I must articulate my position in order to assert it, but articulating it is not yet asserting it. Normally the forward movement of our lives moves us smoothly from cerebration through assertion to action, but often enough we hesitate in a hypothetical state, unable to judge and so incapable of acting. So it should be clear that articulating that something is the case does not yet amount to asserting it. Yet Aristotle regularly conflated the two. The reasons why he conflated articulating and asserting are obvious enough, yet examining them will lead us deep within his cast of thinking. We will be able to appreciate the care which he took to keep distinct yet related the two aspects of substance—a *unity* and a *this-something*—if we attend more closely to what he tended to overlook: the distinct yet related activities of articulating and asserting, or of understanding and judging.[18]

---

17. My debt to C. S. Peirce and his categorial scheme of first-, second-, and thirdness should be evident here. See my "C. S. Peirce: Pragmatism as a Theory of Judgment" (chapter 6 in this volume).

18. This approach has been clearly and persuasively developed in another fashion by Novak, "A Key to Aristotle's 'Substance.'"

There are some obvious reasons why one might overlook this distinction and some clear indications that Aristotle did. The clearest indication is the *Posterior Analytics*, where the premises of an inquiry must, among other things, be true. There is no room for hypothesis here, for a premise fully articulated but not yet asserted. Yet as we have seen, the formal structure laid out in the *Posterior Analytics* is none other than a hypothetico-deductive scheme. The requirement that definitions be assertions and not hypotheses is thus extrinsic to the logical model Aristotle introduces. Among the more obvious reasons for overlooking the distinction is Aristotle's predilection for what is normally the case. Normally understanding issues in judgment, and does so precisely because our inquiries are usually responses to what confronts us. A hypothetical inquiry reflects an "academic question."

Another and more illuminating reason stems from linguistic form. There need be no difference in *what is said*, whether it be tentatively proffered or asserted to be true.[19] To put it another way, which reinforces the first reason given: the normal context presupposes that one is asserting that the yellow stuff is margarine when he says, "that yellow stuff is margarine." And normally he is. Hence an assertion sign or a prefatory phrase like "it is true that" proves superfluous. Asserting or judging is the sort of thing I *do*, not the sort I say. Hence the same expression: "that yellow stuff is margarine" stands for something presently entertained—articulated though not yet asserted—as well as something asserted. So Aristotle's predilection for the normal context of ongoing, self-asserting life, as well as his close attention to linguistic clues, would have led him to overlook a distinction between articulation and assertion. Yet perhaps we can learn most from the manner in which he insisted that inquiry issue in assertion, and under Aristotle's powerful imperative to keep the two together, come to a better understanding of the nature of inquiry and of the peculiar centrality of substance.

Asserting and Making Statements

Recall the way in which Aristotle limited inquiry to the "statement-making sentence—those in which there are truth or falsity" (*de Interpretatione* 16b33). I argued at some length that substance—the *what-is-it?* that every inquiry is after—is reflected not by the noun-function nor by the verb, but by the sentence itself. All that need be emphasized now is what Aristotle took for granted and *we* may have overlooked: that the sentence is a statement-making sentence. When we use a sentence to entertain certain possibilities

---

19. Cf. Geach: ". . . a proposition may occur in discourse now asserted, now unasserted, and yet be recognizably the same proposition" ("Assertion," 449).

but are as yet unwilling or unable to assert it then *what* we are considering takes the form of an intelligible unity and to that extent is considered as a substance. But when we use the sentence to make a statement, and when the object of consideration is an individual before us, then we assert that *this one*—this man—is, say, an effective teacher.

Rather than considering this statement-making sentence as an accidental unity, however, where the noun stands in for the substance and the verb for what is said about it, the previous analysis focuses our attention on the sentence which speaks about the substance so modified or the modification received in it (*Categories* 4a10). If the previous analysis has so far persuaded, it can be extended to the matter at hand. We might be tempted to analyze a statement-making sentence into the noun which reflects the *this-something* and the verb which reflects the *unity*. Something like this might be suggested by the pseudo-statement: "this is a man." Allow me to propose rather that it is the statement-making sentence which articulates the *unity* and our using it to make a statement which reflects the *this-something*.

In asserting what I have entertained about the thing or situation in question, I take a position regarding it, and square off, so to speak, as one individual to another. So long as I am entertaining a particular question about this man or this war, I can put the "this" in brackets, and sometimes should. My task of understanding usually involves spinning out alternatives, comparing this situation with others of similar type, etc. But when I make a statement, I assert that what I have deliberated over is true of *this* situation; or more directly, I state that such is the case here and now.

The individual may be an inert object or a living, growing thing; or it may be a situation which involves or affects objects or living, growing things. All that is required is that it confront the making- or acting-me. For I am an individual *par excellence*—as was Socrates—and my individuality is displayed in my making the statements I make. Hence the full-blown *individuality* of any object or event lies in its capacity to confront me and is confirmed in the statements I make about it, just as the *unity* of any object or event lies in its capacity to be an object of consideration and is confirmed in the statement-making sentences that I propose in an effort to grasp it in its essentials.

Aristotle was able to *affirm* that an intelligible unity and a this-something coincide in substance as the object of inquiry because he was concerned with statement-making sentences and with their issue. He was unable to *show* why the distinct aspects coincide because he seems to have been as unaware of the distinction between articulation and assertion as he was aware that statement-making sentences are for making statements. He was so taken with the culmination which inquiry seeks—is it the case or not?—that he tended to minimize the hypothetical stage of consideration.

I am not saying that he actually proceeded in this way. The *Metaphysics* consists largely of *aporia*—of considerations about the way we consider and put things as we inquire into them—and so with most of his writings. I am rather suggesting that his own awareness of what he was doing and of what we are doing in inquiry was insufficiently reflective, and especially with regard to the related yet distinct activities of articulating and of asserting a sentence. Yet on the other hand, his insistence that consideration seeks a resolution and a stated resolution certainly includes by implication the individual who makes the statement. In other words, his insistence that the stuff of inquiry is statement-making sentences seems to be a naive way of gesturing towards the central role of the language user in turning up the object of inquiry as one and as a this-something.

SUMMARY REFLECTIONS

In summary, to know *what something is* for Aristotle means, in a vague initial way, to be able to state something about it. And we state whatever we do state by using sentences. Hence the *what* about which we are inquiring when we ask: what it is? is a unity of the sort that a sentence is. (His constitutive principles of matter/form flow from this analysis—which gives one an indication of their status.)

To know what something is in a precise and ordered fashion is to be able to state a sentence which serves as a definition. That is, we can use it in conjunction with other statements which delimit the generic universe of discourse, and together with the universal laws of logic derive all and only what *must* be said about the object in question.

Furthermore, when I state of a thing whatever I am able to say about it, that act of stating singles out the individual in question and asserts whatever I have to say of it. There is often an individual in question, and when there is not, the assertion retains its unity but simply has no immediate application. In this respect, whenever we consider anything, we consider it as though it were a substance, under the rubric of intelligible unity; but when we are confronted with an individual thing or event, we take a position vis-à-vis that object by stating something about it. The considerations preceding a statement reflect the unity of the object confronted; in asserting whatever we do, we respond to the individual by exercising our own individuality.

By reflecting upon the manner in which the same statement-making sentence can be used hypothetically during our considerations as well as assertively to state what we have arrived at—without a change in form to announce the change in function—I have tried to show how the "objective correlate" of the sentence, the *what* of the standard query, "what is it" can be at once a unity and a this-something. Furthermore, the analogy with articulation and assertion shows how the two aspects are internally related—as inquiry seeks resolution. Finally, the fact that asserting does not demand further articulation testifies that asserting is not a further consideration but an activity. Since actions are of individuals and terminate in other individuals, inquiry can culminate in saying something about *this* one because what is said is stated. The abstract and the concrete, if you will, are distinguished as the inquiring person inquires, yet united as that same person asserts his conclusions. In asserting them, a person exhibits his own individuality and confirms that of his object.

What people have always admired in Aristotle's earthy respect for the "concrete" comes out, on this analysis, as a respect for the activity of inquiry and the issue that activity seeks. We have doubtless moved beyond him in our feel for hypothetical inquiry, in our appreciation for a studied lag between formulating and stating a point. Yet curiously enough our own preoccupation with hypothetical inquiry has not only tempted us to overlook the internal pressure for resolution, but also fashioned that oversight into a pervasive bifurcation of abstract and concrete, ideal and real, objective and subjective, academic and down-to-earth, etc. The very expression "concrete" is a curiously inert way of referring to what Aristotle found most distinctive of individuals: that they are living, growing things. By keeping to the fore the issue inquiry seeks in assertion, Aristotle allows the living, growing *this*-something to be singled out by a correspondingly active individual who positions the object only in positioning himself.

The textual analysis and conceptual disentangling leads to one inescapable conclusion: any step beyond hypothetical consideration is self-involving. Hence one would suspect that an assertion with far-reaching consequences would demand a degree of awareness and self-involvement correspondingly higher than routine assertions call for. To speak of "degrees of awareness and self-involvement," however, asks for a logic and a language of interiority. It is certainly more than interesting that an analysis of Aristotle on *substance* can lead us back to ourselves in this fashion. And I cannot help but feel this conclusion compelling for any attempt to unravel what is involved in asserting something to be true.

Chapter 2

Aristotle and "Future Contingencies"
Another Interpretation

ARISTOTLE'S CHAPTER-LONG DIGRESSION IN the *Peri Hermeneias* (*On Interpretation*) to remark a restriction of the law of the excluded middle has touched off reams of commentary, logical, metaphysical, and theological. For the theologian, God's omniscience and human freedom were each a stake; for the metaphysician, the status (or reality) of time; and logicians professed to find here an application for their remote exercises in trivalent logics. But whatever be the concern of the commentator, a glance at any one of them is likely to discourage a student from pursuing a question which seems destined only to further entangle itself.

Hence our plan is first to outline Aristotle's argument, supporting our interpretation of key words by parallel passages, and taking the measure of recent discussions as we develop Aristotle's position. Then it will prove necessary to look more closely at the kind of modality implied (Part II), and finally to consider a classic theological application as a test of our interpretation (Part III).

I: ARISTOTLE'S ARGUMENT

The context in which Aristotle raises the question of the truth and falsity of statements about "future contingents" is a frankly logical one. The three preceding chapters (*On Interpretation* 6–8) take up the "affirmation and denial of propositions"—from the logical perspective of contraries and contradictories. From these relations between truth and falsity of propositions one can construct the "square of opposition"—given Aristotle's assumption of a non-empty universe of discourse (chap. 7). A logician is concerned that his relations be as general as possible, and that any restriction be explicable. Aristotle anticipates a difficulty "when the subject [of the proposition] is individual, and that which is predicated of it relates to the future," and chapter nine represents this attempt to "explicate" the ensuing restriction on his logic. The difficulty is the following:

> ... if all propositions ... are either true or false, then any given predicate must either belong to the subject or not, so that if one man affirms that an event of a given character will take place and another denies it, it is plain that the statement of the one will correspond with reality and that of the other will not. (18a34–39)

But we ought not be misled by the Oxford translation[1] into placing the blame on a "correspondence theory of truth." Given the context, it is safer to assume the difficulty to be a *logical* one, arising precisely because the preceding chapters presuppose a general principle:

(A) where "S" is properly used, "S is true (false)" is properly used.[2] Translating his logic of terms into propositional language, Aristotle is concerned lest he be committed to an unrestricted use of what we should call the "semantic definition of truth":

(B) if John affirms truly that *e will take place* (= S), then *e will take place*, since "S" is true ≡ S.

On this account, the ambiguities of a "correspondence theory of truth" would be quite irrelevant to the issue at hand, which is whether one can *say* of a proposition whose "subject ... is individual, and that which is predicated of it relates to the future," that it *is* true or false. To follow Aristotle's argument, one need not espouse a "correspondence theory" except in the noncontroversial sense that he would want empirical propositions to speak about the world, and true ones about the real world.[3] This vague notion of empirical truth is reflected in linguistic usage to the extent that one would

---

1. [Ed. note: Throughout this article, Burrell references Edgehill's translation of *de Interpretatione* (*Peri Hermeneias*).]

2. The formula is taken from Sellars, "Time and World Order," 527–616 (esp. 610), which has also proved immensely helpful in posing the questions correctly.

3. Hence we disagree with Richard Taylor that a "correspondence theory of truth" is an assumption (in the sense of a *premise*) of Aristotle's argument; cf. Taylor, "Problem of Future Contingencies."

not hesitate to let "S will be P" (said before now) be true if S were P now. We feel we have a right to speak of a statement about the future being true if the time comes in which we can *confirm* it—i.e., say of its present-tense counterpart that it *is* true, which means of course knowing that S is in fact P.[4]

Keeping the correspondence issue to one side, however, this simple fact of usage suffices to generate the puzzle Aristotle tried to face. Formulating our intuitions, we have

(1) S *is* P → ("S will be P" (said before now) *be* true)
where "be" is a non-tensed form of "is." By the "semantic definition of truth," we have

(2) "S will be P" be true ≡ S will be P
and by tense incompatibility,

(3) S will be P → ($\overline{\text{S is P}}$)
which, by transitivity, leads to contradiction: S is P → ($\overline{\text{S is P}}$).

Our thesis is that this is the difficulty Aristotle saw, and that his restriction amounts to saying that the consequent of (1) is not well-formed. Roughly speaking, his reformulation places "T or F" in the place of "T" ("S will be P" is T or F), while ours would replace "is T" by "was T," but in either case, one may no longer move through the semantic definition to a contradiction.

But why these restrictions? Aristotle's explanations are in terms of "necessity," "potentiality," "real alternatives," and similar notions puzzling enough in themselves; but when mixed with the intractable character of temporal discourse, they have succeeded in generating a welter of confused commentary. The only justification for adding to that list is our conviction that the source of much confusion has been importing one's own ideas of *necessity* (and the corresponding modalities), while failing to notice that Aristotle's are not introduced to *explain* the vagaries of tensed discourse but arise, as it were, out of the incompatibility of the tenses, and simply try to *formulate* certain of the intractable features of temporal language. This is the sense of Peirce's "Time is a particular variety of objective Modality," which we shall try to catch by insisting that (1) above must read

---

4. We have taken care to assume the weaker formulation that the occurrence of the event is *sufficient* for a statement said about it earlier to be true. One could also argue that it is a *necessary* condition as well. Cf. Ryle, *Dilemmas*, 15–35, esp. 20; and Ducasse, "Truth, Verifiability, and Propositions."

(1') S is P → ("S will be P" (said then) *was* true)
if we are to admit such a way of speaking at all![5]

We may illustrate by Aristotle's first argument: "If it is true to say that a thing is white, it must necessarily be white . . ." (18b1). The next step is to change the tense of the proposition in question to read: "*x* will be white." And if we be allowed to say that, Aristotle concludes that "everything takes place of necessity and is fixed," for

(4) if it *is* true to say that a thing *will be* white, it *will necessarily be* white.

But how is he using "necessarily" here? Certainly he is not taking the "absolute" modal operator, as Donald Williams and some medievals assumed, and asserting that $p \supset Np$![6] Aristotle of all people would not claim the "necessitarian thesis" for a major premise. And he warns us that he is not:

> Now that which is must needs be when it is, and that which is not must needs not be when it is not. Yet it cannot be said without qualification that all existence and non-existence is the outcome of necessity. For there is difference between saying that that which is, when it is, must needs be, and simply saying that all that is must needs be, and similarly in the case of that which is not. (19a22–27)

But what is this "once it is, whatever is is-necessarily"?[7] It is what one might call "temporal necessity" or unalterability. It is the kind of necessity which the lapse of time itself imposes on things. It is not an *absolute* but a *relative* modality, stating that, given *x*, it is impossible (= "too late") for *x* to be otherwise; but says nothing of the character of *x* itself—whether it be contingent or a necessary happening.

This is usually considered to be a trivial or commonplace sense of "necessity," precisely because it seems to obliterate the distinction between necessary and contingent events, making all future happenings contingent and all past ones necessary. And so it simply says (with emphasis) that past

---

5. Peirce's statement is found in his *Collected Papers*, 5.459. Peirce's remarks on this chapter of Aristotle are encouraging: 6.96, 6.368; and his own observations on *time* illuminate them: 1.488ff., 5.459–63, 6.127–31. Albritton argues from the strangeness of this use of "true" and "false" that such questions rather *do not arise* ("Present Truth and Future Contingency," 29–46, esp. 32–34).

6. Cf. Williams, "Sea Fight Tomorrow," 282–306, esp. 291; and Prior, *Formal Logic*, 210–11. Aquinas was not confused in his commentary, *In 1 Peri Herm.* 15.201.

7. The formulation is Prior's (*Formal Logic*, 248).

events are past, and future ones yet to come![8] Yet Aristotle will contend that *time* enters intrinsically into our notion of the modalities—that "no capacity relates to being in the past, but always to being in the present or future."[9] This conception is commonly criticized as "anthropomorphic," in the sense of embodying our feelings about voluntarily influencing the future, but it can be formulated without any reference to will or "occult powers." For the sense in which "capacity" includes an intrinsic reference to the future follows directly from the rule for the use of "possible."

> (C) we may say that *p* is possible if no contradiction follows from assuming that *p* be the case. (Cf. *Metaphysics* IX. 3, 1047a24)

Notice that "possible" can only be used *relatively* according to this rule, which presupposes there be other conditions in conjunction with which *p* may be said to be compatible or not. In the next section we shall consider the points of contact and disparity between this sense of "possible" and the more "absolute" sense of "conceivable," but for now let us examine some of its consequences and its contribution to the thesis: "whatever is, once it is, is-necessarily."

On such an account we cannot say, for example:

> (5) it *is* possible to have won the game we lost yesterday,

since to assume the game won conflicts with the true statement that we lost it. But we can say, until the last moments of play, that it is possible to win a game we are losing (i.e., so long as enough *time* remains to carry out the plays), and we can certainly always say it with regard to tomorrow's game. This is why, then, Aristotle could say that "capacity" cannot be said of the past—indeed if we try to use "possible" with respect to the past, we must convert the past into a hypothetical present or future:[10]

> (6) it was possible to win that game, or
>
> (6') it would have been possible to have won that game.

Now this is the sense of "possible" which gives us the notion of *relative necessity* which Aristotle uses in his argument against saying that *p* is true where *p* refers to a future contingent state of affairs. On the supposition that *x* is white, it is impossible that it not be white, since "Possible (*x* is not

---

8. Cf. Taylor, "Problem of Future Contingencies," 11.

9. *de Caelo* I. 12, 28b13. Peirce's cryptic remark that "hypothetical propositions, unlike categoricals, essentially involve the ideas of time" seems related to Aristotle's point (*Collected Papers*, 3.446).

10. *In* 1 *de Caelo* 29.285.

white)" *means* that no contradiction follows upon assuming it not to be white. Therefore it is impossible that *x* not be white, or it is necessary that *x* be white *on the supposition that it is*.

All this looks quite trivial and even wrong-headed, for apparently it forbids us from saying that this object may very well *not* be white—it seems to entail "necessitarianism." But Aristotle would answer emphatically no, for there is nothing to make us suppose that what is now white *will always be* so. This in fact is precisely what we mean by a thing being changeable, and a property contingent. Hence when we say that *x* may well not be white (= "can be not-white"), we are saying that to imagine it not-white *at some future time* does not entail a contradiction with the true statement that it is *now* white.[11] *Possibility*, then, contains an intrinsic reference to *future time*, and this does not arise because we have conceived it anthropomorphically (in the pejorative sense of that term), but follows directly from its character as a *relative* modality. (We shall see in Part II the consequences of accepting such a definition as basic, and weigh them against other analyses.)

Correlatively, says Aristotle, what is *future*, so long as one can only say of it that it *will be*, for example, *white*, bespeaks the possibility of being otherwise. One cannot operate, in other words, with "*x* will be white" as with "*x* is white," laying it down as the supposition on which it is impossible that *x will not be* white. (This amounts to saying that one cannot move, via the semantic definition of truth, from saying "'*x* will be white' is true" to laying it down that *x* will be white.[12]) ". . . will be . . ." just does not lay down a condition like ". . . is . . ." does, but *embodies* the possibility of being otherwise.

The notion of *contingency*, then, reduces to that of "genuine futurity" in the sense that the event is in no wise occurrent—in fact or "in its causes." By the latter, Aristotle is referring to an invariable set of laws which would link a future event to an occurrent state, and so render it a *virtual fait accompli*. In such a case, since present conditions are what they are (and hence cannot be otherwise), and since they physically imply an event yet to occur, this event is *already*, as it were, subject to the relative necessity which governs *faits accomplis*, and so cannot be said to be contingent because it is not *genuinely future*.[13]

---

11. On the other hand, to say that it *might never have been* white is simply to say that one can *conceive* it as being of another color without contradiction. Aristotle would probably want to say that this "absolute" sense of possibility is derivative from our experience with things now white and later not.

12. Cf. *In* 1 *Peri Herm.* 13.171.

13. Because Taylor does not see this interconnection of "nomical contingency" with "genuine futurity," he must insist that Aristotle assumes a future event to "have both kinds of contingency" ("Problem of Future Contingencies," 14, 21). We can also see the

Since science seeks for *this* kind of knowledge—is concerned with events not *qua* occurring but as exemplifying a law-like scheme (linking future to present state descriptions)—Aristotle's restrictions on using "... is true" for statements about future contingents simply do not envisage scientific prediction. What they do remind us, however, is that "genuine futurity," while uninteresting to science, is nevertheless a compelling fact of our ordinary experience, and central *at least* to our initial conceptions of modality.[14]

Before looking in greater detail at the modality Aristotle uses, let us examine his supporting arguments that:

(7) "S will be P" is true

is ill-formed. The heart of his contention is that "... will be ..." simply does not succeed in laying down the conditions excluding "... will not be ...," so that one cannot say that *it* is true, for what he asserts to be true may *turn out to be* false. (The dual argumentation, of course, holds for *denying* that S will be P.) And if we should try to determine "... will be ..." on the model of "... is ...," we would betray that very characteristic of tensed discourse from which our notions of possibility (and necessity) are derived.

This argument is supported by a *reductio* which will also suggest a finer formulation of the restriction. Aristotle takes the intuitively valid form we have already considered:

(8) if a thing is white now, it *was* true before to say that it would be white (18b10, italics ours)

and moves quickly to "it *was always* true," from which one can easily derive the *atemporal* "... *is* true" or "... *be* true" of the semantic definition, and so arrive at the contradiction embodied in (1) and (3) above. Hence he concludes that "that which was truly predicted at the moment in the past will of necessity take place in the fullness of time" (18b35).

Note that this follows (by relative necessity) because

(9) "was truly predicted at the moment in the past"—

something which we can only say (if we can say it at all) *because* we know that the thing is white *now*—is assumed to be equivalent to

(9') "is truly predicted now" (said then, i.e., where *now* = that moment in the past)

---

irrelevance of Williams's concluding remark that a regular astronomical event in the future would not evoke the same response in us as a sea fight does. Of course not, for the sun's rising is not a "genuine future" to the extent that it is a law-like action.

14. Cf. Peirce, *Collected Papers*, 5.459.

on the model of:

(10) "... was green then"

as equivalent to:

(10') "... is green now" (said then, i.e., where *now* = then).

But Aristotle's statement is not a consequence of our admitting the validity of (8), because the only warrant we acknowledged there for saying that it *was* true to say *x* would be white was its being white *now*.

This means that our native reasoning, formulated in (8), is acceptable only upon clarifying the fact that the "was" in

(11) "S will be P" *was* true

is an *irreducibly* tensed verb, which does not admit the move from (9) to (9'), nor the shift in Aristotle's *reductio* which licenses "... *was* true" = "... *was always* true" = "... *be* true." Its use may be captured in the explicit definition:

(12) "S will be P" (said then) *was* true ≡ "S is P" (said now) *is* true

which means of course (by the semantic definition) that S must be P for the "... *was* true" scheme to be used.

This is, however, simply another way of stating Aristotle's restriction: that one can only say

(13) "S will be P" *is* (true or false)

for both are trying to formulate the fact that a statement about a genuinely future event cannot be said to be true *from the perspective of* the speaker. Each attempts to indicate the modality which time itself embodies for those who "take it seriously," and so each in its own way blocks the use of the atemporal "... is true" of the semantic definition of truth, which leads inevitably to contradiction since it neglects that special character of "... will be ..."

II: RELATIVE AND ABSOLUTE MODALITY

A philosophical discussion of modality usually begins by a division into *real* and *logical*, and nearly as often discards *real* modality as fraught with ambiguity, and settles for a clear-cut *logical* notion. Here too discussion may well ensue as to whether a modal operator must be followed by a proposition or not—i.e., whether modality cannot help but introduce an intensional character to logic. But these distinctions are not immediately relevant to our concerns, which look rather to the meaning one attaches to the modal operator. This is determined of course by the definitions, but these are often so indeterminate that one must look rather to the consequences that result from them. Aristotle was able to draw our attention to the modality inherent in time by using what we have called a *relative* notion of possibility. One might also dub it "existential," since the rule:

> (C) we may say that *p* is possible if no contradiction follows from assuming that *p* be the case

envisages an existing object already possessing properties perhaps incompatible with the one said *possibly* to belong to it. Without prejudicing the issue of many forms of *possibility*—each capable of being the basis of a modal system—we should like to contrast Aristotle's *relative* possibility ("M") with the *absolute* or "essential" possibility of traditional modal systems, namely "logical conceivability" or absence of self-contradiction ("$\Diamond$").[15]

It can readily be seen that relative modality is too confining, and absolute so wide in meaning that it may be undecidable whether it applies or not. Consider the statements:

(14) although *x* be red, it might well not be

(15) if *x* always be red, it is *never* not-red.

And by relative modality, on the supposition of *x*'s *always* being red, we have

(16) if *x* always be red, it is *impossible* for it not to be red.

But something is wrong, for we also want to be able to say that *given x* as always red, it is nevertheless *conceivable* that it not be always so. We want to be able to say *both*:

(17) M ((E*t*) ($\overline{R(x, t)}$)), i.e. it is possible that there be a time when *x* is not red, *and*

(18) (*t*) (R (*x*, *t*)), i.e. but *x* is always red.

Now it is clear that we cannot say both if "M" stands for relative modality, for applying rule C makes us assume that

(17') (E*t*) ($\overline{R(x, t)}$)

be the case, which contradicts (18). And it is almost as clear that all we can *really* say is

---

15 Lewis and Langford, *Symbolic Logic*, 160–61; Prior, *Formal Logic*, 185–93, 248–50.

(19) (t) (Conceivable (R (x, t))) & Conceivable (($\overline{R(x, t)}$))

which, replacing "Conceivable" by "◊," gives us the traditional definition of Contingent (Rx):

(19') (t) ◊ (R (x, t)) & ◊ ($\overline{R(x, t)}$)

These few propositions suggest that while relative modality (via Rule C) gives us rather effective control over the use of "possible," it also forces us to uncomfortable conclusions. Absolute modality, on the other hand, allows us to say pretty much what we want, but at the cost of not being quite sure what we are saying.[16] Without trying any further to explore the *meanings* of one or the other, one might at least recognize that relative modality is linked with an open-ended and undetermined future, when x might not be red even though it be red *now*. Hence the puzzles arise when one wishes to speak of *all time*, for this violates the implicit conditions for using relative possibility by treating time as a *given*, as though it were all *past*. Tactically, then, one has the option to use relative modality, with the understanding that he will not try to say anything about *all of time*, or settle for the absolute notion where he need not worry about such restrictions but is less sure what he means to say by it.

Von Wright has suggested a system of relative modality which incorporates rule C into the symbolism by making it explicit that Mq = M (q/p)—i.e., that "possible" is said relative to other conditions.[17] He notes that such a symbolism can include "absolute" modality as a limiting case, where p is a tautology. Hence

(20) ◊ $q \equiv$ M (q/t).

The first draft of von Wright's paper had as Axiom I:

(21) ~ M (~ p/p)

which we may read as "p is necessary, given p," and might be paraphrased as "p is necessary, given the fact that p." But what of the *fact that p*? We may

---

16. William Kneale has criticized Hume's argument against causality as too free and easy a use of "conceivable," from a sense-data epistemology, in *Probability and Induction*, 78–89. Cf. also Peirce, *Collected Papers*, 5.187; and Geach, *Mental Acts*, 115: it is doubtful that disembodied sensations are really "conceivable" because "too many threads are broken, and the conceptual web has collapsed."

17. Von Wright, "New System of Modal Logic." The four axioms of this paper, however, were originally proposed as the following: 1. –M (–p/p), 2. M (p/h) v M (–p/h), 3. M (p & q/h) → M (p/h) & M (q/h & p) (from a typescript loaned to me by Alan Ross Anderson of Yale University).

raise the question, but this system of modality is not designed to handle it. If we wish, to say that the *fact that p* is contingent, we may write:

(22) M (p/t) & M $(\sim p/t)$.

But to say that something is possible *relative to a tautology* is even less illuminating than to say it is "logically conceivable" or non-contradictory. Yet perhaps this is simply another way of *showing* how difficult it is to pin down the meaning of the absolute modalities. At any rate, von Wright's work has the advantage of providing an example of a modal system constructed on notions similar to those Aristotle was using.

Here it becomes evident that one cannot have both (17) and (18) because the formalism picks up the relative, temporal aspect of (14) by making us say that it is possible that it not be red *even though* it is so *now*:

(23) M $(\overline{R\,(x,\,t)}\,/\,R\,(x,\,t))$.

Now this would contradict von Wright's first axiom (21) unless the *times* be different. Hence

(23') M $(\overline{R\,(x,\,t_a)}\,/\,R\,(x,\,t_b))$ — where $t_a \neq t_b$

which incorporates Aristotle's restriction against using relative modality under the supposition of *all* time—for with "t" universally quantified we could not stipulate that the times be different, and the result would contradict (21).

III: A THEOLOGICAL USE

By emphasizing the central role of the "semantic definition of truth" rather than a "correspondence theory" (even Aristotle's), and by indicting how *contingency* is derived from *genuine futurity*, we have been able to undercut the thorny issue of "real" or "nomical contingency." This often takes the form of an apologia for the *indeterminacy* of the future, and is usually considered as intimately bound up with "Aristotle's thesis on future contingents."[18] It generates puzzles like "there is only one possible past, but many possible futures," and trades on our unwillingness to consider a future event as "something neat and complete awaiting merely the external passage of time in order to be able to appear on the scene, irrelevantly decorated with one date rather than other."[19] Yet when the observations are collated—"there is

---

18. Taylor, "Problem of Future Contingencies," 14, 21–23.
19. Weiss, *Nature and Man*, 12.

no longer any *real contingency* in things past"[20]—and definitions examined, what the "doctrine of real contingencies" says in effect is that "... will be ..." is not reducible to "... is ...," or what amounts to the same thing: that temporal sequence cannot be reduced to a neutral reckoning whereby "now" becomes irrelevant. But this allows no decision as to whether the future be *determinate* or not. It simply insists that it is not *determined* like the present and past are. Hence Taylor's definition of *real* or *nomical* contingency: that it is "really undetermined by anything past or present whether an event of a given description is going to happen," is a fair description of what we could call the "genuine future."[21] For all we know, the future may well be *determinate*, and if the question can be adequately parsed, it might be relevant to note that what will be most certainly will be. In this (tautological?) sense at least, the future is *determinate*. But however we may feel about the question or this reply to it, it is quite distinct from Aristotle's. He is merely insisting, on a much more modest plane, that the future cannot be considered of a piece with the present and the past (i.e., *is* not *determined*), and this is but another way of reminding us that temporal discourse cannot dispense with "now"—that tenses, in other words, are irreducible. That Socrates died in 399 BC, for example, does not tell us whether he has *already been* executed—something we feel entitled to now—unless we can locate 399 BC with respect to our "position" *now*. But the *undetermined* in this sense is not necessarily *indeterminate*, and the distinction is worth drawing because we can comprehend somewhat what it means to say that tenses are irreducible and "now" indispensable to temporal discourse, but the question as to whether the *future* be *determinate* or not seems quite undecidable, being answered at best by the truism: what will be, will be.

Aquinas put this distinction to work in tackling the thorny question of God's omniscience and contingent events.[22] By rightly distinguishing relative from absolute modality, he was able to accept the substance of Aristotle's position (as we have interpreted it), which served to stake out what could be *said* in attempting a penetrating formulation of the Judaeo-Christian tradition on this point.

---

20. Taylor, "Problem of Future Contingencies," 23.

21. Ibid., 13.

22. Aquinas's summary treatment is given in *ST* 1.14.13; but the more extensive and illuminating discussions of *de Ver.* 2.12; *de Malo* 16.7; *In* 1 *Peri Herm.* 14; and *Quodl.* 11.3 ought to be consulted as well. In the last cited, Aquinas invokes the determined/determinate distinction in other terms: "Dicendum quod praedestinatio *certitudinem* habet, et tamen *necessitatem* non imponit."

God, if He is to know future contingent events, must know them *as present*.²³ For if He knew them *as future* (and His knowledge were true), He would determine them. So much follows from Aristotle and his use of relative modality. Only if the future event can somehow be a present event to God can He be said to know it truly without necessitating it. For in that case, He will know it in such a way that it cannot be otherwise, but only because He knows it *on the present condition*—just as our *seeing* Socrates seated is warrant for our saying that he *cannot* be standing, so long as the present condition be fulfilled.

A theologian in the Judaeo-Christian tradition must maintain that creation does not in general necessitate the creature, and the logic of Aristotle's treatment of "future contingencies" suggests this way of formulating the issue. God, then, must know future events as present ones, or *in themselves*. But they are not, by definition, *present*; they do not *as yet* exist "in themselves." Aquinas freely admits this, but goes on to remark that then it must be that there is no "not as yet" for God. Nothing is irreducibly *before* another for Him, because to Him everything is *now*. For God (and for Him alone) time is a pure B-series (McTaggart), and can be viewed as a spatially extended sequence.²⁴

It is important to see how closely these conceptual moves are tied to the logic of Aristotle's position. The objection is (and was) that this is a *merely logical* (or "purely verbal") solution, and the crucial question has long been thought to be: how can God or anyone else know what does *not yet* exist, and indeed know it *as existing*? This is particularly embarrassing to a metaphysical tradition which would hold it as axiomatic that whatever is *known* must to that extent *be*, and translated into these terms, the question becomes: what kind of *being* have these possibles which *will become* actual?²⁵

This formulation tries to force the logical move of restricting "yet" in reference to God into an ontological language which will show up the ambiguities by making one admit some *tertium quid* between the possible and the actual. (Such a position is similar in many respects to that of *sense-data*

---

23. A typical formula, again from *Quodl.* 11.3: "omnia cognoscit tamquam presentia *in sua presentialitate*" (emphasis added).

24. The reference to time as a "B-series" alludes to the discussion of McTaggart in *Nature of Existence*, chap. 33; and the commentary by Broad in *Examination of McTaggart's Philosophy*, 264–323. Aquinas uses the model in the passages cited in 37n22 from *de Malo*, *Quodl.*, and *In Peri Herm.*

25. A good survey of the seventeenth-century discussions can be found in D'Ales, "Science divine et décrets divins"; Weiss in *Nature and Man* discusses it to explode it (12–13); the formula "known *as existing*" is from Aquinas, *de Malo* 16.7.4.

and every bit as unstable.) But let us look more closely at what is claimed. To say that something is possible-but-not-actual is to say that it is as yet *undetermined*. To say that it will-become-actual is to say that from God's point of view it is *determinate*. But such knowledge is not *determining*—that is, the "it" remains undetermined, though it is determinate—unless one be speaking from *within* the time-series, where "now" is indispensable. Only then does a *determinate* knowledge of the future *determine* it. For one to be able to speak truly of a future event, then, it suffices that he attain a perspective whence "now" be dispensable. And correlatively, it is sufficient to preserve the "plasticity" of the future, its undetermined character, that discourse about it be inextricably interwoven with "now."

So the *ontological* question carries us back to the semantic issue, and the only effective objection is to deny that there is such a "perspective," that anyone be capable of assuming it. If the force of the denial be that it is inconceivable to us what knowledge from such a perspective might be like, there is no argument, for Aquinas would freely admit as much. If this be the objection, it envisages all theological statements and not simply the issue at hand.

If on the other hand, the distinction between *determined* and *determinate* be declared unworkable, there is some plausibility to the objection. For the connatural way for us to come to grips with the *determinate* is through the *determined*. This is precisely the role of models in science: to provide the analogies whereby we might have some inadequate but suggestive picture of the entities whose postulation allows an extensive application of theory from other domains. Theoretical entities are usually described, from a more deductive view of scientific theory, in a manner which glosses over their role: simply as *presupposed* to the mathematical formalism. But in either case, there are telling similarities with our distinction, because these entities are not *determined* in the sense that they exist like the models do, and yet the theoretical extensions of science depend on their being and hence their *determinateness*.

But there are dissimilarities as well, and the example offered is but an *indication* that we use a similar distinction in other domains. It may be that the distinction is unworkable, in which case God's omniscience is certainly bounded by the ever-advancing frontier of the present, for there simply *is nothing more to know*.[26] But it is noteworthy that this conclusion is not a simple consequence of Aristotle's insight into the peculiarities of statements about "future contingents," for strictly speaking Aristotle has merely shown that the future is not determined like the past. The logic of his posi-

---

26. Cf. Weiss, *Nature and Man*, 12; Hartshorne, *Man's Vision of God*, 98–104, 327–29.

tion leaves open the possibility of the *future* being *determinate* from *a*temporal "perspective," though it does set the conditions under which such a perspective would not *determine*, and certainly entails that we can have no grasp whatsoever of what such knowledge would be like, since "now" can never be eliminated from *our* temporal discourse.

Aquinas has embodied this fact in his insistence that the only way we can speak of the future being *present* (since by definition, what *will be* is *not now*) is according to the *mode* of knowing proper to God.[27] All we can *say*, then, is that for a knower to whom "now" is dispensable—not in the sense in which it may be irrelevant, as in science, but in the (incomprehensible) sense in which every moment is present—for such a knower there would be no need for "before" or "not yet" because all is *now*.[28] We can say this much by the logic of the theorems at play. Aquinas offers a model of a spatially extended series: a file of marchers viewed alternatively from within the ranks, and from a vantage point whence one can survey the entire line. To more easily apply the example, consider the men marching backwards. Then the position of any marcher marks his *now*, from which he can look back over his past, but gain no insight into the future. From the lookout's vantage, however, no one man's position is absolute, but all are measured by their place in the entire line-up. This image, often misused, is grossly inadequate because it fails to embody the hiatus between the two viewpoints. In the example, the same observer with the same basic powers can be freed from the footsoldier's limited vision simply by being raised to the general's perspective. But in actual fact no man can have the least conception of what knowledge might be from *outside* his temporal perspective. Yet the model remains interesting, especially to us, because it incorporates Aristotle's insight, and says that only God can coherently view time as a B-series alone.

Yet to speak of a determinate though not determining knowledge of the future as proper to God alone accentuates the fact that Aristotle has spelled out the terms of human discourse about the future, and reinforces our suspicion that to inquire whether the future be *determinate* or not can never meet with a determinate answer. By the same token, any speculation as to the kind of *being* the future would have if it were determinate is bound to be fruitless, because the only possible answer would be in a *mode* of knowledge proper to God, and so utterly incomprehensible to us.

It is instructive to note how Aquinas makes use of Aristotle here to formulate the conditions which must be fulfilled if God be omniscient and

---

27. *de Ver.* 2.12.7; and consequently, a mode of willing proper to God alone: *In 1 Peri Herm.* 14.197: "Hoc autem non potest dici de voluntate humana nec de aliqua alia causa...."

28. As Aquinas puts it, God's knowledge is "measured by eternity," in *Quodl.* 11.3.

not necessitating. Once these formal conditions are laid down, nothing more is said. After stating that the future must *somehow* be present to the divine intellect, and noting that this presupposes a distinction between a future that is *determinate* and one that is *determined*, no attempt is made to say what this knowledge might be *like*. In fact, it is expressly noted that we cannot have any inkling of it, since knowledge of this kind would "measure events by eternity," and this is proper to God alone, as our event language is irreducibly tensed.

Though we have carried it far enough as an *illustration*, the theological issue cannot be considered finished. Certainly if Aquinas can avoid any necessitation, can save the *reality* of time and existence *and* have the kind of omniscience with which the Judaeo-Christian tradition has usually credited God, then this view is to be preferred to that of Hartshorne and Weiss. Yet they would question precisely whether Aquinas's move to avoid imposing necessity on future events—that they be somehow *present* to God—has not by that very fact destroyed their "genuine futurity" by denying any ultimate reality to time and occurrence. In Peirce's language, it is claimed that God knows future events in their *secondness* (i.e., *qua* occurring) and yet secondness means to convey exactly that sense in which "now" is indispensable to our speaking of anything in time—as demonstratives are to our positioning anything in space. What Aquinas must claim is that secondness may be intelligible to God and yet remain truly secondness. He can *consistently* make this claim, since he maintains that while man's knowledge is always an instance of *thirdness* (= knowledge by signs or concepts), God's is not, and the logic of the issue we have been considering is one of the strong arguments for his insisting that God's knowledge must be immediate, "intuitive," by "simple presence."[29] And to know *secondness* in this way would not entail its "turning out in the last analysis" as *thirdness*. Hence existence, occurrence, and the *now* of time remain irreducible on Aquinas's account because of the unique *mode* of divine knowledge, but God becomes more and more transcendent, approaches more and more the mysterious "I am" of the Judaeo-Christian tradition. While this was to be expected, since that tradition shaped many of the demands on Aquinas's formulation, one might ask whether these demands, together with the logical theorems at play, produce a philosophically *coherent* view. Since one's answer to this, however, will depend largely on what he requires of a philosophical treatment of God, it is clear that our "example" has outlived its usefulness.

---

29. Among the many places where Aquinas develops this point: *ST* 1.14.4; 1.19.5; *In de Causis* 13; and *In* 12 *Meta*. 11.2614: "the intellect of the first [principle] ... understanding itself understands everything else."

That usefulness—to briefly summarize—was to manifest the strength of Aristotle's treatment of "future contingents" by showing how it could provide the basis for a consistent resolution of one of the thorniest of theological issues. (So thorny in fact that is it usually cast as a perfect dilemma: with God's omnipotence or man's freedom.) It also allowed us to reinforce our contention that Aristotle envisages the correct *use* of tensed discourse, by showing how an ontological puzzle could be translated into a question about use of tenses. (It is no longer likely that anyone will conclude that Aristotle is therefore talking *only* about language, but should anyone want to, it is worth reminding him that he has no *right* to conclude so.) And since it is that very use of tenses which forms the core of Aristotle's modalities, this raised the unresolved issue of relative and absolute modality. Aristotle would certainly want to say that any "absolute" meaning of "possible" is derivative from our experience with things *now* in one state and *later* not—that *relative* possibility is the more connatural conception, and that it presupposes finite spans of time open-ended to what *may become* the case.[30] Von Wright has offered Aristotle *some* support by showing that a form of relative modality may be symbolized which contains the absolute as a limiting case. This would further suggest that "possibility" is an analogous notion and so warn one to move carefully in *using* an absolute (*or* relative) modality borrowed from systematic use. Perhaps the distinction between *determined* and *determinate* can be adjudicated in terms of these diverse modalities: the *determined* containing an intrinsic reference to occurrence; the *determinate* ranging over the conceivable. Be that as it may, we hope to have shown that Aristotle treats of whether the future be determined or not, and that any further conclusions from his position involve either an unwitting confusion of the *determined* with the *determinate* or a forthright denial that any such distinction be tenable. By an analogy from the role of abstract entities in scientific theory, we have suggested that to deny the distinction would severely limit inquiry by demanding that whatever is thinkable be determined—or exist in the same sense as physical objects do.

---

30. Cf. *de Caelo* I. 11 and 12, 283b12.

Chapter 3

Entailment
"E" and Aristotle

"LET US USE THE term 'entails' to express the converse of the relation *q follows from* or *is deducible from p*."[1] The forty or so years separating us from this remark of G. E. Moore has seen a plethora of writing on *entailment*—much of it devoted simply to staking and establishing its claim to a peculiar and proper usage in the face of its competing relatives: "implies," "materially implies," and "strictly implies." One may at least hope by now that using "entails" will appropriately communicate our concern for logical consequence or deducibility, the sense in which the conditional "if p then q" would convey some connection between p and q. For the non-polemical, logical task consists in making as explicit as possible this "inner connection" indigenous to ordinary conditional statements. This is the aim of Anderson and Belnap's system E, and we might be satisfied to say that "q depends on the logical content of p if and only if $p \to q$ is provable in E," were it not that E so frankly invites neighboring consideration, conscious as its authors are of formulating but a part of what men would call "reasonable argumentation."[2] We hope to throw some auxiliary light on the meaning of arrow expressions in E by calling attention to significant similarities between this system and Aristotle's syllogistic. This approach was suggested by the obvious similarities in preoccupation, and has allowed us—in the spirit of a perennial philosophical enterprise—to highlight certain features of the syllogistic in

---

1. Moore, "External and Internal Relations," 291.
2. Anderson, "Completeness Theorems for the System E." Cf. also Anderson and Belnap, "Tautological Entailments."

a rather novel fashion—novel at least in clarity over against medieval commentators, and quite novel in the face of more recent commentary, notably Łukasiewicz.[3]

REVIEWING OPINIONS

Before launching into a detailed comparison, let us briefly review selected articles since Moore to pinpoint the sense of *entailment* operating here.

First of all, Moore's examples are quite explicit:

> We shall then be able to say truly that "p entails q," when and only when we are able to say truly that "q follows from p" or "is deducible from p," in the sense in which the conclusion of Barbara follows from the two premises, taken as one conjunctive proposition; or in which the proposition "this is colored" follows from "this is red."[4]

We are neatly outside of a merely truth-functional relation.

Paul Weiss, writing some ten years later (1930), is concerned to distinguish "entailment" from "implication" (*not* simply "material implication"), and lays it down that while both fail on "T implies/entails F," that nevertheless the antecedent of an *entailment* always is contained in (or contains) the alternatives of the consequent, while this is never true of *implication*.[5] Similarly, *entailment* is always necessarily true, while *implication* never is. Entailment, meanwhile, divides irreducibly into *extensional* and *intensional*, where extensionally, a part entails the whole of which it is the part, and intensionally, the more specific in meaning entails the more generic. While Weiss will argue incisively that the *extensional* notion is conceptually dependent upon ("logically secondary to"; Strawson) the *intensional*, what concerns us is his insistence that there is no common notion underlying these two. Entailment, then, is not a generic, but an analogous notion, realized in two distinct and related, yet irreducible ways. "Material implication"

---

3. For an incisive medieval commentary on what the syllogism is reaching for and what its elements presuppose, cf. Albertus Magnus, *Commentarium in Priorum Analyticorum*, 1.1–2; 4.6. For a general appraisal of scholastic commentary on Aristotle, cf. Bochenski, "De consequentiis scholasticorum earumque origine," 106–9. The modern commentary on Aristotle, now standard, is Łukasiewicz, *Aristotle's Syllogistic*. Moody in *Truth and Consequence in Medieval Logic* comments in a similar tenor on the scholastics.

4. Moore, "External and Internal Relations," 291.

5. Weiss, "Entailment and the Future of Logic," 143–50. On the level of commentary, "contains" and "is contained in" manifest an ambiguity hard to eradicate.

of PM turns out to be *extensional entailment*, where the tautological entailments ($q \supset pv-p, p.-p \supset q$) are valid only because there is no real deduction here, since PM's logical propositions merely stand for an exhaustive set of alternatives, which is certainly entailed by an proposition. We shall see how valuable many of Weiss's remarks will prove to be—notwithstanding the obscurity of the original "implies" with which "entails" is contrasted.

Norman Malcolm, writing ten years after Weiss, wants to sharpen Kant's criterion, namely: "p entails q when the consequence is contained in the antecedent," which he formulates as follows: "p entails q when q is not a 'further fact in addition to p'."[6] He would doubtless accept Prior's subsequent translation of this criterion from fact talk to proposition talk, but the difficulty remains: presumably q *looked* at first like a distinct fact from p; otherwise analysis would have no job to do. Yet if we are told that entailment is used to bring to light what is *implicitly* contained in p, this simply restates the problem. What does it mean for q not *really* to be a further fact in addition to p, when it *looks* like it is? It means some astute philosopher can show q to be deducible from p.

Jonathan Bennett and A. N. Prior are willing to grant the "connection of meanings" indigenous to entailment systems, but rather than try to formally eliminate the paradoxical entailments (Strawson apparently failed and Smiley can only come up with severely limited systems in reward for his efforts), they would convince us in Hegelian fashion that there *really is* a "connection of meaning" in paradoxes.[7] "Any proposition asserts (at least implicitly) something about *all* objects whatsoever" (*hence $p.-p \supset q$*), and "a necessary proposition is implied by all since it can always be introduced" (so $q \supset p \text{ v} -p$). Now to *introduce* is not to *deduce* (as Weiss has noted), and one might question just *how* any proposition *asserts* something about everything? (Even should he want to say that a *judgment* of its truth or falsity is "implicitly total," it would not follow from this operation that anything could thereby be deduced from it. Judgment in this sense is not understanding.)

Finally and most recently, von Wright and Geach have insisted that entailment is a frankly *intensional* notion: "p entails q if and only if it is possible by means of logic to come to know that truth of 'p entails q' without coming to know the falsehood of p or the truth of q." In other words, entailment is *essentially* relational and cannot be understood truth-functionally.[8] (Von

---

6. Malcolm, "Nature of Entailment," 333–47, esp. 341; Prior, "Facts, Propositions and Entailment."

7. Bennett, "Meaning and Implication," 451–63, esp. 462–63; Prior, "Facts, Propositions and Entailment"; Strawson, "Necessary Propositions and Entailment-Statements"; Smiley, "Entailment and Deducibility."

8. Von Wright, "Concept of Entailment," 166–91, esp. 181–82, 175. Cf. also Geach, "Entailment," 157–72, esp. 164.

Wright's remark that it is the "⊃" understood *intensionally*, only reflects a straining to communicate his thesis in a truth-functional atmosphere. The "⊃" has no meaning but an *extensional* one!) Von Wright's insistence *inter alia* that the "problem of entailment ... leads ultimately to the problem of the conditions and meaning of demonstrability" is yet another warrant for a detailed comparison with Aristotle.[9]

Now there is a way, of course, of showing that $p \to q$ independently of truth-functions, by treating it as set inclusion and use Euler's circles. It is perhaps worth recalling that this handy pedagogical device neatly begs the question of relevance by presupposing it. There is no concentric representation of the paradoxical implications. And the further fact that relevance becomes purely extensional, making deduction and proof a trivial affair of inspection ought to warn us that the solution is too easy. The thrust of this maneuver was to make the syllogism mechanical, so allowing one to move to more flexible systems. But for Aristotle, συλλογιξειν is not something mechanical and if the syllogism be inflexible, the explanation is tied to reasoning itself, a native process which the "syllogism" rests on and certain aspects of which it seeks to codify—not legitimize.

Codifying is fascinating and necessary. It reflects reason's aesthetic side and in the drive to simplicity may demand greater formal freedom than Aristotle's syllogistic. But simplicity and transparency are not the *only* regulative principles of reason, and the subsequent efforts of Procrustean codifiers to so persuade us strikes one as dangerously internecine, though the relations are too abstract to see. Indeed, to try to break logic off from its roots in reasoning is self-defeating, and that not for "metaphysical" or "psychological" reasons merely (though these may well be relevant), but simply because an ideal of purely formal freedom coupled with an aesthetic preoccupation with simplicity can lead to greater *restrictions* on reason than Aristotle dared imagine. In short, there is another kind of flexibility that the "rigidity" of the syllogism was made to exhibit. This is the "argumentation whereby one proceeds from what is known to what is unknown," reason as the tool of inquiry, of our "coming to know."[10] How little of this process need be germane to an axiomatic system can be judged from Weiss's observation that a "deductive" system with inference defined truth-functionally and allowing substitution and detachment, useful as it may be structurally, has in fact frozen out *deduction*. "Follow from" has very little hold where there

---

9. Von Wright, *Logical Studies*, 135, 165, 188; viii: "The concept of entailment is closely related to the concept of demonstrability. And the demonstrable is that which, by means of logic, we *may* come to *know*."

10. Albertus Magnus, *De predicabilibus* 1.1; Geach, "Entailment," 164.

is no first or last, where what comes before or after is largely a question of aesthetics.

But what is *deduction*? What are we saying when we assert that q can be deduced from p? We are at least making explicit what was hitherto but implicit. And vague as this contention may be, it already suggests the inadequacy of Euler's circles as more than a preliminary tool. Everything there is already transparent. The fact that one circle is contained within another is something to be *seen*, not unpacked. Nothing remains to be shown, and most would agree that deduction is a process *showing* that something is implicitly contained in another, and in the process, exhibiting it *as* so contained by explicitly bringing out its "grounds." This, at any rate, is what it means to *demonstrate*, and von Wright reminded us of its affinity with entailment.

Aristotle treated this aspect of the syllogism, its use as a tool in coming to know, in drawing out the implications of our common notions, in the *Posterior Analytics*. Here the stringent conditions which implicitly define demonstration are conditions on *predication*. But this is simply to remind us that Aristotle took the subject-predicate form as normal to assertion, and modeled on it his "logic of terms." Assertion itself is complex, molecular, and yet is also an element in reasoning, where it is called a "premise."[11] These "premises" fit the mold of the syllogism, itself shaped with a view to handling the premises. We want to explore the analogies between the Aristotelian subject-predicate model and a propositional one which preserves the essentials of his predicative relation, and manifests even more perspicuously the role of assertions as premises and premises in argument. We offer the following reconstruction of Barbara:

I. *If*   if for all x, p, then for all x, q
         and
         if for all x, q, then for all x, r,
   then if for all x, p, then for all x, r.

(where "for all x, p" may be read as "all x is p" or "all x exemplifies p" and so on.) That is:

II. *If* $(x)\,(Px \to Qx)$ and $(x)\,(Qx \to Rx)$ *then* $(x)\,(Px \to Rx)$, which is:

III. $(x)\,(((Px \to Qx)\ \&\ (Qx \to Rx)) \to (Px \to Rx))$, which abbreviated is:

IV. $((p \to q)\ \&\ (q \to r)) \to (p \to r)$

---

11. Cf. Albertus Magnus, *Commentarium in Priorum Analyticorum* 1.3.

Interpreting the arrow in the sense of Anderson and Belnap's E, we want to examine the syllogism in the light of E, and E in the light of Barbara, for what mutual illumination this might gain for the meaning of entailment.

ANALYSIS OF ARISTOTLE

Our thesis is multiple but converging. It is invited by Alan Anderson's concluding remark: "... but for expressions involving the arrow we know no suitable definition of 'true'"[12] and encouraged by Moore's choice of examples for entailment: the "if ... then ..." of Barbara, and a statement of enveloping generality: "this is red" entails "this is colored." Together, these point to the medieval contention that Aristotle's theory of the syllogism rests firmly on a doctrine of predication: that what permits one to draw necessary conclusions is precisely the order of enveloping generality among the premises. (If what is red is colored and what is colored is extended, then what is red is extended.) The position of the premises is irrelevant, their relative universality is decisive. These two: position of premises and relative universality were distinguished by medievals as *artificial* and *logical* form, respectively.[13] Barbara is perfect, because the two forms coincide: the external or artificial form lucidly *manifests* the logical relationships involved, which license deduction. (For the scholastics, the *perfection* was that of art perfectly "imitating" nature.) The fundamental logical relation, that underlying all the others, is *predication*, and Barbara is paradigmatic since all of its premises are universal.

What is important to notice here is that one may conclude logically without Barbara, for it is not Barbara but the order of enveloping generality which licenses deduction.[14] But Barbara is not completely superfluous for it *shows* us that this is the case.[15] The heart of deduction is interlocking universality; the anatomical model designed to display its functioning in cut-away fashion is called "Barbara." Hence it is significant that Moore's examples are exactly the model and the kind of inclusion the model was constructed to manifest. And similarly, we shall find in medieval writings a continual shifting from the model to what it is meant to show, as Plato hit upon the state

---

12. Anderson, "Completeness Theorems for the System E," 216.

13. Cf. Albertus Magnus, *Commentarium in Priorum Analyticorum* 1.2.

14. Cf. *In 2 Post Anal.* 8.486–88, where Aquinas speaks of a certain kind of definition validly *concluding* to what a thing is, and only differing from a (demonstrative) syllogism *incidentally*, i.e., in the order and position of terms.

15. Albertus Magnus, *Commentarium in Priorum Analyticorum* 1.2. On this as a logical ideal, cf. Wittgenstein, *Tractatus*, 4.022.

and its functions to manifest the inner workings of its citizen, man. We shall see also how Barbara precisely manifests the predicative relationship, carrying over to the conclusion the kind of predication found in the premises.

Predication

But first, what is this "predication"? There is little doubt that it is fundamental to entailment—from Aristotle's defining it at the outset of his theory to recent controversy on the definition of "⊃" as set inclusion. Aristotle himself defines it in terms of *inclusion*: "That one term should be included in another as in a whole is the same as for the other to be predicated of all of the first. And we say that one term is predicated of all of another whenever no instance of the subject can be found of which the other term cannot be asserted."[16] The definition is of universal affirmative predication; but "to be predicated of none," he says, "must be understood in the same way." It is significant that "to be predicated of" in the sense of "be included in" is defined here to cover indifferently what the *Posterior Analytics* will speak of as accidental and essential predication, where *essential* bespeaks an intrinsic tie between subject and predicate ("all men are rational"), and *accidental*, the explicit absence of (knowledge of) such a tie, where one must have recourse to enumeration ("all swans are white"). The "all (no) . . . is P" form, then, is indifferently extensional or intensional on Aristotle's definition.

But is there a notion of *predication* still more basic that is at work here, the sense of "predicate" which applies to the ordinary declarative sentence? This question is suggested by the fact that syllogistic premises are not ordinary sentences—if only because singular terms are prohibited and the same term must be able at times to serve as both subject and predicate.[17] Now Aristotle insists in the *de Interpretatione* that there is something natural about the way subjects and predicates fall out in ordinary speech, and we certainly use sentences to speak about individuals.[18] What is the difference between the ordinary sentence and a syllogistic premise, and how can we express it?

The difference, we suggest, is as follows. The "*s* is *p*" of an ordinary declarative sentence *asserts* something of a subject. Analyzed, there is something said ("is *p*") and something of which it is said (*s*). This relationship, we would want to hold with Aristotle, is primitive. Aquinas likens it to matter-form, the "predicate being as it were the formal part; the subject,

---

16. See Jenkinson's translation of *Prior Analytics* I.1 24b27–29.

17. For Aristotle's syllogistic and singular terms, cf. Łukasiewicz, *Aristotle's Syllogistic*, 5–7.

18. *de Interpretatione* 4–5.

the material."[19] The "is p" is like form; it will give the assertion a direction or "sense." But it *needs* the subject to complete itself; it is, as Frege would have it, "unsaturated," while "s" alone *says* nothing.

The "all s is p" or the syllogistic premise, however, does not so much assert something of another as it asserts a relation holding between two things that can be said of another— relation of greater or less generality. The subject is, as it were, suppressed—or rather underlies *both* terms.[20] Aristotle has extended the "s is p" model of ordinary speech to a technical use, and instead of reflecting that extension in the *form* of the premise, chose to introduce restrictions on the kinds of terms permitted. This required twisting the predicate into noun-like form, and forced the medievals to fabricate a theory of transformations to assimilate both insights: the radical difference between subject and predicate in ordinary speech, and the fact that in a logical premise the same term may be used as subject or predicate.

FROM STATEMENT TO PREMISE: AN HYPOTHESIS

What Aristotle is really saying by "all s is p" is, we suggest: "if anything is (has) s, then that thing is (has) p." A model syllogism would look like the following:

> IF   if x is rational then x is risible
>   and if x is a man then x is rational,
> THEN if x is a man then x is risible.

We have written the syllogism as a principle of inference, making explicit that the line in the form of argumentation answers to "if . . . then . . . ." We have emphasized that the *form* of argumentation that is Barbara was constructed with an eye to manifesting the relation of enveloping universality holding among the terms of the premises. This way of recasting the premises shows the strictly parallel use of "if . . . then . . ."—as the schema of each premise and of the entire paradigm. (As an abbreviation of this interweaving use of "if . . . then . . ." we may now introduce the arrow [→], freighting it along the way with subsequent remarks and waiting until the end to discuss its relation to the arrow of E.)

This form has the added advantage of retaining Aristotle's insight into the irreducible character of the subject-predicate relation by allowing the terms whose relative generality will carry the deduction always to *function*

---

19. *In 1 Peri Herm.* 5.54, 8.95–96; *In 1 Post Anal.* 36.309–13. Cf. *In 2 Peri Herm.* 2.215.

20. Cf. Moore, "External and Internal Relations," 296–97.

as what they are, predicates.[21] The relation "x is rational" or simply "x rational" remains irreducible even if it be not the same in all cases, as in "x rational" and "x man," where the categories of the predicates differ. A set theoretic interpretation may help illustrate the point. Whereas one can, if he wishes, consider the relative universality expressed by "if . . . then . . ." as set *inclusion* ("the set of all rational items is included within the set of all risible ones"), it is hardly illuminating to try thoroughgoing set-theoretic reconstruction by reading the "x rational" relation as set *membership*. For the statement: "if anything is a member of the set of rational items, then it is a member of the set of risible items" only makes us wonder what it means—what one has to be or do—to belong to the set of rational (risible) things. When reformulation only forces the issue to change its verbal apparel, one suspects that something fundamental is at stake. What remains true—and what the reformulation exhibits—is that whatever "category" the predicate may exemplify, what is essential is that it is said or asserted of the subject. To say that this relation cannot be reduced to set-membership (without investing "ε" with the same properties, which belies the reduction) merely recalls in this context what has been frequently noted elsewhere: the inherent difficulty in carrying through a radically extensional interpretation of logical inference.

Connection: Accidental and Essential

There is a sense of "extensional," however, corresponding not to the truth-functional, but to the Aristotelian *accidental* "all swans are white." This usage is applicable, then, not to the relation "x swan" or "x white" but to the "if . . . then . . . ," and it says in effect that being a swan has nothing to do with being white, so far as we can tell, but merely that every specimen we have come across happens to be so. What is interesting here is that the overarching "if . . . then . . ." of the syllogistic form—the principal arrow in the abbreviated "$(p \to q) \& (q \to r) \to (p \to r)$"—transmits faithfully from premises to conclusion the *character* of the relative generalities holding in the premises—denoted by the "secondary arrows." Whatever the premises may exemplify, *accidental* or *essential* (necessary) connection, is carried over into the conclusion.

---

21. Lest our concern for the *predicate* look archaic, we may refer to Sellars, "Grammar and Existence," 499–533, esp. 501, 512–13, 517. "The fundamental difference between 'triangularity' and '*that* x is triangular' would be that the latter makes explicit a *gappiness* or *incompleteness* which is perhaps implicit in the former." Cf. also Geach, *Reference and Generality*, 31–34.

PERFECT PARADIGM

But of course these questions do not arise until one essays an interpretation or application of the logic. Aristotle speaks of them in the *Posterior Analytics*. Whatever be the connection between the propositional variables of a premise, one presumes that the connection between premises and conclusion in Barbara is an intrinsic or necessary one. Indeed it was meant to be, and the interlocking generality (be it accidental or essential) is so arranged that it will be. This of course suggests a further parallelism of "principal" and "secondary" arrows: a perfect form of Barbara intimated by Moore's example "if anything is red then it is colored," where the premises reflect the necessity of Barbara so that *every* arrow denotes an intrinsic or necessary connection.

This is Aristotle's notion of "scientific demonstration" or simply "demonstration," which allows us not only to construct necessary chains of reasoning, but to reach necessary conclusions when we can come to know the (necessary) premises. The conditions for demonstration are what the scholastics called the two "modes of perseity,"[22] and on our reconstruction they stipulate for each premise that either

(1) the predicate of the consequent of a premise be contained in the predicate of the antecedent of the same premise, or

(2) the predicate of the antecedent be contained in that of the consequent. Thus

(1') "If anything is a number, then it is divisible" (x Number $\rightarrow$ x Divisible)

(2') "If anything is a number, then it is odd or even."

There is little doubt that these stipulations, added to Barbara, allow us to construct entailments with every arrow denoting a necessary connection of meanings, but the result is a theory of demonstration so tight that Aristotle sees that nothing but geometry—and that Euclidean geometry—can conform to it.[23] If we take it as a model for natural science, then the connections must be "for the most part," and necessary conclusions give way to probabilities. But in spite of these grave inconveniences, Aristotle never ceased to regard the "strict demonstration" of the *Posterior Analytics* as the very paradigm of scientific reasoning. Besides the necessity it promised, we suggest that a strong motivation was that it allowed him to show Barbara off to perfection, achieving what our reconstruction manifests: a perfect parallel or symmetry between principal and secondary arrows, be-

---

22. For the meanings of *per se*, cf. *In* 1 *Post Anal.* 10.

23. At least one can say that Aristotle usually proffers only mathematical examples of his demonstration; Aquinas saw that only mathematics (à la Euclid) fit: *In* 1 *Post Anal.* 4.43bis; *In* 2 *Post Anal.* 12.525.

tween the necessity of concluding from such interlocking generalities and the necessity of the premises so interlocked—which together, yield the same necessity in the conclusion. This is the crowning success of a paradigm: it can be made to *produce* the necessity it was constructed to lucidly illustrate. It is as though Michaelangelo's *David* were able to come to life.

Its Meager Utility

But logicians are traditionally content with bare bones and lifeless models. In scholastic terms, they will settle for the *necessity of the consequence*, and do not demand to be handed over the *necessary consequent*. So whether the connection internal to the premises be accidental or essential, the enveloping universality of Barbara is enough to assure the conclusion's following of necessity. So the construction of the *Posterior Analytics*, useless as it is for working scientific methodology, seems also redundant to logic, except that it illustrates dramatically the kind of contrapuntal relation between form of premises and form of inference that Barbara actually is, the relation holding on our analysis between principal and secondary arrows.

WHAT THE SYLLOGISM SHOWS

By employing the arrow as an abbreviation for the "if . . . then . . ." that Barbara contains and manifests, we have meant to give an interpretation to the primitive relation of E. This is *prima facie* quite unexceptionable since E means to axiomatize that same common notion of *entailment* which most have no difficulty seeing as perfectly exemplified in Barbara. But is the interpretation useful? Does it throw any light on a meaning of "true" for expressions involving the arrow? Aristotle would of course reply that any such statement is true if it can be reduced to Barbara (or Celarent), reduced that is to a finite series of premises each of whose antecedents is "less universal" than its consequent, and consequent of the kth premise is the antecedent of the $(k+1)$th *seriatim*. But what is this *reduction*? As a part of the process of logical proof, it will itself be subject to formulation—and what is to validate the ensuing "laws of reduction"? Here we have, according to Łukasiewicz, the "fundamental flaw in the Aristotelian theory of proof." What Aristotle apparently did not realize was that there was another system of logic operating here, a system more fundamental than the theory of the syllogism: the logic of propositions. Or if he did realize it—as certain expressions suggest—it had to wait for another half century to be formulated by the Stoics.

Such at least is the contention of Łukasiewicz, exposed as well by Bocheński in his CS (formalization of the categorical syllogism).[24]

But recent work by Strawson has made us wary of accepting any one logic as "more fundamental" than another, and to say that Aristotle's arguments "rest on" the logic of propositions sounds suspiciously as though one believes *this* logic *legitimizes* and not merely codifies rational inference.[25] But however one may react to the thrust of Łukasiewicz's remarks, it is interesting that the logic of propositions he claims Aristotle had to employ as an "auxiliary theory" contains not a few theses which are invalid in E.[26] Because of the affinity between entailment as envisaged by E and demonstration for Aristotle, one might suspect that something more (more *fundamental*?) than the "logic of propositions" is operative in the Aristotelian "reduction"—perhaps indeed the same sense of "universality" which Barbara exploits and arranges in an enveloping series to present a paradigm of logical inference.

But let us examine our suspicion. Both Łukasiewicz and Bocheński, accepting the "logic of propositions" as *fundamental*, interpret each premise of the syllogism as a proposition. Hence

    IF   all *s* is *m*
              and
              all *m* is *p*,
    THEN all *s* is *p*

becomes "If *p* & *q* then *r*" (C*Kpqr*). Then the "law of exportation," which allows us to pass from categorical to hypothetical syllogism looks like

  (3) CC*Kpqr*C*p*C*qr*   (Łuk. VII, Boch. 10).

Now if "C" be material implication, the law is valid, but if "C" is the arrow of E, it is invalid, since by substitution and *modus ponens*, we may derive C*p*C*qp*, where *p* is quite irrelevant to C*qp*. Guided by our premonition that Aristotle would not be "relying upon" logical laws invalid in E (a system with preoccupations so cognate to his), we might ask what permits this discrepancy. It seems clear that the interpretation of each syllogistic premise as

---

24. Łukasiewicz, *Aristotle's Syllogistic*, 44, 47–48, 88–94; Bocheński, "On the Categorical Syllogism." Cf. also Moody, *Truth and Consequence*, 78.

25. Cf. Strawson, "Reply to Mr. Sellars," but also *Introduction to Logical Theory*, chaps. 1, 2, 8, and passim.

26. Łukasiewicz's "auxiliary theory" is listed in *Aristotle's Syllogistic*, 89. It includes the laws of simplification (C*p*C*qp*), exportation, and others invalid in E. We shall deal expressly with the corresponding list of Bocheński in "On the Categorical Syllogism," 41–42.

itself a proposition, by neatly suppressing the dove-tailing structure of the syllogism, opens the door to a kind of substitution in which Aristotle simply would not have indulged. For example

(4) CCK*pqr*C*p*C*qr*, when for *r*, we put *p*, yields CCK*pqp*C*p*C*qp*, and by *modus ponens* (since CK*pqp* is logically true)

(4') C*p*C*qp*.

But Aristotle would not have lingered over the corresponding

(4") IF   all *s* is *m*

and

all *m* is *p*

THEN all *s* is *m*,

which is the detached CK*pqp*, since there is no concluding, no συλλογιξειν here.

Now here we notice a move common to Aristotelian and medieval logic: an appeal at critical moments to the rational ground of the whole enterprise, a ground *presupposed* to the systematic development and not a formal part of it. Hence the appeal must be entered in the form of extra- or meta-logical commentary.[27] This allowed the scholastics to develop two logical systems side by side—that of the categorical syllogism and a theory of "consequences" quite unrelated to it. Where these other "consequences" lacked the logical following that characterized the syllogism, this was accounted for by commentary, so that the notion of *consequence* became encrusted with distinctions. No one who knows medieval logic can find a trace there of the "anti-formalist" polemic of some neo-medievalists, but he will certainly notice an unresolved tension between a basic commitment to Barbara as the paradigm case of "logical following" and the drive to a symbolic calculus.[28] It would be more faithful to their insights into Aristotle

---

27. So Abelard may say "the perfect inference of a syllogism ... does not depend on any connection between the terms, ... if it has the structure of the syllogism, it stands unshaken" (*Dialectica*, 328). But Moody citing this text in *Truth and Consequence* goes on to note that the syllogism was conceived in use, presupposing a natural language communicating something (19–20). Hence, for Moody the "connection" Abelard renounces is merely a "material" one of content, not a logical following (15n).

28. As early as Albertus Magnus, the need for "transcendental terms" or symbols was clearly recognized (*Commentarium in Priorum Analyticorum* 1.9). Yet, Moody tells us that "perhaps principally, the syllogism is a *formal* consequence," and at least for Buridan, "material consequences are only evident, logically, insofar as they are 'reduced' to formal consequences"—and here "material" includes "simply material" which is our "material implication" (*Truth and Consequence*, 73, 76).

to try to resolve the tension somewhat by incorporating into our symbolism as much of the commentary as we can.[29]

This we have tried to do in interpreting the syllogistic premise as itself two propositions, united by the same relationship which Barbara is constructed to manifest. Historians of logic will recognize this tack as that of Theophrastus, transmitted by Alexander as "analogical" or "totally hypothetical syllogism." Theophrastus, however, was not clear on the distinction between term and propositional variables, and his formulation does not *manifest* the parallelism between the form of Barbara and the form of each premise. As Bochenski notes, this would have forced him to an "intolerable" Greek construction beginning each rule with a double "εἰ" ("if"). Yet on our interpretation, his rules, reflected into formulae, constitute more of a *link* than a "curious half-way house between the logic of Aristotle and that of the Stoics." Theophrastus's "inaugurating a logic of propositions and yet thinking all the while that he was continuing the Aristotelian syllogistic" becomes more plausible if the two turn out to be inextricably related.[30] By this reconstruction, we had hoped to avoid a prior commitment to the propositional calculus as "more fundamental," taking rather as "fundamental" the relationship ($\rightarrow$) which Barbara both contains and reflects, exhibiting by our use of arrows this contrapuntal construction. Applied to the "law of exportation" we have

(3') $(((p \rightarrow q) \& (q \rightarrow r) \rightarrow (p \rightarrow r)) \rightarrow ((p \rightarrow q) \rightarrow ((q \rightarrow r) \rightarrow (p \rightarrow r))))$.

On a substitution similar to the previous, this form clearly shows us why Aristotle need not have bothered. For replacing r by q:

(3") $(((p \rightarrow q) \& (q \rightarrow q) \rightarrow (p \rightarrow q)) \rightarrow ((p \rightarrow q) \rightarrow ((q \rightarrow q) \rightarrow (p \rightarrow q))))$.

Since the antecedent is detachable, we have the consequent as a theorem of E, where the very form of "$q \rightarrow q$" manifests why it is superfluous (in a way which "$CpCqp$" cannot).

But a closer look at (3') reveals some interesting logical facts. Together with similar reconstructions of the remaining theorems of Bochenski's CS which were originally invalid in E (the antilogism and what he calls "direct reduction"), in every case antecedent and consequent are singly theorems of E, but the entailment is not. But the antecedent in each case is Barbara (($p \rightarrow q$) & ($q \rightarrow r$) $\rightarrow$ ($p \rightarrow r$)), so that formulae such as

---

29. Cf. Bochenski, "De consequentiis Scholasticorum earumque origine," for an appraisal of scholastics on Aristotle.

30. Bochenski, *La Logique de Théophraste*, 111–16. Also in his *History of Formal Logic*, 103–4. Theorems 37–41, reconstructed from Theophrastus's rules and listed in *La Logique de Théophraste* (114) are valid in E.

(5) $(p \to q) \mathbin{\&} \overline{(p \to r)} \to \overline{(q \to r)}$,

(6) $((s \to t) \to (p \to q)) \to (((s \to t) \mathbin{\&} (q \to r)) \to (p \to r))$,

while themselves valid in E, cannot be shown to *follow from* the syllogism. Yet we arrived at the true consequents by reconstructing the theorems of a propositional theory of deduction on the model of Barbara. This encourages our suspicion that the syllogism Barbara is not to be construed as a *principle* (in the formal sense) of an entailment system, but is rather more *presupposed* to the whole enterprise, as manifesting most clearly the basic relationships at work.[31]

Our reconstruction also accounts for Aristotle's marked preference for Barbara over other forms of the first figure: Celarent or Ferio. Neither is deducible from Barbara, yet either one taken together with Barbara yields the other. Their "imperfection" lies rather in the structure of their negative and particular premises. So long as these are treated in the fashion of a logic of terms, however, it seems that Aristotle was simply showing partiality for "all" over "no" and "some," for "all *p* is *q*," "no *p* is *q*," and "some *p* is *q*" are hardly that diverse. Interpreted propositionally, though, they come out:

(7) $(x)(Px \to Qx)$,

(8) $(x)\overline{(Px \mathbin{\&} Qx)}$,

(9) $(\exists x)(Px \mathbin{\&} Qx), = \overline{(x)\overline{(Px \mathbin{\&} Qx)}}$

"No *p* is *q*" and its negation, "some *p* is *q*," do not speak of the irreducible relationship modeled on predication which Barbara manifests, for their propositional expression contains no arrow. In spite of Aristotle's original definition, then, there *is* a difference between universal predication and its contrary.[32] The fact that "no *p* is *q*" and "some *p* is *q*" can be converted, while "all *p* is *q*" and its negation, "some *p* is *q*," cannot—a fact Aristotle knew very well—calls attention to a difference which the general similarity of the sentential form left obscure. That difference is clearly manifested by our propositional interpretation: whereas "all *p* is *q*" goes into an arrow statement and may be fruitfully interpreted as "logical following," "no *p* is *q*" sidesteps the issue, "no *p*" merely denying that anything exemplifies both *p* and *q*. Since this premise (and its negation), then, do not *internally* reflect the basic structure whereby the syllogism concludes, they are "inferior" in

---

31. For the use of "presupposes" in this quasi-technical fashion, see Strawson, "On Referring," and *Introduction to Logical Theory*, 175.

32. Cf. 49n16. Aristotle speaks of the priority of the first figure in *Prior Analytics* I. 23, 40b13, and *Posterior Analytics* I. 6.

logical form to the universal affirmative premise, and the same may be said for the syllogistic figure containing them.

Concluding Remarks

What may we conclude from these converging indications of our thesis? That whatever the "other logic" may be that is operative in Aristotle's systematic reduction of syllogistic forms to the first figure, it cannot be said to be simply and without qualification the "logic of propositions." Common logical relationships are no doubt at work in Aristotle and *Principia Mathematica,* and Aristotle can speak of the premises of the syllogism *in globo* as single propositions,[33] but something else is controlling Aristotle's reductions as well. We have suggested that it is the paradigm of Barbara and the kind of *universality* the first figure is made to manifest. This is not to say that "the *dictum de omni et nullo* . . . is the axiom on which all syllogistic inference is based," a proposition J. N. Keynes attributes to Aristotle and Łukasiewicz roundly criticizes.[34] The notion of *universality* is not a "principle of the Aristotelian syllogistic" in the sense of a thesis entailing all the axioms. It is rather presupposed to the entire endeavor—a meaning of "principle" that Łukasiewicz leaves room for, but confesses (in advance) not to understand.[35] Our propositional reconstruction of Aristotle's first figure has meant to bring into the open as much as possible exactly what is being presupposed. By using the arrow in each premise in a fashion strictly analogous to the line separating and uniting the two premises from (and with) their conclusion, we have meant to show at one and the same time how Barbara concludes in virtue of interlocking universality and that one's most accurate guide to the *nature* of this universality is the manner in which Barbara concludes. If the relative universality is radically *in* the premises—which themselves reflect the absolutely irreducible subject-predicate relation that suggested *universality* in the first place—it is in the kind of "logical following" which the syllogism is constructed to yield that we are *shown* what this universality *is* by seeing what it can *do*. As Weiss has remarked, and this relative universality allows of both extensional and intensional interpretations: of a part entailing the whole of which it is a part, or of the more specific entailing the more general. And what is more, there seems to be no common denominator to

---

33. *Prior Analytics* II. 4, 57b1: "modus tollens"; II. 8, 59b3: the "antilogism."
34. Keynes, *Formal Logic,* 301; Łukasiewicz, *Aristotle's Syllogistic,* 46–47, 73–74.
35. Łukasiewicz, *Aristotle's Syllogistic,* 47: "It is a vain attempt to look for the principle of the Aristotelian logic, if 'principle' means the same as 'axiom.' If it has another meaning, I do not understand the problem at all."

the two. Each represents a "logical consequence" and *not* in virtue of some more fundamental law. (Whether the *extensional* is conceptually derivative from the *intensional* is a further question and beyond our scope. One can only say that it *seems* as though it is, Weiss argued that it is, and the latest work in analysis is taking on the burden of *showing* that it is.)

So the truth of expression involving the arrow, whether they be interpreted extensionally or intensionally, may be said to depend on the *relative universality* of their propositional variables, so arranged as to conclude after the fashion of Aristotle's first figure, even if not so manifestly as Barbara. (The second Belnap property: that every propositional variable of a tautological entailment must be both an antecedent and consequent part of the formula, where these parts are rigorously and recursively defined, assures such an a "arrangement."[36]) Whether this actually throws more light on what we mean by the truth of an arrow statement than "provable in E" does, is probably one of those matters of epistemic preference. Perhaps it would not be remiss to add that using Aristotle to "throw light on E" is not to *reduce* E to the theory of the syllogism. Quite the contrary, it has doubtless been evident how much this reading of Aristotle has profited from the researches embodied in E.

---

36. Cf. Anderson and Belnap, "Pure Calculus of Entailment."

Chapter 4

How God Achieves His Ends according to Saint Thomas Aquinas

The Council of Orange, in the shadow of Augustine, demands we take Saint Paul literally: it is really God who "accomplishes in us both good will and the accomplishment of that will," all to carry out his loving purpose:

> Hoc etiam salubriter profitemur et credimus, quod in omni opere bono non nos incipimus, et postea per Dei misericordiam adjuvamur, sed ipse nobis nullis praecedentibus bonis meritis et fidem et amorem sui prius inspirat, ut et baptismi sacramenta fideliter requiramus, et post baptismum cum ipsius adjutorio ea quae sibi sunt placita implere possimus.[1]

But his will is infallible. What remains of human freedom? of the human agent? So the questions arise, one after another, as the dogmatic fonts threaten one's philosophical moorings. The honest student has no choice but to follow the lead of the Church and of his intellect, as Saint Thomas did. If he turns to him for guidance, however, he may become more profoundly unsettled, for Saint Thomas unhesitatingly affirms: God actually moves the

---

1. Denzinger, *Enchiridion Symbolorum*, n200, Phil 2:13.

will,[2] moves it presumably to his end,[3] and being God moves it infallibly.[4] More specifically, if this act comes about in virtue of *gratia operans*, then there is no chance of failure.[5] Here the inquirer will demand: if God infallibly works his ends, must he determine man's freedom to do so? Yet if man remains free, how is God certain of achieving his purpose? Those who have already seen through this difficulty will want to go further into the heart of the mystery itself, to ask: why is it that God permits some to fail and sees to it that others do not? This is certainly the final question, but we must stick with the first, answer the difficulties as to *how* God moves the will, and so help bring the inquiring believer to the threshold of the mystery of God, enabling him to ask the final question, personally, to God Himself.

So once again, if God's action is infallible, how can the supernatural act be fallible? Yet must not every human act be able to fail? The immediate response is implicitly contained in Saint Thomas's treatment of actual grace in the *Summa Theologiae*, where he breaks down actual grace ("the divine assistance by which God moves us to right willing and acting") into two aspects: operating and cooperating.[6] One and the same grace moves us to perform one complete supernatural act. But as the act can be distinguished into the willing of the end and then the actual performance of that will, so God's motion can be broken down into two effects: one moving the will in such a way that the will is not a mover (operating), the other moving it so that the will moves itself (cooperating). God's action is simple, the supernatural act is one; but the created effects of divine motion correspond to the two components of the human act: willing the end, carrying through to action. If the supernatural act could be completed by operating grace, we

---

2. *ST* 1–2.9.4c: "Unde necesse est ponere quod in primum motum voluntatis voluntas prodeat ex instinctu alicuius exterioris moventis. . . ." The argument is from *initium consilii* (cf. 67n26), and article 6 of the same question asserts that it is impossible that the extrinsic principle that moves the will directly be any but the cause of the will itself: "ipse Deus, qui est universale bonum."

3. *CG* 3.94.10: "Quaecumque vero eorum aliquid operantur, instrumentaliter agunt ab eo mota, et ei obtemperando ministrant, ad ordinem providentiae ab aeterno, ut ita dicam, excogitatum explicandum in rebus. Si autem omnia quae agere possunt necesse est ut in agendo ei ministrent, impossibile est quod aliquod agens divinae providentiae exsecutionem impediat, sibi contrarium agendo."

4. *de Ver.* 6.3.4m: "Et ideo ordo divinae praedestinationis quamvis sit cum suppositione voluntatis humanae, nihilominus tamen absolutam habet certitudinem. . . ."

5. *ST* 1–2.111.2. This is the capital text whose moorings form the field of this study. For a taste of the dimensions of a truly adequate study, see the concluding remarks to the series of articles in *Theological Studies* by Lonergan on the respective range of Augustine's and Aquinas's concerns: "Thomas' Thought on *Gratia Operans*."

6. *ST* 1–2.111.2.4m: "Dicendum est quod gratia operans et cooperans est eadem gratia, sed distinguitur secundum diversos effectus. . . ."

could remove the source of failure, for the contingency of the human agent would no longer be involved. But by the same token, the act would cease to be human. In as much, then, as the supernatural act is effected by both operating and cooperating grace, the human will re-enters as an agent, and with it, the possibility of failure, of refusal, of sin.

The response apparently saves philosophy, but the response is technical. Understanding is not so easily satisfied. It raises disconcerting questions. Does not this possibility of failure compromise God's omnipotence? Does it not set conditions on the unconditioned: B will necessarily follow *if* A does not fail? What if we should switch the question to a positive form: can God move the will, move a man, irresistibly to will the good? If the answer is yes, then, pray tell, how?

But first a word of explanation for anyone who may be appalled at our daring to reopen this tortuous chapter of theology. They may remember it as tangled in verbosity, overladen with partisan footnotes, hopelessly inconclusive. For these we offer, not an apology for opening an old question anew, but a justification for posing it afresh: a justification and a promise. Distinguished voices have been pointing out for some time that the seventeenth-century posing of the question could only abut in deadlock.[7] And they have suggested the reason why as well as the remedy. The weakness inherent in the controversy on *auxiliis*, and in all those who saw fit to take up the arms of one side or the other, may be called a lack of philosophical artistry in coming to grips with the transcendent.[8] Philosophical categories behave strangely at the limits of proportionate being, much as infinite series do at their limits. And as the nineteenth-century saw mathematics come into possession of methods for operating at the limit without contradiction, so it seems that our times are propitious for a finer grasp of the philosophical nuances of transcendence.[9] Yet rather than offer the startling advances of

---

7. Notably Sertillanges, *Saint Thomas d'Aquin*, 255–68. Broglie has also recognized in his notes on *De Gratia* that nothing short of repeated application of the theorem of participated being could do justice to the question, and Finance, by showing how *esse* allowed Saint Thomas to do just that, succeeds in posing the question in its full metaphysical perspective (*Être et Agir*, 230–40).

8. Cf. Hawkins, "Two Conceptions of Freedom in Theology," where the author suggests that Molinism was an attempt of the Renaissance to make its mark on theology—and that the formulation must suffer from the inadequacies of such a humanism. One is reminded of Lubac's censure of Baius: a weakening in the "sense of God" (*Surnaturel*, 24–25). Presumably he means the inability of Baius and his contemporaries to *express* the encounter of God and man.

9. Such a sweeping statement gains credibility from the testimonies of two divergent philosophical schools, as interpreted by perceptive theologians. For German phenomenology, cf. Balthasar, *Science, Religion, and Christianity*; and for British analysis, cf. Daly, "Knowableness of God."

symbolic mathematical method, our *prise de conscience* of the dimensions of transcendence seems but to return us, with fuller appreciation, to Saint Thomas's formulation of the question. Yet this cannot be a simple "return," for the philosophical and cultural movements that have forced us to a more refined grasp of God's transcendence will inevitably color our reading of Aquinas, giving our reconstruction of his thought an unmistakable contemporary tone.

Such a return to Saint Thomas was the remedy suggested by those challenging the frozen problematic of Baroque theology, but to exhort is one thing and to stake out the route quite another. No return journey could have hoped for much success until the systematic surveying had been done. It was a matter first of recapturing the context and flavor of Saint Thomas's usage, and this quite independently of later theologians who, though working in a problematic quite foreign to his, do not hesitate to present their "solution" as Thomistic.[10] This study has been done, effectively and thoroughly, by Bernard Lonergan in 1941.[11] Our brief attempt to recast the movement of Saint Thomas's thought with a certain freshness would have been impossible without the guidance of that study. It depends on it at crucial points to be noted, and will achieve its aim if it incites but a few to pursue in detail Father Lonergan's methodical research.

Let us return now to our question, follow Saint Thomas as he comes to grips with it, and watch his thought unfold to reveal the "classical" positions of Báñez and Molina as each inadequate to the task. This was our promise: to shed new light on a well-worn question by training on it the beacon of a yet fuller tradition.

THEOREMS NECESSARY

The question: can God move the will, move a man, irresistibly to will the good? Saint Thomas answers yes: God can move a man to will the good and move him irresistibly, provided one understands how it is that God moves something. God's irresistible motion does not determine.[12] In itself, the will can still fail. This is the keystone of his speculation on Providence: the theorem of *divine transcendence*. What sounds like specious double-talk

---

10. Cf. Garrigou-Lagrange, *De Gratia*, 359–74.
11. Lonergan, "Thomas' Thought on *Gratia Operans*."
12. *CG* 3.94.11: "Cadit igitur sub ordine divinae providentiae non solum hunc effectum esse, sed hunc effectum esse contingenter, alium autem necessario, et secundum hoc quaedam eorum quae divinae providentiae subduntur sunt necessaria, quaedam vero contingentia, non autem omnia necessaria."

is really nothing but an obscurity on our part, as the negative statement of the theorem makes so clear: *to act, to cause*, is used equivocally if it is applied both to the first principle of all things, and to a secondary principle producing a specific thing.[13] God's moving the will and the will's moving itself are not the same thing. They are, if you will, on different levels. But let us go on, for understanding needs more tools.

The theorem of divine transcendence includes another as co-extensive and complementary to it: that of *universal instrumentality*. The created agent is a secondary agent who not only exists but acts in virtue of a primary agent.[14] The theorem suffers various formulations according as the point of reference is cosmological: universal and particular agent; descriptive: principal agent and instrument; or metaphysical: primary and secondary agent. The terminology is fluid and each pair is so readily interchangeable with the other that what is to be understood is one.[15] The understanding, however, is not easy, for while analogies for potency and act abound, creation offers no example of an act of an act: of a higher-order agent moving another to be agent in its own order. Among creatures, what is not in act is in potency to act; one is the agent, another is the power by which it operates. A man knows *by* his intellect; the intellect is said to know only improperly, as that by which the subject knows. But man himself is not a mere principle *by which* God works his end. Saint Thomas, in assuming the Aristotelian doctrine of substance, affirms both primary and secondary agents to be proper agents. For but one example among countless, consider one of the frankest of texts on divine motion in the soul: "The soul of man is moved by God to know, will, or do something (*ad aliquid cognoscendum vel volendum vel agendum*)." So of all creatures: "God looks after natural creatures so as to move them to natural acts." Although moved, it is the soul itself which understands, wills, acts, as every creature *performs acts* natural to it.[16]

---

13. *In 8 Phys.* 2.974: "Et quia omnis motus indiget subjecto, ut hic Aristoteles probat et rei veritas habet, sequitur quod productio universalis entis a Deo non sit motus nec mutatio, sed sit quaedam simplex emanatio. Et sic *fieri* et *facere* aequivoce dicuntur in hac universali rerum productione, et in aliis productionibus." Remember that analogy is generically equivocation.

14. *de Pot.* 3.7 is the classic locus.

15. Compare the affirmations *per transennam* of *ST* 1.104.1; 3.62.1; 1.19.1.2m. Compare especially the general statement of the theorem in *ST* 1.60.1.2m with the distinction drawn between a *causa secunda* and a mere instrument in *ST* 1.36.3.4m. That this is an *ad hoc* refinement and not systematically employed by Aquinas is clear from later writings.

16. Cf. *ST* 1–2.110.2, where the distinction is made between grace as a motion and as a habit, but within a context whose sweep reveals what "creature" means for Saint Thomas: ". . . non est inconveniens quod Deus minus provideat his quos diligit

Art provides an image of this unique relation, and nature will offer a revealing, though remote and inadequate analogy. Just as a tool, extending the power, dexterity, and plan of the artisan to his object, seems to participate in his power, dexterity, and intelligence, so long as it remains an active instrument, so the existence and act of the creature is totally dependent on that of God, is indeed a participation of God's act of existence.[17] This power of art (*virtus artis*), this transitory actuation somehow possessed by the active instrument, is likened to the incomplete being of corporeal motion,[18] which turns out to be the only analogy we possess to the created agent standing under the uncreated, acting only by its act, inescapably carrying out its designs.

AN ANALOGY

Motion is the act of a thing existing in potency, and considered precisely as in potency.[19] The definition is well known, yet its import is many-sided. Because we need a precise understanding here, we take the liberty of a humble illustration. Consider an apartment building in progress. What is now up, say the steel or concrete frame, is certainly something over and above the previous vacant lot—"motion is the *act* of a thing"; but this is not all. It is the frame of an apartment building—"... act of a thing existing in potency," and it is this second aspect that dominates. The excuse for all the dirt, noise, and human traffic surrounding the frame is not the steel or concrete structure already up, but the building that is to be—"the act of a thing existing in potency, considered precisely as in potency."[20] An aerial photo could "catch" this motion, slice the time-continuum with a split-second section that would be true, but leave the explanation right out of the picture. The crane platform in mid-air, the cement mixer in the act of dumping its contents, the concrete skeleton itself—all these things, real as they are, are incomplete in themselves. They are pointed to something beyond, part of something greater, phases realizing a master plan which had to include them all: the architect's mental elaboration of a contemporary apartment. Motion in

---

ad supernaturale bonum habendum, quam creaturis quas diligit ad bonum naturale habendum. Creaturis autem naturalibus sic providet ut non solum moveat eas ad actus naturales, sed etiam largiatur eis formas et virtutes, quae sunt principia actuum, ut secundum seipsas inclinentur ad huiusmodi motus."

17. For participated existence, see *ST* 1.44.1; for act, see *CG* 3.67.

18. *ST* 3.62.4c: "... virtus autem instrumentalis habet esse transiens ex uno in aliud, et incompletum; sicut et motus est actus imperfectus ab agente in patiens."

19. *In 3 Phys.* 2.285.

20. Ibid., 2.289.

itself is something, it is true, but something incomplete, remaining to be explained, a kind of middle term between potency and act.[21]

So we can look at man like the photographer looks at events, catch him as he is something, as he acts, moves himself to think, reflect, and make decisions. And we must do so, for we can only understand what is in act, can only grasp a motion when we stop it.[22] But a philosophy which stops at man leaves out the explanation, just like the photograph. Yet philosophy, unlike the camera, is a spiritual activity, able to realize its limitations, know its explanations *as* incomplete. So it will speak of the creature's being as participated,[23] offer the image of the instrument,[24] and analogy of the incomplete being of corporeal motion—all manners of speaking, images, analogies, for just as motion cannot be directly conceived because it is already pointed towards something beyond itself, neither can the creature in so far as it is incomplete, "in the hands of God." Yet the imperfect, analogical act of theological understanding seeks to do just this: to reconstruct the human act as it is actuated by God. Philosophy can prepare the way by reflectively recognizing that what is act to the creature would be potency, material to the divine architect. Man, if he is to be explained, must first be understood as *in motion*, as pointing beyond himself.[25]

To set up, then, the theorems of universal instrumentality and divine transcendence, we must first see that man is not his own explanation, and better yet, show with scientific precision, *how* he is not. Saint Thomas's mature expression is in psychological terms, taking its lead from the *Liber de Bona Fortuna* of Eudemus, and the need there proposed for some beginning

---

21. Ibid., 3.296.

22. The biologist has become acutely aware of this in trying to define the status of his science, to proceed from a naive to a critical use of physico-chemical methods. Reflection on the organism as a whole, as something in process, has proved to him that his slides cannot tell the whole story. But he continues to slice and dye living tissue, thereby dissecting the unity and arresting the process, because there is simply no other way of knowing it scientifically.

23. *de Pot.* 3.7.3m; *ST* 1.44.1; 1.61.1.

24. *de Pot.* 3.4; 3.8.19m; *CG* 3.67; *ST* 1.105.5.

25. This general theorem for all of nature is especially verified in the case of man, whose intellectual nature has a natural propensity for the infinite (cf. the focal text: *ST* 1–2.3.8). But what Saint Thomas affirmed in countless places was not to see its full development until the more frankly anthropological orientation of philosophy in our times. (Cf. McCool, "Philosophy of the Human Person.") Inversely, however, nothing manifests so clearly how phenomenology cannot stand on its own as the inability of many of its foremost exponents to break through a cultural atheism to give full range to their humanism. What is at stake, more often than not, is sheer incomprehension of the theorem of divine transcendence.

of counsel (*initium consilii*) that man actually will the good here and now.[26] The argument hangs on the principle of sufficient reason: man moves himself, it is true, but by the powers of intellect and will. Once the process is started, the causality is mutual, but the first step depends on the will. No one thinks about medicine until he wants to get well. But because men do not always really want to get well, something must move them to do so. This sounds like too fine an analysis until we recall those hospital patients whom all of us have known, usually without relatives or friends, who have given up the "will to live." Abandoning hope of recovery, no one can induce them to *try* to do this or that, for any such effort is meaningless without the enduring will to live. And just as the will to live is prior to the will to get well, so at the root of all voluntary action is the actual willing of the good *as good*. Once he actively wills this most universal end, the person can bring himself to will others as means to it, by virtue of counsel. But how does one come to will the good as good? It is the natural object of the will, we know, but this is not enough, for by as much as potency falls short of act, the internal disposition of a power fails to explain its actual exercise. In more refined terms, *action* is a further perfection of the existing subject, one that *esse*, taken autonomously, cannot explain. This will become clearer, closer to our experience, when Saint Thomas will use it to show the need for some actual help beyond habitual grace, precisely to make our choice of the final end operative in this concrete deed.[27] Let it suffice for now that some external agent must move the will to actively will the good as good. God who creates an intelligent being must act in it if it is to fulfill the finality bestowed upon it.

Another line of thought, present from the beginning and finding its most apt expression in the *de Potentia*, is more frankly metaphysical: what is "most common to any change," what is "first and more penetrating than any other effect" is that the new thing is *real*. Something *exists* afresh or at least in a way it did not exist before.[28] But a cause cannot produce along a certain line without something of the power that causes the whole species. Man can form an artifact to the extent that it embodies a pattern originating in his imagination. But in so far as it offers a new combination of all the materials,

---

26. *Quodl.* 1.4 2. For the background of the *Liber de Bona Fortuna* and the place of this argument in the development of St. Thomas's thought, see the chapter devoted to it in Bouillard, *Conversion et grâce*, 123–34.

27. *ST* 1–2.109.9. For a detailed examination of the relation between *esse* and *agere*, see Finance, *Être et Agir*, 214–53 (chap. 7: "Le Plus Être").

28. *de Pot.* 3.7: ". . . nec aliquid agit ad esse nisi per virtutem Dei. Ipsum esse est communissimus effectus primus et intimior omnibus aliis effectibus; et ideo soli Deo competit secundum virtutem propriam talis effectus: unde etiam . . . intelligentia non dat esse nisi prout est in ea virtus divina." Also *CG* 3.66.5.

a new manner of existence, his action is dependent on the power that causes being itself. He is acting as an instrument of God.

This is the seed of revolution: philosophy realizing that its proper object does not offer its own explanation, but points beyond itself. It belongs to the new intellectual polity of theology to conceive this object afresh without destroying the unity of the concrete existing thing, of this human act; to see how divine act explains created act not by adding anything to it, but by constituting it from within. For to say that all of nature is an instrument of God is to posit an *order* between God and nature whereby the operation of nature is also the operation of God's power. How shall we, how *can* we conceive this order?

THE LIMITS OF CONCEPTION

If we are willing to deny ourselves the satisfaction of *imagining* this order between a transcendent first principle and a particular created agent, if we will follow the created images and analogies as they lead beyond themselves, we already possess the theorems necessary to give a response that will lead the intellect to the heart of the mystery.

Can God move the will irresistibly to perform a supernatural act? Or more accurately: can God move an intelligent self-mover irresistibly to exercise a supernatural act? We have already seen that God can move the will, and move it immediately to will an end.[29] But can He move it to performance as well? Yes, if the intelligent self-mover, moving himself, retains the possibility of resisting. No, if in moving himself, he *must* exercise the act. For if divine actuation determines what it causes, then the act is no longer human. It would no longer be the action of a free agent, so could not be supernatural nor meritorious.

What seems to limit God's omnipotence, however, will really force us to a much more exalted sense of it. The principle intruding here demands that every human act retain the inner possibility of resisting, or more accurately,

---

29. *ST* 1–2.111.2c: "Operatio enim alicuius effectus non attribuitur mobili, sed moventi. In illo ergo effectu in quo mens nostra est mota et non movens, solus autem Deus movens, operatio Deo attribuitur: et secundum hoc dicitur *gratia operans*." Note how this formulation has become more incisive as Saint Thomas moves to a finer psychological grasp. The same reality is just as strongly affirmed in *de Veritate*, where, however, the *movendo tantum* of actual grace is fitted in a context of moving the will *mediante inclinatione* (*de Ver.* 22.8), and the empire of *gratia operans* is weakened by a final hesitation: "Hoc enim donum (justificatio) sola gratuita divina voluntas causat in nobis, nec aliquo modo eius causa est liberum arbitrium, *nisi* per modum dispositionis sufficientis" (*de Ver.* 27.5.1m).

of failing. The free instrument reserves to itself the privilege of breaking in the hands of the divine artisan. Nothing shows more dramatically the gulf between spirit and nature, between the conscious agent and the one that merely follows its innate bent. The intelligent agent adds a contingency of his own to the unpredictability of matter that he shares with all of nature, a contingency on the side of *form*. He can not only fail in acting, he can fail to act; he can not only fall short of achieving his end, he can fail to even follow the sign posts pointing towards that end. Before failing to realize his nature, he can fail to follow its very lead. And while the contrariety of matter finds its ultimate explanation in God who created it contingent, the failure to act, to follow form, has no cause whatsoever![30] It is simple contrariness, a surrender of freedom in favor of slavery; reason abdicating its rule, allowing what is not dominant to dominate.

Such a metaphysical reversal has no explanation. There is nothing to understand, so nothing dependent on God, nothing He can control. We can only say: if Socrates does not resist, he exercises a supernatural act.[31] Note that the condition is negative: if anything is accomplished, it comes completely from God. The creature can only claim for himself what is *not*, what he failed to do, what lacks intelligibility. So we might be tempted to say: although God would prefer that Socrates not resist, his specific desire is conditioned. He wants Socrates to do thus and so *if he* does not resist. God wants him to act, but act according to his own nature.

But have we gone far enough? Is this really divine omnipotence, if God ends up taking his chances? By insisting on the demands of human freedom, we have succeeded in avoiding necessity, but what remains of the certitude of Providence, which must extend to each rational creature?[32] Have we not removed it from the realm of explanation, reduced it to the matter

---

30. Cf. Lonergan, "Thomas' Thought on *Gratia Operans*," 3:547–52. The exposition is bold as it must be, for the point is crucial to a metaphysics, i.e., for a world view that would affirm final intelligibility. In fact, one might say that no single stumbling block looms so large to our contemporaries as our apparent impotence before the "problem of evil" (cf. Flew, "Divine Omnipotence and Human Freedom"). The history of theology has presented more than enough scandalous and contradictory "solutions"—forcing us to "choose between divine governance and divine sanctity"—to make us welcome the tri-valued system Lonergan proposes as the thought of Saint Thomas. Only by establishing sin as a complete surd in the intelligible order can we recognize how it can be a "ground for punishment in a way in which merit is *not* a cause of glory."

31. ST 1.19.8.2m: ". . . ex hoc ipso quod, nihil voluntati divinae resistit, sequitur quod non solum fiant ea quae Deus vult fieri; sed quod fiant contingenter vel necessario, quae sic fieri vult."

32. Cf. *de Ver.* 5.6: "Et ideo dicendum quod bruta et omnes eorum actus cadunt etiam in singulari sub divina providentia; non tamen eo modo quo homines, et eorum actus: quia de hominibus etiam in singulari est providentia propter se. . . ."

of fact, subjected God's will to a created condition? If God's action does not and cannot necessitate the free creature, how does He achieve his ends infallibly? How does he move the will irresistibly to perform a supernatural act, without determining it?

The Baroque attempts to answer this question were reluctant to aim high enough. They ignored the potential as well as the limitations of philosophical categories, in their desire to remain within them. What is at stake is the dynamic order between creature and Creator, between the particular and universal agent. But an order or relation which is frankly transcendent cannot be affirmed except analogously. It cannot be systematized but rather asks to be understood in an act that drives the created intellect to capitalize on its limitations by candidly recognizing them. If we try to conceive directly such a relation, work it out in terms consonant with experience, the very attempt to conceive what cannot be conceived sets up its own smoke screen, throwing obscurity rather than light on the mystery.[33] This is the sense in which it is insoluble—if one approaches it as he would a *problem*![34]

So the expression: "God knows that Socrates *will* not resist . . ." is easily ruled out as naively anthropomorphic. All things are present to God; there is no future. But its refinement is more tempting: "God knows Socrates *as* not resisting and *so* moves him beyond willing the end to perform the deed." This saves the possibility of resistance and avoids the temporal involvement as well. But God remains conditioned, the creature reappears as autonomous, nothing is said of a secondary agent. Must not God be the cause of his not resisting as well as the act that follows?[35]

33. This is the central flaw in Báñez: a practical denial of the theorem of divine transcendence by a finitist application of causality. Vesting God's moving of the will in a created entity disregards the warning of the *Commentary on the Physics* (*In 8 Phys.* 2.974), and compromises the transcendent *order* involved in any divine-human encounter. This led Garrigou-Lagrange to the dilemma: God is either determining or determined; and allowed him to propose as an analogy of God's operation the vital influx of a plant, or (better) the influx of our will enlightened by intelligence on our hand as it directs it to write. While proposed as "mere analogies to support the imagination and aid the intelligence," they betray a kind of type-fallacy in theology (cf. *De Gratia*, 372).

34. The primary locus for the contrast "problem" and "mystery" is Marcel, "Presence as a Mystery."

35. Most will recognize this readily as the common formulation of Molina's teaching, together with the objections usually brought against it. (A good standard exposition is Lennerz, *De Gratia Redemptoris*, 382–91.) We do not intend a critique of *scientia media* as such, but of the formulation: "God knows . . . *and so* He . . ." which has God looking to his creatures for guidance (cf. Lonergan, *Insight*, 662–63). Indeed *scientia media* is an unfortunate term for a kind of knowledge necessary to assure God's choice of this world order as a wise one, and unconsciously suggests what, most profoundly, must be God's knowledge of "possibles," as against our own abstract grasp (cf. Finance, *Être et Agir*, 179–84).

Saint Thomas's early tussle with the question draws on a fine sense of the complexity of human action to assure God achieving his ends. The will is not really pure indeterminacy, but tends to follow the inclinations set up by habit. Environment, early training, commonly accepted ideals, set up behavior patterns that allow mere psychologists to establish with an increasing degree of certitude how we will react to different sets of conditions. But God has all these factors under his control: the number of children in the family, the economic conditions, educational possibilities, the neighborhood in which we live. He can even adjust the conditions under which his favorites will be asked to exercise their freedom, by so timing the actual moment of decision as to find the person favorable to accepting his will, or by so adjusting events as to prepare him for an arduous choice. And any creature, any occurrence, may be the instrument God uses to intimate his will: a friend inviting me out for dinner, a beggar pleading for some kind of help, the death of an intimate friend. By holding the strings that control and direct all the contingent events of nature and history, God can arrange all the elements that naturally incline the will one way or another. Although the will *can* fail to follow his lead, nevertheless God so arranges that it *does not*, by an overwhelming convergence of factors that condition choice without determining it, for it is precisely the nature of human freedom to operate within such a framework of conditioning: "So by his innumerable supports, God props up salvation, assuring that one does not fall, or if he should fall, that he rise up again; supports such as exhortations, prayers of others, gifts of grace, and many others."[36]

In other words, Saint Thomas has God circumscribing the freedom of the secondary agent to such a high degree of probability[37] that his end is *in fact* always achieved. This unique explanation not only illuminates the concrete workings of all that is human in human freedom, but goes on to illustrate many facts of divine transcendence by showing the ingenuity and unbelievable adaptability of God as He works out his plan for mankind, sweeping up into it every individual man, as he is in himself and in all his relations with others. The human agent remains contingent, retains the privilege of resisting, yet the *fact* that he does not resist most certainly comes completely from God.

36. de Ver. 6.3c (*in fine*): "Liberum enim arbitrium deficere potest a salute; tamen in eo quem Deus praedestinat, tot alia adminicula praeparat, quod vel non cadat, vel si cadat, quod resurgat, sicut exhortationes et suffragia orationum, donum gratiae, et alia huiusmodi, quibus Deus adminiculatur homini ad salutem." An earlier statement, more external still, is found In 2 Sent. 28.1.4.3m. The contextual nature of freedom is incorporated into the developed treatment of ST 1–2.9.1, 3, 4, 6.

37. [Ed. note: Burrell's margin note written after publication of this article changed this phrase, "a high degree of probability" to "statistical certainty."]

This speculation, reminiscent of Bellarmine,[38] is more of a springboard than a fixed position for Saint Thomas. Systematically, it is significant for what it does *not* say. God's pattern of conditioning factors makes it not impossible, but infeasible, for Socrates to resist. By refusing to go any further, Saint Thomas obscurely affirms here what he will later explicitly develop: that Socrates does not resist is not *explainable*, but simply a fact: "From the simple fact that nothing resists the divine will, it follows not only that those things come about which God wills, but that they come about contingently or necessarily, as he wills them."[39] Explanation means causal relations, and causes as we know them determine their effects. So if it were susceptible of explanation, Socrates would not be himself a mover, but reduced to something moved. This is the inevitable logic of the philosophical theorems in play, but the negations of logic can be the impulse for intelligence to transcend its own limits by affirming them. The principles of explanation are present to the knower, though they lie beyond his grasp. They affirm that there can be no explanation because it must be a transcendent one. This is the final position of Saint Thomas, revealing a grasp of metaphysics so fine that he could exercise its primary categories at the limit of experience, making them bend back upon themselves, to realize their infinite extension.[40]

38. Bellarmine, *De gratia et libero arbitrio*, 1.14.296a–b. For a favorable, contextual interpretation of Bellarmine, see Hens, *Die Augustinusinterpretation des hl. Robert Bellarmin bezüglich der wirksamen Gnade*, 5–19, 54.

39. *ST* 1.19.8.2m. See 69n31.

40. The verbal play here may be disconcerting. "Explanation," like "cause," may well be an analogous notion, but it is so only in function of a determinate, this-world usage. Now to use the finite notion in reference to God is a patent philosophical howler, laid bare by Kant as a transcendental application of categories proportioned to this world. Although this remains what many "Thomists" end up doing in practice while displaying the audience-card, "Analogy," Saint Thomas knew better. We have cited one text (64n13) on causality and creation. The burden of the essay and the crucial argument against such erstwhile "Thomists" is to do the same for "explanation." For them, the explanation for God's moving the will is a created entity added to it. For us, the way to explanation is a more profound, necessarily dialectical grasp of the *order* between Creator and creature, an order which defies conception but which can be affirmed *as* intelligible. The "explanation" does not lie in a created efficient cause we can get our grips on, but in a deeper understanding of the limits of our power to properly explain. Hence our desire to celebrate this refined understanding by calling it a *theorem*; the theorem of divine transcendence, whose first formulation, we recall, is negative, yet whose thrust is positive. It affirms a final intelligibility that remains transcendent. The clearest expression in Saint Thomas is found in *In 1 Peri Herm.* 14.17–22 and *In 6 Meta.* 3.1222, although it was already expressed in *In 1 Sent.* 38.1.5. Aquinas's explicit option for a transcendental *order* uncluttered by "explanatory entities" is found in *de Ver.* 6.3.9m: "Sed praedestinatio non importat productionem alicuius effectus temporalis secundum suum nomen, sed tantummodo ordinem ad aliquid temporale, sicut voluntas, potentia, et huiusmodi omnia: et ideo, quia non ponitur effectus temporalis esse in actu, qui

Socrates as a mover is also moved, but in such a way as to remain a mover. Such an agent is inconceivable if we employ univocally the Aristotelian theory of motion where motion is *in* the thing moved but *from* the mover. According to the ordinary sense of this formula, a thing could never be mover in the same respect in which it was moved.[41] Yet in the supernatural act man is mover precisely to the extent that he is moved. In fact, whenever a free secondary agent moves and is not moved, he rather "nihilates" than acts.

The sole condition for the fulfillment of God's will was that Socrates not resist. But his will can have no real conditions. So the *fact* that Socrates does not resist must finally be explicable, must finally depend on God and find its explanation in God as the absolutely unconditioned.

So logic pushes us to admit that there must be an explanation and that the explanation lies beyond our comprehension, lies in the very makeup of the primary agent whose act grounds all act, who provides each thing and every event to be and to be necessarily or contingently according as not only effects, but causes and even modes of being are dependent on Him.[42] To God there are not things already out there to be coaxed or manipulated. To say that his act is the ground of all act means that all things are present to Him in the act whereby He is completely present to Himself. In this presence, creatures are understood to be and to be at a definite time and in relation to other creatures and to fulfill either freely or necessarily the divine intention. Furthermore, the "divine intention" is not something added on, but part and parcel of the conscious act whereby God is eternally present to Himself.

Far from the activity or failure of the creature being a condition placed on God, the very concept of an agent among creatures is derivative. Possessing its very existence from another, the created agent cannot move itself to act independently, but points elsewhere for its complete explanation. And

---

est contingens, non oportet quod praedestinatio sit temporalis vel contingens: quia ad aliquid temporale et contingens potest aliquid ordinari ab aeterno et immutabiliter."

41. The logic of the position is inexorably finite: in so far as something is moved, it is not a mover. (Cf. discussion of self-motion: *In 8 Phys.* 7.1023; 7.1028.) Thus if another pushes me, I do not move, but *am* moved. For both Báñez and Molina, God is suspiciously like just another mover: for Banez, by moving within a created entity; for Molina, by moving by "boxing in" the will. In neither case have we penetrated truly *within*. Saint Thomas formulates the transcendental situation in *de Malo* 3.2.4m: ". . . cum dicitur quod aliquid movetur ab altero, ponitur aliud esse movens et aliud motum. Manifestum est *autem* quod cum aliquid movet alterum, non ex hoc ipso quod est movens, ponitur quod est primum movens: unde non excluditur quin ab alio moveatur, a quo habet hoc ipsum quod se ipsum movet. . . ."

42. *CG* 3.94.11. Cf. 63n12.

beyond this root dependence of the creature lie the dynamic consequences: given existence and actuated by another, it cannot help but carry out the intentions of the transcendent agent, act towards its ends, even though it be consciously opposing them.[43] So the created agent as a thing in-itself, the philosophers' reference point of individual substance, becomes a methodological abstraction. For while the creature truly subsists by an existence that is not its own, it subsists among other subjects. The relations which express this "togetherness" make up a common world and guide the subject's development by conditioning or determining its activity. These sets of relations are the created counterpart of divine Providence, which by positing certain creatures in existence at a definite time and in varying proximities to one another, creates a milieu, so allowing them to influence one another that they act as instruments carrying out his design.[44] But flattering as this picture may be to an intelligence able to integrate so many factors into a coherent and operating pattern, it falls short of the mark so long as it remains a picture, so long as it conveys the image of God manipulating actors already on the scene.

For nothing is a *given* to God, neither actors nor scenery nor script. He not only knows his actors as contingent, as apt to fail at any moment, but goes on to endow them with the power to refuse his lead and set out on their own. But no matter that number of plays within the play, the plot remains in his hands. Why? Because even the supposedly independent pieces must take whatever sense and unity they have from the first truth, and end up serving as subplots of the whole. How? That is God's secret, locked in the identity of existence, understanding, and willing that is the divine essence; in the single eternal act of full subjectivity that allows Him to comprehend Himself as producer and director *par excellence*, comprehending and possessing at the same time secondary agents, real beings who are at once his instruments as well as producers and directors in their own right. They are not present to Him from without, as objects to be manipulated, but transparently in their innermost subjectivity. He possesses them from within as "projects" of the act by which He completely possesses Himself.

43. *ST* 1.103.8; *de Malo* 6.1.5m.

44. *ST* 1.116.1–4: "Sic igitur inquantum omnia quae hic aguntur, divinae providentiae subduntur, tamquam per eam praeordinata et quasi praelocuta, *fatum* ponere possumus . . ." (*ST* 1.116.1c). "Et ideo dicendum est quod fatum, secundum considerationem secundarum causarum, mobile est: sed secundum quod subest divinae providentiae, immobilitatem sortitur, non quidem absolutae necessitatis, sed conditionatae; secundum quod dicimus hanc conditionalem esse veram vel necessariam: *Si Deus praescivit hoc futurum, erit*" (*ST* 1.116.3c). This last telescopes the treatment of causes transcendentally ordered, as Saint Thomas clarified it in the texts supplied at the end of note 40.

Chapter 5

What the Dialogues Show about Inquiry

RIGOR IS ONE OF those issues germane to any discipline and always subject to review. Whenever we do turn about to scrutinize the ways in which we have been proceeding, there is no doubt that we are diverting attention from our avowed goal, yet at the same time we cannot help feeling even more forcefully engaged in pursuing it. This curious fact already reveals something about inquiry. In fact, it points us to that feature of understanding which outreaches an ordinary pursuit, where the quarry, seen, needs only to be bagged. Strength, agility, and wit serve well enough in the chase; reflection would only delay the issue. But what if the object is not of a sort to be seen or bagged, but something to be understood—like student protest, democracy, or who-am-I-to-be?

In these cases—and they represent the majority of our concerns—we dare not even try to locate the topic without having made some effort to understand what it is we call by that name. So we must pursue it before we can locate it. And the only way we know of alleviating the paradoxical ring in that observation is to suggest that the original pursuit metaphor has served its purpose. But to make a suggestion like that gathers our attention to the way in which *we* have been proceeding, and introduces a reflective moment into *this* fledgling inquiry. And that reflective moment represents an increment of understanding and so carries us closer to our goal.

We cannot conduct an inquiry, then, without reflecting on the way in which we are proceeding. Method is an integral part of any discipline because there is no other way of coming clear about the goal. For if we already understood, inquiring would be superfluous. Yet while the demand for reflection is ever present, some feel more at home with it than others, and these we have come to call the "philosophical" types. When they cluster together to reflect upon what they are doing, the results tend towards a new discipline: philosophy. But if my myth of origins is accurate, then this new discipline will be of a special sort: call it a "discipline." Otherwise these professional reflecters will find themselves being reflected upon, these seasoned students of method will be themselves subject to methodological scrutiny.

What keeps us from vertigo also restrains philosophy from pretension—a generous lacing of irony. Philosophy cannot be anything but a "discipline," for the entire enterprise is simply too precious. One engages in it because he must, because he is driven there. Until we appreciate how peculiar a compulsion philosophy is, we will be inclined to consider it a discipline among others. And the reflective impulse will aspire to one meta-level vantage point after another. Honesty requires of the one who scrutinizes others' methods, demanding rigor and reflective lucidity, that he be most exacting of all upon himself. And so he should, but in a manner which reflects the peculiarities of that "discipline" which takes upon itself the reflective task germane to any inquiry whatsoever, yet so notoriously elusive of formulation and hazardous in execution.

SOCRATES AS PARADIGM

The philosopher shows his seriousness of purpose most candidly by acknowledging how impossible his task really is. And he acknowledges the pretension most humbly and honestly by allowing this awareness to shape his own discourse, showing itself in the manner in which he elucidates what reflective, critical consciousness is up to. Certainly there is no better witness to this high seriousness than Socrates. And yet he witnesses to it by threatening its very respectability. For Socrates insisted upon "talking about cobblers and fullers and cooks and doctors, as if we were discussing *them*" (*Gorgias* 491a). His entire manner seemed calculated to resist the pull to moor philosophy among the disciplines. And of course it was, for the Socrates we know is Plato's. By knitting philosophy so closely to the figure of Socrates, Plato is insisting that it is not one among many but a "discipline" as unique as the spirit of Socrates.

Not only does Socrates figure as the central *dramatis persona* in nearly every dialogue, but his spirit weaves the dramatic *form* as well. I want to show how Plato executes this in one dialogue after another, displaying the manner in which constant preoccupation with the reflective aspects of inquiry constitutes a "discipline." Methodical and insistently logical, this mode of reflection itself requires something even more ruthless than logic. It demands a style of living which shows by its finite, even pedestrian concerns how to live with the devouring infinity of reflection. By a simple and unaffected persistence, Socrates shows how to live with the pretensions of reflection, and by continuing to ready himself to begin questioning afresh, he shows how the task beckons man beyond himself.

A SCHEMA FOR INQUIRY

What I propose to unravel is *not* Plato's conception of philosophic method—though it amounts to that. It is rather Plato's way of displaying what any inquiry is all about. What results is a sophisticated example of what we would call "philosophic method." But Socrates stands to remind us that any discussion which comes to close quarters with its subject, however pedestrian, will have to bear the traits which Socrates's way of questioning embodies and elicits. It goes without saying that I cannot claim to have comprehended all of Plato's contributions to philosophy by laying out the essential features of inquiry as they are exhibited in some of the dialogues. Nor am I prepared to present all the evidence which could be mustered; and I freely acknowledge that the pattern seems completely absent from the later dialogues. I shall have little or nothing to say about his metaphysical constructions. But I do endeavor to show how Plato's artistry informs his philosophy precisely by allowing him to *show* what he found himself unable to *say*. By adopting this tactic consciously, Plato acknowledges his Socratic origins. He also succeeds in eliciting from anyone who consents to take part in the dialogues a living awareness that philosophy is that sort of activity which demands the utmost in rigor yet is nowhere removed from the concerns of everyman. As a "discipline," it is indispensable to the school of life itself and it demands of its explicit practitioners not only the wit but the integrity of Socrates.

I shall take as Plato's central question:

(A) what does it amount to to know that something is the case?

and its operative form:

(B) how do we arrive at this state?

I want to show how Socrates responds to this question—as logician, dialectician, and witness to the truth—by showing how logician and witness are focused in the dialectician to bring us to an ever-increasing awareness of the commitments which our very language bodies forth. What follows is a more personal responsibility for the way we use that language and a marked fidelity to the style of life into which responsible discourse leads or drives us.

How do we come to know that something is the case? The general outlines of Plato's response are clear: we ask questions, like the one we asked about knowledge itself. Since we can ask bags full of questions, a shrewd way of conducting our inquiry into questioning itself would be to concentrate not on what is asked but on the way we ask it. The *form* of any question is (or can be transformed into) *what is it*? Hence: what is knowledge? or what is it to know that *p* is the case? Aristotle will canonize this shift to the form of the question or of a statement in a formal logic, and exploit it for a method of methods in the *Metaphysics*. Yet the maneuver is Plato's and it operates consciously throughout the dialogues.

The next salient feature about knowing is that we come to know. We cannot ask every question at once; some come only after others have been answered. Furthermore, we learn to discriminate leading from misleading questions only by having asked plenty of them. So the metaphor of a journey, a quest, with beginning and end, suggests itself as an apt initial answer to the question: how do we come to know something? The metaphor implies that we ought to ask someone who has travelled there how to get there. And this pattern remains constant throughout the dialogues. Its meaning will shift almost beyond recognition: the best guide of all, Socrates, will claim to know nothing at all, and Plato's artistry will conspire to show us how this very unknowing makes him the best of guides. But this paradoxical gloss does not vitiate the original pattern, for Socrates designs to guide us right there: to unknowing. What the pattern eliminates is any suspicion that one who knows can succeed in simply telling it like it is without making the effort to guide us there himself. The pattern asserts that such a one could not know whereof he spoke for he has not traversed to it. For had he traversed from ignorance to knowledge he would realize that there is no other way to come to know—and would never attempt simply to tell it.

STAGES OF THE JOURNEY

However we may have to modify the journey metaphor respecting the *end*, the issue of a starting point is more immediate and imperative. Nothing reminds us so forcibly that we are gripped by a metaphor as the fact that the starting point can be an issue. Ordinary journeys begin from here: where we are standing now; the journey of understanding can only begin from an understanding of where it is we stand. The history of philosophy makes sophisticates of us all by offering several alternatives: experience, sense data, innate ideas, phenomena, unthematized foreknowings, and the rest. Plato himself suggested a few of these in later dialogues, but Socrates represents an uncomplicated stage. Socrates simply begins. He dissolves the issue of a starting point by starting a conversation. The material, the fodder, or the fuel for the journey is provided by the opinions commonly shared and bandied about the marketplace. Socrates begins with these—with what people hold, think, and say—and gets things moving by asking about them.

All this is effectively yet deceptively uncomplicated, of course. The shrewdly analytic fact is that none of the standard candidates that might occur to us can really qualify as starting points for the journey of understanding. To take the vague term "experience" or the more technical "sense-data," in each case we are dealing with a precondition for inquiry, a *sine qua non* rather than an actual starting point. My suspicion is that most of the candidates proffered for starting points are really offered as moorings—the concern resting not so much with inquiring as with its "foundations." Preoccupied with certitude, we were concerned to guarantee the issue of an inquiry by securing its initial stage. But note how the very language of "securing" weighs upon the journey metaphor. What this shows in telegraphic form has been elaborated in critique after critique of phenomenalism: to construct a world out of sense-data precludes any genuine inquiry. There is no journey, no discovery, for the exciting questions have all been settled (or begged) by postulating sensa of a sort sufficiently well-defined to serve as building blocks. So the starting points offered in the interest of certitude ill serve the project of inquiry. More like foundations than an initial stage, they are neither elements in our experience nor appropriate first steps of any inquiry.

What is missing is faith—the faith a Socrates has in human reason to begin a journey, chart its own course, and recognize when it achieves or falls short of its goal (*Phaedo* 90–91). The simplicity and intrepidity with which Socrates puts common opinion to the test bespeaks this faith. Armed with the question form: what is it?, Socrates patiently unfolds the consequences of those opinions commonly and unconsciously held. In his hands, logic serves to confront us with ourselves, as the undergirding structure of language allows him to make clear to us the things to which we are already committed as well as the conversions demanded of us. A homely example will display the major stages of awareness Socrates wants to secure.

Common Sense

If I were prompted at a gathering to ask, about someone who just entered, who (or what) is he?, the various responses could well be—beyond his name—"a vice president," "an administrator," "a desk warmer." Each of these descriptive tags serves as a kind of name in the milieu in which it functions. Names identify, and for the world of common sense, identification normally fills the bill. Conversely, of course, common opinion suffices to formulate an identifying tag.

The set of answers immediately offered to satisfy what is it? reflects a domain of discourse: common opinion, and bespeaks a style of life: the common-sensical. It is not a perfectly self-contained world, for the question form (what is it?) proves embarrassingly iterative, and the answers themselves often reveal this. So the three given above could be ranked in increasing range of scope and of interpretation: vice president, administrator, desk warmer. Yet there is sufficient cohesion to speak of a domain of discourse with a style of life appropriate to it. Trading on Plato's image of a divided line, I would offer the naming or identifying response as the first stage or level in inquiry.

Studied Opinion

The wit who named the gentleman a "desk warmer" has already pushed out beyond an identifying remark. Note that he accomplishes this by a response which transgresses those proprieties which secure the common-sense style of life. If someone were playful enough to take him up, the conversation would move explicitly beyond the first stage and an inquiry would be in process. In the telescopic form of ordinary repartee: "so that's what you think an administrator is—eh—a desk warmer?"

The question form is at work on the answer, and moves the inquiry beyond the arena of common opinion to that of more expert advice. If a wiseacre triggers the move, a more respected voice must resolve it. For we are no longer simply classifying (e.g., "a VP is an administrator") but evaluating, and opinions are bound to differ. Hence the need to appeal to a more expert, studied opinion. For the commonest experience we have of common opinion is that it is interlaced with differences and that those who differ lack the tools for resolving these differences. Hence, commonly, we have recourse to other tools or to violence unless an overweening presence can spark a consensus.

An expert opinion suffices where the man speaking has earned a hearing. So, as we shall see, Socrates's opinion is readily accepted among his disciples. Too readily, even, so that Socrates himself often welcomes the probing demand of a critical outsider for his credentials. There is, of course, a way of producing credentials which simply embellishes the fact that one has been acclaimed an expert. Commonly called "an appeal to authority," this may be the only recourse available, but it does not advance the inquiry. The only way to do that is to produce the credentials for the opinion offered—by bringing forth *reasons*.

Giving Account

Reasons distinguish knowing from opining, for they can tether an opinion to something more than esteem. It is indicative that the question form shifts from the apparently innocent what is it? to its more needling variant: why is that so? If we had accepted a respected elder's view on what a (good) administrator was to be called—say, an inspirer of men, an efficiency expert, or an enabler of enterprises—someone who yearned to understand the matter a little better might be tempted to ask: why does proceeding in that way succeed in administrating well?

The question asks overtly for something more comprehensive than a name, and even than an evaluation—at least of the sort that can be summed up in a phrase. The question *why*? pushes out to demand a framework within which even the studied opinion of an expert can be assessed. It is no respecter of persons; rather it seeks for a ground which can be shared in common but does not require the support of anyone—expert of group—for it can establish itself. Whether it is introduced to resolve conflicting expert opinions or simply to ground the one which can muster the most expertise, what is offered as an explanation resulting in knowing why it is that something is the case.

There is no single pattern of explaining for Plato. He usually signals his intent to secure understanding in this way by explicitly introducing an hypothetical framework "in terms of which" the opinion can be "tethered down." This method of hypothesis makes the logical point that explanation only functions within an established framework of discourse. But no specific framework is regarded as privileged, even if certain ones are preferred. Plato contented himself with making the generic logical point about framework-dependence, and left open the question of which hypotheses could constitute a proper framework. He could afford to leave the question open not because he naively overlooked it but because explanation does not terminate inquiry for Plato. A further question remains—and it is one which must be answered not in overriding terms but in those proper to the inquiry itself. The further question reiterates the why-is-that-so? form, directing it to the framework introduced to provide an explanation for the expert opinion. It asks: why do these terms constitute an explanation?

The Worth of an Account

The question: why is this explanation an explanation? might sound somewhat perverse, but it stems legitimately from the logical fact that any explanation depends on the framework chosen. It is quite natural to ask: why choose this hypothetical structure rather than another?[1] Our first query ought to be whether a question like this one admits of an answer. And if it does, the answer must be of a manifestly different sort than the way the explanatory framework sought to ground the expert's opinion. For if we answer this question about the framework itself simply by offering another, presumably wider framework, then someone has the right to raise the question all over again. And so on . . .

Notice that the further question arises quite independently of the type of explanation we are considering. By calling our attention to this fact, Plato assures that this level of inquiry remain distinct from the preceding one of explanation. He also readies us to grasp *dialectic* as the crowning phase of an inquiry thoroughly imbued with human concerns, and whose entire course can also be described as "dialectical."

Difficult though it may be to describe this final, reflective stage, we cannot renounce the search for an appropriate idiom. Otherwise the entire enterprise of inquiry is threatened by arbitrariness in one's choice of hypotheses and hence of explanations, and thus to the ridicule of serious students who cannot help but debunk it as a *game*. What sort of a description will do the job? Certainly not a straightforward one, as we have just seen. A more comprehensive framework will not do the job. Then why not an indirect, reflexive one? The question form itself—how does the explanation

---

1. Aristotle's restrictions on those definitions appropriate as proper principles of demonstration in effect limited explanation to one privileged framework. In this way he felt he could answer once for all the embarrassing question about how an explanation explains, and avoid a similarly embarrassing plurality of purported explanations. In doing so, however, he managed to throttle subsequent scientific inquiry by placing it under literally impossible restrictions. For his model pattern could not be employed in investigative research but would only function in an enterprise constructive and nearly tautologous, like geometry.

explain?—is overtly reflexive. Perhaps the most fruitful way of approaching this question is to treat it as a question for reflection.

A Reflective Response

We need not be entirely clear on what we mean by a "question for reflection" to adopt it as a way of responding to the difficulty of justification. Certain features readily appear, however. Reflection will not come up with an *answer* in the customary sense, for to do so would be to offer an opinion or supply another explanation. We have seen how introducing a wider framework to explain why explanations explain sets up a formal regress without any inherent way of stopping the question and hence of answering it. A regress of course is not always damaging. It could usefully exhibit a structural feature of inquiry itself: say, its ongoing and ever tentative character. The wider framework scheme for answering the embarrassing questions arising from pluralism fails rather more seriously, and certainly more significantly, by mistaking the form of the question itself. The question about explanation itself is *prima facie* a question for reflection and not a request for further explanations. It deserves to be treated appropriately.

On the other hand if one's decision about frameworks were simply a matter of opinion and incapable of any firmer footing than that, then no regress would result, but skepticism certainly will. And it has, as we can experience among a generation taught by astute researchers well aware of the relativity of their scientific conclusions yet incapable of responding to the reflective question with other than "it's a matter of opinion; take your choice." Like tomato or vegetable soup, say their students; then it's all a game. If inquiry is to be more than a professional exercise, but germane to all men's quest for understanding and for their own humanity, then we must discover how to confront this question. What sort of answer will it tolerate?

Plato's way of responding is quite simple yet inescapably paradigmatic. Since the question form itself suggests a reflective response, that is the kind it receives. Plato responds to the question about the propriety of his own explanation by literally *reflecting* the response into the very structure of the dialogue itself. In this fashion, the form of the explanatory discussion itself *shows* why its terms are appropriate to meet the original question in an explanatory way. If there is any actual discussion devoted explicitly to meeting the reflective question about the dialogue's explanatory power, that discussion only serves to direct the reader's attention to the structure of the dialogue itself—where the answer to the question will be displayed. For no ordinary answer can be given, as we have seen. In other words, why an explanation explains cannot be *said*. Yet this fact does not leave us prey to mere taste. For the question can be met, and the answer, appropriate enough, exhibited.

What Dialogue Shows

Exhibiting is what the dialogue form is all about, complete with the active figure of Socrates who structures the inquiry as it moves along, and so bodies forth the entire process in his person. Wittgenstein's distinction between *saying* and *showing* provides the key for this interpretation of dialectic in Plato, but Plato's use of it also sheds light on the distinction itself. Wittgenstein was obviously trading on the formal features of logic and mathematics, and the plain fact that one knows he has a proof when he arrives by repeated application of the transformation rules at a formula of the desired shape. Plato does not restrict himself to *ad oculos* manifestation, but will show how the propriety of other forms of inquiry can be exhibited by making manifest certain inescapable things about the inquirer himself.

Once put this way, we can recognize the concern which permeates Socrates's manner of questioning. We can also see why there is no answer to the reflective question about explanation unless one is willing to engage in dialogue with Socrates. And if he is willing to sustain the inquiry in this fashion, he will come to realize how and to what extent the reflective question has been answered. He will recognize it in the understanding he has come to acquire of the original subject matter and of his grasp upon it. Recall Wittgenstein's reflective observations about the *Tractatus*: "My propositions serve as elucidations in the following way: anyone who understands *me* eventually recognizes *them* as nonsensical [*am Ende als unsinnig erkennt*], when he has used them—as steps—to climb up beyond them" (emphasis added).[2] What is at stake is a process resulting in understanding the matters broached and in self-knowledge on the part of the inquirer himself—the very thing which Plato proposed in the Socratic dialogue form. Active participation is not only invited but demanded. An explanatory framework can be laid out and examined for consistency; but the further question about its power requires another sort of understanding which cannot be divorced from self-understanding nor from the sort of interior growth which only sustained engagement in inquiry provides. The name Plato gave to the entire process, and also reserved in a special manner for the final stage which brings the process itself to consciousness, was *dialectic*. A few examples will show how he carried it out.

2. Wittgenstein, *Tractatus*, 6.54.

DIALECTICAL PROCESS IN SOME DIALOGUES

I have chosen four examples to illustrate the schema elaborated in the previous section: *Euthyphro*, *Meno*, *Phaedo*, and *Republic*. I have noted that the scheme is less applicable to the later dialogues; there is in fact solid evidence that Plato was up to something else there.[3] I am confident that it can illuminate many other dialogues as well, but will leave that to the participating reader. (The *Gorgias*, for example, would be a fruitful and paradoxical example, where Socrates, lacking anyone with sufficient resolve to sustain a full-fledged inquiry, is forced to turn rhetorician, thereby showing the limitations inherent to Gorgias's way of proceeding.) I have not pressed for the scheme itself as authentically interpreting Plato's own explicit image for inquiry in the divided line, though I have argued this point at greater length elsewhere.[4] For present purposes the scheme is offered as *an* interpretation of Plato's remarks on the method of inquiry, and proposed on the strength of its power to elucidate what Plato is up to in at least some of the dialogues.

Generally, the shift from one stage of inquiry to another is managed, appropriately enough, by posing the original question afresh. There is a kind of pause where some are satisfied, yet others find objections. Socrates usually holds back, allowing others to note that the resolution is only apparent and to push the question further, but the final reflective question normally belongs to him to raise. It is the office of the wise man to wonder even in the face of the security offered by an explanatory scheme.

The shift from opinion to knowledge—explanation and reflective understanding—is marked by a definite break. In the interlude Socrates is wont to give a kind of pep talk underscoring the role of reason and celebrating its power. For opinion—even expert opinion—still takes its bearings from what surrounds us. The move to explanation carries us beyond the familiar to a perspective whence the relativity of our own opinion is made manifest. Rising to this perspective implicitly involves a kind of self-knowledge, and the reflective step demands that we understand even more explicitly where it is we stand. Since the type of growth that self-knowledge requires seems universally unwelcome, Socrates's reassurance forms an integral part of the inquiry process—showing what is at stake.

---

3. Cf. Sayre's careful and ground-breaking study: *Plato's Analytic Method*.

4. The strength of the case rests inherently on the power of this scheme to elucidate what Plato is actually doing, and it can best be defended against other interpretations (notably those which align the first level with sensation) by insisting that the line and its division into objects of sense and objects of intellect is itself an *image*. The argument comprises a chapter in my *Analogy and Philosophical Language*.

Euthyphro

Socrates, charged with impiety, happens upon Euthyphro at the entrance to the law courts, where he is piously bent upon prosecuting his father for murder. The irony is shamelessly staged, though not totally contrived. What about the avowed motive of piety (reverence or holiness)? Socrates inquires this of Euthyphro, convinced that by forcing him into words, he will be carried by the matrix of language to face up to what the reader sees so openly: the irony of his own pretension. "Then tell me: how do you define the holy and the unholy?" Euthyphro's answer is illuminatingly typical: "I say that the holy is what I am now doing, prosecuting the wrongdoer who commits a murder or a sacrilegious robbery, or sins in any point like that, whether it be your father or your mother, or whoever it may be. And not to prosecute would be unholy" (5d).

Euthyphro goes on to substantiate his claim by invoking current stories about the gods. Since the charge against Socrates centers on his attitude towards such stories, he cannot feel comfortable with substantiations like these. So he presses Euthyphro for a more sophisticated response: "Yes, but what is holiness? . . . I wanted you to tell me what is the essential form of holiness which makes all holy actions holy" (6d). Not yet an explanation, the attempt to formulate does yield a more studied opinion: "What is pleasing to the gods is holy" (7a). Socrates's response is enthusiastic yet pressing: "Perfect, Euthyphro. Now you give me just the answer that I asked for. Meanwhile, whether it is right I do not know, but obviously you will go on to prove your statement true."

Euthyphro has not said much and has given no reasons for what he did say, but his response is still *perfect* at this juncture. For he has supplied enough with which to take up the inquiry, and the difficulties arising from his statement will force the explanation stage upon him. Difficulties do arise because the gods are so unstable a reference point—Socrates's impious contention, of course. Yet the formula can still be used, this time to launch the quest for reasons: "Now think of this: is what is holy holy because the gods approve it, or do they approve it because it is holy" (10a)?

The question urges the very meaning of predication upon us: how have we implicated ourselves when we make a simple statement? We have put together two different things: *holiness* and *pleasing-to-the-gods*; and now must be able to show what it is which unites them. To say that x is y is not to remark that they are the same, but to acknowledge their difference, yet assert that somehow they belong together. The "somehow" asks for some *reason*, and thus far has Socrates brought Euthyphro. He does not understand what is being asked at first, so Socrates must help him see. The interlude is delicate; predictably enough, Euthyphro points at Socrates: "I simply don't know how to tell you what I think. Somehow everything that we put forward keeps moving about us in a circle, and nothing will stay where we put it" (11b). He is even prone to blame Socrates for this errant behavior, but Socrates takes the opportunity to recall him to the need for understanding the logic of a language in which such motion occurs ("if so . . . I am an unwilling artist, since I would rather see our arguments stand fast and hold their ground") and presses the inquiry on to make his point.

Socrates suggests a possible explanatory tack: if holiness is *a part of* justice, then maybe we could proceed to explain what it is from what we know of justice. He introduces part/whole by different analogies and so establishes the condition. And what is justice? Euthyphro is unable to state anything more about this than about holiness—thereby showing that containment does not open a useful route to explanation. Yet this much at least *is* known, and not just about *reverence* but about anything into which we are inquiring: classification only invites further questions.

Now Socrates: "And so we must go back again, and start from the beginning to find out what the holy is. As for me, I never will give up until I know" (15c). Euthyphro has not the stamina to start all over again: "Another time, then Socrates, for I am in a hurry, and must be off this minute" (15e). To prosecute his father. Yet if he had only continued, would they have discovered what holiness or reverence is? They most assuredly would not have found a formula which would stand still, but many a formula would have been examined and its explanatory mettle tested. So whatever explanation did ensue we could certainly trust, for the researchers would have *demonstrated* that reverence for which they were seeking by the very manner in which they continued to seek after it: "as for me, I never will give up until I know."

Socrates of course professes ignorance at the end: "What are you doing, my friend? Will you leave, and dash me down from the mighty expectation I had of learning from you what is holy and what is not, and so escaping from Meletus's indictment" (16a)? The irony is charged with a poignant reminder that Socrates will not escape. Yet most striking of all is the manner in which the dialogue itself *shows* the truth of the oracle. For his professed ignorance is the sign that he does know what reverence is, and hence will never "succeed" in formulating it, but will exhibit his understanding by continuing to try to understand.

Meno

The same scheme proves useful in unraveling the *Euthyphro*'s far more sophisticated analogue: the *Meno*. It too apparently takes up the subject of virtue (αρετη) but is "really" about coming to know and understand—yet *shows*, like *Euthyphro*, that it is really about virtue after all. The treatment here will be extremely schematic since the dialogue is so complex and interwoven. The scheme cannot claim to bring every new theme into line, but will prove especially useful in a dialogue so rich as this, by providing an illuminating way of capturing the overall movement of the inquiry. Specifically, the close parallels between *Meno* and *Euthyphro* will become quite evident.

The dialogue begins abruptly: "Can you tell me, Socrates—is virtue something that can be taught" (70a)? This query of Meno's demands of course that we inquire what virtue or moral excellence is. After a spate of examples, Socrates asks for "some common character that makes them all virtues" (72d) and awaits the answer which will reveal the expert in human affairs, the perceptive man of insight.

Many answers are offered but none proves acceptable. Perhaps that is significant; perhaps *the* expert in human affairs would be just the one to eschew defining *arete*. Yet so far, we stand perplexed. And if Socrates can only produce perplexity, how can any of us hope to come to know anything? This is the point, on the schema, for Socrates's explicit reflection on the role of reason, for a *coraggio* to move onwards. What follows is the famous illustration to the slave boy that he *really* knows already.

On our interpretation, what has been seen as the heart of the dialogue becomes an interlude. There is no difficulty here, however, for the illustration is clearly just that—an illustration—and the interlude explicitly taking up the cause of reason might well be considered at the heart of a dialogue so thoroughly concerned with coming to know. Plato's own words at the end of the episode underscore the illustrative and motivating role of the story in the dialogue's forward movement:

> I shouldn't like to take my oath on the whole story, but one thing I am ready to fight for as long as I can, in word and act—that is, that we shall be better, braver, and more active men if we believe it right to look for what we don't know than if we believe there is no point in looking because what we don't know we can never discover. (86b)

Meno then restates the original question: can virtue be taught? And Socrates converts it to: is virtue knowledge? The move is strikingly similar to *Euthyphro*, though explicitly conscious of its hypothetical character:

if virtue were (a part of) knowledge, then it could be taught. What would follow from that? There would be teachers for it, of course. Yet it proves difficult to find anyone who will claim to teach virtue or whom we would acclaim to have taught it. In examining this consequence of the hypothesis, a dramatic parallel to Euthyphro enters in the person of Anytus. He is properly scandalized at Socrates's dispassionate analysis of Athenian heroes, and refuses to have any part in such an impious inquiry. We meet him again as Socrates's accuser at the trial.

Unable to find any teachers, we must conclude that virtue is not (a part of) knowledge. Again, we have not turned up a formula for virtue, but have come into possession of a useful feature of the art of giving reasons: *reductio ad absurdum* argumentation. Although we have not reached an answer in the form sought, we have been proceeding in a manner proper to the level of explanation. The only thing to do is start all over again (96e). And we are able to do so knowledgeably since we can pinpoint where we have been misled: "in insisting that knowledge was a *sine qua non* for right leadership" (97a), since this led us to the absurd conclusion that "there are in fact no good men at all" (96d). Absurd not simply because it conflicts with common estimation but more pointedly because we are in the presence of Socrates.

What follows is carried more exclusively by Socrates than the preceding—a sign that we are into the fourth or reflective level of inquiry, dialectic proper. Further indications are (1) that he does not propose an alternative explanation but seeks to show *why* we were misled by taking virtue to be part of knowledge, nor (2) does he claim to have discovered what virtue is (100b). What he does do is reflect on the role of reason in tethering opinions so that they will stand still, and suggest that the successful statesman is one who accomplishes what he does—in himself and others—only by divine inspiration (99c). This is not so much an explanation as it is confessing one's incapacity to explain. But it is not thereby worthless, because Socrates himself can find no better way to "explain" his own life. And it is, after all, he who has shown—by his relentless and fearless pursuit of the question— what excellence or virtue is all about.

Phaedo

Even more ambitiously, we can submit the *Phaedo* to the same overall scheme for inquiry. The treatment here will be even more schematic than the *Meno*, and for the same reason offered there: the greater the wealth of detail, the more schematic the display of the movement of inquiry. Typically, one level or stage of inquiry is marked off from another when the questioning process reaches a kind of finish. It can be taken up only when someone questions whether the proposed answer is an adequate one. There will also be an interlude between the second and third stage, to mark the crucial move from opinion to knowing.

The setting is thoroughly dramatic: Socrates, on the threshold of a death to which he has freely submitted, agrees to inquire into life itself in the face of death. The question posed is whether or not suicide is legitimate; Socrates's manner is playful.

> I suppose that for one who is soon to leave this world there is no more suitable occupation than inquiring into our views about the future life, and trying to imagine what it is like. What else can one do in the time before sunset? (61e)

Furthermore, the entire dialogue affords respectful dramatic distance on this event since it is not presented "live" but as best Phaedo can recall it.

The first reflections could be summed up as opinions commonly shared by all those present—Socrates's students and friends: man is body and soul, the soul needs to be freed to realize its powers; wisdom, not pleasure, provides the key to a full life (60–70). Cebes acknowledges that everything said about the soul seems excellent to him but would leave the average person quite at sea, for it flies in the face of the facts:

> Of course if it still existed as an independent unity, released from all the evils which you have just described, there would be a strong and glorious hope, Socrates, that what you say is true. But I fancy that it requires no little faith and assurance to believe that the soul exists after death and retains some active force and intelligence. (70b)

So Socrates insists: "If that is how you feel, we had better continue our inquiry" (70c), and goes on to give several "arguments" that converge upon the point at issue: whether or not the soul *lives*. These are that opposites come from opposites, that learning is a form of recollection, that if the forms exist so does the soul, and finally that there is no reason *why* it should disintegrate (70–84). Although these are purely rational arguments, they function more like studied opinion in the dialogue since they do not *argue* the specific point. (In Aristotle's terms they may be universal but they are not commensurately universal.) They represent the cumulative effect of many other things of which Socrates's lifetime inquiring has convinced him, and note that nothing short of a soul which lives would be in harmony with these convictions.

The result is silence. But Socrates realizes that doubts and objections remain; to Simmias and Cebes: "Why, do you feel that my account is inadequate? Don't hesitate to . . . point out any way in which you think my account could be improved" (84c). What follows is the interlude introducing the last two phases of the inquiry. Simmias raises his objection: why is not the soul like the attunement of an instrument? and Cebes, his: why can we not think of it like a cloak which may outlast several owners but finally disintegrates itself? Socrates does not meet these counter-proposals head-on, but takes time out to remind them of the role of logic and of reason in inquiry, and especially of the dangers attendant upon a failure to trust in reason. "We must not let it enter our minds that there may be no validity in argument" (90e) lest we allow ourselves to be led by our own anxieties and persuaded that what we want to be true is in fact the case. Nor does he fail to turn this advice to himself, considering what it is they are inquiring into and where it is that he himself stands (91a). He goes on to meet their objections by exposing the metaphors in each case, yet acknowledges that an adequate response "involves a full treatment of the causes of generation and destruction" (95e).

The most significant dramatic point to this section is that Socrates takes his own advice and undertakes a dispassionate explanation of the matter—in terms of *causes* (96–106). The arguments are designed to have a cumulative effect and, if I am right, amount to proposing a language of "source" and "principle": what makes the body live must itself be alive. If we use this form of language to explain in many domains, then we must accept this conclusion here.

Cebes and Simmias are convinced. It is Socrates who realized precisely how the explanation is incomplete: it is based on assumptions which still need consideration—like asking how appropriate it is to use the language of "principle" here. Yet Socrates *believes* that "if you and your friends examine them closely enough, you will arrive at the truth of the matter, in so far as it is possible for the human mind to attain it, and if you are sure that you have done this, you will not need to inquire further" (107b). What he goes on to speak about is not offered as a further explanation but is simply a statement of his own beliefs. Cast in moral terms of judgment, it is a description—hence a myth—of how things will be for the soul (108–15):

> Of course, no reasonable man ought to insist that the facts are exactly as I have described them. But that either this or something very like it is a true account of our souls and their future habitations—since we have clear evidence that the soul is immortal—this, I think, is both a reasonable contention and a

> belief worth risking, for the risk is a noble one. We could use such accounts to inspire ourselves with confidence, and that is why I have already drawn out my tale so long. (114d)

Having submitted to the rigors of a dispassionate inquiry, he can afford to inspire himself with a likely story. He no longer fears claiming it to be true because he wishes it so. For the truth of the account—Socrates's response to the reflective question—does not rest with the story but with the actions which follow. It is his manner of living and now of dying which testifies to the reality of the "source" or "principle" within him. There must be something *animating* Socrates, "who was, we may fairly say, of all those whom we knew in our time, the bravest and also the wisest and most upright man."

Republic

The *Republic* exemplifies the scheme more straightforwardly than many others. This very fact lends support to our working interpretation of the divided line, since it would be expected that Plato's reflective remarks about method (*Republic* VI) would be reflected most artfully into that dialogue which contained them. The clues for discriminating levels of inquiry are unmistakably telegraphed—at the end of I, IV, and VII, and each level reflects an appropriate way of proceeding.

Thrasymachus does Socrates the favor of proclaiming in the crassest manner possible what many feel about society and its claims upon them: good guys finish last, so why be good? The ethical question is confronted with human life as it is, and becomes the thematic question of the dialogue: is the life of the unjust man better than that of the just, or is that of the just better than that of the unjust? Thrasymachus characteristically cannot sustain the heat of discussion, and refuses after a point to move with Socrates. So his position gets put down but not refuted (354b).

At the opening of Chapter II, Glaucon proposes a thought-experiment to continue the inquiry: a man who possesses a magic ring and so can be perfectly unjust—including appearing to be a paragon of justice. We sense something fishy about the proposal—appearance and reality just don't divide that neatly—but the only way to expose it is to lay bare enough of the conceptual connections so that latent contradictions will stand forth. This Plato accomplishes by his large-scale picture of the state as a blow-up of the soul (II–IV). The picture need not be accurate in its details, for its job is not to explain. It simply reminds us of things we already know but may have overlooked, and reminds us of them forcibly by bringing them into a unified view. Hence anyone who would seem to be utterly other than he is would end up with so many aspects of himself running at cross-purposes that the net effect would be an explosion. The only way to introduce order and simplicity into an organism of many parts is to find a principle of harmony. Without some such unifying principle, the very multiplicity of parts threatens chaos, and a program of explicit disharmony assures it. This is the advice of a wise man—one who has seen much and long—recalling us to our senses.

The picture does not explain, it reminds. But to do its job, it must, like any expert advice, enjoy the force—the verisimilitude—of truth. With a picture, furthermore, any single unwelcome feature can skew its entire effect. And this is precisely what happens to Plato's picture of the harmonious society; it stipulates that wives and children be held in common. Adimantus, finding this offensive, speaks for us all. Socrates's response must explain why this element is included by proposing new principles of judgment so that what once offended will be welcomed. He does this by addressing himself to that element of the state which accounts for its unity, for its being a state: a class of men who care not for themselves but for the common weal (V–VII). Under the rubric of a theory of education for the guardians, Plato takes the opportunity to present his own account of the levels of inquiry—in this chapter which accounts for the good of the state (or the soul).

The task is apparently finished—for everyone but Socrates. He is alone in demanding it, but nevertheless does demand a review of the procedures followed (543c), and goes on to show why the account rendered should be accepted as one (VIII–X). He does this first by contrasting the polity described with various decadent forms, showing how easily these could arise by displacing one or more key elements from their place in the harmonious pattern; and then relates a myth which "will save us if we believe it" (621c). His way of proceeding in these chapters is not obviously reflective and so does not seem to exemplify the subtle movements of dialectic proper. Yet recall the initial query: is the life of the unjust man better than that of the just, or vice versa? The inquiry presses after what is better, or the good life. There is no way to recommend an account of "the good" other than to bring it back home to those primitive feelings which signal whether or not we are living closely with ourselves. In fact, the sophisticated construction of the *Republic* can be offered as elucidating the pregnant phrase "living closely with oneself." So by contrasting the ideal state with repugnant, decadent forms, and by daring to describe what things would be like were "the good" to hold sway. Plato directs the explanation to its roots in human feelings of joy and repugnance. Feelings refined by sustained inquiry, but—the message reads—all the more sensitized for that.

SUMMARY

What I have been able to say about inquiry is not much, yet Plato succeeds in showing a great deal. He does not tell us what explanation is, but does show us what sort of question that is, and gives instances demonstrating how one would go about answering it. The four-level scheme is not a method, but indicates the stages which will constitute any methodical inquiry. Presumably, then, the "philosopher" cannot be expected to come up with a master key to inquiry, and ought not be consulted about the proper method in advance. For he will have nothing to say.

Yet we do have a right to look to him to help us ascertain what it is we are about. He dare not present himself as superior to other men, but should be exceptionally exercised in those qualities of reflection which men tend to find annoying and beside the point. Reflection, however, is a paradoxical task, a humbling profession. For it does not really *get* us anywhere, nor dare it claim to. Yet we dare not—any of us—overlook it, lest the normal hubris of our minds blind us to what we are doing: inquiring into what is in fact the case.

How better characterize this skill in reflection than to call it "judgment"? What we admire in Plato—and in Aristotle and every thinker who continues to inspire us—is the artistry exhibited by his *feel* for the subject matter, the deft mastery with which he puts every systematic tool he touches to the service of inquiry. This clearly demands more than expertise. That something more I have suggestively labeled "judgment." It asks of a philosopher not that he be smarter than the rest of men but that he be more self-aware, not that he understand more than they but that he understand better where he stands. Judgment demands something yet more demanding than expert intelligence: it asks for the humility and the integrity of Socrates. Yet, ironically enough, these demands cannot be announced as criteria, for Socrates himself would never own up to them.

The Socrates we know is Plato's way of showing what it is to do philosophy and what sort of an activity it is. His questions are often skeptical but never his manner. The dialogue form is offered as an exercise. By doing it, we can develop the skills necessary to pursue questions like those the dialogues take up. Plato is too expert a teacher to relieve us of the undertaking by trying to state some typical conclusions. For conclusions can only conclude an inquiry; they cannot be read off a page. In this sense, philosophy has nothing to say, but a skilled philosopher will. Lest Plato's methodological purity lead us to believe that philosophizing itself yields no positive results, however, we have the witness of Socrates. If inquiry results in being like him, it has shown its worth. Plato exists for emulation; Socrates for edification.

Chapter 6

C. S. Peirce
Pragmatism as a Theory of Judgment

BY SHEER ARTISTRY AND sense for perspective, C. S. Peirce has left a logical canvas of sign and meaning able to carry us to the very threshold of *judgment*. Since this paper means to take Peirce up at precisely that point and extend his random remarks into a *theory* of judgment, we shall have to assume a general acquaintance with his overall picture of signification.

The salient features of signification for Peirce may be summarized as an inescapable vagueness characteristic of signs in virtue of which they always invite further determination, a sense of the *continuity* of intentional process as the implicit substrate for any "association of ideas," and the schematic dovetailing of the logical forms of abduction-deduction-induction to explain how we bring our initially vague and general ideas to greater precision. These functional elements are corroborated by his "phenomenology," which seeks to establish three irreducible categories, present in and penetrating the structure of anything real. "Thirdness," as the core of communicability ("A gives B to C"), becomes the heart of the sign-relation; and *as* a pervasive element of our experience reveals itself to be a feature of nature as well. Yet thirdness is never manifested without virtually containing—or *presupposing*—the "brute out-thereness" of experience, which Peirce calls "secondness." And each of these in turn, by the mere fact that they are *present* at all, reveal their "firstness"—a category whose role and significance we shall have to examine later.

But if Peirce's theory of meaning is supported by the phenomenological categories, it is not completed until the doctrine of *pragmatism*, which would explain how *thought*—itself a continuous on-going process of signifying—manages to culminate in a *judgment*. This converging-to-judgment is crucial for Peirce lest his preoccupation with signs and signifying betray our common experience that consideration moves towards decision and understanding is perfected in judgment. It is also needed to give flesh to his normative notion of truth and to support his sophisticated realism—by showing how we can in fact (and not just "at the limit") *assent* to a proposition; and by so *anticipating* the ideal, be said truly to "know reality" and not just "experience existents." And that signs come to apex in judgment is important for us as well, if we are to grasp the connection of Peirce's pragmatism with his theory of signs. This alone, it seems, will allow us to understand his continual insistence that "pragmatism" cannot function without an epistemological realism nourished by cognitive dispositions or "habits," and hence can be *mi*staken for a simple "verificationism."

To call pragmatism a "theory of judgment," then, has the advantage of showing its connection with Peirce's work on signs and emphasizing his contribution to the philosophical analysis of judgment. We shall have to take for granted a certain consensus about judgment: that it is (1) not another piece of knowledge, another fact about a thing; and (2) yet is the natural consummation of inquiry. But what it is, exactly *how* one consummates an inquiry, is much more difficult to say. Peirce endorses (1) by placing judgment beyond the logician's concern and eschewing any hope for a logical diagram of it, and he accepts (2) pointing out that judgment is nothing other than an inquiry's achieving its *purpose*. This suggests the analogies of action, volition, and function (or uses), and provides an opening to realize the prime feature of judgment—the one preventing it from being "pictured" like the sign-relation—its capacity to analyze and correct itself. *Purpose* highlights this feature since we can presumably know the purpose of our inquiry and in the face of new facts or a developing understanding review our past judgments with respect to the purpose as we see it now. At any rate, this will be our thesis: that judgment as we experience it is the focal point of *pragmatism*. Our program will be to examine Peirce's statements about assertion or judgment according to the successive analogies he invokes: action, volition, and purpose, showing at each phase the central role *assertion* plays, and to consider incidentally some disputed interpretations and at least one other view of judgment in human knowing. Finally we shall offer an interpretation of the category of "firstness" which would lend support to our view of judgment in Peirce.

ASSERTION AS ACTION

Peirce tends to speak interchangeably of propositions, judgments, and assertions as conceptual signs, conveying a *representamen* to an interpreter, rounding out and completing the role of a sign by embodying thirdness and virtually containing secondness as well. He also has "propositions asserting" (5.569), and even asserting *their own* truth (5.340, 4.282).[1] This seems to deny any hiatus between meaning and assertion, and even suggests an opening to the radically "pragmatic" slogan that "all meaning lies in the consequences."[2] Yet Peirce emphasizes again and again that this is *not* what the "pragmatic maxim" means to him, that pragmatism entails the reality of general ideas (5.428, 5.504), and that it is a program for *determining* meanings, not bestowing them.

When pressed for precision himself, Peirce readily recognizes that *assertion* is something over and above *meaning*, and accuses the Germans of confusing the issue by using *Urteil* indiscriminately for *assertion* and *assertible*.[3] But the accusation is leveled against logicians, who are supposed to *distinguish* what ordinary usage assimilates into one. Ordinary usage cannot be accused of "confusing" *act* and *ability* because its role is *not* to be precise but to be vague. By using notions interchangeably, it shows how closely interwoven they are. Meaning and assertion are certainly related in the general sense that we only come to know of an ability through its act. Act is its normal completion, what it is *for*. "The sole vehicle in which a concept can be conveyed to a person's cognizance" is a judgment (5.547). A proposition *asks*, as it were, to be asserted. But if this be true, what does assertion *add* to meaning? Certainly not "more meaning," for we have already suggested that the two are incommensurable, as act and ability. But once it is admitted that assertion is not a "purely representitious event" (5.547), the search for an "assertory element" poses "a difficult question" (4.56).

Aristotle's notion of *act* as a generalization of *energy* suggests Peirce's category of secondness (4.542). In this sense, "the *judgment* . . . involves an act, an exertion of energy, and is liable to real consequences and effects" (5.547). This emphasizes the fact that we have noticed: assertion is not a further increment of meaning: "neither the predicate, nor the subjects, nor both together, can make an assertion. The assertion represents [rather] a

---

1. Peirce will be cited unless otherwise noted from *Collected Papers of C. S. Peirce*, where citation (in this article) will be given in the standard volume and paragraph number fashion: thus 5.161 is taken as referring to volume 5, paragraph 161.

2. Dewey, *Reconstruction in Philosophy* (1920), chap. 6; (1948), 154–56.

3. For the distinction of assertion and meaning, see Peirce, 2.252, 2.309, 2.315, 2.437; 5.30, 5.86, 5.424n.

compulsion . . . to attach the predicate to the subjects as a sign of them taken in a particular way" (3.435). Although this activity is reflected into the structure of an *assertible*, which must contain an indexical element (2.337, 4.56), a well-formed proposition is *not yet* a judgment—"the logician does not assert anything" (4.79, 4.352, 4.397). Rather, "a judgment is an act of consciousness in which we recognize a belief and a belief is an intelligent habit upon which we shall act when occasion presents itself" (2.435). That *recognition* "may come very near action, . . . but in general [is a] virtual resolve, . . . a peculiar act of the will." What accounts, then, for "*assertion* seeming so different from other sorts of signification is its *volitional* character" (2.436), and since "volition involves action and reaction" (2.437), it seems that we have at least "pegged" the *assertory element* as a kind of *second*.

If we were to stop here, however—with a "categorical explanation"—we would be violating Peirce's pragmatic maxim and misusing the categories. But it might be helpful to take stock of what we have said by making the plus-factor of assertion a "kind of second," and incidentally to remark the correct role of phenomenological categories in inquiry.

Peirce had already assumed a firmly anti-Cartesian posture: negatively, by showing that knowledge simply is not the kind of thing that needs unshakable foundations to build upon, nor does it even *reductively* demand a clear and indubitable basis from which further progress might be *explained* (5.263). This amounted to a rejection of deduction as the paradigm of human knowledge. Peirce was to replace this by *abduction*, which simply labels the pervasive features of scientific method: "studying facts and devising a theory to explain them. Its only justification is that if we are ever to understand things at all, it must be in that way" (5.145). This allowed him positively to develop a theory of perceptual judgments as the "limiting case of abduction" (5.186), and so incorporate the body of Aristotle's *Posterior Analytics* by giving an effective meaning to the metaphor of the routed army making a stand. Aristotle is perfectly clear that what he called "induction" is the "originative source" of all scientific knowing, since it alone can yield the definitions or proper principles. As relatively determinate, these can shape the direction of an inquiry; and as containing much that is yet vague, they still leave room for the process of explicitation which is science.[4] By giving "induction" a logical status as *abduction*, Peirce removed it from the role of a genial and inspired preamble to scientific inquiry, and did Aristotle the favor of redistributing the weight of the *Posterior Analytics* in a way that Aristotle's own reflections beg to be done (5.144).

4. For this view of science as coming to know more distinctly the virtualities of the definitions, see Aristotle, *Posterior Analytics* I. 1–3; and Aquinas's commentaries *In de Sensu* 1; *In de Caelo* proem.; *In de Meteor.* proem.; *In 1 Phys.* 1.

From this new kind of "foundation," then, inquiry was capable of launching hypothetical forays carried by the continuous relation of thirdness, which allows each significative moment not only to pass on but to contribute to the initial momentum. The whole meaning is the trajectory which relates any single stage to the target. But how is one assured of being "on target," what is to count as a hit? To extend the metaphor a moment, in a "high-powered" inquiry what is to prevent one from losing control and orbiting about the goal indefinitely? In fine, how can one know that an inquiry is consummated? This is of course the question Hegelianism poses for philosophy, and Peirce intended to capture in his sign-relation of thirdness: the heart of Hegel's dialectic (1.491, 1.544). Hegel demonstrated in spite of himself that "thirdness" does not consummate inquiry of and by itself. We have seen how Peirce apparently answers this dilemma by invoking secondness. If we were to treat this as his reply, we should be able to oppose him neatly to Hegel, and show him as the progenitor of "pragmatism" in one fell swoop; inquiry is consummated in *action*.

But this is *too* neat a reply. We have Peirce's testimony: "If pragmatism really made Doing to be the Be-all and the End-all of life, that would be its death. For to say that we live for the mere sake of action, as action, regardless of the thought it carries out, would be to say that there is no such thing as rational purport" (5.429); and his warning that a search for the "assertory element" raises a "difficult question." Peirce does not use words lightly, so we ought to be surprised to have arrived so quickly at an answer. But the real reason for objecting is that this is not a reply. Coming up with a categorial niche does not *answer* a question so much as it directs and guides further inquiry. The categories do not provide an explanation but offer a program; they are not terminal, but heuristic. What is needed now is a *model* which can serve like the diagrams in mathematics to *focus* our experience, now *guided* by the category, on the salient features of assertion and *suggest* fruitful associations (5.148).

RESPONSIBLE ACTION

Peirce carries on the search for what is peculiar to the act of assent under the guiding analogy of *willing*. But while he laid stress on the elements of action/reaction in 1893, ten years later he will focus on the peculiar twist which volition gives to action, in particular its demand that action be *responsible*. In the Pragmatism Lectures of 1903 he speaks of judgment as "an assertion to oneself" whereby one personally assumes responsibility for the truth of what he says (5.29–30). Such an act is quite clearly above and beyond "apprehending meanings," and is more like *adopting* a proposition as one's own (5.115).

There are two aspects to the act, which Peirce recognized in 1897: the *intention* of "the judger ... [is] to impress upon himself the truth of a proposition," but the paradigm case is "going before a notary and assuming formal responsibility for its truth" (2.252). What appeared to be distinct, however, is gradually recognized as closely related: "to *assert* a proposition is to make oneself responsible for it" (5.543). Responsible to whom? Not merely to oneself, but to oneself *as belonging to* the community of inquirers: "solitary dialectic is still of the nature of dialogue" (5.546). Judgment, then, will be explicated on the model of intersubjective discourse, but what suggested the model? The fact, perhaps, that "every new concept first comes to the mind in a judgment" (5.546). Thought is essentially a to-be-asserted, and after accurately recognizing that the proposition-sign "retains its full meaning whether it be actually asserted or not" (2.252), one must nevertheless admit that *unasserted* it remains somewhat emasculated—incomplete and unconsummated. The close relation between *assertible* and *assertion*—as reflected in ordinary speech—must be brought to light to counterbalance the realization "that the act of assertion is an act of a totally different nature from [that] of apprehending the meaning of a proposition" (5.30). And both viewpoints must be held firmly to keep an *effective* balance:

> The *volitional element* is quite extraneous to the substance or "meaning" of a concept.... For it is no pragmaticistic doctrine that responsibility attaches to a concept; but the argument is that the predication of a concept is capable of becoming the subject of responsibility, since it actually does become so in the act of asserting that predication. (5.547)

The example Peirce uses to accentuate the "assertory element" in judgment is a "very formal assertion, the features of which have purposely been rendered very prominent." But the forfeit is no smaller for being unnamed, and

> This ingredient, the assuming of responsibility, which is so prominent in solemn assertion, must be present in every genuine assertion. For clearly, every assertion involves an effort to make the intended interpreter believe what is asserted, to which end a reason for believing it must be furnished. (5.546)

> When a writer makes an assertion, his principal purpose is to induce the reader to believe in the reality of the fact asserted. He

has the subsidiary design of causing the reader to follow along his line of thinking. . . . (4.353)

Once one's attention is directed to assertion as the natural completion or fruition of an assertible (meaning), and thence to the intersubjective dimension of thought, observations like the above begin to pour in. "Implication" ceases to be a purely formal operation and one is sensitized to the "pragmatic implications" woven into the texture of ordinary speech; logic is expanded to make room for *statements* as well as propositions, to consider *use* in addition to form.[5] The added dimension is *point* or *purpose*, the end for which a proposition is *used*. This introduces the most fruitful element in pragmatism, and suggests Peirce's most mature view on the "difficult question" of assertion. But before looking further, let us consolidate the gains made under the guiding principle of *responsibility*.

The most striking is perhaps the personal element: "the words 'reasonable' and 'perverse' imply that assent is as free as choice ever is, and so proclaim their volitional strain" (1.330). There is something essentially communitarian about thought, and yet the assertions which culminate and initiate it demand that one be willing to step out of the ranks and stand up to the community, personally backing his thoughts by the act of asserting them. But the two dimensions are only superficially antithetical. As we are finally realizing after the demise of that individualism which so rankled Peirce, genuine community demands self-assertion, and assertion in turn becomes less defiant and more effective the more one acknowledges his own radical need for the community. The analogy of responsibility leads to the further simile of thought:assertion::community:person, underscoring the essentially Hegelian insight that what *distinguishes* judgment from consideration will also account for their being so closely *related* in function.

But to admit the personal dimension is to raise the question of ethics—especially when one speaks of "assuming responsibility." So we are given a clue to Peirce's insistence that *logic* presupposes and is governed by *ethics*—a strange even unwelcome notion at first blush, yet one which promises to put us on the "trail of the secret of pragmatism" (5.130). Peirce's scheme presumes the interrelatedness of thought and assertion that we have remarked, specifically the fact that formal analysis is developed to clarify the process of functional argument, to elicit the logical doctrine virtually contained in *any* act of reasoning. *Logica utens* must be the final judge of any *logica docens* proposed to explicate it (2.186ff.). A systematic picture

---

5. For "pragmatic implication," see Grant, "Pragmatic Implication"; Black, "Presupposition and Implication"; and Nowell-Smith, "Contextual Implication and Ethical Theory."

gives a clarity and perspicuity which makes it useful as a ready measure for any actual course of reasoning, but the final measure of reason can be none other than *reasoning itself*. And reasoning takes place in a community, via *judgments*, as the "sole vehicle in which a judgment can be conveyed to a person's cognizance or acquaintance" (5.547). Now if judgments are the kind of thing that one personally adopts, so must the reasoning process be which culminates in adopting them. So Peirce insists that one may not be able precisely to *formulate* the general habit of thought determining a judgment, but it is essential that he "*approve* it as conducive to true knowledge" (2.773, italics ours). "If we did not approve, we should not infer" (5.130). And since "self-approval supposes self-control . . . , *logica utens* is a particular species of morality" (5.108, cf. 4.540).

Note how this distinction of *logica utens* and *docens* and the subsequent move through *use* to responsible use or morality draws upon the fact that *propositions* as logic must study them are "incomplete"—their very construction bespeaks assertion and so presupposes their actually being used in making judgments for the sake of inquiry (e.g., 2.337). We analyze what we *find*, and what we find is actual use: *form follows function*. This introduces us into Peirce's most mature (and most "pragmatist") treatment of assertion as relative to a *purpose*, which will also permit us to do justice to his pregnant remarks that if logic be regulated by ethics, ethics in its turn is subject to esthetics. This is of course a challenge to the view we have just outlined—to develop its virtualities further. For fruitful as it is to recognize the role of *approval* in reasoning—and useful as some contemporaries have found it in reestablishing the relativity (and hence utility) of distinctions like analytic/synthetic—there is something wanting thus far.[6] It is of course the sense of expectancy one always feels at being told that a certain course of action is ethical. Why? And the "why" cannot help but implicitly call the whole procedure into question—since ethics does not, cannot, answer its own most threatening questions. Something more is always needed—something which may well not be able to be *said* but finally only hinted at. In the meantime, however, more must be said, if only to frame and give a perspective to Peirce's startling remark that "he who would not sacrifice his own soul to save the whole world, is, as it seems to me, illogical in all his inferences, collectively. Logic is rooted in the social principle" (2.654).

---

6. Cf. Sellars, "Counterfactuals, Dispositions, Causal Modalities," 225–309, esp. 287–88.

ROOTS OF RESPONSIBILITY

Judgment may be considered *a* limit point of inquiry. Since there is nothing in the sign-relation to assure its convergence, however, the preliminary heuristic tack was to assume the "assertory element" of judgment as a kind of second. The model suggested was *volition*, which captured the sense of personal responsibility evidenced in the range of postures we assume in proposing our thoughts to the community (= to ourselves and to others). As *responsibility* invoked ethics, however, the model carried us well beyond secondness to show the instability of the pragmatist slogan: "Inquiry is consummated in action." For if action be human action, then it had better be responsible; and to request the criteria of responsible action is to initiate a further inquiry. We are back in "thirdness," then—well inside the cognitive realm of inquiry—when we ask, as we must: When may one *approve* a course of reasoning, when is one *justified* in asserting an idea? The classical response was in terms of *purpose*: whatever fulfills the purpose envisaged for it may be said to be correct or justified. "Good" is closely associated with "aim," "end," and "function," although it cannot be said to be *defined* by them.[7] Peirce unabashedly adopts this heuristic scheme to temper his insistence that inquiry *per se* is potentially endless, and so must always be kept open, with the willing permission to halt any particular inquiry *when its purpose is served* (5.212, *ad fin.*).

Lest the terms in which we have cast the issue suggest that it be a mere systematic difficulty for Peirce, it is worth recalling that we are faced here with the substance of the *Meno* question: "How do we recognize the truth when we find it?" For *judgment* has been traditionally associated with truth, and to know when to terminate an inquiry is to say that one has satisfactorily answered the question posed, has arrived at the truth. Posed in this way, however, it sounds foreign to Peirce, for we know that he regards *truth* as a regulative ideal which inquiry (hopefully) approaches as a limit (2.113, 5.407). But nevertheless he speaks of the "main points [of an analysis being] pretty near to the truth" (2.322), of there being "reasons to think there is some truth in pragmatism" (5.35); nor does he hesitate to say of a provisional "rude division of triadic relations" that "we need not doubt [it] contains important truth, however imperfectly apprehended" (2.234). The image seems to be that of a finer and finer approximation to the truth: o is contained within the interval ± 1/2, as it is also within ± 1/8, ± 1/1000, and

---

7. Nowell-Smith concludes his article "Contextual Implication and Ethical Theory" by suggesting that "Aristotle was right, both in commending those who said that 'good' means 'what things aim at' and in refusing to commit himself to this as a definition of 'good'" (18); cf. *Nicomachean Ethics* I. 6.

± 1/n (n ≠ 0). *Continuity* assures both that a continuous function within any of the intervals will take 0 for one of its values, and that a closer approximation will *always* be possible. But once this has been said the mathematical image shows more by its inadequacy than by what it can *say*. For the clarity and precision of mathematics stems directly from the fact that the general *purpose* of the inquiry is severely delimited and hence transparent to the inquirer. One is interested in no more than the formal relations that can be manifested among the distinct objects of an (assumed) collection, once they are subjected to a set of defining properties. *Because* the purpose of the inquiry is so explicitly contained, judgment in mathematics is reduced to *checking* whether the operations have been carried out as defined.[8]

This, we might add, does not mean to *reduce* mathematics to logic, for mathematical inquiry, as Peirce has seen so clearly, has a peculiar "diagrammatic" character which suggests otherwise unsuspected affined uses in a manner defying formal logic (3.364, 4.642). The most fruitful areas of modern algebra—in group theory, for example—even trade on a kind of *vagueness* in the initial axioms which encourages one's attending to different groupings of formal relations. But in every case, the way one *judges* whether he be *entitled* to lay down a proposition as a theorem is by means of a proof amounting to a step-wise check of the applications made of the defined properties and operations.

The example together with our critique of it *as* an example suggests two salient features of judgment. The first is that one should be able to say, as he easily can with the example, that while the interval ± 1/1000 contains 0, nevertheless ± 1/n (n > 1000) approximates it *better*. One must be able to say, in other words, how *well* a proposed response corresponds to the question posed—fulfills the *purpose* of the inquiry. Outside of mathematics, it is doubtful whether this can ever be estimated with exactitude, nor can one hope for a "perfect fit" in anything outside of logic—indeed anything beyond the propositional calculus.[9] What we need is the ability to judge an approximation *as approximating*—that is, as *both* approaching *and* falling short of its goal. Hence Peirce says of his general theory of signs in 1902: "Close examination encourages the student to believe that this is something

---

8. The observation is made by Lonergan in *Insight*, 310.

9. This is the crucial role of continuity: to always leave room for a better approximation yet assure that each contains the limit, and even that after a certain point it is *adequately defined*, i.e., further approximation becomes *irrelevant* (cf. Lonergan, *Insight*, 59–60). The fact that continuity is so important even to mathematics lends a formidable *rhetorical* force to Peirce's use of it, but one is inclined to agree with Murphey's final judgment that he never succeeds in *showing* how continuity plays the systematic role he says it does (*Development of Peirce's Philosophy*, chap. 18, esp. 405–7).

like the truth, but so far as it has been carried, excites doubt whether this be the whole story . . ." (2.322). Now this requires, of course, that in some way we *already know* the goal about which we are inquiring. Here we have the *Meno* paradox, and Peirce's answer is substantially the same as Aristotle's (though much more sophisticated in its attention to method): of course we already know the goal, but only vaguely—in such generality that the knowledge can be of no *use* except to entice us to inquire more about it.

In Peirce's terms, this means that we *can* survey the purposes of our inquiries, and so know in general what to expect them to turn up. And this implies the second feature of judgment, which was manifested in criticizing the use of a mathematical example to illuminate the process of inquiry. One object or state of affairs may be subjected to many *styles* of inquiry, and we would want to be able to say that at least *some* were more revelatory than others. The capacity to survey the purposes of our inquiries, to take stock of the general "points of view" from which we are considering something, may not *logically* entail the ability to adjudicate amongst them, yet in fact we *do* evaluate at least some of them, and feel warranted in doing so. (The relative merits of viewing man as an object of economics, sociology, or psychology may be hard to assess, but one can certainly contrast them as a group with physiology.) There is no doubt, however, that judgments of this kind are more tenuous than the first, so that one of the practical tenets offered by pragmatism is tolerance and pluralism in admitting forms of inquiry. Even the most unlikely projects can unwittingly witness to the truth—like the "nominalist" campaign to reduce meaning to denoting and so analyze thirds into seconds (1.344).

Both facets of judgment—appraising an inquiry as approximating its aim, and evaluating the adequacy of diverse aims to the object—suggest an *assessment* of sorts, and yet one radically different from ordinary assessing in that we have no preconceived standards. That the aims of an inquiry can be scanned and so the general outlines of its goal known *before* inquiry does not say that the object can as yet properly be conceived. *This*, in fact, is the goal of the inquiry. So the vague, general grasp which serves to *elicit* inquiry can hardly double as a *standard* with which to measure its success. It simply is not determinate enough to be *used*—in this way or in any other. By contrast, in taking Plato's metaphorical "solution" to the *Meno* problem literally, and accepting the assessment model at face value, Neoplatonists like Augustine were compelled to postulate a primordial intuition of truth, against which "imperfect truths" could be measured and their inadequacy read off. Since they tended to treat knowledge on the model of *vision*, judgment became a unique kind of *seeing*, or "intuition."

But how can one assess without a standard? He can be constructing one as he moves along, gradually *approximating* one. And such a solution does not initiate a regress because it is simply a manner of describing the critical faculty which can assess without a standard because it "tends to correct itself." Peirce cites this feature as

> ... one of the most wonderful ... of reasoning and one of the most important philosophemes [*sic*] in the doctrine of science ...; namely that reasoning tends to correct itself, and the more so, the more wisely its plan is laid. Nay, it not only corrects its conclusions, it even corrects its premises. (5.575)[10]

One would look in vain, however, for rules of correct self-correcting. The consequential role of reasoning may be codified with some success; the reflective, assessing role involving self-correction cannot be, under penalty of regress—*quisnam custodes custodiet*? This capacity of the deliberately formed habit to be self-analyzing—"self-analyzing because formed by the aid of analysis of the exercises that nourished it—[makes it] the living definition, the veritable and final logical interpretant" (5.491). Now the "final logical interpretant" is defined three years later in the letters to Lady Welby as the "one Interpretative result to which every Interpreter is destined to come if the sign is sufficiently considered."[11] As "that towards which the actual tends," it is the normative factor of inquiry which defines *the* truth as its ideal consummation. The self-analyzing or reflective dimension of habit, then, would be its psychological analogue. (Traditionally, this would have been attributed to the reflective nature of the faculty, but as nature must manifest itself in habits of operation, one might as accurately point to a dimension of *habit*. Furthermore, Peirce has rhetorical reasons for using one term, "habit," to call attention to the all-pervasive factor of *thirdness*.)

More must be said of the systematic consequences that the self-correcting capacity of reasoning holds for Peirce's theory of signs. But some observations are needed at this point to quiet a skeptical query whether

---

10. Compare Plato: "Then the dialectic method proceeds alone by this way, demolishing the hypotheses as it goes, back to the very beginning itself, in order to find firm ground; the soul's eye, which is really buried deep in a sort of barbaric bog, it draws out quietly and leads upwards, having the arts we have described [mathematics] as handmaids and helpers" (Rouse translation of *Republic* VII. 533b).

11. Peirce, "Letters to Lady Welby," 414. We are deeply indebted to Fitzgerald for the loan of his PhD dissertation, "Peirce's Theory of Signs as the Foundation of His Pragmatism," which contains the interpretation we have adopted here (92–93). One might also cite Peirce, 8.184: "[the final Interpretant is that] which *would* finally be decided to be the true interpretation if consideration of the matter were carried so far that an ultimate opinion were reached."

Peirce has not invoked the *deus ex machina*. What is this power of self-criticism, that is, *how* does it *operate*? One factor stands out; unlike reason's role in drawing consequences, this self-analyzing, reflective role is not rule-like. At least its rules are not perspicuous like those for consequences, nor, if a set of them *could* be drawn up, would one use them for assessing, in the same literal manner in which (some) logicians would have us following theirs in drawing conclusions? This discrepancy merely reflects the fact that the faculty of judgment is precisely what explains our insistence that a systematic logic, functional as it is, remains but the bare bones of reasoning, and why we can challenge the pretensions of some logicians to be giving us more—to have captured, for example, the "cognitive content" or "if . . . then . . ." by *material implication*. The terms of the challenge are usually: "But we don't *use* it that way . . . ," and the way we *use* our ideas (in language) has the peculiarity about it that we can *recognize*—once our attention is subtly drawn to it—*how* we used and tend to use certain expressions. One might also say "how we *intend* to use them," to suggest how use overflows rules—at least in the usual sense in which rules invoke games or commands. For one can always ask what was *intended* by that rule, and since no rule can give its own instructions for application, the overriding intention of the legislator—of *this* one and, more importantly, of legislators in general—will have to guide our observance.[12]

By illustrating the difference between reason in its *consequential* and in its *assessing* roles on a parallel with rules of procedure vs. moral rules, we have helped reinforce the analogy of judgment with volition and ethics.[13] To take up the lead once again, the recent (and profoundly traditional) insistence that neither moral decisions nor evaluations can effectively be made *in abstracto* illuminates the "contextual" factor of *judgment*. Reason cannot correct itself once and for all, but only in *inquirendo*. We look to encyclopedists for *knowledge*, but for an evaluation we turn to someone who has a working familiarity with a field. (Newman calls him "the expert," and one of his prime arguments in favor of liberal education is that those who later become *experts* in a specialized field be able to articulate their experience, so the world can profit from their *judgment*.[14]) Peirce has expressed this by noting that the deliberately formed habit *is* "self-analyzing because [it is] formed by the aid of analysis of the exercises that nourish it." We ought not be put off by the circularity, because the fact that "control may itself be

---

12. The intention of the legislator *in general* is meant simply to emphasize the general characteristics of lawmaking and enforcing, so as to avoid a "voluntarism" of observance.

13. For instance, Hare, "Decisions of Principle."

14. Newman, *Grammar of Assent*, chaps. 5–6.

controlled, criticism itself subjected to criticism" (5.442) is exactly what is at issue. It is noteworthy that only the person expressly engaged in forming a specific *habit* of inquiry will stop to analyze the exercises designed to develop it. One who is content to "learn about" a field can do so simply by going through the paces; critical analysis will be an incidental by-product of his mental acuteness. But someone who *needs* both the durability and flexibility of a habit of inquiry cannot afford to leave his position untested as he moves along. And correlatively, a greater ease and familiarity in employing the habit helps him to discern what might count as a *test* or analysis of its procedures.

Here we have the bite, then, of the pragmatist insistence that judgment is tied up with the *purpose* of an inquiry, and that the one who can most effectively assess how well an inquiry is serving its purpose is the *actual inquirer*.[15] Although the "final logical Interpretant"—the truth sought for—is an ideal limit, reason's self-corrective power when used by an expert with a *feel* for his subject gives us an assurance of being *on course*, of being "pretty near to the truth." The familiarity or *feel* of the expert assures that this solution be a *human* one—not a godlike, intuitive one. For all that, however, the fact that human knowledge is "a self-correcting enterprise which can put *any* claim in jeopardy though not *all* at once," ought not lessen our *wonder* at this unique power.[16]

AN INTELLECTUAL SYMPATHY

But what could one possibly mean by the "familiarity or *feel* of an expert" for a field of inquiry? This statement invites development by its excessive vagueness, and yet already suggests Peirce's schematic resolution of ethics. Before examining this in detail, however, let us collate the few remaining statements on *assertion* which highlight this final aspect. Peirce defined "judgment" in 1893 as "the actual calling to mind of the substance of a belief, not as personal to ourselves, but as holding good, or true" (4.53). "Belief" is said to be a "habit of which we are conscious," and the negative clause apparently corrects an earlier definition (1880) when he had been content to call judgment a "representation to ourselves that we have a specified habit" (3.160). "Holding good, or true" is explicated (in 1896) as the "conditions [to which] an assertion must conform in order that it may correspond to the 'reality,'

---

15. Cf. Gallie, *Peirce and Pragmatism*, 130–31.

16. The citation is not from Peirce but from Sellars, "Empiricism and the Philosophy of Mind," 300. Peirce's remarks on the "lumen naturale" of Galileo are interesting, however (1.80–81; 6.477).

that is, in order that the *belief it expresses may be stable*" (3.430, emphasis added). Peirce goes on to show how one comes to accept a belief as stable, and gives his most lucid account of assertion:

> Neither the predicate, nor the subjects, nor both together, can make an *assertion*. The assertion represents a compulsion which experience, meaning the course of life, brings upon the deliverer to attach the predicate to the subjects as a sign of them in a particular way. (3.435)

"This compulsion," he explains, differs from mere secondness in that while it "strikes him at a certain instant, he remains under it forever after." Hence the need to embody it in a proposition, to give it the "permanent conditional force [of] law." The sign that the proposition so embodies a judgment "is the *copula* of the assertion."

In this passage, Peirce manages to incorporate the functional relatedness of proposition and assertion as well as do justice to their intrinsic difference: the "assertory element" is like a *compulsion* but one which the "course of life"—not a single staccato event—brings upon the inquirer. What is it like for "the course of life" to "bring something upon one"? It seems very close to Peirce's description of "*deliberately*—that is to say *reasonably*—adopting an ultimate end of action." This "must be a state of things that *reasonably recommends itself in itself* aside from any ulterior consideration." For Peirce, this is enough of a lever to move us into his schematic resolution: "Since the only kind of goodness that such an ideal *can* have" is that it be *admirable*—"namely, esthetic goodness . . . , the morally good appears as a particular species of the esthetically good" (5.130).

We have supplied the associations too freely and so moved too quickly, but a little reflection should fill in the gaps. *What* finally convinces us we are entitled to make an assertion, adopt a course of action? *Finally*, nothing but the fact that after *weighing* the arguments and evidence, we *feel* it is correct to do so—where the use of "feel" rather than "see" conveys at once the intimately personal and the esthetic elements. But the resolution remains schematic. The best clue Peirce can give us to the nature of this *feeling* is that

> It is a sort of intellectual sympathy, a sense that here is a Feeling that one can comprehend, a reasonable Feeling. I do not succeed in saying exactly *what* it is, but it is a consciousness belonging to the category of Representation, though representing something in the Category of Quality or Feeling. (5.113)

It is an "intellectual sympathy," very like the *feel* (or familiarity) of the expert, because while it does license *assertion*, the latter is put forward with a certain *consciousness* of its inadequacy.[17] If our judgments are to respect continuity, they will be aware of approaching and yet not touching the truth of the matter. This is manifested by a "habit's being ready to be broken in case reasons should appear for breaking it" (2.315). That is, we can recognize *in what respect* our judgments are vulnerable, can accept or reject a criticism as relevant or not, which presupposes an awareness of the extent to which we have committed ourselves. Because this awareness is direct—conscious, but not self-conscious—it is not expressible, but discloses itself only upon further inquiry, in the recognition with which one greets criticism (cf. 5.300). This sense of approximation is corrigible and perfectible, as one is usually unsure in the beginning of an inquiry which objections to count as relevant, while the expert hand betrays itself not necessarily in being able to respond to every such challenge, but by knowing which ones to take seriously and which to discard.

A SUGGESTED REVISION

Bernard Lonergan, in a study of general methodology which bears remarkable affinities to Peirce throughout, makes *judgment* as we have described it the basis for one of his three fundamental categories. Working out from Aquinas, he shares with Peirce the axiom that the categories of intelligibility are those of "being," and in architectonic fashion develops the analogies between the three "levels" of experience: description, explanation, and judgment, and Aquinas's ontological hierarchy of potency, form, and act.[18] Lonergan has amassed the evidence elsewhere to show the crucial importance of *act* for Aquinas, and its novelty in the Aristotelian scheme.[19] If *act* was indistinguishable from *form* for Aristotle, it becomes quite diverse from it in Aquinas, where the real distinction between *essence* and *existence* forces a separation.

Much of this was already familiar from Gilson, but by using the basic axiom linking "ontological" and "epistemological orders" Lonergan was able to explicate act and its difference from form on the analogue of judgment and understanding (assertion and proposition).[20] Judgment is not a further

17. On judgment as "feel," see Smart, "Theory Construction," 238, 241.

18. Lonergan formulates the axiom in *Insight*, 552; Peirce, for example, at 6.417, 6.477. Lonergan's treatment of potency, form, and act is to be found in *Insight*, 431–34.

19. Cf. Lonergan, "Concept of *Verbum*," 8:408–13, 8:418–29; and *Insight*, 434n.

20. The position of Gilson may be gleaned from his readily available works: *God and Philosophy* and *Being and Some Philosophers*. Lonergan's development is found in *Insight*, 434–51.

act of understanding but the limit of rationality when the mind gains—in so far as this is possible—a reflective grasp of the conditions under which it is knowing its object, and so is able to make a judgment of the quality we have sketched—a judgment Lonergan calls (after Kant) the *virtually unconditioned*.[21] This means simply that it can do the things which Peirce's epistemology demands that judgment be able to do: point towards the ideal (unconditioned) by estimating that one's ideas are "on the track." Hence it fulfills the twin *desiderata* of being sure of being on the path and yet remaining always revisable. By thus distinguishing judgment from understanding, Lonergan is able to assimilate all that Peirce says of thirdness and its rule-like quality into *understanding*, and by means of *judgment* account for the further dimension of *using* these rules, or assessing their adequacy.

For Peirce, on the other hand, "a Feeling that one can comprehend," the *feel* or familiarity licensing assertion, is inexplicable because it crosses categorial lines. It must actively exhibit the characteristics of *both* firstness and thirdness—and so account for the *compulsion* (or secondness) that we feel. (Everything, it is true, displays all three categories, but one alone must predominate: so communication presupposes demonstratives, and a sharp blow "asks" to be identified.) This seems to be a serious objection to Peirce's categorial structure—given the central importance of the "assertory element," the self-analyzing dimension of habit, in giving *content* to the limit-concept of truth. There is a "way out," suggested by Lonergan's work (which we can only invoke here as an example), but only the strain of further inquiry can tell whether it is more than a mere verbal patchwork. This would be to take the drift of Peirce's *examples* rather than his explicit statements, and make *firstness* what we ordinarily mean by "consciousness." (Lonergan suggests this, since he made all three of his categories of consciousness designed to manifest the "polymorphism of human consciousness.") But at least one emphatic denial, "I do not mean [by firstness] the sense of actually experiencing these feelings" (1.304), may be taken as denying that firstness is self-consciousness, for Peirce was clear on the distinction we have noted between consciousness and self-consciousness (5.225, 5.289). On the other hand, if one looks at his examples and reads the attempted descriptions, expressions like "the present in its direct positive presentness" (5.44) and other remarks about *mere feeling* (as yet unascribed) are certainly reminiscent of the notion of *consciousness* which Lonergan develops out of Aquinas's thought.[22]

21. Lonergan introduces the notion in *Insight*: "To grasp evidence as sufficient for a prospective judgment is to grasp the prospective judgment as virtually unconditioned" (280), and relates his development with Kant (339–42). (For elaboration of the "virtually unconditioned" in *Insight*, cf. index.)

22. For Lonergan, see *Insight*, 320–28, for example, "By consciousness we shall

Although these few remarks are manifestly insufficient to calculate the ramifications of identifying firstness with consciousness, at least one would not be tempted to *describe* "presentness" and so run the risk of assuming (mythical) given qualities in experience, as much of Peirce's writing on firstness does.[23] Judgment could then be "explained," much as Lonergan does, since thirdness, as presupposing firstness, would now be imbedded in consciousness, and the gradual coming-to-consciousness, or better, to self-consciousness, of one's manner of using the signs he does—of the scope and purpose of an inquiry—would "bring upon" the inquirer that "compulsion . . . to attach the predicate to the subjects as a sign of them *taken in a particular way*."[24]

CONCLUSION

We have traced the development—logical and chronological—of Peirce's search for the "assertory element" in human knowing, from action as compulsion to action as responsible, to a compulsion which is *felt* to be rational. We have tried to indicate how this development not only coheres with the *normative* dimension of pragmatism, but assures its *effectiveness* as well. Moreover, it appears that judgment *must* be very close to the reflective, self-correcting disposition which we have rounded out from Peirce's remarks. This conviction forced our reappraisal of *firstness*, in the light of Lonergan's scheme, to provide some categorial support for the *role* judgment has to play in consummating Peirce's doctrine of signification. Whether our interpretation of the categories be viable only further inquiry can tell, but we hope to have shown at least that *some* new reading of them is required by the crucial function of judgment in sounding the obscure epistemological depths of pragmatism and so revealing the role which that doctrine plays in rounding out what is missing to any theory of signs, or meaning.

---

mean that there is an awareness immanent in cognitional acts." It is "not to be thought of as some sort of inward look . . . ; a conscious act is not . . . an act to which one attends . . . , a deliberate act." But "to affirm consciousness is to affirm that cognitional process is not merely a procession of contents but also a succession of acts." Further, "one cannot deny that, within the cognitional act as it occurs, there is a factor or element or component over and above its content, and that this factor is what differentiates cognitional acts from unconscious occurrences." A clue to Aquinas's notion may be found in *ST* 1.87.1, where by the formula "ipsa mentis praesentia," consciousness is widely separated from knowing.

23. Cf. Peirce, 5.41–44, and Gallie, "Metaphysics of C. S. Peirce," 50.

24. Cf. Lonergan's attempt to clarify his position on the three functional levels in human consciousness: "Cognitional Structure," 530–42.

Chapter 7

Classification, Mathematics, and Metaphysics
A Commentary on St. Thomas Aquinas's Exposition of Boethius's *On the Trinity*

IN PHILOSOPHY, STOCK WAYS of saying things have a way of hardening into dogmas. In fact, they can serve a useful function. Cutting like broad expressways through the settled areas of discourse, they can carry us quickly to the untrammelled expanses of the philosophical frontier. But if they should, in the process, have actually diverted us from a view to be treasured or even steamrolled over intriguing outcroppings of the native landscape, then their convenience may be dearly purchased. And even though highways in thought may not do the permanent damage of concrete and macadam, they may well take years to reroute. And this for an understandable reason. For the efforts to dislodge them are often contradictory, as a few perceive their harmful effects but cannot pinpoint why; and most would rather rest secure in well-travelled paths then risk the perils of discovery. And such a conservative posture is needed to remind one and all that it is not sufficient to destroy. One must also offer a better alternative, doing what he can to establish it. In the economy of human thought, though, the first essays must needs be negative. If we may take it, then, that the familiar "three degrees of abstraction," long a hallmark of Thomistic writing, has been laid to rest, let us begin by registering our indebtedness to those who first had to destroy before we try to reconstitute a division of the sciences more cognizant of the facts and more faithful to Aquinas's thought.

For their work can now be summarized.[1] From Aquinas's exposition of Boethius's *On the Trinity*, Question Five, Article Three, where the different modes of scientific consideration are taken up in detail, it is clear that there are, to his mind, but two kinds of abstraction, properly speaking, and not three. These two answer to physical science and mathematics as Aquinas knew them from Aristotle. Metaphysics, on the other hand, has nothing to do with abstraction at all but neatly distinguishes itself from any other mode of inquiry by an initial negative judgment or *separatio*.

Yet while this text is clear, others are not—hence come the origin and persistence of the "three degrees of abstraction." However, we not only have the general principle of interpretation—a general and passing treatment is to be elucidated by the specific and apposite development—but the very application of this principle is adumbrated in our basic text. "Abstraction" may certainly be used to cover any rational consideration whatsoever[2]—and so one may speak of "three degrees"; but this general sense may also be restricted to the considerations of the apprehensive power, to human reason's method of fashioning itself a *proportionate* object—and in this sense there are but two degrees. And such is precisely the tactic of Aquinas in our text as he carefully prunes metaphysical considerations from those proper to human science. That the restricted sense is the proper meaning of "abstrac-

---

1. The earliest appears to be Regis's penetrating critique of Maritain: "La philosophie de la nature, quelques 'apories.'" Geiger combined textual and philosophical reasoning in the trenchant "Abstraction et séparation d'après saint Thomas." His reasoning was eloquently and independently confirmed by Robert, "La métaphysique, science distincte de toute autre discipline"; and most recently by Merlan, "Abstraction and Metaphysics" (cf. 129n54).

The reactions—notably Leroy, "Abstractio et separatio"; and Simmons, "Three Degrees of Formal Abstraction" (with full bibliography)—see no particular reason for doing away with the triple division and invoke the argument of chronology. *Expositio super librum Boethii de Trinitate* is early, the general expression invariably later. Yet the fact that chronology is irrelevant here can be seen from this: that Aquinas accepts the triple division as already standard in *In de Trin.* 5.3, where his specific concern to distinguish calls for a precision in the accepted terminology. In other contexts, where the question is resumed, often to give a general preview of a whole science (cf. 122n26), the standard division will have to do. (To further reduce the significance of *In de Trin.* 5.3 to a polemic with Platonism is gratuitous.) But the basic decision is strategic: Which division better reveals the thrust of Aquinas's thought? This article tries to show why our conclusions will be radically at variance with Simmons's: "There is enough proportional sameness to speak of three degrees, and this is not to ignore . . . the basic difference between *separatio* and the other two formal abstractions, which are as between themselves [sic!] radically disparate in nature" ("Three Degrees of Formal Abstraction," 64).

2. General uses of *abstrahere* and *separare* can be found in: *In 1 Phys.* 1; *In de Sensu* 1; *In Meta.* proem.; *In de Meteor.* proem.; *In 6 Meta.* 1.155–65; *In 1 Post Anal.* 41.361–71; and most notably in *ST* 1.85.1.1–2, although this last recognizes explicitly the precision of *In de Trin.*, even if it fails to use *separatio*.

tion" is corroborated by parallel loci, where Aquinas, considering the intellect's power to abstract, proceeds to illustrate the two ways this can be done.[3]

These points, we may take it, are now well established and may constitute our problematic. For while the dogma is dethroned, the alternatives are far from evident. Yet one thing is clear, that metaphysics occupies a unique position. So one might have expected that most of the reconstruction work would be in this direction—given as well the powerful pull of ontological questions and the once-pressing need for an apologetic against positivism. (Indeed the chief harm of the doctrine of the three degrees was that it obstructed a clear view of the utterly unique character of metaphysics, that it misled one in fact into a feeling that there was always another, more profound dimension hidden from him—as though anything that was to be known admitted of three degrees of comprehension.) Yet the subsequent writing about metaphysics has not always respected the uniqueness it meant to exploit. For the knowledge one can glean from a negative judgment is certainly not very much (in any ordinary sense), and our considerations about that knowledge ought to be equally wary. In short, the suggestion of *de Trinitate* (5.3) is that a consideration of the negative judgment is the "way in" to a preview of the object of metaphysics, just as the abstraction of whole from part defines natural science and the abstraction of form from matter defines mathematics. But the negative judgment is tricky and nearly impervious to frontal attack, as more than one foray has demonstrated. So we would begin with an appropriately negative tactic by considering first the two kinds of abstraction to which it is opposed. Isolation may prove the most successful strategy.

CLASSIFICATION

These two modes of consideration would establish objects proportioned to rational inquiry (hence scientific objects), while the metaphysical, though it remains an object of intellectual pursuit, is always somewhat beyond the reach of reason.[4] Yet even here, one object is more proportionate than another. This has been abundantly illustrated by Ernst Cassirer in the early

---

3. Cf. *In 3 de An.* 8.714–16; 12.781–85, where *abstraction* is defended in the case of mathematics and physics, and the possibility of knowing otherwise, in a manner proper to pure intelligence (716), is controverted (785). The theological application in *ST* 1.40.3 is also important for what it assumes, as well as *In 2 Phys.* 3.161–63.

4. Cf. *In 2 Meta.* 1.278–85; *In 10 Ethic.* 11.2105–10. The distinction of Broglie between a proportionate object of apprehension and an adequate object of affirmation serves us well: "Sur la place du surnaturel dans la philosophie de S. Thomas," 5–53, esp. 14.

sections of *Substance and Function*, which drive hard to establish the superiority of the serial order of mathematics over classification as a scientific method. Construed as a polemic against abstraction as such, it cuts down to proper dimensions in fact the "potential" abstraction of a classificatory method to vindicate the "formal" abstraction of mathematics as the more proper and powerful scientific tool. As such, it represents a valid and long-overdue critique of a pseudo-traditional logic and methodology of science, a legacy of later Scholasticism. But a student of Aquinas finds himself strangely at home in an argument laying bare the inherent weakness of generic abstract concepts only to extoll another more penetrating kind, whose meaning, "if we are still to speak of 'abstraction,' . . . is not totally different"[5]: the formal abstraction of mathematics.

The fact that Cassirer made his own task of destruction easier by choosing the generic concept of sensationalist ontology need not detain us. For Aquinas, possessed of an even more viable general concept, can also be eloquent on how feeble a knowledge it yields. As he conceived it, abstraction of whole from part, which yields the generic concept, has none of the inner inconsistencies of sensationalist doctrine; but it remains a potential abstraction, issuing in knowledge as vague and ambiguous as it is sweepingly general.[6] Its perfect counterpart would be a knowledge as concrete as it is all-embracing, the ideal which we would that metaphysics were.[7] (And if it were, of course, it would not be misleading to speak of three degrees of abstraction, though it would still be incorrect, since such knowledge could never be called abstract.) But since such an ideal lies quite beyond our ken, the actual counterpart of vague, general knowing by potential abstraction is that with which it is usually paired and often opposed: mathematical knowing by *formal* abstraction. It is this knowledge which, while short of the ideal to which we aspire, remains that most proportioned to human knowing. (This is why it is both misleading and incorrect to speak of three degrees of abstraction, for it offers no clue that two of the degrees are proportioned to reason while one is not.)

---

5. Cassirer, *Substance and Function*, 25.
6. Cf. *de Subst Sep.* 15.134; *de An.* 15; *In 1 Post Anal.* 4.43; *In 2 Post Anal.* 16.557.
7. "Because the human understanding receives metaphysical truths from sensible things, and proceeds to understand them in a discursive manner proper to reason" (*ST* 2-2.180.6.2), principles first in themselves will always retain a certain confusion for us (*In 1 Sent.* prol.; 1.2). Hence metaphysics cannot escape a duplex motion (*In de Trin.* 6.1.3): it is presupposed to the other sciences and yet depends on them (*In de Trin.* 5.1.9), and for this reason is intrinsically imperfect (*In 2 Meta.* 1.278), never being able to dispense with examples (*In de Divin Nom.* 7.2.711).

MATHEMATICS

Now if Aquinas in his time could cite Ptolemy to prove his point, we may use Whitehead in ours, for the point is the same: "The generality of mathematics is the most complete generality consistent with . . . our metaphysical situation."[8] And this admission, more than anything else, will permit us to isolate the proper object of metaphysics. For it will permit us to manifest quite clearly the limits of tolerance permitted a proportionate object of human understanding and so to suggest how (and to what extent) what transcends these may be an object.

The privileged position of mathematics in human knowing is a recurring theme in Aquinas, and the basic melody is always the same; namely, that mathematics alone perfectly exemplifies the Aristotelian ideal of scientific knowing.[9] The ideal was inspired by Plato: a knowledge more worthy of the name than opinion, delivering over to man a certain and unerring grasp of what he could properly know.[10] Aristotle felt the need to delineate more strictly the specifications and tolerances of such a knowing. Nor was this an easy task, for it had long since been recognized that the certitude demanded of scientific knowing often had to be won at the price of exactness. And while such might confirm a Platonic realism, it could but nag the more empirical Aristotle—unless mathematics were there to comfort. And large comfort it was, providing nearly every illustration for scientific method in the *Second Analytics*. The inspiration here was doubtless Platonic as well, but the use vastly different. Aristotle could not permit himself the easy chair of *mathesis universalis*.[11] "Science" admits of many meanings; and if mathematics provides the model, other less perfect procedures may well prove more appropriate when the subject to be investigated does not call for such a rigorous exactitude.[12]

---

8. Whitehead, *Science in the Modern World*, 27. Ptolemy: "Let us call the other two kinds of theoretical knowledge opinion rather than science: theology indeed on account of its obscurity and incomprehensibility; physics, because of the instability and obscurity of matter. Mathematics alone will give the inquirer firm and unshaken certitude, namely demonstrations carried out with unquestionable methods." Cited in *In de Trin.* 6.1.2.

9. *In 1 Post Anal.* 1.10; *In 4 Meta.* 5.588.

10. Cf. *Republic* VII; *Theaetetus*, 184b-186e, 200d-201c.

11. The reference is always to Aristotle's contemporaries in the Academy; cf. *In 3 Meta.* 4.385; *In 1 Post Anal.* 43.387-90.

12. Without this realization, certain people are "apt to require a mathematical certitude in everything" (*In 2 Meta.* 5.334), whereas science must be tailored to its object, mathematical or natural (*In 2 Phys.* 10.239-40), as demonstration admits of many degrees of conclusiveness (*In 1 Post Anal.* 42.373-74; *In 2 Post Anal.* 12.525).

But what makes mathematics the model of scientific method? The fact that it alone matches certitude with exactitude.[13] The reason lies in the peculiar mode of consideration whereby our manner of knowing perfectly coincides with what is known to yield a transparent object.[14] But this is only possible because the mathematical object is as much constructed as it is known—indeed, *known* insofar as it can be constructed.[15] Constructivity and intellectual freedom mark mathematics not simply because it is abstract, as any rational considerations must indeed be, but because it alone considers the abstract as abstract. But intervening philosophical positions make such a formula less than happy, as Cassirer's struggle with abstraction shows so well. Aquinas in fact does not say just that but rather the untranslatable: "Mathematicus considerat *res abstractas* secundum *considerationem tantum* . . ." (italics ours).[16]

The meaning is that what is already abstract becomes an object of free play to the mathematician. So the system of integers can serve as the basis for rigorously analogical extensions which defy construction but exhibit an operational isomorphism. Nor do such extensions conflict with Aquinas's insistence that mathematics never transcend the imagination and must always resolve to it.[17] Such statements were meant to assure rather than restrict the freedom of mathematics. For what distinguishes the imagination from sense is precisely its comparative autonomy. With some little data from experience, it can construct fantastic worlds—the more so in fact as it is cut loose from the control of the sensible world, as for example in sleep.[18]

---

13. In 2 *Meta.* 5.336; In 1 *Post Anal.* 41.357–60. We are indebted to De Koninck's remarks on the ambiguity of *acribeia*, meaning both "certitude" and "exactitude," which two are often incompatible in human knowing.

14. In 1 *Post Anal.* 4.43bis.

15. In 9 *Meta.* 10.1888; In 3 *Meta.* 13.509, 13.513. To attribute an "intuitionist" position to Aquinas is of course anachronistic.

16. In de Trin. 5.4.7.

17. In 6 *Ethic.* 7.1211; In de Trin. 6.2.

18. Hence Aquinas's remarks that Aristotle can "extend the term 'imagination' to denote something intellectual . . . for imagination can function, like reason or intellect, in the absence of exterior sense-objects" (*In 3 de An.* 16.837). And he himself does not hesitate to speak of the mathematician treating what is "only comprehensible to the intellect" and not to the senses (*In de Trin.* 5.3.2), of mathematical objects as "intelligible singulars" (*In 7 Meta.* 10.1494), though imagination is the proper faculty of mathematics (*de Ver.* 15.2). We are especially indebted here to the unpublished dissertation of Mullahy, "Thomism and Mathematical Physics," chs. 5–6; see esp. 291, 304, 345, 409. [Ed. note: The original citation for this source lists pages beyond the page range of the latter published dissertation. Burrell refers to pages in the unpublished dissertation, pp. 551–59, 952–57. The sections cited here are broad, but most likely indicate the crucial passages. Editor discussed this emendation with Burrell.]

And yet mathematics is not ever restricted to this degree of freedom in the sense that it must temper its pace to the imaginable. All that is required is that it finally resolve here, that the vast reaches of mathematics be rigorously reducible to a fundamental set of properties whose understanding presupposes something imaginable. The "successor relation" would do. The fact that neither Aquinas nor Aristotle suspected the wonders hidden in the logic of relations did not prevent Aquinas from specifying the sense in which mathematics "falls under" the imagination. The condition is negative. Mathematics will never transcend the imagination in the specific sense that it must always resolve thereto—not immediately, however, but finally.[19]

From our vantage point, then, we may say that mathematics as a whole can never transcend the imagination and for this reason represents the "most complete generality consistent with our metaphysical situation." For that situation is an embodied one, and this entails, on Aquinas's testimony, a continual appeal to images. Hence is it "simply impossible for our intellect, united as it is to a receptive body, to understand anything without the aid of images—and this holds not only for the acquisition of a science, but also for the use of one already acquired." "For the image is, as it were, the permanent foundation of intellectual operation" so that "anything we can connaturally understand is known by comparison with sensible things"—the reason being that the "proper object of the human intellect, embodied as it is, must be the laws and regularities manifested by the material things which embody them."[20] It is not hard to see, then, how a mode of consideration which is capable of fantastic generality while still respecting these limitations on the proper object of human understanding—and offers to boot the perfect model for scientific demonstration—might well be considered the highest of the human sciences. And the indications are that Aquinas considered it just that, without once ceding to the Pythagorean temptation. (In fact, the antimathematicizing polemic in Aquinas [following Aristotle] has nothing to do with mathematics as such but with its indiscriminate application by the followers of Plato.[21] Aquinas would say that by hypostasizing mathematics, they were not only in danger of leaving themselves out on a limb but of toppling the spreading oak of mathematics itself. For its universal applicability is but a facet of its proper remove from nature, following upon the freedom of constructivity.[22])

19. The "falls under" of *In de Trin.* 6.1.2, becomes "resolve" of *In de Trin.* 6.2, whose general sense is given *In Post Anal.* proem.6, as a rational process terminating in the formal principles constituting the object as intelligible.

20. Quoted in order: *ST* 1.84.7; *In de Trin.* 6.2.5; *ST* 1.84.8; *ST* 1.84.7.

21. Cf. *In 1 Meta.* 13.204–5; *In 3 Meta.* 4.385; 7.422; 13.513.

22. *In de Trin.* 5.3.6.

TWO ABSTRACTIONS

Before sounding the implications for metaphysics, a final comparison of the two proper modes of abstraction will help highlight that science which, if it be not the noblest known to man, remains the highest and most formal he can possess, and that precisely because its most daring generalities do not "transcend the imagination." We have already contrasted the potential generalities of classification with the more formal ones of mathematics. Comparison is even more fruitful, especially for us, for what Aristotle and Aquinas barely divined we can know and experience. This is, of course, the application of the ordering principles of mathematics to the study of nature to produce the kind of revolution in method which Cassirer so eloquently describes. Such an application was adumbrated by Aristotle with reference to the Greek forays into harmonics and astronomy. (Aquinas, sad to say, can bring forth no new examples.) In each case, mathematics proffers the formal element, suggests the reason why the facts lie as we see them, by offering a set of explanatory relations.[23] Natural science, proceeding by way of generic abstraction and classifying sensible properties, is tied to the senses; and while these may sometimes show us the reason why, more often than not they can but make us aware of a problem for scientific analysis, without even being able to adequately set up the problematic.[24] What is needed is a more powerful ordering instrument, capable of proposing an hypothesis at once comprehensive and testable. We have seen that mathematics can perfectly fill this gap with a generality that need not sacrifice exactitude and is always compatible with the spatio-temporal conditions of sense and imagination. No wonder, then, that the few examples Aristotle could cite and the many we know all point to the organizing power of mathematics. All this does not, of course, deny that a science of nature must resolve to sense, as Aquinas insists,[25] but shows us how remote such a resolution can be from the upper reaches of a science—as far indeed as transfinite arithmetic is from the imagination; so far, that is, that it may seem to transcend it.

But can we say that "proposing a comprehensive and testable hypothesis" adequately conforms to Aquinas's notion of mathematics coming to the aid of natural science to propose the reason why their classifications were so distributed? We think so, for in spite of an experiential lacuna, Aquinas explicitly recognized, in the introduction to each of his commentaries on Aristotle's scientific works, the need to progress from a vague, general knowledge

23. Especially *In 1 Post Anal.* 25, and also 17.145; *In de Trin.* 5.1.5; *In 2 Phys.* 3.164; and in operation: *In 1 de Caelo* 2.14.

24. Cf. *In 1 Post Anal.* 42.381 and 17.145.

25. *In de Trin.* 6.2; *In 1 Phys.* 1.

to a more explicit, particulate grasp.²⁶ Such is the inner thrust of every investigation of natural science, "all the way to the elements."²⁷ To frustrate it is to block the natural desire of reason to progress from the potential to the actual, from an indeterminate to a more determinate knowledge. To implement it is to have recourse to the schema of *scientia media* we have sketched above—to borrow from the powerful ordering capacity of mathematics. Not that the ordering relations of mathematics will meet equal success in all domains. What indeed seems to be required is that the changes to be studied must be reducible to local motion before mathematical relations can be said to be explanatory.²⁸ Otherwise, functional correlations can suggest explanatory hypotheses but not provide them, as in the social sciences.²⁹ Be that as it may, in those domains sufficiently homogeneous to admit functional correlation as explanatory, classification is reduced to a prelude, a prescientific gathering of the facts, preliminary to a more explanatory organization of them. This corresponds to Aquinas's grasp of the movement proper to science; and while not to be construed as a despising of classification, it does deflate its scientific pretensions, reducing it to the ancillary role of description vis-à-vis explanation. Such is indeed the relation Aristotle saw verified in his time in harmonics and astronomy, where the natural science (which proceeds by way of general *abstractio totius*) made known the facts and mathematics (from the vantage point of an *abstractio formae*) provided the explanatory hypothesis. That the process is not always so simple as he imagined does not undermine the fundamental relationship, for as more prolonged fidelity to description fed scientific wonder with more and more problems to be solved, so the development of mathematical analysis and group theory provided yet more comprehensive tools of organization. That scientific knowing became more and more hypothetical was an inevitable consequence of its straining for a more specific and determinate knowledge of the material universe. (Aquinas's principles predict it; and if some of his subsequent followers were alarmed by it, that can only be the effect of centuries of commentators subtly substituting for his affirmation of "man's natural desire to know" their own timorous "need to be secure.") Nor does the hypothetical character of much of modern mathematics threaten its generality, any more than it obviates its final "resolvability" to the imagination—in the

---

26. Cf. *In de Sensu* 1; *In de Caelo* proem.; *In de Meteor.* proem.; *In 1 Phys.* 1.
27. *In de Caelo* proem.1.
28. Cf. *In de Trin.* 5.3.5; *In de Caelo* proem.3; *In 5 Meta.* 15.985. For the sense of "explanatory" and "descriptive" as used here, see Lonergan, *Insight*, 291–92, 504–5.
29. Such would be the role of *in plus* characteristics: *In 2 Post Anal.* 13.533.

sense explained.[30] It remains the formal element par excellence in physical science, and that because we are possessed here with "the most complete generality consistent with our metaphysical situation."[31]

TOWARD THE METAPHYSICAL OBJECT

Is there any room left for metaphysics? Let us pause to ponder this question. For until we realize how stubborn a query it is, we have not succeeded in cornering the object of metaphysics. Indeed, much of the contemporary apologetic against positivism has but added fuel to the critics' fire. Part of a strategy of defense, emanating from deep within the fortress, composed with evangelical ardor—such can only confirm the wavering. Metaphysics most certainly is nonsense! We hope to show how a serious consideration of certain objectors can shed much-needed light on some neglected facets of tradition.

As Aquinas sees it, what is left for metaphysics to talk about? His answer is straightforward: whatever is separated or separable from matter, from the conditions of space and time.[32] In other words, whatever cannot, properly speaking, be conceived because there is no corresponding image to "come home to."[33] Hence the careful choice of *separatio*, to distinguish metaphysical consideration from what is properly human by neatly extracting its formal object from the confines of man's apprehensive powers to locate it in his judgment.[34]

The positivist wine, then, while well adulterated, owed a good deal of its body to a time-tested vintage. There is a perfectly traditional sense in which metaphysics is inconceivable, the sense in which its object "transcends the

---

30. In passing, one can only try to straddle the conflicts in contemporary philosophy of mathematics, though one may ask whether the present division of opinion really succeeds in posing the question accurately (cf. Körner, *Philosophy of Mathematics*). Aquinas, if only for the fact that his remarks are so general, could hardly be assigned to any single camp, although a program such as that of Weyl in *Das Kontinuum* bears certain marked affinities to the direction of Aquinas's thought.

31. For similar reasoning as to the intrinsic possibility of mathematics as an explanatory instrument, cf. Lonergan, *Insight*, 509–14.

32. *In de Trin.* 5.1.3; 5.4.4; 6.1.3.2; *In 7 Meta.* 2.1299–1305; 11.1526; 11.1534–36; *In 8 Meta.* 1.1682–85. There is more to be said, but it must be said with these texts in mind. Cf. 125n42 and 129n54.

33. *ST* 1.84.7; *In 3 de An.* 13.791.

34. This thoroughgoing interpretation of *In de Trin.* 5.3 has been unmistakably confirmed by one of the last articles of Simon: "On Order in Analogical Sets." Cf. my discussion in the same journal, "Note on Analogy."

imagination"[35] and so cannot be known by abstraction. Indeed, should one overlook this warning light and proceed doggedly on to defend metaphysics as yielding a yet greater and more fruitful generality than that of mathematics, he soon finds himself overshooting the limits of conception and discourse, and racing—like the ubiquitous cinema cartoon—to find some support in the airy reaches of the general, empty concept. There is evidence that such was the metaphysics Kant dethroned, and Ayer's early and truculent critique presumes a superscience ready to deduce a world order from principles invulnerable because inconceivably general.[36] Nothing, in fact, can break through the positivistic logic but a frank recognition that the metaphysical object does lie outside the power of human apprehension but is not for that totally beyond man, since it is constituted by the judgment. In fact, nothing lends such an authentic ring to anti-metaphysical polemic as an apologetic which retorts on the limited ground of apprehension.

But what does Aquinas mean by the judgment, indeed the "negative judgment" or *separatio*?[37] And how can it be said to constitute the metaphysical object? The severe limits he places on human knowledge of a properly metaphysical object provide a clue. We can only know that such things exist and have a more or less vivid grasp of what they are not.[38] This removes metaphysics immediately from the rank of deductive science, for the fact that something exists is never deduced but either pointed out or arrived at by a series of pointers which serve as evidence for a reasonable judgment to the effect that "something like this must be." But unlike the murder weapon, metaphysical objects could not be pointed out if they were to turn up—indeed they never do "turn up." Hence their vulnerability to loaded description like "shadowy." We can only know of them what they are not; and while this knowledge can be more or less penetrating, it remains forever negative.

---

35. "... transcendunt imaginationem et requirunt validum intellectum" (*In 6 Ethic.* 7.1211).

36. Ayer, *Language, Truth, and Logic*, 33. That metaphysics is not a "superscience" for Aquinas, cf. *In de Trin.* 5.1.6.

37. That the *separatio* of *In de Trin.* 5.3 is clearly negative: *In de Trin.* 6.2.4; 6.3.5; *ST* 1.88.2; *In 5 Meta.* 7.865; *In 10 Meta.* 4.1990; *In 3 de An.* 11.758.

38. *In de Trin.* 6.3.5 contains the entire process in capsule, summarizing what is affirmed elsewhere: (1) that the proper metaphysical object is not properly knowable—(*a*) for psychological reasons (*In 1 Post Anal.* 30.254; *In 9 Meta.* 11.1905–7); (*b*) for semantic reasons (*In 7 Meta.* 17.1669–71; *In 9 Meta.* 11.1901–4; 11.1910–16; *In 11 Meta.* 2.2189)—(2) though at the same time it does not completely exceed the intellect, since the fact that it is can be known through a negative judgment (*de Ver.*10.11.4–5; and 124n37 above), which admits of manifold degrees of penetration (*In de Trin.* 1.2).

Yet Aquinas insists that rather than the objects themselves being shadowy, the reason for our ever imperfect grasp of them is their too-intense light.[39] The formula is ambiguous for us, for we tend to retort, "Who's to decide?" Yet his meaning can be elucidated by other remarks, revealing the proper function of the judgment here. What sets off the metaphysical object from every other is its pervasive universality. When we speak of the structure presupposed to discourse and reasoning itself, we are not designating an object like any other, for this one does not turn up but is implied in any one which does. In fact, as Wittgenstein has cautioned, we cannot properly speak of such "things," for our language cannot double back on itself thus without employing the very structures we are seeking to isolate.[40] We can only point to, manifest them, and that but indirectly. So Aquinas constantly reaffirms that one can only be led on by the hand, as it were, toward metaphysical objects;[41] and the moment he thinks he has grasped them, he has deceived himself. For one understands this object only to the extent that he realizes he has not grasped it.[42] We must, so to speak, back into a knowledge of it.

The image of *manuductio* is carefully chosen. Things we can easily know and talk about, sensible things, must lead us into this domain, taking us by the hand as one would a blind man. This is a poignant reminder that we cannot know what these things are that metaphysics tries to manifest but only more or less what they are not. For Aquinas considered sight the power most able to give us a working grasp of what things are. But what permits these myriad pointers to converge on an object, one which cannot for all that be singled out and identified? The judgment, the same power which weighs evidence in a murder trial or decides a sample is representative enough to use for statistical purposes, here picks out recurring patterns

---

39. *In 2 Meta.* 1.282–85.

40. Wittgenstein, *Tractatus,* 5.6–5.641. Aquinas for his part notes that "'quiddity' and all such terms are used quite equivocally when said of sensible things and of these [separated] substances as well" (*In de Trin.* 6.3.1).

41. *In de Trin.* 6.3.2 summarizes a wealth of uses of *manuductio* in diverse contexts: the classroom (*ST* 1.117.1; *de Ver.* 11.1), arriving at ethical principles (*In 1 Ethic.* 4.53), basic notions in metaphysics (*In 9 Meta.* 5.1826–27), knowledge of any spiritual being (*ST* 1.51.3.1; *de An.* 16), and especially in knowing God (*ST* 1.12.12; *de Pot.* 7.5.3–4; *In de Divin Nom.* 7.4.731).

42. Such is at least Aquinas's position on the highest of metaphysical objects: God, known as the ultimate presupposition, since his existence underlies not merely the most basic patterns of discourse but anything's being at all. Hence "the highest knowledge we can have of God is to know that He is above and beyond whatever we might think of Him" (*de Ver.* 2.1.9; *In de Divin Nom.* 7.4.731). A proportion by which the same may be said of any properly metaphysical object is suggested in 129n54.

of thought and expression to decide that there must be some explanation for them, even though it lies beyond our proper capacity to formulate. And since one must always know something about a thing to assert its existence, we can justly say here that the professed inability to formulate the object, the negative judgment, is what constitutes it.[43]

A random example happily turns up in Thomas Gilby's treatment of community and society. What makes it all the more useful is to note the turn his lucid prose is forced to take when he wished to introduce a properly metaphysical notion. Master of the Anglo-Saxon idiom, he deftly manages the shift from apprehension to judgment. While it is the purpose of community and society alike to secure a common good, the term "common," he reminds us,

> has a double meaning, for it can be read either collectively, to mean the sum total of all the parts, or distributively, to mean what all share in whether they be taken singly or all together. . . . Collectively, the common good stands for a heap-value, the integrity of a whole body, the majority benefit according to individualistic utilitarianism, the racial or proletarian lump according to totalitarianism. To the collective good all partial and particular goods are, rightly and naturally, subservient: the hand goes up to protect the body, private interest gives way before public benefit, a minister surrenders his own opinion in the corporate decision of the Cabinet. Distributively, the common good is a freer value, more versatile, and *not so easily imagined*. It is *not* an accumulation of particulars, but a whole that can be repeated again and again. As in the logic of predication so in the philosophy of society, a whole is formed which suffers *no* diminution or subtraction from the presence or absence of particular subjects.[44]

The distributive notion is properly metaphysical. Its roots lie in the conception of "nature of," as he reminds us further on:

> *Mankind*, or the *human race*, are collective ideas, but the bare philosophical idea of human nature, which is precipitated in our experience of men and women, *is not like* a common stock

---

43. That linguistic reference cannot be without a sense is recalled in *In de Trin.* 6.3.3 and *In 2 Post Anal.* 8.484. The negative judgment ("Quando omnia quae sensus vel imaginatio apprehendit a rebus huiusmodi *separamus* . . ." [*In de Trin.* 6.2.4]) constitutes precisely by distinguishing from all else (*In de Trin.* 2.2.2).

44. Gilby, *Between Community and Society*, 89 (italics added).

which can be dealt out in bits and pieces, but is a single meaning exemplified without addition in every fresh instance.⁴⁵

But baffling as they may be to the imagination, the fact remains that distributive terms are freely employed. There is something about the relationship of the person to society, of Peter to mankind, that cannot be forced into a Procrustean collective notion. We do not know what it is, this unimaginable relationship, but we are compelled to admit that it is and give it a rubric such as "common good" or "human nature." Any attempt to describe it, however, slides off into negatives, as Gilby's prose illustrates. These are the irreducible linguistic facts which remain compelling even though they do not elucidate.⁴⁶ And yet this very need to characterize the subject negatively, by contrast to ordinary imaginable relations, provides the key to the mystery, the final clue which permits us to see that all the others converge on an object, which must be "something like that." The negative judgment constitutes the metaphysical object.

AQUINAS AND METAPHYSICS: SOME PECULIARITIES

But how, then, can Aquinas be so terribly sure about mysterious things like "common good" and "natures of" things? The question is crucial, for a failure to answer it has misled both enthusiasts and critics. While warnings such as we have culled can be had for the looking, the landscape of Aquinas's writings remains bathed in affirmation. The scandal of the schematic set of reasons adduced, ostensibly to manifest the existence of a God, is notorious. Where is the natural skepticism which must needs accompany such an employ of human reason? It is there; but it is apart from the mainstream, which rushes on to speak of the attributes of such a God and of the order in the universe!⁴⁷ The same may be said of his apparently naive objectivity. Where is the critical hiatus of subject and object—or their intentional union? Again, it is there— but as a diminished, secondary theme, barely yet firmly recognized; never quite worked out.⁴⁸ But what is this except to say that Aquinas was a man of his time? The questions that vexed his contemporaries were to preoccupy him as well. Yet that his thought is not frozen in the

---

45. Ibid., 108 (italics added).

46. Lest this sound too modern for an exposition of Aquinas, cf. *In 1 de Caelo* 2.13. For an illustrative example, see Strawson's critique of reduction of all to conjunction, in *Introduction to Logical Theory*, 183–84.

47. *ST* 1.3–21; 1.34.

48. For example, prime loci such as *de Ver.* 1.9 and *ST* 1.87.1 are corroborated by hints like *de Ver.* 10.12.7 and *In 11 Meta.* 6.2240.

directions he felt called to develop it, that it contains abundant indications of variant readings, awaiting as it were the problematics of ages other than his own, is simply to recall that he was a great philosopher. Any suggestion, then, that a student just acquire a medieval *Weltanschauung* to assimilate his thought is in fact to deny Aquinas the title of philosopher. To say that any problematic—critical, phenomenological, linguistic—is per se foreign to his thought is to relegate him to a moment in history, which, whatever its touted brilliance, is forever past. As P. F. Strawson has reminded us—though we should not have needed it—

> If . . . the central subject-matter of descriptive metaphysics does not change, the critical and analytical idiom of philosophy changes constantly. Permanent relationships are described in an impermanent idiom, which reflects both the age's climate of thought and the individual philosopher's personal style of thinking. No philosopher understands his predecessors until he has re-thought their thought in his own contemporary terms; and it is characteristic of the very greatest philosophers, like Kant and Aristotle, that they, more than any others, repay this effort of re-thinking.[49]

And, we would add, Aquinas. Yet how do his buoyant affirmations about natures, about metaphysics as treating the "most common things," about being, not as subject and object but as being—how do all these resound in a contemporary idiom and square with our (and his) insistence on the negative judgment?

Taking them one at a time, our hardest job will be to reconstitute Aquinas across centuries of commentators and digesters. "Nature of," for example, has not the brittle ring for him that it acquired through later Scholasticism. Far from being frozen to an "inner core of meaning," it is loose and ranging enough to admit any knowledge of what a thing is.[50] And if one wishes to speak of the essential nature, then he had better be indirect about it, for Aquinas insists we cannot properly know it, whatever the case may be.[51] For while "nature of" is a methodological device, the (essential) nature is a metaphysical notion. The most we can know is that there must be such a thing to explain the fact that all we can properly know points to it. Should

---

49. Strawson, *Individuals*, 10–11.

50. *In 2 Post Anal.* 4.484. In any inquiry we may say indifferently that it is a thing's nature to be (subsumed under) the general notion we are using or that such a notion helps lead us to its nature. Cf. for example, the inquiry into will from election (*ST* 1.83.3).

51. *de Spir Creat.* 11.3; *ST* 1.77.1.7; *CG* 1.3; *In 2 Post Anal.* 13.533; *de Ver.*10.1.6.

we try to describe it, we could only begin with the various aspects, or accidents, that fall within our apprehension.[52] Any attempt to get closer would have to end by recalling that they were not the nature they converge upon. Without the benefit of the model of hypothetical science, Aquinas could not have underlined the converging status of empirical knowledge as clearly as one can today; yet his dual insistence on the fact of a central intelligibility together with its intrinsic unknowability by human methods grounds at once the possibility and the posture of authentic scientific inquiry.[53]

But what of metaphysics as the science of things "most common"? Aquinas often speaks in this vein, and many have seen here the reflection of an Aristotelian ambiguity about the subject of metaphysics.[54] Yet Aquinas

52. *In 1 de Gen et Corr.* 8.62; *In 1 de An.* 1.15; *de Ver.* 4.1.8; *In 7 Meta.* 12.1552; *de Pot.* 9.2.5.

53. Aquinas's reminder that *differentiae* are infinite in number for us (*In 3 Meta.* 8.435) suggests a human science always approximative. Lonergan has worked out the tension in terms of central and conjugate forms (*Insight*, 79–82, 434–37).

54. The tension between the most common notions (like "being," "one") and the separated substances (or causes of being) in Aristotle's metaphysics has been pointed up forcefully by Jaeger, *Aristotle*, 216–19. It is retained by Aquinas in *In de Trin.* 5.1.3; 5.4.4, as the *separabilia* (what can be without matter and motion) and the *separata* (whose very *ratio* is to be separate from matter). But Aquinas says further that metaphysics treats of the *separabilia* (most common notions) as its subject, and the *separata* as the principles of this subject. This has led to the distinction of general from special metaphysics, which Merlan accepts, correlating them with the third degree of abstraction and the *separatio* respectively (cf. 115n1). Yet such a distinction hardly does justice to the dynamic latent in the order Aquinas notes. *Separata* are principles of *separabilia*, and metaphysics alone of all the sciences investigates into the causes of its own subject (*In 6 Meta.* 1). Hence metaphysics strains towards the cause of all by a consideration of the most general notions—to the principle through the subject. The very amplitude of a general notion such as "substance" as "that which is," or of its constituents "matter" and "form" arrived at from considering recurring structures of predication (*In 7 Meta.* 2.1287–89; *In 8 Meta.* 1–2), allows one to estimate the range of a "principle of all." But to go on then to express "that which the first principle is" is impossible except through a negative judgment, since such substance is not composed, as is any substance we can talk about. As long as the concept of "that which is" remains vague and common, it is open to both substance and the principle of all substance; but once we wish to use it specifically of the principle of all, we cannot. (Aquinas expressed this by saying that God is not within a genus, not even the genus of intelligible things, except as its principle [*In de Trin.* 1.2.4] and by noting that one must alter the very structure of predication to speak of Him [*ST* 1.13.1.2]).

Thus we have one metaphysical movement, which utilizes general notions yielded by logical (or better, semantic) study (*In 7 Meta.* 3.1308) to move to the point where it affirms the principle of all via a negative judgment. The move is from subject to its principles, from "being as being" (*In 6 Meta.* 1.1147) to the "common causes of being" (*In 6 Meta.* 1.1164); and yet the last stage can never stand on its own, as it were (*In 6 Meta.* 1.1165), since it is constituted only by negating the mode of understanding which leads us to it (*In de Trin.* 6.3.5). The manner of grasping is increasingly negative,

himself realizes how misleading this way of speaking can be and, while accepting it as inevitable, suggests how one might compensate. General notions like "contrary" seem to fall to the metaphysician by default. No one else can treat them; and yet because they are so general, his treatment of them will fall dangerously close to "dialectics."[55] That is, he must consider contraries in complete generality, "as per se dividing being,"[56] and to do so must consider being as though it were a thing—indeed the most general thing of all. But what distinguishes the true metaphysician from the dialectician, says Aquinas, is his power. This means, concretely, his ability to reduce any of the multifarious meanings grouped under the rubric of a common notion like "contrary" to one primary signification. Every related meaning will be employed with reference to this one, and the metaphysician is aware of these nuances of similarity and difference concealed in the common notion, while the dialectician is not.

And what is this awareness but a finesse in judgment? Only judgment can add the torque of personal understanding which allows us to put our concepts to work, employing them where we want them. The person with judgment can illustrate his point, for he grasps the bearing of the general heuristic notions on the material at hand. Without this added sense supplied by the judgment, the temptation would always be to apply the general term indiscriminately to each of its instances, as though its meaning were exhausted in the definition given. (Such is indeed the constant temptation of metaphysics, where notions like "being," in spite of Aquinas's insistence that they must be verified in one primary instance, always retain something of the generic about them.[57])

The implication is that while the dialectician treats the general notion as a first-level generality realized univocally in its instances, the metaphysician recognizes that he is faced with a second-level notion admitting of proportionally different first-level meanings. "Living," for example, can be said of four different kinds of activity, ranging from mere vegetation to the immanence of consciousness.[58] Yet we do not study life but living things, for "'to live,'" Aquinas remarks, "means simply 'to exist in such and such

---

as semantic considerations remove one from imaginative familiarity to speak of bare linguistic necessities (*vide* Gilby), and the move to affirm a yet higher intelligibility must needs negate those very connatural structures. These remarks were inspired by a preview of the dissertation of Doig. [Ed. note: Doig dissertation later published as *Aquinas on Metaphysics*.]

55. In 4 *Meta*. 4.571–81. One can almost substitute "transcendental dialectic."
56. Ibid., 4.589.
57. Compare ibid., 4.587 with 4.546 and the warning of 4.547.
58. *In 2 de An.* 3.255–56.

a nature,' for which 'life' is the abstract expression."[59] The general notion is derived, to be sure, from a basic experience of things moving on their own, more evident in animals than in plants; but a subsequent definition of "life" as "the capacity for self-motion" is more a rubric than a concept. It is meant to provide a rule for uses of "living" and, like any rule, must be applied judiciously. In fact, to apply it, one must be sensitive to the primitive experience that "life" initially conveys and have a sense of further meanings as proportioned to this. Our example is further complicated by the fact of our own personal experience, whose intervention enables a yet further extension to consciousness—for "self-motion," Aquinas reminds us, can be understood of immanent as well as transitive activity.[60]

A detailed examination of Aquinas's treatment of common notions shows his concern to reduce them to a primary meaning native to human experience. Any more refined usage must not only be in terms of this but consciously proportioned to it. The most sophisticated use of a term will be announced by the negative judgment, which denies any imaginative rapport with the primitive usage to mark the absolute limit of its range. This is the properly metaphysical notion: "life" as used of God, while the metalinguistic "analogous concept" belongs to the realm of logic or semantics.[61]

What, finally, of Aquinas's apparently naive objectivity, his easy way of moving right into being without seeming to be aware of the crucial division into subject and object? Perhaps this was more of a stumbling block to our predecessors than it is today, after a generation of phenomenology has illustrated how much of the subject-object problem was *malposé*. Yet be that as it may, there is an authentic core to the problematic which cannot be arbitrarily overlooked, unless one is willing to leave rich philosophical acreage fallow and plead guilty to the charge of obscurantism.

Again, the indications are there: the privileged place of man in the universe because he alone of all material things is also spirit, the unique factor of consciousness which allows natural science to issue in a demonstration of the "soul."[62] Where we would want to hear "subject," he will invariably employ the more objective "spirit," reserving "subject" for the more neutral grammatical, logical, or metaphysical sense. Yet even here, the example of a substance is invariably man, the human subject. One can construct as well

59. *ST* 1.18.2.
60. Ibid., 1.18.1; *CG* 3.46.9.
61. That *analogy* is primarily a logical (or semantical) doctrine in Aquinas is the striking thesis of McInerny, *Logic of Analogy*. For an application of this interpretation to metaphysics, cf. my review, "Religious Language and the Logic of Analogy" (chapter 10 in this volume).
62. Cf. Koninck, "Introduction à l'étude de l'âme."

an epistemology from his writings, utilizing texts which betray a fine sense of psychological and critical questions, but one must indeed construct it;[63] the main stream is a straightforward ontology of knowing. Yet we have already noted how a philosopher tends to develop the questions controverted in his day. The sign of his greatness is not that he answered all questions in advance (which would make him more sophist than philosopher) but that the finished landscape conceals seeds which will germinate in the light and heat of later problematics. So the fact that one can construct a viable epistemology from the indications Aquinas gives belies those critics who see no need to return to anyone before Kant, as well as the enthusiasts who would continue reading him as though there had never been a Kant. The fact is of course that no one can read anyone the same after Kant, and the particular resilience such a reading gives to Aquinas only shows the greatness of them both.

What is at stake is the notion of being. Paraphrased dialectically as "all that is," it is defined as the answer to a question—the twofold question we ask of anything, whether it is and what it is.[64] The order may be inverted, depending on whether we first meet it or first hear about it; but normally one implies the other, like sense and reference. So the form of these questions will reveal the basic constituents of being, but not so much their external form as the act of understanding which they strive to attain. It is not the set forms of language but their wellsprings in meaning which are isomorphic with reality for Aquinas.[65] These will be expressed not so much in static forms of expression as in basic yet superficially shifting elements of structure, linguistic and conceptual equipment that perdures through the supple and differentiating drive of understanding to encircle and secure a knowledge of everything. That the intellect can become all things, is the obverse, if you will, of being itself. So the prevailing structures of understanding as revealed in expression will manifest the basic constituents of being.[66] This is Aquinas's metaphysical way of justifying descriptive metaphysics. It is the supreme recognition of the unique role of the subject who can question being: to admit that the very form of his questions manifests that same being. A study of the role of predication and the well-formed question in Aquinas's metaphysics promises to show that, borne as it was on the wings of Aristo-

63. Cf. Lonergan, "Concept of *Verbum*," 7:349–92; 8:35–79.
64. *In 2 Post. Anal.* 1; Lonergan, "Concept of *Verbum*," 7:364–73.
65. Cf. Crowe, "St. Thomas and Isomorphism."
66. Aristotle's preliminary affirmation is recorded *In 3 de An.* 7.681, and the final commentary is *In 3 de An.* 13.787. This is the fundamental theorem of Lonergan's *Insight*, affirmed on p. 444 and amplified on pp. 499–502; applied to metaphysical method, pp. 520–29, and to verification, pp. 535–56.

telian objectivity and theological affirmation, much of it is more descriptive than hitherto suspected.[67] Such promises, however, can only be delivered in the contemporary idiom.

METAPHYSICS AND JUDGMENT

We have taken up three peculiarities of Aquinas's approach to metaphysics and roughed them out in language a little closer to our own. That many of the details and even some of the bold outlines of our sketches would be controverted by Thomists is unavoidable. For the present, we can only document these brief summaries, referring the incredulous to studies which expose and more than adequately substantiate the line of development we have espoused. What gives each sketch its body and marks its fidelity to Aquinas is the role played by the judgment. Evident in the first two, it is even more necessary in the final resumption of the critical question. What marks Aquinas off from Kant, it has been noted, is precisely the recognition of human judgment as "virtually unconditioned," as definitive within quite conscious limits, as absolute because revisable.[68] The man of judgment can recognize what new facts count against his theory, for he knew what was relevant to its support. Judgment can carry the burden of responsible assent because it bespeaks the zenith of consciousness, operating from that reflexivity which best manifests man's transcendence over a purely material order and his participation in the intellectual.[69] The same power which can help us decide whether or not the sensible properties of a thing adequately manifest what it is—not of course all at once, but normally, over a period of time allowing for concerted experience to collect the clues, creative intelligence to suggest an organizing scheme, and imagination to devise viable methods of testing—the power which judges so the bearing of our schemata on the data is the same which can make us aware of our intellect as polarized on reality. Once again, the affirmations of Aquinas are more ontological in tone. "Truth is the good of the intellect," which then tends to what is true as by a "natural appetite."[70] Yet such a dynamic can only be explained by a deep-seated connaturality, a certain structural isomorphism with its

---

67. As it is the logical genus of substance which reveals to us the substantial manner of existing (*In 5 Meta.* 9.890), so it is the well-formed question which provides manifestly what metaphysics is searching for (*In 7 Meta.* 17.1648–68; *In 8 Meta.* 3.1720–21) and which yields matter and form at the limit (*In 8 Meta.* 1, 2, 5.1766–67).

68. Cf. Lonergan, *Insight*, 339–42.

69. *de Ver.* 24.2; *CG* 4.11; *ST* 1.88.2.3.

70. *de Ver.* 22.11.3; 22.5.9; *In 1 de Caelo* 2.13; *In 1 Phys.* 10.79.

object.⁷¹ Hence the way is open for a post-Kantian grasp of a metaphysical object. In formulating "being and its properties" (and in grasping its unity of immanence in diversity), we are not so much studying objects as the nature of any possible object. The first principles, denoting the way all things must be thought, are defined by their immanence in every idea and judgment. Hence to speak of them is to grasp the essential constituents of subject and object in the necessary structure of judgment.⁷²

CONCLUSION

Genuine metaphysics, then, far from pretending to deduce the universe from unassailable generalities, will represent rather the aspiration of human understanding for an intelligibility which it knows must exist and recognizes it cannot apprehend. That such an intelligibility must exist metaphysics would manifest by myriad examples, signs, illustrations, designed to take the intellect by the hand, as it were, and lead it by the principle of converging evidence to recognize something beyond its proper ken. That it may not enter this privileged reserve is expressed by the intellect itself in the crucial negative judgment. The object indicated is affirmed to be properly unknowable! Things we can know, reflections on our proper experience, serving as examples, lead to some recognition of an overriding metaphysical intelligibility; the negative judgment defines it as the inexpressible limit of our understanding.⁷³

All this is another way of saying that the proper objects of human scientific knowing can never adequately introduce man to the metaphysical understanding to which he aspires.⁷⁴ In fact, metaphysics is not properly human at all but answers to something of the divine in man, something which man can only express imperfectly if at all, something he does not possess so much as participates in.⁷⁵ These final qualifications of Aquinas should convince the most literal that his precise designation of metaphysics by the

---

71. "In appetitu autem naturali, principium huiusmodi motus est connaturalitas appetentis ad id in quod tendit..." (*ST* 1–2.26. 2). "Nihil... potest ordinari in aliquem finem nisi praeexistat in ipso quaedam proportio ad finem..." (*de Ver.* 14.2).

72. Cf. Geiger, "Synthèse de St. Thomas."

73. Cf. ibid., 351. The examples are the rungs of Wittgenstein's ladder (*Tractatus*, 6.54), which nothing short of mystical vision can induce us to throw away and yet which judgment alone can license us to use. The peculiar role of self-consciousness, the mere fact of its presence and not any particular results it might yield (*CG* 3.46.8–11; *ST* 1.88.1.1), reminds us that the subject is the limit of the world (*Tractatus*, 5.641).

74. *In de Trin.* 6.1.2.2; 6.4.4.

75. *In 10 Ethic.* 11.2105–10.

separatio or negative judgment was meant to denote a disproportion between this and the properly human sciences of nature and mathematics—a disproportion hardly conveyed by the familiar three degrees of abstraction. And if our manner of exploiting certain aspects of Aquinas's thought would bring him dangerously close to positivism for the comfort of some, we would assure them it was intentional. For an authentic tradition recognizes its critics—not its self-styled defenders—as its most loyal friends. Only when the adventitious growth has been ruthlessly pruned away can the trunk manifest its true vitality. Once again, a new problematic—or a more vigorous and consistent presentation of an old one—has helped us organize scattered remarks to bring into the foreground a theme hitherto but secondary: the transcendent nature of metaphysics. And as usual the service is mutual, for such a reading of tradition can give the contemporary style a dimension it lacks. The real question is the one Pascal put to humanism: Is man, or is he not, "infinitely more than man"?

Chapter 8

How Complete Can Intelligibility Be?
A Commentary on *Insight*: Chapter XIX[1]

INTELLIGIBILITY IS THE KEY to transcendent knowing for Lonergan. Not just an intelligibility which is sought after, but one which is experienced whenever an inquirer judges his formulation of a state of affairs is indeed the case. So the inquirer himself, living and moving in the intellectual pattern of experience and hence aware of the demands of rational reflection, offers the key to understanding what "intelligibility" means for Lonergan. This needs to be made explicit, for Lonergan's highly abstract treatment of transcendent knowing might lead one to miss the fact that it culminates a journey—a journey wherein the demands of rational consciousness are illustrated and exercised until the pilgrim has made consciousness of them part of his own expanded consciousness. But "intelligibility" may easily become a trademark and a slogan. The purpose of this paper is to test the bases of Lonergan's account of transcendent knowing. Its focal task will be ascertaining whether Lonergan succeeds in tying the term "intelligibility" to a use determinate enough to make it the axial notion in formulating and affirming the reality of God.

At the risk of scandalizing the temerarious, let us begin our analysis with Lonergan's summary argument for the existence of God: "If the real is completely intelligible, God exists" (672). At first blush a gratuitous

---

1. Lonergan, *Insight*. [Ed. note: In-text citations in this essay are to page numbers in *Insight*.]

affirmation since the antecedent could never be asserted. One is simply at a loss for a determinate method of pinning down what it might mean. But Lonergan claims to be able to assert it, and offers the trip through *Insight* as the way of discovering what it means to say that the real is completely intelligible. The journey consists of three stages (675):

(1) identifying the real with being;

(2) identifying being with complete intelligibility;

(3) identifying complete intelligibility with an unrestricted act of understanding.

Lonergan claims the first moment is the expansive one. That seems a matter of one's current philosophical perspective. It certainly is so once one understands Lonergan's notion of being. For it is that notion which allows one to move from stage (1) to (2), from the real to complete intelligibility. But the notion of being turns out to be little more than a place holder. It is *intelligibility* that does the work.

For to undergo the conversion to the intellectual pattern of experience that *Insight* requires is to acknowledge the inherently heuristic character of *being*. Being is known in every act of knowing in the sense that any conscious act of understanding is an implementation of an unrestricted desire to know. "Being" is the name we give to the object of this desire (676). We know the desire is not vain; it does lead towards an object because we have experienced knowing what is the case. We know what it is like to know in the full sense if we have ever dared to claim correctness for our understanding of a situation. Any such claim is always conditioned, it is true, but when we have ascertained the conditions to be fulfilled, the resulting judgment that we have correctly understood the situation deserves the title of "virtually unconditioned."

It is executed and in that sense no longer conditional; but executed with an awareness that it does depend on certain conditions. These conditions are both factual and criteriological. My judgments about American involvement in Southeast Asia depend in part upon my knowledge of the factual, historical situation and also on a set of moral and political criteria for determining whether military intervention is a viable course of action. My judgment is unconditioned insofar as these conditions are fulfilled, yet only *virtually* so, since there may be other factors—both factual and criteriological—that have escaped my attention. To the extent that my judgment is conscious, I will be able to recognize whether new factors must alter it or not—in short, I am possessed of an ability to discriminate relevant objections from irrelevant. This is the final sense in which a judgment is said to be *virtually* unconditioned.

Anything that is claimed to be the case is of course claimed to be *really* the case. Hence knowledge culminates, if you wish, in being: in knowing that something is indeed the case. And since inquiry culminates in reality something is affirmed to be real to the extent and after the manner in which it is known to be the case. This may sound redundant but it is opportune to emphasize it in the face of a nativist conception (which Lonergan calls "extroverted consciousness") that all knowledge is a construction placed on a reality antecedently and primitively encountered. (The semantic analogue is Frege's insistence that terms refer via their sense and Wittgenstein's recognition that language makes reference through its use or actual employment. The psychological alternatives consist in supposing that genuine feelings exist in a naked state behind all masks or insisting that one's true feelings can only be recognized through a gradual process of articulation.) Once one eschews the model of knowing as direct vision and recognizes the effort to articulate as inherent to one's coming to know, then he can confidently say that "the real" is grasped in affirming something to be the case. What is affirmed is my articulation. And the affirmation is conscious in the virtual manner we have described—with an awareness of the conditions which must be fulfilled and of the manner in which they have been fulfilled. And this awareness includes an ability to sort objections into relevant or irrelevant, into those which demand that my judgment be revised or those already met.

It is the judgment as a reflectively conscious activity, then, which allows one to speak of something actually *being* the case. The unrestricted desire to know does attain *reality* in individual judgments, hence we can speak of *being* as its object. And the *being* that is thus known is intelligible, for what is affirmed is a specific understanding, an articulation, and it is affirmed consciously. This, I submit, is what is meant when one says with Lonergan that being is intelligible.

It is intelligible in what Lonergan calls "the profounder sense" since this affirmation—namely "being is intelligible"—can only be understood by elucidating what understanding is (647). Only by unraveling the conscious activities of understanding and judgment have we been able to show how it is that one affirms something to be the case. And in doing so we have identified the real with the being that is rationally affirmed. Reality then is intelligible in this deeper sense which identified it with intelligence in the act of affirming something to be the case (648). Hence we can say that being, as the objective of an unrestricted desire to understand correctly, is intelligible. It is intelligible in the sense that any intellectually responsible judgment affirms that something *is* the case, conscious of the conditions under which it is making this claim and conscious of their being fulfilled. One is conscious, if you will, of laying hold of reality in an articulated fashion. Hence whatever he grasps in this way will be intelligible.

But *being* taken here as the objective of an unrestricted (and in fact uncompleted) desire to understand, is an inherently heuristic notion. I am unsure what it could mean to say it is "completely intelligible." For being to enjoy complete intelligibility would seem to demand that it lay aside its heuristic character, cease to be the *objective* of an unrestricted *desire* to know, and be affirmed as the *object* (and content) of an unrestricted act of understanding. But I submit (and Lonergan agrees) that we have no experience of such an act on any pattern of experience (643). And if we have no such experience, we simply cannot affirm that being is completely intelligible because we cannot conceive what the judgment would be like which affirmed that all intelligent questions were in and all answered correctly (673).

What corroborates my skepticism regarding Lonergan's extrapolation from restricted acts of understanding to an unrestricted act (670), from the *notion* to the *idea* of being (643), is the manner in which he must describe this unrestricted act of understanding. "It grasps everything about everything in a single view (651) . . . inasmuch as it understands itself" (650). It is, more handsomely,

> the eternal rapture glimpsed in every Archimedean cry of Eureka. Understanding meets questions for intelligence and questions for reflection. The unrestricted act meets all at once; for it understands understanding and all the intelligibility based on it; and it understands its own understanding as unrestricted, invulnerable, true. (684)

Any experience we have of understanding truly is had through a specific judgment. We can understand what it means to truly understand by reflecting on what happens when we affirm that something is the case. But we cannot, I submit, understand what it is to grasp reality outside of a judgment—"in a single view." Hence we cannot understand what it means to say that being is completely intelligible.

And if we cannot understand what it means to say that being (or the real) is completely intelligible, then we cannot affirm anything about "complete intelligibility"—most notably, that it exists (674). And if we cannot affirm that complete intelligibility exists, we cannot complete Lonergan's argument to the existence of God (674). On the cumulative force of other arguments Lonergan advances, we can found a belief in God's reality as most plausible and a decision to live by our grasp of it as eminently reasonable. But if my objections are sound and, as I believe, faithful to Lonergan's original unfolding of "intelligible" as he uses it throughout *Insight*, then the generalized argument offered for God's existence cannot be offered as a conclusive demonstration.

One clarification might be useful at this point. In claiming that we haven't the slightest inkling of what an unrestricted act of understanding would be like and hence that "complete intelligibility" can have no meaning for us, I am not judging either notion to be a contradiction in terms (676). What I am rather objecting to is an idle use of language, an extrapolation beyond the conditions wherein the term is effectively used. I am not claiming that Lonergan has pretended to grasp the unrestricted act of understanding. He is explicit about this: "what is grasped is not the unrestricted act but the extrapolation that proceeds from the properties of a restricted act to the properties of the unrestricted act" (670). I am questioning the extrapolation, and precisely because the intelligibility of being to which we can attest is that realized by reflection on the rational act of judgment. Yet the unrestricted act does not proceed by way of judgment, since it does not proceed at all but understands everything "in a single view inasmuch as it understands itself" (650). Since the highest awareness available to us is that of a rational consciousness operating in the intellectual pattern of experience, our understanding of the way in which being is intelligible is linked to that experience. A "complete intelligibility" which follows upon an intuitive act of understanding everything would seem to have cut so many ties with our experience that it is literally inconceivable. It is the act of judgment which provides us the key to what we mean when we say that being is real and intelligible. How then, when the unrestricted act lacks this very focal point, the judgment, can we pretend to extrapolate to it from the properties of a restricted act?

What can Lonergan show, then, about transcendent knowledge? I would suggest that his battery of illustrations appealing to the limitations of specific inquiries does establish "the negative conclusion that knowledge of transcendent being cannot be excluded, if there is proportionate being, and being is intelligible" (655). And if we couple the fact that specific inquiries end at unexplained matters of fact with the unrestricted desire to know that animates them all, we find eminently plausible a belief in the reality of God as ground of the intelligibility of being and source of inquiring intelligence. And this belief would be plausible even though we do not know what it would be like to "be capable of grounding the explanation of everything about everything else" (655). For what we would be believing would be beyond our capacity to affirm, but in the line of that conscious desire which operates in every genuine affirmation. And since a decision to believe is an affirmation of reality (albeit of a unique kind) it elicits in its train a decision to shape our life by what we believe to be true. But since plausibility has neither the force of demonstration nor of an imperative, the affirmation of God's reality requires an intervening decision that is at once personal and free.

Chapter 9

Truth and Historicity
Certitude and Judgment

PRELIMINARY REMARKS AND A TACTICAL MOVE

PHILOSOPHY OUGHT TO REFRESH and lighten the Academy, but it more often burdens it with courses and topics too ponderous for words even to bear. So let us unburden ourselves at the outset by recalling that, concerned as we all are about truth, we seldom ask in so many words whether something is the truth. That anxious or perplexed expression on a person's face is usually wondering how judicious that observation was, how perceptive the analysis, how accurate the description. The "... is true" form is just that—a form which is kind of shorthand for a string of expressions concerned with appraising how faithfully other expressions represent the situations they purport to describe or do whatever other job they set out to do.

Academic philosophy has of course succeeded in systematically repressing the variety of jobs which we call upon language to do, and isolated description—physical or metaphysical—as a paradigm task of language, and wondered about its fitting the world. Theories of truth tended to presuppose two things or domains: language (or thought) and the world, and then wondered aloud how they were related and what we might know about that relation. But if philosophy is to enlighten the Academy, it would seem to fulfill its purpose better by elucidating than by theorizing. How better to begin than by reminding its own academic outgrowth that whatever else might be said, one would look silly trying to *say* how language relates to the world—unless he could come up with a special language in which to phrase *that* statement.

In a similar vein, a philosopher might remind his academic self that *truth* is a concern we all share but not a question we ask. We ask—in various ways which focus upon the items at stake (observations, analyses, theories, etc.)—whether what someone said is true or not. As tradition has it, *ens et verum convertuntur*. *Veritas* (or "truth") is reserved to coats of arms, titles for addresses to philosophical societies, and the rest. And it is so reserved because it evokes one of our deepest concerns, but if we would capture that concern we need a careful method to expose it. The simple reminder that the question form is "is . . . true?" recalls us to what footing we have.

CRITERIA AND FRAMEWORKS

Yet the question immediately arises: how can I/you/we tell whether a statement is true? (Try to hear here: is the report accurate? the analysis perceptive? the observation judicious?) Let us try out the new question form: how can we tell whether the desk will fit in that corner? the phone is connected? someone is a good teacher? The first two are easy, the last one worrisome: how about asking his students? which ones? The perceptive ones. How can you tell which ones . . . ? At some point, we are tempted to shout: "Oh, you can tell!"

Have we just lost our patience? Perhaps, but losing our patience can sometimes signal the end of the road and not just the end of our rope. Philosophers intent on explaining have found a reason where most of us simply find ourselves at a loss: "Oh, you can tell!" reflects an *intuition*, they say. But this turns out, of course, not to be a reason after all. And that fact offers yet more evidence that philosophy ought to content itself with elucidating rather than trying to explain. Furthermore, an explanation in terms of *intuition* proves harmful to the growing inquiry precisely because it offers itself as an answer to the how-can-we-tell question. Yet it is an answer only if knowing amounts to taking a look—which of course it doesn't. Otherwise, whoever proposes intuition must present it as a criterion which can afford overlooking the ways in which criteria function.

For "how can we tell whether . . . ?" is asking for criteria. Hence whatever one might *say* about *intuition*, it functions as a criterion insofar as it purports to answer the question. And once it has been invoked in response to the question, it functions as an answer. Criteria, in general, constitute those conditions sufficient for locating a statement within a functioning linguistic framework, so that one can assess it at work and ask whether it articulates a situation adequately or faithfully. They are sufficient conditions: there is more than one way to check whether the phone is connected, and any one will suffice. Furthermore, criteria serve to

(a) locate the statement

(b) within a framework

(c) that is functioning.

How can we tell whether the desk will fit into that corner? Measure them both. But what if we find when we bring it home that it doesn't fit at all, because—"well, it's ungainly, and I've worked so hard to make this room attractive." "Fit" functions in more than one way, obviously, and so one is free to introduce aesthetic as well as geometric criteria. But in each case, the criteria themselves function like specifications guiding an assessment: criteria for admission to college or for taking on this job. Can we speak, analogously, of criteria for a statement's being true?

Remarking how perceptive an analysis is or how judicious an observation certainly involves some assessing. So we spontaneously cast about for criteria. Yet recalling that criteria function like specifications, one would be at a loss to *specify* what is going on in calling something perceptive, judicious, penetrating, or true. We are driven to look for criteria, but chances are none will be available, because we are not that sure what we are up to in judging something to be true.

Furthermore, tradition reminds us that *verum*, like *ens* and *bonum*, transcend any framework. Just as "good" cannot be formulated without remainder as "good for," so ". . . is true" cannot be limited to a single job description. "How can I tell whether a statement is true?," then, admits of no direct answer. What it should succeed in doing, however, is to launch us on the project of locating the statement within a framework which is functioning. In the process of locating the statement and assuring that the framework is functional, appropriate criteria for assessing it will arise. So it is not pointless to ask for criteria in our search for truth—so long as we have begun to pinpoint which of the many forms of ". . . is true" we are out to secure. Criteria, by the way, may be vague as well as precise. It all depends on the job. If someone had asked whether the desk would fit in the corner and with the rest of the furnishings, besides instructing him in the use of a ruler, we would have recommended he bring his wife along.

FUNCTIONAL FRAMEWORKS

The homey examples mentioned so far remain within what I have summarily called a "functioning framework." By "functioning framework" I mean the set of implications both logical and pragmatic which allow a statement to go to work and articulate a situation. (I shall resist the temptation throughout to try to clarify what it means for a statement to "articulate a situation." The best I can hope for is that we become more comfortable hearing it. Those fixed in the language-R-world model would fault this expression for begging their question. But *that* question was already out begging.) The observation about our examples reminds us, however, that none of those so far chosen raises the truth-issue in an interesting way. Since they so obviously function within a clearly functional framework, their meaning is clear or can easily be clarified, and procedures for realizing their application are available if not always formulable—like *taste*.

A functioning framework, then, renders reflection superfluous. What works is true, and what has proved reliable can be held to be objectively true. Yet any single statement can be seen to function only because the framework does. What do we mean, then, by a "functioning framework"? How can we tell when a framework is functioning?

In some ways, this is easy. When Nelson blasts: "England expects every man to do his duty," and nearly every one does, something is working. On the other hand, when a spiritual leader enjoins obedience and meets argument, something is not. When a new language—think of Newton's—proves more illuminating by clarifying what had been obscure and unearthing hitherto unsuspected similarities, then it replaces its predecessor as the functioning framework in the field. "Functioning," then, is not far from "in possession": the network of convictions which are better described as presuppositions than assumptions, because we seldom entertain them enough to be said to be assuming them.

One may always ask, however: is it *good* that this set of convictions be "in possession"? At this point the reflective question of truth arises most dramatically. "Why should I—an Englishman—do my duty?" Sea captains can rarely supply an answer to this question. In the main, Nelson's exhortation exhausts the matter for them. It is one of those limiting statements which—like axioms—shape the contours of one's life and discourse. Someone of a more reflective nature might bring supporting reasons to bear, but such a person would be even more vulnerable than a Nelson to a question like: "how do you or I know that *resistance* is not my duty? It always *could* be, you know."

The dramatic alteration which "duty" undergoes here will help us summarize and clarify the framework notion, as well as offer some leads on how a framework functions. "Duty" can play one or both of two distinct roles: a descriptive or predicative role and a transcendental or impredicative one. Value terms share this ambivalence with time-honored transcendentals like ". . . exists."[1] In the one case, "duty" describes a round of activities; in the other, it sanctions these activities as responsibilities. The first role lies well within the perimeters of a seldom questioned framework: the descriptive, *zuhanden* one. The other role, the transcendental or impredicative one, explicates the manner in which certain activities—already adequately described—can no longer be regarded simply as things to be described, but also weigh upon us as part of our very destiny.

The descriptive language continues to function but it is brought to bear in a new way. The formal notion of *framework* seems helpful to elucidate this process. It is like making explicit the fact that a girder bridge also serves as an electric ground and so exhibits one structural pattern while functioning as part of another, electrical pattern. The example is useful in another respect: the anchored steel structure can always serve as a ground, yet it functions within a distinct electrical pattern only when it is so charged. A round of activities is normally open to being a round of responsibilities, but something must be done to so freight them. Words like "duty," "should," and "ought" remind us that two frameworks are interwoven here, and that the activities are to be assumed as responsibilities as well.

So when a term like "duty" is used in this way, it does not describe anything, but indicates how the descriptions are to be taken—as prescriptions as well. Metaphorically, this function could be described as (a) showing how the descriptive language is functioning here, or (b) indicating that another framework—one which engages the subject's own destiny—overlies the descriptive language here. (I shall adopt the first way of describing it, for rhetorical purposes.) The peculiar role which "duty" is playing comes through clearly in any case: it is an expression which does not describe anything but reflects into language something of the manner in which the language itself is functioning. To make explicit the fact that one can wield a language in this way, I have employed the framework—metaphor.

Examining the Functioning—Metaphor

While we might find "framework" a little arch and ask for cause to use it, talk about a framework's "functioning" is likely to go by unnoticed. Yet one form

---

1. Preller, *Divine Science*, chap. 1.

of speech is just as metaphorical as the other. Furthermore, by assuming that "functioning" meant one thing and one thing only, many were misled into seeking *the* criteria for truth or *method* of verification. As the example about activities-become-responsibilities shows, the question is not simply whether a language (or linguistic framework) is functioning—in gear and not idling—or even how well it functions. We must also ask *how* it is functioning. Just as expressions have different roles within a language frame, so the frameworks themselves can function differently. The analogy is both a formal and a moving one. That is, an expression *plays* its role—actually functions—only when the framework is functioning. And the manner in which the role is played is determined by the way in which the framework is functioning. So the truth-question—the adequacy of an expression's performance—must envisage how the framework is functioning.

For example: is an account of U.S. military actions or student uprisings in *Time* magazine substantially accurate? It reads like a piece of reporting, doesn't it? Well, yes and no. The prose is carefully weighted with knowing sophistication, the tone is somewhat supercilious, and the focus invariably centers on the piquant episodes. A contestable appraisal, no doubt, but proposed in self-defense: to render explicit the appraisal already operating in *Time*'s conception of reporting. Hence accuracy is not simply a matter of degree—like functioning better or worse—but a matter of perspective as well. *Time* reporting functions within *Time*'s general conception of its role, and one's query whether the report adequately or faithfully articulates a situation must be met with this overall function (or perspective) in mind.

I am simply adverting to a truism of literary criticism: the genre determines one's interpretation of a text; it directs the performance of the expressions which compose it. And of course the genre is determined by the expressions chosen and the way they enter into composition with one another to make the piece. There is no independent way of discerning it. One seldom finds a framework which is not already doing some sort of job. But to determine what that job is, to characterize the way it is being used, is the task of a reflective critic. The sort of appraisals he makes are of a piece with what we have abstractly called the truth-question: whether a statement adequately or faithfully articulates a situation.

Perhaps this will help us to see how the issue of truth is co-extensive with human life itself, for language is, after all, a way of life. A comparison with Aristotle's schematic rendering of "good" is certainly germane. The tradition has often elucidated intellect and will, knowing and doing, "true" and "good" one in terms of the other. For Aristotle, we can call something "good" when we have determined that it is fulfilling its nature, that it is functioning properly. We know *how* something should function when we adequately apprehend what it is, its nature. Hence the appraisal whether or not it is *good* is simply a matter of deciding whether it is functioning up to par or not.

This schema is a suggestive one. It is formally the same as that we have been using to unravel the truth-question. But we cannot apply it in a straight-forward manner to anything but artifacts, for we only adequately apprehend what we ourselves have made. (This epistemological theorem is displayed in many other ways, notably in the recourse scientific inquiry has to models.) Does this fact jeopardize the schema as a device for understanding how to use "good"? No, it simply underscores the fact that it is a schema, and hence too abstract to be a formula which only needs to be applied to yield an appraisal of every matter at hand.

Reflective Awareness—or How Is the Framework Functioning?

The fact that men can determine their goals and purposes, the fact that it belongs to man's nature, if you will, to shape himself by determining the aims which will norm his conduct, shows why it is one thing to appraise a motorboat and another to appraise a life or even a lifestyle. We are tempted to say that one can be settled while the other cannot. Consider again a piece of reporting: is it accurate or not? The analogue with a deciding whether the motorboat is a good one would be an account which perfectly fits the facts—which could be laid on top of them, as it were. There might be complicating elements—like rules of projection—just like the motorboat buyer ought to know enough to examine the engine, as well as simply take it for a spin—but the process would remain a straightforward one.

But reporting obviously does not function like a motorboat. Though it is regarded as the most straightforward use of human language, it is clearly subject to that capacity for modifying its own aims which characterizes man generally. How, then, can we hope to settle a question about accurate reporting? Or to use a vocabulary fashionable in some circles, how can we break out of or at least render harmless the "hermeneutical circle"? Once again, the question form "*how* . . . ?" seems to envisage a method or set of procedures to be followed. Yet at this juncture, no method will be forthcoming; for we have already seen that there is no straightforward way of determining the accuracy (read: truth) of a piece of magazine reporting. Perhaps we can meet the question, however, if we can become more reflectively aware of the obstacles to giving a straightforward response to it.

It will help to contrast Nelson's sturdy seaman with the protestor. The seaman need only ask, if he has any questions left: what is my duty? The protestor is demanding: what is duty? And in doing so, he brings an entire framework into question. For "duty" is one of those expressions which proclaims that that portion of the language which describes our activities will also prescribe them as responsibilities. By asking whether resistance might not be his duty, he is in effect challenging the settled connection between a certain set of activities and one's responsibility. For he asks whether "responsibility" cannot set in motion an utterly different response than hitherto.

Note that this is not simply asking where his duty lies, as though "the ethical" were a free-moving spotlight which illuminated now this, now that range of activities. A particular set of activities currently functions as responsibilities for the patriotic person. The protestor is questioning that functioning framework by asking whether some other set of actions, outside of and at variance with the established set, should not be deemed his responsibility.

We might perhaps conceive of duty being put to an even more radical test, where the question: what is duty? could be interpreted: why should one do his duty/be responsible? I shall try to show why this way of putting the question is inoperative, unless "duty" or "responsibility" is implicitly linked to a range of activities. For the use of "should," "deem," or other cognates of "duty" and "responsibility" seems inescapable. Furthermore the protestor's way of asking: what is duty? is radical enough, for it challenges those very criteria which normally settle for us whatever is *objectively* right or wrong. As the sociologists of knowledge have abundantly demonstrated, claims of *objectivity* have always been just that: claims. They have never succeeded in simply pointing out: that's the way things are. In fact, the plausibility of the claims has always rested upon the surrounding frameworks functioning in accepted ways. This is not, of course, to gainsay the *intent* of the language of *objectivity* to articulate how things are, but rather to remark how that aspiration is translated into practice. In fact the protestor is met with a solid front of *objective* norms—an organized matrix of activities deemed responsibilities—and accused of preferring *subjective* judgment.

REFLECTION: SUBJECTIVITY AND OBJECTIVITY RE-LOCATED

In this respect the sociologist of knowledge is vindicated and the defender of established order speaks more wisely than he realizes. For the very capacity to question duty in this fashion evidences subjectivity, freedom, or spirit. From Socrates on, "what is *x*?" has been recognized as a formal rendering of that very wonder which singles man out from the universe and germinates philosophy as at once inescapably and pathologically human. Plato's dialogues represent carefully structured attempts to show how the question can unfold organically into a way of life.

Carnap proves an unwitting witness by carefully distinguishing between *internal* and *external* questions.[2] He notes that it is only proper to ask whether a statement is true *within* a functioning framework. The pattern would hold analogously for *right* or *wrong*. To ask whether a framework is functioning appropriately or not—as the protestor does—is to ask an *external* question, and these do not admit of an answer. The reason is simple enough: an answer must itself be formulated within a framework, about which the question could again be posed. And since nothing can prevent an indefinite reiteration of the question, issues of truth or falsity (and of right or wrong) would never be able to be settled. The best we can do is opt for a framework; better truth settled by choice than never at all.

The entire framework analysis, of course, has been inspired by Carnap and allied contemporary analysts who have introduced a renewed form of logical expertise into epistemological and metaphysical inquiries. That Carnap opted for option and choice does not jeopardize his formal analysis of the logic of a truth-assessment. It simply invites us to articulate more carefully how it is that we handle *external* questions like that of the protestor when they are upon us. The language of "option" and "choice" carries all the pejorative connotations of "subjective." But there is another language in the neighborhood which will prove more fruitful: the language of "decision."

It is commonplace now to assert that *right* and *wrong* are a matter of decision, and only slightly less popular to speak in the same way of *true* and *false* assessments. Yet what separates *decision* from *choice*—right from "I want to" and true from "it looks O.K. to me"—is *reflection*. And reflection traditionally introduces subjectivity, freedom, and spirit. We begin to locate reflection when we recognize that questions which call into question a settled explanatory or ethical framework—like wondering whether a scientific account is appropriate or whether resistance might not be one's duty—cannot be met by yet further explanation. At some point another style of thinking must take over. This logical fact was recognized by Plato and handily formulated by Carnap in the internal/external distinction. Yet Plato went on to show that another style of thinking was available to us at the very interior of logic. He showed it by literally *reflecting* into the very structure of the early and middle dialogues the mode of consideration and the style of life which embodied it.[3] That mode of consideration and that

---

2. Carnap, *Meaning and Necessity*, 214–21.

3. I have tried to argue and to illustrate this point in my study of Plato: "What the Dialogues Show about Inquiry" (chapter 5 in this volume).

style of life—epitomized in the *persona* of Socrates—is what we have come to call reflection.

A Pattern for Reflection: Subjectivity Put to Work

Reflection begins with an awareness of the fact that we operate with and within linguistic frameworks which structure our perception of the facts by articulating them in certain settled patterns. At this initial stage any simple opposition between "objective" and "subjective" or "inner" and "outer" is already overcome. This initial awareness, however, admits of gradual thematizing, as we become yet more aware of the various ways in which *we* use these frameworks, the expectations with which we freight them, and the conditions according to which we decide—in one field or another—when we will replace one by another.

The initial awareness brings with it a kind of resignation, a sort of cynical wisdom, when we realize, for example, what "accuracy" means to the *Time* re-write staff. When we go on to thematize the ways in which we come to recognize how pliable "accuracy" can be, however, we are able to realize ourselves in possession of a new power: that of critical reflection.

This power, like most any power, has a destructive as well as a creative potential, and it seems uniquely suited to destroying us. Kierkegaard often spoke of the "devouring infinity of reflection." Is not a reflective awareness open to the same potentially endless—and hence fruitless—repetition as a pattern of ascending explanations? Plato's way of responding to this anxiety is to confront us with the *persona* of Socrates. What sets Socrates off from the sophists—what distinguishes philosophy from academia—is not his wit so much as his style of life. Socrates frequents that marketplace; he "never stops talking about cobblers and fullers and cooks and doctors" (*Gorgias* 491a), nor presumably with them. He is driven to understand the most pedestrian yet pressing facts of his own life, and he cannot sidestep the fact that he is an Athenian.

Plato is showing in this dramatization of Socrates one of those "facts" which deserves the honorific title of a "truth" because it reflects the very structure of reflection.[4] It is characteristic of these "facts" that they are far more effectively exhibited than discoursed about. Yet one may be allowed to sketch how they might be shown. What "Socrates" shows is that one has

---

4. I am indebted to Zemach for this distinction, among other things, from his essay "Wittgenstein's Philosophy of the Mystical," 359–76, esp. 362: "Let us refer to formal features of facts . . . as 'facts' . . . The factual character of the world is a formal property of the world. We can say that is it a . . . 'fact.'"

no options about continuing to inquiry, unless he wants to opt out. And those who opted out found themselves compelled to try to stifle inquiry by stomping out Socrates. The *ought* embodied in inquiry is inescapable, unless one wants to destroy all that is noble in himself as he sees it personified in Socrates.

And the way in which Socrates lives out the human demand to inquire after "the truth of things" shows that reflection need not be a devouring infinity even though it never comes to an end. What it must rather do is to come to terms with my life as I am living it. Reflection as Socrates carries it out is a way of participating in the world and the community of which he is a part, for the manner is always intent upon understanding where he stands. While this understanding admits of continual pursuit, and is even compatible with not understanding, the fact that it is he who is living where he is—no one else nor nowhere else—cannot be gainsaid nor undermined by further reflection.

With deference to Owen Barfield and Brian Wicker, I can risk labeling this style of lived reflectiveness: "participatory thinking." Heidegger aspires to fill the same logical space with *nachdenken* or, as it has become rendered: "primal thinking."[5] Both ways of speaking attempt to articulate the fact that the truth-question will not down and to capture as well the fresh terms in which it now arises: out of a living recognition of the relativity of linguistic frameworks. Hence no one is claiming to have stumbled upon a method or a way—how to determine whether statements adequately/faithfully articulate things as they are. Rather we have come to recognize, with Socrates, that it's *not* "all a matter of how you look at it." One cannot simply use linguistic frameworks as he pleases; he *must* engage in a long-termed process of inquiry which respects the logic of the languages involved and the fact that he lives where he lives. Furthermore, this program demands to be lived and not just talked about.

We have moved from an initial realization that one cannot escape language and its various uses—to the fuller realization that language is a way of life whose internal norms are the logic of the inquiry in question. And if one would inquire into inquiry itself, he discovers a way of life demanding the most stringent fidelity of all: that of Socrates.

---

5. Cf. Barfield, *Saving the Appearances*; Wicker, *Toward a Contemporary Christianity* and *Theology and Culture*. The Heidegger comes to me through Ott, *Denken und Sein*; for a discussion of this use of Heidegger, cf. Robinson and Cobb, *Later Heidegger and Theology*, 7–63.

Summary Reflections

How likely a story is the one I have sketched? It is certainly shaped by the traditional locution, "truth-judgment," yet accents the more receptive side of judging: recognizing and understanding where I stand. After all, the practical analogue of judgment—decision—seems in its most intimate forms to be precisely that: recognizing where it is I have arrived. There is plenty of room, of course, for the more active, commitment side of judgment or decision—if we can but recognize how these arise out of commitments already acknowledged. The roots of freedom reach to accepting necessity.

But how do I know that the style of life and inquiry sketched out will let me in on things as they are? I don't, of course. Yet I have tried to show that no obvious way opens out to answer this direct question. And the way sketched does articulate a plausible pattern for inquiry: from scuttlebutt to expert opinion to an explanation, and then on to reflection upon the entire procedure. Reference to the *persona* of Socrates also succeeds in halting the process of reflection without asking us to step outside of discourse. And that same reference brings each of us home to ourselves and to the fidelity demanded of us as persons with a history. It asks for a refined sensitivity with which to assume and assimilate the standpoints of our predecessors, passing over from ours to theirs and then illuminating our own with theirs, for we are also persons within history.[6]

Where does all this mesh with so-called "theories of truth"? I have gained much from wrestling with them, but do not propose these remarks as one among them. For what I have said could hardly be called a theory; it consists merely of what logical observations I could make, capped over with a likely story—a myth, if you will—when I reached the limits of what logic could show. But can stories like this be *true*? Only in the measure that the style of living and inquiring described here comes to life. And then it is no longer a story.

---

6. The theme of "passing over" from one standpoint to another, and the consequences for judgment, are delicately presented in Dunne, *City of the Gods*, as well in his work *Search for God in Time and Memory*.

Chapter 10

Religious Language and the Logic of Analogy
Apropos of McInerny's Book and Ross's Review

IN THESE DAYS WHEN nearly everyone is too busy sifting through anthologies and publishers' notices to sit down and read, a truly exceptional book may go unnoticed. And so one must risk aggravating the situation by going into print to warn the wise and selective: this book is worth your while. Such is particularly necessary in the case of Ralph McInerny's *Logic of Analogy*, where the fact of a Dutch publisher means little advertising to catch the eye.

McInerny's proposal is quite modest: "An Interpretation of Saint Thomas," and his results, revolutionary. Yet the author would be the first to insist: it is not he but St. Thomas who works the revolution. His task has been but to remove the accretions of other times and men to allow the reader to discover St. Thomas. The principal accretion, of course, is Cajetan, and the author's balance is sorely tested as he firmly pursues the train of St. Thomas's thought without allowing his basic disagreement with Cajetan to assume the proportions of polemic. For McInerny maintains—as many have felt—that Cajetan simply missed the boat, and supports his contention with a quite straightforward counter-thesis, appealing to the many uses St. Thomas made of analogy. Nor is he content to show that *there is* another view of analogy in St. Thomas by indicating texts which Cajetan sidestepped. Indeed there could be many such, now that we realize Aquinas did not always speak formally. Rather, McInerny claims that St. Thomas held *one view* on analogy, a view capable of myriad applications because it is above any of them. To prove this, he does not fear to tackle the very texts which served Cajetan as a *clé de voute*, only to show them ill-fitted to bear the strain once the extraneous matter is removed—fill added, of course, by Cajetan.

The argument is undeviating: analogy has to do with the use of terms, and so is a logical, not a metaphysical doctrine.[1] It simply recognizes that, while terms may be used in many different senses, it is always the case that one sense or usage is more basic than all the others, and sometimes true that the other senses are proportionately related to this basic or primary usage. When can we say that two or more terms are proportionately related? When a *ratio communis*, a common notion, has developed by linguistic convention and includes them both. Properly *analogous* usage is but metaphor domesticated, according to rules of linguistic propriety.[2]

The reader familiar with St. Thomas will want to concur, for analogy as a *habitudo unius ad alterum* is a constant theme in his writings, as well as his care to preserve a first meaning of any analogous term, a meaning proper to our mode of knowing. But the same reader will hesitate, for what has become of the famous distinction of analogy of attribution and analogy of proportionality? If our sketch of McInerny's thesis is complete it has simply vanished. And that it has, for the distinction, we recall, was based on whether the analogical attribute was actually present or not in the subject of which it was predicated. (Thus health is present in the bodily constitution but merely *attributed* to medicine, while both man and God are good, but *proportionally*.) Yet logic is quite indifferent to all this. While intrinsic or extrinsic denomination may be an interesting property of different domains denoted by analogical terms, it does not cause a major division in analogical usage. Things signified and their modes of existence are quite extraneous to a study of words and their meanings.

As a sign that such is the feeling of St. Thomas, McInerny takes the text which served Cajetan as a cornerstone: *de Veritate*, question 2, article 11, and recalls that the example of urine and health, which we have come to accept as a prime example of "analogy of attribution," is brought forward here as an instance of *proportionality*. What is more, "proportionality" is set off against "proportion" only to emphasize an indeterminate extension of the original meaning, a meaning which is definite and mathematical. So in

---

1. "Logical" is used here in the comprehensive Scholastic sense of the science of the argumentation whereby one proceeds from what is known to what is unknown (Albertus Magnus, *De predicabilibus* 1.1–2). As such it includes the study of words and their meanings as preliminaries to reasoning, as well as formal deductive procedures. We should say rather: "analogy is a semantic doctrine."

2. McInerny, *Logic of Analogy*, 150–52.

reality "the text of the *De veritate* does not deny that there is a proportion *unius ad alterum* in names common to God and creature. Rather it stresses that some things named analogically are separated infinitely, something clearly the case with God and creature."[3] He considers as well an apparent contradiction of the *Summa Theologiae* and *de Veritate* to show how the same two words can be considered analogous on the level of meaning, and disparate when one shifts to their foundation in reality.[4]

The fact, then, of intrinsic and extrinsic denomination, which has to do with the objects denoted, is quite accidental to analogy as such. For analogy is concerned with the various senses of a term as they are related—or proportioned—to one meaning which is connatural to us. The formulation: "a:b::c:d," has no canonical force. It is but an example used by St. Thomas to illustrate his point. And what is his point? That the several usages of a term must be related to *one*, and that a familiar one, for us to pretend to use the term properly in a strange context.

Is this hard to accept as the thought of Aquinas? For some it may sound too simple; for others, too contemporary. For yet another, however, it may be more than welcome on one or both of these counts. Not that *Logic of Analogy* is easy reading. Such a departure from "tradition" to seek an authentic tradition demands close and careful documentation, as well as widely ranging illustration. McInerny comes off well on both counts. We have seen something of his treatment of the *de Veritate* text. He examines Cajetan's other footing in the *Commentary on the Sentences* with even greater care,[5] and then goes on to test the interpretation by allowing it to range over a greater part of the domain where St. Thomas applied analogy, considering successively: analogical causality, knowledge by analogy, and divine names. The result is a simple theme, amply orchestrated with harmonies of St. Thomas himself, lacking but the amenity of a graceful style.

CONTINUING THE REVOLUTION

Two questions arise in particular: the status of the *ratio communis*, or common notion, which distinguishes properly analogical usage from

---

3. Ibid., 87. For such an extended sense of "proportion," see Crowe, "St. Thomas and Isomorphism," 178–80. There is a proportion that is a relationship between one quantity and another, and a proportion that is any relationship at all: *de Ver.* 26.1.7.

4. McInerny, *Logic of Analogy*, 89. The opposing texts are *ST* 1.13.10.4 and *de Ver.* 2.11.8. In the former, "animal" is said to be used analogically, and not purely equivocally when said of an animal and its picture. In the latter, the opposite is held. The context reveals the decisive shift of emphasis.

5. *In* 1 *Sent.* 19.5.2.1 (McInerny, *Logic of Analogy*, 96–124).

metaphor,[6] and a more rigorous testing of the thesis in the area of religious discourse, the touchstone of any theory of analogical predication. Since the remarks we will make owe fully as much to the incisiveness of McInerny's thesis as they pretend to add to it, they would be best styled "precisions," which the author graciously invites.

By extending the range of McInerny's work, we can manifest the extent of the revolution he calls for. And to make this even clearer, we propose these remarks in the light of another recent study on analogy, by James F. Ross.[7] Seeking to lay bare the semantic structure of analogy with appropriate rigor, Ross makes use of I. M. Bochenski's pioneering efforts in symbolic expression, and professes a doctrinal reliance on Cajetan. If his article illustrates the advantages of such a technique, it betrays as well this dependence on Cajetan. Finally, as both studies are frankly concerned with analogy as a semantic issue—analogy of names and terms—comparison should prove fruitful.

Since Ross is primarily concerned with analogy as it permits us to speak about God, let us first look into the question of divine names. If McInerny is right, Ross's acceptance of *proportionality* (a:b::c:d) as the normal form of properly analogical discourse is at best misleading, and so would be likely to carry him somewhat astray of the main issue. At the same time, we may try McInerny's thesis in the domain where logic and semantics meet the supreme test.

ANALOGY AND DIVINE NAMES

Now saying anything about God—of "naming" Him, in Aquinas's terminology—comes down to this: certain properties or attributes can be discerned as not limited to the mode of occurrence in which we come to know them. These properties are affirmed to be in God, and to be verified therein most properly.[8] On the basis of such an affirmation, we can construct the familiar: "God:good::man:good," but the form is more than misleading. For not only is the "::" not to be construed as the "=" in mathematics (as many have remarked), but even what is *qualitative* in this proportion cannot be grasped!

---

6. McInerny, *Logic of Analogy*, 150–52, 135.

7. Ross, "Analogy as a Rule of Meaning." For Bochenski's symbolic formulation, cf. "On Analogy." The author acknowledges there the efforts of Salamucha and Drewnowski in applying formal techniques to the texts of St. Thomas in an effort to reveal the structure of his thought. At least one such has been published in English: Salamucha, "The Proof 'Ex Motu.'"

8. *de Ver.* 2.11c (*in fine*).

We all know that the proportion between God and his knowledge cannot be known. Such was indeed the very reason for recourse to the "a:b::c:d" form. But what the form hides is that the proportion between the proportions, the pseudo-equality, really stands for a relation of exemplarity, that of creature to Creator, which cannot be known as such, but only affirmed to be.[9] So the supposedly normal form not only hides a proportion *unius ad alterum*, that is, a relation to a usage of the analogous term that is connatural to us, but also glosses over the fact that in divine names such a relation is affirmed in and through a negative judgment. Is it any wonder, then, that theologians and philosophers caught in such a form of discourse should be compelled to make so many subsequent reservations that the end product sounds like parliamentary double-talk?[10]

Thanks to an authentic view of Aquinas's position, however, it now appears that we are able to order the givens of theological discourse within a viable theory of meaning, which will help us distinguish the different levels of apprehension and judgment, of knowing and affirmation. By a "viable theory of meaning," I mean one that takes full account of St. Thomas's dictum that the proper object of the human intellect is the material thing. Not *as* material, certainly, for that belongs to the senses, but the most the intellect can hope to know is "what material things are."[11]

This means, then, that any statement which purports to talk about things other than those which are a part of our world must bear *some*

---

9. Is this not what Simon was getting at when he said, "... the proportional resemblance here is irreducible, in other words, no analysis, abstraction, or manipulation can ever reduce it to a resemblance that is not proportional"? (Cf. "On Order in Analogical Sets," 33.) We shall have occasion to return to this remarkable essay.

Cornelio Fabro, in his *Participation et causalité selon S. Thomas d' Aquin*, concurs in reducing *proportionality* to something more fundamental, which he calls *intrinsic attribution* (509–37, esp. 528–35). Yet he wants to hold on to both as expressing, respectively, the Aristotelian and Platonic "moments" in the Thomistic synthesis (535). He does not seem to worry about the fact that by making attribution "intrinsic," he has undercut the very reason for Cajetan's division into two forms. Perhaps it is that he can afford to overlook such niceties, being concerned with the forms only in so far as they may be suggestive of a direction of thought, viz. Aristotelian or Platonic. As we hope to show, a clear-cut distinction of the roles of apprehension and judgment would have brought clarity where "dépassement" leaves the crucial question of transcendental predication quite vague (531–32).

10. For a fair appraisal of this critique, see Flew, "Theology and Falsification," 96–99, 106–9.

11. ST 1.85.1; 1.84.8: "proprium objectum intellectui nostro proportionatum est natura rei sensibilis." To speak of knowing the *nature* of a thing means simply being able to give some sort of answer to the question, "what is this?" And this question, of course, admits of a variety of answers, from descriptive to explanatory, from a name to the ideal of a proper definition. Cf. *In 2 Post Anal.* 8.484.

relationship to an ordinary statement such as we might use to describe things we meet from day to day. McInerny's central achievement is to establish that this is what St. Thomas means when he speaks of analogous predication: using a word in an extended sense, but a sense always *proportioned* to one which is connatural to us, and so dubbed the *primary* sense. Indeed, one might have drawn the same conclusion from but a cursory reading of the main loci in St. Thomas[12] had not Cajetan shifted the discussion to a question of qualities inherent or not, and so laid disproportionate stress on one text, presenting the *ad hoc* solution therein as the *normal form* of analogy.[13] This form, the familiar "a:b::c:d," suppresses the fact that the term is used properly in one sense and analogously in the other, and gives the impression that there is some "objective content" to be understood here, as symbolized by the "::."[14] This led to a search for the "analogical concept" and the ensuing semantic muddle. Because of the key role of analogy in religious discourse, such confusion proved a convenient lever for a sophisticated skepticism. Indeed we can say that much of the contemporary attitude towards religious statements is quite justified, in the face of the semantic explanations usually offered. What we propose here builds on the foundations laid in the *Logic of Analogy*: an analogous sense of a work is always proportioned to a proper usage which is quite ordinary, and turns as well on the distinction of understanding and judgment, Aquinas's key to the antinomies of Aristotle.[15] From such a base, we can show clearly how St. Thomas can say that, when a name is common to God and creature, it is the creature who provides the proper meaning of the name, but God who *realizes* it most perfectly. This has led to a number of paradoxical formulations,[16] and to a search for a theory of

12. Cf. *In 1 Sent.* prol.2.2; 35.1.5; *CG* 1.35; *de Pot.* 7.7; *ST* 1.13.5.

13. *de Ver.* 2.11. Cf. Ross, "Analogy as a Rule of Meaning," 500–501, paras. 4, 5, 6.

14. In a three-page footnote in his article "On Order in Analogical Sets," Simon exposes the view of Blanche in "L'analogie," who rightly saw that a reference to a first analogate is essential to the understanding of any secondary analogate in *any* kind of analogy. Simon espouses this view, indeed develops it, in the article in the notion of an ordered set of analogical meanings. But he feels impelled to a number of subtle distinctions to harmonize this position with the traditional form of proportionality (see "On Order in Analogical Sets," 35n27).

15. The distinction between understanding and judgment is the correlate of that between essence and existence, and is indeed the only way we have of grasping the latter (cf. *de Ente* 4). For Aristotle, *form* accounts for intelligibility and actuality, while *matter* is the principle of physical plurality, of individuality. Yet it is the individual, he insists, which is primarily substance or actuality. For St. Thomas, *form* still accounts for intelligibility, but a new principle, *esse*, for actuality. For St. Thomas's thought on judgment, cf. Lonergan, "Concept of *Verbum*," 8:36–61.

16. For example, McInerny: "Some things can save the *ratio propria* of a name and yet be said to receive the name with reference to something else. This is true of 'true' and of all names common to God and creature" (*Logic of Analogy*, 98).

analogy tailored to the dilemma. We can now show that this is a special problem *for* analogy, a privileged instance of its use, but does not create a new subdivision, demanding a formal solution all its own.[17] And while the problem itself is bigger than analogy, it could not hope for a neat solution in the absence of a precise view of analogical predication.

Now if analogy is a semantic theorem having to do with the use of language, then its proper concern is meanings. In the language of St. Thomas: "Signification, and this will include equivocation and consequently analogy, pertains to the logic of the first operation,"[18] the act of apprehension or understanding. But if transcendental discourse cannot be achieved through direct signification, but only by means of the negative judgment,[19] then while metaphysics will *use* analogy, it will be as a tool. The semantic statement, then: "'being' is analogous" becomes, in metaphysical idiom: "being is divided into being *per essentiam* and being *per participationem*." The first: "'being' is analogous" has to do with the concept of being, with the use of the term, which all admit is but a logical consideration. More precisely, as Ross notes, any talk about the uses of an analogical term is properly metalinguistic.[20] It has to do with a notion which is not *one notion* on the object level, but which we can consider as such by viewing it from another level, at one remove. This, I take it, is what is meant by the "analogous concept."[21] The second statement: "being is divided into what is *per se* and what is participated" has to do with being itself, which is not comprehended but asserted

17. Ibid., 153.
18. Ibid., 66.
19. Ross, "Analogy as a Rule of Meaning," 499–500.
20. Ibid., 491. Logic, of course, in the Scholastic sense, included these levels, but contemporary work has brought them into focus.
21. Here again, a frankly semantic theory cuts neatly through a great deal of confusion. Consider for example "life." We do not study *life*, but living beings; we speak of many different kinds of life, and even extend the notion to include immaterial realities. (Cf. *ST* 1.18.2, and note the care with which St. Thomas *extends* the notion.) A definition of "life," then, such as "what has the capacity to move itself," is not meant to denote some minimal characteristic present in each, as Aristotle says clearly (*de Anima* II. 2, 413a20–30). What it rather provides is a rule, by which one might decide whether he could talk about computers being "alive" or not. Such is a meta-linguistic common notion, glossing over the fact that correct usage of the word "life" depends on our understanding of its primary meaning, and how the extension in question is proportioned to that meaning. [Ed. note: Burrell's later margin notes reflect these corrections to the previous sentence: "Such is a meta-linguistic common notion, glossing over the fact that *sensitive* usage of the word 'life' depends *upon our accepting a* primary meaning, and *realizing* how the extension in question is proportioned to that meaning." (Italics indicate his latter corrections.)] Which meaning is primary is not always easy to determine, however. "Life" is a particularly touchy example. Is its primary meaning more akin to our proper experience, or to a minimal organic structure?

to be so divided. But the word "being" is *used* analogously in this sentence. The *judgments* of metaphysics require analogous elements.[22]

And how are such judgments justified? Not from *analogy*, since analogy is but the *sine qua non*. We could not assert that God is *good*, that men and animals *know*, if there were not terms admitting of such extended use. (And of course, if the world were not so constructed, but that is precisely what we want to show. To say that the analogy of being is the foundation of the analogy of "being"—or better, that the fact that being is divided into *per se* and participated is the reason why "being" is analogous, is true but gratuitous. We can only know being in the myriad ways in which we are led to use "being"; we can only speak of a dog's knowledge because of the countless circumstances in which we are forced to say "Fido knows that . . ." The only alternative is to propose an intuition of being as participated and unparticipated which is of course proper to God alone.[23]) As men, we have to begin from things as they appear to us, from language as we have it. Such language is in part analogous—it contains expressions whose meaning can only be determined by relating them to a privileged case—and this permits us to use a certain class of terms as elements of a transcendental assertion.

But what justifies our making the assertion? Our power of judging, or more explicitly, the finality of the intellect as it is realized in our ability to make judgments. Though mysterious, this is not occult, for we use it every day, unless we suffer from a schizoid inability to face reality. For man, to live is to make decisions. And much as an hypothesis leads on to a verification (or not), so the perception that a term can be used analogously suggests a transcendental affirmation (or denial). And by the same token, just as verification is a step beyond hypothesizing, so affirmation is beyond the threshold of apprehension. To make this step is the supreme achievement of intelligence, what really sets man off as *rational*.[24] For St. Thomas, the intel-

22. The shift in expression from the use of the word to the metaphysical theorem is frequent in St. Thomas. For example: ". . . non dicitur res 'bona' nisi ex habitudine ad Deum, ex qua habet rationem causae finalis. Et . . . dicitur quod creatura non est bona per essentiam sed per participationem" (*de Ver.* 21.1.1.). Compare *de Ver.* 21.4.7.

23. The penalty for making light of the operative distinction of understanding and judgment is recourse to "intuition" to give reality to one's speculation. But a super-apprehension is, for all that, still on the level of understanding, and cannot do the work of the judgment. Indeed, to postulate that it can is to invite skepticism regarding the kind of insight that *is* properly ours: that of grasping a pattern or unity in the singular. The fact that discerning relevant from incidental is similar in form to an insight does not permit us to telescope the levels. "Intuition," as it is often used, becomes a conceptualist's substitute for the judgment. Cf. 165n38.

24. The existentialists have driven this home by concentration on the personal decision, which is an emotive response of the "whole man," including affective and intellectual elements. If our position is more coldly analytic, it is nonetheless the ground of theirs.

lect makes this step because it is intellect. Not because it somehow inspects the eternal verities, as Augustine's Platonic background led him to insist, but because the ground-structure of the intellect is an anticipation of being itself.[25] The intellect judges not because it *sees*, but because it *must*. There is no single criterion for discerning what is relevant.[26] It is this distinction between apprehension and judgment which will allow us to rough out the semantics of affirmations using analogous terms, present our program in contrast to Ross (in so far as he relies on Cajetan), and end on a note of gratitude to the skeptic and of challenge to the Thomistic philosopher and theologian.

ASSERTIONS USING ANALOGY

Everyone is familiar with the usual critique of Scotists for their position on analogy: when all is said and done, they really make it univocal, for they ground the sameness of an analogical term on a residual content of meaning common to every use. Yet not many have recognized how this is wedded to a conception of knowledge as "taking a look" which forms the backbone of much good solid Thomist "realism."[27] Similarly, many, while neatly refuting Scotus on analogy, go on to use analogy or talk about it in a manner which betrays their allegiance. In maintaining that there is something the same or similar in the use of "good" in "God is good" and "man is good," the tendency is always to search for some minimal *something* that both have in common. Scotism is much more tied to the mind's normal way of proceeding than is St. Thomas. For normally every judgment is made in function of some apprehension; every affirmation and negation is pronounced upon a directly meaningful statement. And so when we affirm that God is good and man is good, we feel justified in asking: what do you mean by "good"? Yet we know that we can only make these statements because there is no *one* meaning for "good" operating here. Otherwise we would be speaking univocally, putting God into a genus—even if the identity in meaning were *minimal*.

---

25. St. Thomas's thought is capsulized in *de Ver.* 1.9. Cf. also *de Ver.* 10.8; 10.11.12, to see how far he can go along with St. Augustine. Many of the difficulties regarding "consciousness" clear up when we discover that it means not one thing, but three. In us, consciousness is at once empirical, intellectual, and rational, and only as such an ordered and discriminating unity can it be self-authenticating. For a contemporary treatment, see Lonergan, "Self-Affirmation of the Knower."

26. Cf. Will reviewing von Wright: "Justification and Induction"; and Nielsen, "Sampling and the Problem of Induction."

27. Cf. Lonergan, "Concept of *Verbum*," 10:28–40; or *Insight*, 371–74.

Ross has recognized this, as of course he must. Yet because he has not recognized the gap between apprehension and judgment at work here, his formulation falls back into the search for *something common*. He has recourse to an expedient suggested by Bochenski. Recognizing that there cannot be a material element common to the meanings of "good" as it is used of God and man, he stipulates that what is common be purely *formal*.[28] This means in effect that when we say that God is good, we are actually saying that certain formalities such as symmetry and reflexivity hold between good as known by us and good as realized in God.[29] Ross extends this to include the formal properties following upon a merely linguistic set of axioms, axioms "presupposed by implicit language rules governing the employment of the analogous term." The fact that such axioms would be hard to come by does not invalidate the proposal, for such recurrent structures do exist in our usage, and a solution along these lines promises to be more in harmony with St. Thomas, who credited men with enough insight to recognize relations as sufficiently similar to extend the usage of a term.[30]

Now to say that nothing carries over but the formal properties of relations certainly seems to save the "unknowableness" of God. If all we are saying when we say "God has knowledge" is that his knowledge, like ours, is reflexive, asymmetric, and intransitive, then we do not know very much. And this is as it must be, for God is outside any genus, beyond any direct similarity with things. From goodness as we know it to goodness as realized in God, nothing is carried over of the ordinary meaning of the term, nothing but a set of formal properties, which we hardly mean when we say someone is good, but which is all we can hope to mean when we say that God is good as well.

It is this set of formal properties which is presumably the *res significata*, what we "intend to mean" when we attribute something to God, and

---

28. This needs to be clarified for the rigorous: Bochenski stipulates relations between what is *signified* by the word, the *ratio* or objective content, and the thing *denoted* thereby. So when we use "good" in "God is good," the meaning "good" is here related to God's goodness by relation P. Similarly the meaning we have for "good" in "Socrates is good" is related by Q to Socrates's goodness. When relations P and Q concur in the formal properties they can possess as relations: reflexivity, symmetry, transitivity, then we can use the proportional: "Socrates:good$_1$::God:good$_2$" and have proper proportionality ("On Analogy," 442). We have seen fit to drop the P and Q, however, and speak of the *rationes* as sharing or not in the formal properties of relations. This is partly to ease the expression, but also because the *ratio* is precisely that aspect under which things are denoted, and so already contains a relation to the thing.

29. Ibid., 443. This is an interpretation of Bochenski's 19.4, where "R" is no longer a relation but a set of formal properties of relations.

30. Ross, "Analogy as a Rule of Meaning," 496–97.

what survives the utterly diverse *modes of signification* to save the proper proportionality of creaturely and divine goodness by being predicable of both.[31]

Now this solution is manifestly brilliant. A common core of meaning has been established which has nothing to do with our ordinary fashion of naming things and with our this-world use of language. Yet this set of purely formal properties can be verified both in creature and Creator. It is precisely the realization that certain sets of formal properties can be shared by God and creature, together with the perception of certain creaturely characteristics as reducible, in their essential structure, to such properties that permits us to extend a name to describe God. It can properly describe God because it has no descriptive power left. The *mode of signification* proper to "good," say, as we have come to know it and learned to use it, has been "cancelled out."[32]

The response is cast in the mold of the problematic of analogical terms, as Ross conceives it: how is it possible to have words which are the same in *meaning* but differ in *intention*?[33] It is possible only if we distinguish, as Saint Thomas does, the *mode of signification* from the thing signified (*res significata*). Now the mode of signification has to do with the way we come to know things, with the spatial and temporal connotation of terms as we ordinarily use them. This goes to make up the *intention* of terms as we commonly employ them. And because our discourse is usually about this world and well within space and time, this constant reference to our manner of understanding is quite overlooked. Only when we are trying to speak beyond these confines are we forced to distinguish those terms whose meanings are firmly tied to their mode of signification from others which appear to admit a core of pure meaning, a *res significata*. "Knowing," for example, would be one such, while "sensing" would not. So the *res significata* (of "knowing") is what is common to all activities which we can call "knowing."[34] The statement is Ross's, who notes, to be sure, that such a common significance is never more than logically or artificially separate, but doubtless feels that such a position is necessary to preserve *some* kind

---

31. Using the example of "knowing," Ross notes that the "*res significata* is what is common to all activities we can call 'knowing'" (ibid., 493). "Mode of signification" is treated at length (ibid., 487–93).

32. Cf. Ross's application, ibid., 497–500.

33. Ibid., 487. "Intention" is defined with respect to term "T" as "the conjunction of all other terms each of which must be applicable to anything to which the term 'T' is correctly applicable" (ibid., 473, def. 1–2).

34. Ibid., 493.

of similarity between God and creature.[35] By reducing it to purely formal characteristics, he can safely say that the similarity is proportional and not direct, since the common *res significata* has neatly abstracted from any this-worldly use of the term, from any representational meaning we might give to "similarity."[36] Finally, it is the recognition of these formal characteristics that permits an analogical extension of the term.

Cajetan's theory is deftly saved[37] and the whole result is *almost* right. What is missing (the distinction between apprehension and judgment) leads to a search for similarity on the level of apprehension, which gives us what is misleading: a common *res significata*. Ross has apparently confused the common notion (*ratio communis*), which is meta-linguistic, with the *res significata*, which is on the level of meaning. Now the fact that he clearly recognized the common notion as meta-linguistic suggests that he was led by the normal form of proportionality ("a:b::c:d") to seek an "objective content" common to both uses of the analogical term.

At this point, one might well object: there must *be* a similarity to recognize if one is to extend a proper notion to cover an entirely new usage. Our response would distinguish: as long as we remain within this world, with analogical uses such as "Plato knows" and "Fido knows," yes, indeed. But when we use a term to apply to God, one need not *recognize* a similarity, not even a purely formal one. All that is necessary is that we perceive that certain terms admit of usages that are somehow independent of their space-time denotations,[38] and then judge that such occasions need to be explained. We *do* recognize the possibility of extending the proper meaning to form a common notion, but we simply affirm that what we know in a way that is proper to us is most perfectly *verified* in God as in its source. This does not say: there is a common *res significata* which is realized but imperfectly in the creature, yet perfectly in God. Such a statement would give the impression of some common, neutral "core of meaning" as the "a:b::c:d" form seems to demand. This says rather that what we know as goodness,

---

35. Ibid., 498n33: ". . . Aquinas is not committed to the absurd notion that God is entirely different from creatures. In fact, the analogy theory is designed to permit expression in language of the similarity between God and creatures while protecting our discourse from a claim that God is directly similar to creatures." By grounding what similarity there is in the orientation of rational consciousness, rather than in an underlying *res significata*, we would pinpoint how it is by no means *direct*, and indeed, how God could be said to be "completely different," according as "different" is ordinarily understood.

36. Ibid., 499–500.

37. Ibid., 471n6, where Ross affirms his theory to correspond to that of Cajetan, "not merely by election, but by selection."

38. Cf., for example, Ginnane, "Thoughts."

authenticity, etc., and recognize as capable of indefinite perfectibility, is so realized in God, who is its source and final explanation for being what it is.

Clearly the commanding element here is the drive of the intellect to complete intelligibility, which forces the issue and says that the indefinite perfectibility is realized, as the universe is intelligible. What is not said is *how* the perfectibility is realized or *how* the universe can be said to be intelligible. Inaccurately called the "principle of cause and effect" and misleadingly "the principle of sufficient reason," what is at stake is the dynamic orientation of the intellect towards the intelligible,[39] or in common language: the ability to discriminate the relevant from the irrelevant as evidence for the truth of a statement, the power to evaluate whether or not an inference is sufficiently warranted, the capacity to judge the adequacy or not of an explanation.

This power is at the heart of any statement about God, for as Ross has recognized: "All natural knowledge of God consists basically in showing that certain relationships with possible worlds actually obtain between things that exist and God."[40] The most fundamental such relation is the *reason why*, for it is the ground of all intelligibility, and it is this relation which the intellect affirms to exist between the world and God, and so allows it to speak of God in terms whose proper meaning can be extended to a common notion detached from all limitation. But it is not the *common notion* which is asserted of God. Rather, He is affirmed to be the source and final explanation of the property that we know and from which we receive the proper notion of, say, "knowledge." And as such, He is judged to realize it most perfectly.[41]

Of God's mode of possession, we can know nothing, except that it is totally different from ours—so different that it breaks the very structures of our language. (We are forced to say, for example, not only "God is good," but "God is goodness" as well, for all of its "logical barbarity." And Saint Thomas

---

39. Cf. Finance, *Être et Agir*, 157–58, note 113: "L'intellect *vit*, à sa manière, sur le mode propre de l'affirmation, non sur celui de l'intuition ou de l'idée, le lien existentiel qui noue les êtres à l' Être. En suivant jusqu'au bout ses exigencies, il accorde son activité à la loi qui régit l'ordre ontologique.... L'orientation dynamique de l'esprit n'est pas seulement prérequise à la connaissance analogique; elle y est sous-jacente, et sans elle la proportionnalité n'aurait aucun sens." And when the *form* of proportionality loses its canonicity, the true powers at work become all the more evident.

40. Ross, "Analogy as a Rule of Meaning," 500, par. 3.

41. And since the mode of realization is beyond our power to conceive, we might suspect that "verification" will have to be extended too. This is exactly what St. Thomas does when he speaks of the *rationes* which we attribute to God being "in God as radically verifying" them (*ut in radice verificante has conceptiones*); he goes on to remind us that such notions are not false if they imperfectly represent the one thing which corresponds to them, but only if there were nothing corresponding (*de Pot. 7.6c fine* and 7.6.4).

explains why we have recourse to such revisionary forms of speech.[42]) But if the modes of signifying are utterly diverse, and if we cannot take refuge in a common underlying meaning—a *res significata* which remains after all that is connatural and earthbound has been stripped away,[43] what *does* carry the meaning?

We have suggested that it is the drive native to the intellect to seek the relevant, a demand of rational consciousness to recognize the fact that there must be an explanation, even when equally aware of its incapacity to grasp what that explanation might be. In practice, this is very similar to what goes on in inductive procedures, and in fact, this is the very analogy Saint Thomas uses when he compares the way in which the mind is led on by what the senses apprehend to something further, to the way in which things understood lead it on to some knowledge of the divine.[44] Much as the descriptive features of individuals act as springboards to pattern recognition, so the normal ways of understanding certain things, as betrayed in ordinary language uses, act as so many pointers beyond our proper experience. (The diverse yet related meanings of "knowing," for example, revealed in the myriad expressions our experience must take, can point to a knowing which totally transcends ours.) And just as induction stubbornly resists analysis in terms of logical warrants, refusing to be compressed into the form of inference, so transcendental predication overflows the bounds of "meaning" as we ordinarily use it within the confines of *apprehension*. It is here that we must recognize the further function of *judgment*, and so extend our notion of "meaning" to include that which the intellect *attributes to* what it cannot know when it uses a word well beyond its proper meaning, *intending to express* thereby what it is pushed to affirm by the inner demands of rationality.[45]

---

42. *ST* 1.13.1.2.

43. The similarity to the pseudo-Scholastic notion of *substance* as something underneath the properties is striking. That such a notion is utterly foreign to St. Thomas goes without saying. That it has, however, passed into common repertoire only proves that popular philosophy took its notions of Scholasticism from the prevailing manual treatment—simplistic and so inevitably Scotistic.

44. *de Ver.* 10.6.2: "Unde pro tanto dicitur cognitio mentis a sensu originem habere ... quia ex his quae sensu apprehendit, mens in aliqua ulteriora manuducitur, sicut etiam sensibilia intellecta manuducunt in intelligibilia divinorum."

45. The significant turns of phrase "intend to mean" and "attribute to" are established in *ST* 1.13.5: "Sed cum hoc nomen de Deo dicimus, non *intendimus significare* aliquid distinctum ab essentia..."; and *de Pot.* 7.5.3: "... intellectus noster manuducitur a similitudine creaturae ut huiusmodi Deo eminentiori modo *attribuat*," and *de Pot.* 7.5.4.

By clearly distinguishing the intellectual functions of apprehension and judgment, we are not only able to signal where and how we propose to extend the notion of meaning, but find ourselves in harmony as well with a recurring remark of Saint Thomas in the context of naming God: that names signify things *as we know them*. The meaning of the names we use is derived from our apprehension of the things denoted, and our intellect apprehends them according as they are found in creatures.[46] There is a principal meaning, then, which is quite simply the one betrayed by our ordinary discourse. When we are able to delineate this meaning sharply enough to recognize that it signifies a peculiar kind of property: a perfection admitting of indefinite perfectibility, then we can proceed to form a meta-linguistic *ratio communis* (common notion), which announces, as it were, that this word is open to use in other contexts, even as an element of a transcendental assertion. The meaning of the word in such an assertion will be determined, not by some prevailing substrate carried over from a this-world use, but by the matrix of judgments, mostly negative, of which it forms a part. These will give direction, as it were, to the pointers provided by the connatural meaning of the term, but in no way bestow a new meaning similar to the first. ("Meaning," too, we note, is analogous. It admits of an extended use always to be related to the primary one: the "what is apprehended.")

CONCLUSION

It should be evident by now how a study of analogy which peeled away such irrelevancies as extrinsic and intrinsic predication to lay bare its original form of "proportion of one to another" has taken the courageous first step in a renovation of the semantics of religious discourse, one which permits a clearer view of Saint Thomas's sophisticated view of the question. Cajetan's interpretation, by adopting the "a:b::c:d" form as normal, suggested that there be some residual common meaning. The semantic consequences were grave, grave enough, as has been suggested, to justify a rather thoroughgoing skepticism.

By accentuating the incommensurability of apprehension and judgment, we have tried to cut the final tether with Scotus, suppress from the outset any tendency to seek out some increment of meaning common to God and creature, and to do this by showing how "meaning" too functions analogously in divine discourse. This permits us to start off in agreement with many skeptics that religious statements are simply *meaningless*. For they have hit upon a capital truth, a pillar of a truly adequate semantics

---

46. *ST* 1.13.3 (initio); *de Pot.* 7.5.

of religious language. Of course such statements are meaningless if one is thinking of ordinary representational meaning, as we usually are.[47]

The next step, however, is more difficult. Ross's treatment of *modus significandi* would be an excellent move. But if we are right, to move on with him and pose the fundamental question of analogy as the search for a meaning which is univocal within an equivocal intention would not contribute in the end to a viable semantics. What one would have to do instead is to point up, in one domain after another, the function of the judgment in human knowing, establishing it as an imperious need of the intellect itself. This alone could lead to a breakthrough in the ceiling imposed by Kant on transcendental affirmation, imposed because he failed to grasp the proper role of judgment as the *virtually unconditioned*. This work indeed has been done, but that is another and a much longer book, one requiring an introduction weightier and more skillful than this.[48]

---

47. Cf. *In de Divin Nom.* 1.1.27–35; 1.2.72–74, for St. Thomas's careful use of "cognition" and "comprehendere" when speaking of God.

48. The book is Lonergan's *Insight*, whose relevance is demonstrated if only by its range. But paradoxically it is that very range which frightens many a reader and has dismayed the best reviewers. On the relation with Kant, see *Insight*, 339–42.

Chapter 11

Beyond a Theory of Analogy

THEORIES OF ANALOGY HOLD promise of clarifying both what classical thinkers like Aquinas were up to and what we are doing when we speak in a religious vein, but they are rather formal affairs. They are concerned to lay bare the structural connections among the uses of those privileged terms designated "analogous" in order to preserve "cognitive meaning."[1] Their goal is to locate sufficient sameness within difference to assure meaningful discourse. One instrument is a "transformation rule" and the model sometimes suggested is an implication scheme. No theorist would claim, certainly, that the diverse uses of a term which are related closely enough to be called "analogous" are thereby related so closely that they can be said to follow logically one from another. The implication scheme is rather offered as an analogy itself, as are the "transformation rules" which form its connective structure.

We hardly need to remind ourselves, however, that an implication scheme and its transformation rules will help us to understand the structural connections among analogous uses of a term precisely in the measure that it leads us to recognize features relevant to analogous sameness. In short, an analogy is useful to the extent that it is leading, and a useless analogy would not deserve the name. So anyone attempting to account for the cognitive continuity among analogous uses without attending to the characteristics which prove to be leading ones would fail to give an account by missing the point. For any such theory seems fated to employ models (or analogies)

---

1. For a good example, see Ross, "New Theory of Analogy."

in offering its account, and these will be acceptable only if they prove to be useful in leading us to the appropriate recognitions.

Furthermore, Peirce offers an interpretation of implication itself which locates the connection in a propensity to lead an inquirer on to a more satisfying or integrating articulation of the manner at hand.[2] Lest this sound too vague and evocative, it might help to recall that the implication process intends to display how we go about making explicit what was implicit. This movement seems to be at the heart of coming to know anything at all, and there are grounds for seeing it operative in that most primitive of all relations in logical grammar: predication.[3] On the other hand, an account of implication which locates its linkage in "transformation rules" looks to be more straightforward than Peirce's, thanks to its "formal" appearance. But this may prove quite misleading, for both "transformation" and "rule" are highly analogous terms, and each is employed quite metaphorically in applying an instrumentality from formal systems to a functioning language.

I am not saying that a transformational model for implication is misleading. I am simply remarking that it is a model offered to explain a process we regularly engage in, just as implication itself was offered as a model for the sameness proper to analogous terms. The technical language of "transformation rule" might mislead one into thinking that it succeeded in displaying the basal "formal" structure of the matter such that any other account would be an "interpretation."

Hence it behooves one to offer the same therapy for theories of analogous usage which attention to analogies accomplishes for our intuitions regarding straightforward discourse. Whoever once looked for sameness now settles for family resemblance. Yet this blow to our naiveté should not unsettle us about the entire venture. Aristotle's divisions recognized certain recurrent semantic patterns: classifying terms do behave quite univocally when contrasted with terms more useful for assessing—even if every classification exercises discriminations laden with assessments. Furthermore, that subclass of equivocal terms named "analogous" does appear qualified to play certain overt roles better than any other group.

These are the terms we have recourse to when we want to call attention to the fact that classifying involves discriminating. Our habitual use of language exhibits an inertial tendency, however, whence recurrent expressions appear to be given rather than expressive of a discriminating activity. So when we need to get in touch with that activity, we may need explicit reminders. Hence a man may wonder whether the procedure whereby he

---

2. Peirce, *Collected Papers*, 2.442–44 (esp. note 1); 2.227–73.
3. Cf. my "Entailment: 'E' and Aristotle" (chapter 3 in this volume).

was led to an acceptable salary was an acceptable one. Or anyone might question whether the equitable distribution of goods prevalent in a capitalist economy is equitable, as someone who has reflected on the ecological rapacity of a *laissez-faire* society might ask whether an ethics focused on individual behavior can be ethical.

More generally, I would like to locate our recourse to analogous terms in a reflective moment when we need to become more aware of the manner in which we are using many expressions we normally use. If this description will not succeed in characterizing every analogous use of language, it does capture the more interesting ones, as we shall see. Furthermore, describing our recourse in this way provides appropriate place for the metaphorical side of analogous terms. Analogies never cease to be metaphors, yet theoretical accounts of the usage tend to find this improper. The metaphorical angle appears to give direction to the analogy, and so would account for its success or failure to lead one to recognize relevant features about the subject in question.

This fact also keeps us from relegating the metaphorical aspect of an analogy to a purely perlocutionary role, as though it were meant primarily to shock us.[4] Shock us it must, out of our settled ways of employing descriptive language. But metaphor can unsettle us with a carefully aimed jolt, so that its final effect is to move us in a definite direction. The difference between a mere jolt and a well-aimed one lies with the quality of control the context is able to provide.[5] It is enough here to note that metaphors can play an irreducibly cognitive role.[6]

The analogous uses of language which I want to explore, then, comprise those which succeed in calling our attention to the contours, if you will, of the language we are using. They will normally do this with an eye to preparing us to use this language in a yet more refined way, or in hitherto quite unexplored regions. Of course, it is not the terms which are doing this; we are. Yet in doing so, we find ourselves relying upon the capacities built into certain expressions: capacities to jar us into awareness and to offer some direction to that newfound awareness.

One upshot of all of this is that our analogies will prove effective the more we attend to the point we wish to make in using them. Hence an account of analogical usage must know how to include that dimension of

4. I signal the weakness in Wisdom's otherwise arresting account, *Paradox and Discovery*, 1–22, 114–38.

5. Note how Ross depends on context: "New Theory of Analogy," 77ff. See Harris, "Distributional Structure," for a linguistic essay.

6. For the relation between metaphor and analogy, see McInerny, *Studies in Analogy*, 67–94, and my *Analogy and Philosophical Language*.

consciousness associated with "making a point." I shall argue that analogous terms enjoy the structure they do precisely because they express something of our distinctively human purposes, and that one employs them more accurately the more human he has allowed himself to become. Alternatively, the discriminating employment of analogies is the only index we possess for that quality of judgment which we tend to associate with a developed humanity.

A CLASSICAL EXAMPLE

Allow me to risk an illustration from one of Aquinas's references to analogous usage. The example will prove a particularly crucial and fruitful one, for it illustrates language reaching for God. I want to show first how a formal theory can help us appreciate how Aquinas consciously puts different dimensions of language to work. Then I would like to show what more is involved; or better, what guides us in putting language through these paces.

In prosaic terms, we may be said to have some sense or feel for what outreaches expression. What this comes to is a rather acute consciousness of ourselves having a stake in what we are doing. It is that consciousness which directs our choice of expression and the ways we have of directing them. Turned towards the instrument of language itself, the theoretic side of that consciousness can discern the structures which allow us to use these expressions as we intend to use them—of God. So the "analogical use of language" refers both to the linguistic structures which make such usage possible, as well as to the quality of consciousness which guides the way we actually proceed.

The example is taken from question four of the first part of the *Summa*, where Aquinas begins to draw out all that the previous question implied when it forbade every recognizable statement form to be used with "God"— by asserting that God is to be. That very statement announces the complete absence of any resemblance between God and man. Creator and created can hold no features in common; not because God is so different from us, but because God is utterly unlike us. God's very manner of being God allows for no features whatsoever.

Yet we can count on a kind of resemblance, Aquinas concedes: "precisely as possessing existence [things] resemble the primary and universal source of all existence."[7] The likeness that a thing bears to the transcendent first cause of all things "will present the sort of analogy that holds between all things because they have existence in common." The focus on existence

7. *ST* 1.4.3.

is understandable. The basic form governing whatever else might be said of God states that God is to-be, and in the same context of questions Aquinas describes "created existence" as the "proper effect of God... since it is God's nature to exist."[8] Yet existence (to be) is not a feature nor a genus. It is precisely not the sort of thing which can bear a likeness nor be held in common. So the very terms which might allow for some resemblance of creatures to God forbid us any way of characterizing that resemblance. Aquinas ends up being consistent, but vulnerable to a charge of misrepresentation.

ANALYTIC CONSIDERATIONS

Yet Aquinas has indicated a way through the dilemma if we are skilled enough to negotiate it: "precisely as things possessing existence [*inquantum sunt entia*] they resemble the primary and universal source of all existence [*primo et universali principio totius esse*]." But how is it that anything can be said to be a being? After its appropriate manner of being what it is, of course. Most generically, the field divides between what exists in itself and what exists in another—between beings properly so called, and manners of being. And then we know how the manners divide into conceptually distinct modifications. And whatever exists properly cannot help but be modified as well.

So that is how things are what they are. Hence it is the only way we have of suggesting how "existence" might be held "in common": by the analogy which links these ways of characterizing anything's being what it is. But what links them together? An attention to forms of discourse, to the "categorical" differences imbedded in our language. I say "imbedded" because we do not normally call attention to these differences; we simply work within them. We only notice them when someone entertains an expectation or offers an account that seems inappropriate—like expecting a good musician to be a good man. That is why these differences are at once profound and commonplace—why we think a grammatical joke profound—for they show the very structure of our language-world, the structure which guides our discourse so effectively that we can take it for granted.

Could Aquinas be saying that we will begin to look at things—anything—in a new light once we are sensitized to their manner of being what they are? Is he suggesting that by schooling oneself to read sentences not simply for what they say but for what their very form shows about the structure of the subject, that such a trained eye would be able to note divine traces invisible to others? Curiously enough, I think he is saying something

---

8. Ibid., 1.8.1

like that. To defend my interpretation, however, I shall want to head off most of the leads which the visual metaphors offer.

On Aquinas's account of the action of the first cause of all, there need be no visible traces; and by his account of the manner of being of the first cause of all, there could be no visible traces. We would be quite unable to identify a divine trace, for there can be no such thing as an identifiably divine feature. Whatever access we might have to divine things is inescapably mediated, and mediated through a highly reflective consciousness of what we are about, called a "negative judgment."[9] This activity can issue in a determinate awareness, however, if we are clear about what it is we are denying; and that awareness will prove more revealing the more central are the features we clearly deny.

Now the "features" to which the categories call our attention are quite special features. Wittgenstein will call them "formal features," and so did Aristotle and the scholastics. For they succeed in marking out the "formal parts" of an object even if one could never locate them as material parts.[10] These "features" only arise when we adopt that reflective attitude towards the form of our discourse peculiarly adapted to making metaphysical points.

Aquinas would then be saying that exercising this sort of attentiveness will help us develop an attitude towards things quite different from the matter-of-fact one which just takes them as "empirical objects." Attention to the "formal features" of things attunes us to considering them as receiving what it is they are—from another. Of course, the exercises which we have engaged in since Kant have attuned us to thinking of things as receiving what it is that they are from the structure of the language we use. Aquinas did not enjoy our accumulated sophistication, but he showed himself astute in handling language in different ways and quite aware of what he was up to in doing so.[11] Furthermore, his own theory of knowledge demanded a

---

9. So Aquinas: "Having recognized that a certain thing exists, we have still to investigate the way in which it exists, that we may come to understand what it is that exists. Now we cannot know how God is, but only how he is not; we must therefore consider the ways in which God does not exist, rather than the ways in which he does." McDermott, "Simplicity and Unity (Ia 3 & 11)," 213. Cf. my "Religious Life and Understanding" (chapter 13 in this volume), especially pp. 208–15, for an introduction to Preller's genial way of handling these issues in his *Divine Science and the Science of God*.

10. For a guide to the *Tractatus* on this issue, see Zemach, "Wittgenstein's Philosophy of the Mystical." For Aristotle, see *Metaphysics* VII. 1034b20–1036a12.

11. "Hence: 1. In talking about simple things we have to use as models the composite things from which our knowledge derives. Thus when God is being referred to as a subsistent thing we use concrete nouns (since the subsistent things with which we are familiar are composite); but to express God's simplicity we use abstract nouns." *ST* 1.3.3.1; cf. ibid., 1.13.1–2.

role for intellect so active that an accomplished interpreter could sum up his overall view of things as "placed between two knowing subjects, ... between the Divine and human minds."[12]

So attentiveness to the ways our manner of discoursing at once determines and exhibits the structure of the subject can accustom us to the thought that things might receive what they are from another. "The sort of analogy that holds between all things because they have existence in common" would be represented by the manner in which diverse forms of discourse structure their objects. We would then be in a position to appreciate things receiving their existence from "the primary and universal source of all existence." We would have no clues to the manner in which it is received, but we would be able to conceive of things resembling their source without having to recognize any particular traces.

Furthermore, this interpretation explains how Aquinas can maintain that resemblance is asymmetric here: "we can say in a way that creatures resemble God, but not that God resembles creatures."[13] If any ordinary sense of "resemblance" were at stake, the statement would be inane. But since the only accessible resemblance is that which is shown by the form of a statement couched in a working language, we have access to a resemblance where our language is tailored to its subject, but never in the case of God.

The nature of God escapes us not simply because we lack descriptive resources but because the form of our language reflects (and manifests) a composite ontological structure. The best we can do is to use our language to announce this fact, as the statement "God is to be" does. We can understand that statement if we are skilled in detecting the ways our language has of reflecting upon itself to meet questions of adequacy. We would utterly fail to grasp its import if we tried to make "to be" express some recognizable feature. To say that God in no way resembles creatures is another way of calling our attention to these semantic facts about "God." It also tests whether we understood the highly qualified manner in which creatures could be said to resemble God.

ROLE OF ESSE

These grammatical remarks suggest how the resources of language may consciously be tapped in an effort to clarify what we cannot know in an area of concern to us. It is worth noting how the terms functioning in the discussion itself were pressed into playing extended roles—terms like

---

12. Pieper, *Silence of Saint Thomas*, 53–54.
13. *ST* 1.4.3–4.

"resemblance." One way of understanding what is going on is to attune oneself to the way in which certain expressions can be employed in a reflective as well as straightforward way. We normally associate resemblance with matching features. But we can also use it to call attention to those "features" which do not themselves appear yet which are displayed by the form of our discourse. The overriding reason for using the same term seems to be our concern that language interpret our world to us, in one way or another.

The role of a theory of analogy is to note the ways certain expressions have of appearing in diverse contexts—to map those uses and to try to account for the same expressions being used. Whoever works to construct such a theory cannot help be impressed with the resources latent in language: taken as language-cum-language-user. He will also be pressed to refine his own logical and grammatical skills: to sharpen his ear for the different roles available to expressions within a working language, and to come up with more effective models for relating those roles to one another.

But beyond all this lies the point of it all. We may be taken up with analogy because we are fascinated by the resources hidden in our language, but we find ourselves pressed into using expressions analogously only because we are drawn into inquiries that concern us. We reach beyond the pale of descriptive discourse when we are concerned about how things ought to be. We venture into those metaphysical regions where we must tread with acute consciousness of how we put whatever we say only when something utterly vital is at stake: like asking whether the whole business makes any sense at all.

This query presses on the entire activity of discoursing and of inquiring. Hence it admits of no answer. We can of course devise different strategies to meet it, yet each represents a way of reminding the inquirer how his query already adumbrates a response in the manner in which it is cast. Metaphysical inquiry will be designed to lead a person back to what his manner of living and being presupposes.[14] The most radical presupposition of all is that I exist, just as the question which opens up the region of the divine is "why is there anything rather than nothing?"

"Does the whole business make any sense?" is not cast in a way which admits of our using any part of the business to respond to it. We would likewise be at a loss to come up with something which explained why there was anything rather than nothing. This predicament marks the point where the analogous resources of language are given their most severe test, and also shows what is at stake, namely, everything. Aquinas's way of dealing

14. That is why metaphysical *theories* are always distracting: because metaphysical issues arise out of that tissue of connection between question and answer, problem and explanation, which a theoretical account must take to be settled.

with this is to lay claim to an expression—*esse*—which reminds us of our stake in the business of understanding of the incredible wonder that there is something rather than nothing.

The deliberately malformed "God is to be" states the case, first by showing that no expression will be adequate to state what this reality is, and then by reminding us how our very existence is at issue. The infinitive *esse*, when taken as a verb, goes some way in making this point. Yet it loses most of that ground when it plays the role of a noun, for one is led to ask what *it* is which God is and which defines the range of inquiry itself as the "primary and distinctive object of intellect."[15] To this question Aquinas supplies a whole set of answers: it is "what is formal with respect to everything else which might be said about a thing," for it is "more intimately and profoundly interior to things than anything else."[16] Nevertheless, because it is not anything and cannot even be expressed by a predicate of proper categorical status, by using *esse* in this way Aquinas seems to be gesturing towards that which is presupposed to any inquiry by providing its point.

Hence, it would appear less strange that God could be said to be *it*, and quite understandable that we could not understand what *that* would be like. In fact, the only likenesses we have of this "to be itself" lie imbedded in the activity whereby we become aware of how things as we know them bear traces of the manner in which we know them. Thus, the only access we have to such likenesses will lie in becoming more conscious of our vital concerns being interpreted in and by language as we use it. The analogous resources latent in language people this Pandora's box, and our own concerns open it. Though there is no measure available to men but man, we outreach our own limits in the ways we use our distinctive propensity for language-making.

---

15. *ST* 1.15.2.
16. Ibid., 1.8.1.

Chapter 12

Reading *The Confessions* of Augustine
An Exercise in Theological Understanding

THIS ESSAY IS NOT intended to swell the bulk of Augustiniana but rather to assist anyone who would engage himself in a work as engaging as the *Confessions* with some hope of advancing his theological understanding. The essay offers assistance in two ways: by leading one to take up the text once again, and by leading the same person to examine what he continues to bring to that text. For one advances in theological understanding in the measure that he understands a little better what counts as understanding in matters religious. Hermeneutic or interpretation or more simply, understanding, is more secure the more reflective it is; this essay proposes to display that thesis. Hence the initial and final justification I shall offer for considering Augustine's *Confessions* to be primarily an exercise in theological understanding lies in the fact that they can be read that way with unsuspected fruitfulness. The thesis of the article, then, concerns hermeneutics more than it does Augustine, but the benefits of a fresh understanding of Augustine are more than incidental.

USE AND INTERPRETATION

The tools offered for helping us to understand an historical figure often seem to interpose themselves in the way of the very quest they are designed to assist. How can we use them to help us achieve the quality of understanding we are after? It is one thing to learn enough about the various currents which have influenced an author to be able to offer a plausible reconstruction of his world view. Yet something more is needed if this understanding is to advance us in our quest for self-understanding as well. The scholar may argue that this second kind of understanding is not relevant to his work; and the querying individual will then be tempted to wonder to what end the scholar's work. When claims of irrelevance invite charges of irrelevance, one suspects that illumination, if at all possible, lies elsewhere.

Yet illumination is possible. The plethora of scholarly material surrounding Augustine and the *Confessions* in particular plays a distinct and specifically ancillary role in understanding that work.[1] It can bring us to a sharp appreciation of the schemes which dominated Augustine's shaping of the work. These schemes provide the material rules of inference which license some implications and restrict others. To identify them is to explain why questions are posed in the terms in which they are, and why certain issues are taken up and others dropped. For purposes of discussion I should like to call this contribution "dialectical" in the straightforward sense of positioning the issues. Anything which helps us to understand why the discussion is framed as it is clearly claims our interest and contributes to our enlightenment.

Beyond the interesting, however lies the critical. How does Augustine structure the book—given the influences which parameter his decision—and why? How does he use the schemata offered to him? And a correlative question: what do the obstacles I feel in approaching the text tell me about what is going on in the unfolding of Augustine's exposition, or in myself? When a question is posed in what seems to be an untoward way, it could be that a scheme is operating in Augustine's exposition of which I am innocent—or that I am employing a scheme in my reading which inhibits my following what is a quite linear path for Augustine. One could easily show that these two ways of describing a difficulty in interpretation come to the same thing. In fact, they do: such is the reciprocity between text and reader. Yet their sense is different, and this difference determines what steps we will take to correct the distortion. The road from Athens to Piraeus is the

---

1. Among the more useful works I have found are Courcelle's *Recherches sur les Confessions de saint Augustin* and *Les Confessions de saint Augustin dans la tradition littéraire*. The most valuable single introduction to the life and work of Augustine I have found is that of Brown, *Augustine of Hippo*. Brown's fidelity to his subject and his hermeneutic sophistication encouraged me to believe that it is possible to read and to learn from Augustine. The text of the *Confessions* upon which I have relied is that translated by Pine-Coffin, where the breakdown is offered into books and chapters. Hence, 1.13 signifies book I, chapter 13.

same that leads from Piraeus to Athens, yet it usually helps to know which direction we are traveling.

Granted that Augustine's world view is vastly different from my own, how can I read him not only to understand what he is saying but also to come in greater measure to grips with what I wish to say? Is it not hard enough to expect someone living today to understand what Augustine was saying, without expecting him to have something to say to me? The challenges posed by a consciousness of historical and cultural relativity contain the elements of their own response. For it is clear that we can never hope to understand what Augustine is saying until we become aware that we are reading him in a certain way. The very factor that tends at first to paralyze us actually turns out to empower both kinds of understanding—the historical and the critical. Once we realize that what looks like a straightforward question is already a reflective one, then the task of reflective understanding does not seem so prohibitive. The trick is surely to discover whence the misreading comes and so where to direct the therapy: to Augustine and his world view or to me and to mine?

Points of conflict, then, turn into points of contact, as I become aware of my own canons of interpretation in attempting to lay hold of Augustine's. What we have in common are the issues we each must face. But we will most probably differ in the formulation we give to them. Once we have been able to voice some of these differences, we are free to turn our attention to the way we each work with the conceptual apparatus available to us. For what we share with each other and with Augustine are the skills required to meet an issue. The way we handle the frameworks we have indicates the quality of judgment we possess; and as Wittgenstein has reminded us, "To share a language is to share in . . . judgments."[2]

To test this observation, consider what reading Augustine's text adds to reading a summary account in any history of philosophy. Assuming that the summary is an accurate one, we will learn little more from the actual text. Yet the text, we feel, gives us more of the man. The manner in which he comes to grips with questions shows us how much the question is his question. If we respect this fact, we will be less and less tempted to take home what he says as an "answer." For what Augustine says, he has worked out in response to his question. Yet in compensation we will have learned a little better how to meet our questions, by participating in his attempt to formulate his. In this manner, reading becomes exercising, as learning passes over

---

2. "If language is to be a means of communication there must be agreement not only in definitions but also (queer as this may sound) in judgments. This seems to abolish logic, but does not do so." Wittgenstein, *Philosophical Investigations*, par. 242.

from learning about to learning how. Let us bring these reflections to bear on the *Confessions*.

Plan of Exposition

The clues we have to follow in understanding another and coming to grips with the obstacles we erect to such an understanding are invariably structural or logical clues. Even relatively "straight" questions of historical influence, we are told, cannot be answered uniquely by finding literal citations from one author in another.[3] It seems natural to speak of the "sense and structural unity of the work," as if in the same breath. The reason attention to form is so telling is at once simple and profound. Both fourth- and twentieth-century authors must organize their work. Hence, the task is an understandable and a comprehensible one, no matter what general set of views one espouses. The manner in which a work is organized can be counted on to shed light on the set of judgments which control what a person does with the schemes at hand. The order decided upon says something about relative weighting and this will prove all the more true in the case of Augustine's *Confessions*, where the mode itself is not inherited but consciously adopted.

In what follows, I shall begin by proposing some general and hypothetical remarks about the role of the *Confessions* in Augustine's life and literary output. I shall then propose a way of reading the work suggested by paying careful attention to some obvious structural features of its composition. Bringing these two sorts of observations together will allow me to present the *Confessions* as a project in understanding. Finally, I should like to compare and contrast this way of proceeding with some recent psychological analyses. This specific comparison with another method of interpretation is offered as a test of the hermeneutic remarks proposed in the section on "Use and Interpretation."

THE ROLE OF THE *CONFESSIONS* IN AUGUSTINE'S LIFE AND WRITINGS

The difference between the *Confessions* and other works of Augustine is immediately and dramatically evident. Linguistically, the *Confessions* is a carefully and a highly constructed work. It is fashioned and chiseled more like

---

3. For example, O'Connell writes, "The solution here proposed will both test and confirm previous suggestions that the Plotinian sources active in the Saint's earlier works are still exerting their influence in the *Confessions*, and that, in their light, the sense and structural unity of the work is laid bare" (*St. Augustine's Confessions*, 5).

a work of art than an account. It is clear from comparative studies that this work not only differs from the rest of Augustine's output, but stands without any clear precedent, initiating a novel literary genre.[4] The choice of form illustrates better than anything else Augustine's feel for theological understanding. What is most remarkable about the choice is its apparent naturalness; to adopt an autobiographical form in the way he does is to exhibit its appropriateness. It is not so much to credit Augustine with special insight as to charge others with oversight. For what we have is a crafted response to the biblical recommendation that we praise God for what he has done in and to our lives. This format is central to the Jewish blessing and consequently to the Christian anaphora.[5] It forms a standard motif for celebration and for increasing the faith which triggers celebration. Augustine adapted the recommendation from the arena of God's people to the field of his own personal history: Where fathers were to relate the great deeds of God to their children, Augustine recalls his own childhood to relate God's deeds there to himself now—for the child is the father of the man.[6]

In this way Augustine finds a recommended way of coming to grips with the question central to every Christian life, but nettling for a professionally religious person—the question of faith. I speak not of the neurotic desire to find certitude where none will be forthcoming, but of the troublesome issue of one's own genuineness. As bishop and as theologian, he must speak of God and the things of God. But where does he himself stand? How can he responsibly speak of such things, as distinguished from analytically or defensively? Perhaps this is too modern an hypothesis to foist upon Augustine, but I think not. For the very manner in which he undertakes the *Confessions* suggests it, as well as the way he organizes the material. He undertakes it publicly, as befits his character, and as he must, being a magisterial figure in a church whose founder resented being called "master." The irony of such a position could not be lost on a psyche as sensitive as Augustine's. Furthermore, the double sense of "confession" is well served by this hermeneutic hypothesis—praising God for all that He has made him and confessing how much he yet remains in need of purification.

That part of the authenticity question which can be tackled in a work of human crafting might be roughly called establishing the criteria or the warrants for speaking responsibly of God. How, on what evidence, do you

---

4. For the place of Augustine's autobiography in the history of autobiography, see Misch, *History of Autobiography in Antiquity*, 1:17; 2:625ff.; 2:681ff. Also Pascal, *Design and Truth in Autobiography*, 21ff. I am indebted to John S. Dunne (see 183N6) for these references.

5. See Audet, "La 'benediction' juive et 'l'eucharistie' chretienne."

6. Dunne, *Search for God in Time and Memory*.

say what you do? By choosing the autobiographical format, Augustine could show how a person's understanding of God is interwoven with his personal development. Certain questions arise at certain times, and until they do, a language crafted to respond to them remains idle. Correlatively, this logic feeds back on the writer to apprise him of where he now stands. This special understanding of where he stands comes to an author directly as he retraces his own steps up to the present. But the form also allows him to have a reflective insight, were he to try to ascertain why he selected one episode rather than another, and why he organizes his history in the stages that he does.

To look carefully at the genre is to appreciate its severe demands. What Augustine undertakes is to trace his way to God, the manner in which the relatedness of every creature to the Creator was exhibited in his case. Here the plan betrays a metaphysical scheme: for the Christian, "to be" is "to be related to God the Creator." Yet Augustine continued to frustrate the operation of this scheme; his innate propensity to be autonomous kept preventing this (true) scheme from being true. The sign that he was bucking a metaphysical fact was, of course, its revenge; every effort at autonomy resulted in increased dependency and enslavement. Metaphysical schemes become dramatized when the context is the history of human subjectivity. So runs Augustine's genius.[7]

Furthermore, by focusing on his intellectual development, Augustine was able to unfold one hypothetical scheme after another, showing what made them look plausible and how he came to reject them. Exercise in revealing the springs of one's judgments along the way allows him to examine the judgments upon which he is presently operating. This is Plato's recommendation for dialectic: that it exercise itself in becoming aware of the hypotheses which it has adopted, that it become skilled in bringing them up for examination. It is significant that this recommendation does not lend support to the search for a definitive scheme or a foundation for understanding. Nor does Augustine propose anything like that. He rather casts his work into a format which will illustrate the relatedness of all things to God by unfolding the drama within his spirit, which can become all things. By exposing his life right up to the moment of composing, he places himself

---

7. One is reminded of Carl Jung's observations about method in *Aion*: "Once metaphysical ideas have lost their capacity to recall and evoke the original experience they have not only become useless but prove to be actual impediments on the road to wider developments. . . . If metaphysical ideas no longer have such a fascinating effect as before, this is certainly not due to any lack of primitivity in the European psyche, but simply and solely to the fact that the erstwhile symbols no longer express what is now welling up from the unconscious" (34–35).

in an admirable position for taking stock of the premises governing his thought and life at present.

We are clearly in the presence of someone who cherishes and relies upon intellectual skill. Yet these skills are just as clearly placed at the service of living one's life, of helping one to understand, and to live into that primary relatedness which being alive is. The autobiographical form shows this fact more easily than it could be said. For we are not speaking of a yet higher scheme, but of the manner in which any scheme may be utilized. The form will also exhibit how Augustine is driven to adopt an epistemological model quite different from that available to him in neo-Platonism. The model he proposes is the very one, of course, which led him to adopt the developmental format of an autobiography. Understanding what something is demands more than insight or vision; it will also require an appropriate discipline so that we can articulate what we understand in a word which faithfully expresses our present situation. In things that matter, there is no knowing short of becoming, no articulation short of a faithful expression of where it is that one is.

The reason for this, as we shall see below, is that the hypothetical scheme one is employing is not nearly as important as the manner in which one employs it. This fact imposes itself in "things that matter," because this phrase describes those subjects of inquiry which are presupposed to any inquiry, those topics toward which we cannot help but be positioned whether we have taken a position or not. Hence, understanding cannot escape self-understanding, and taking a position often involves disengaging oneself from the position in which he already stands. To say that Augustine succeeds in dramatizing metaphysics is another way of noting how he firmly subordinates conceptualization to living, schema to use, understanding to judgment, and judgment to action. For if "to be" is "to be related," then any affirmation of what I am includes an assessment of what I must become. Let us illustrate these general contentions in the unfolding of the work.

MODE OF COMPOSITION

The divisions in the work are clearly demarcated and more or less adequately announced by the initial chapter in each book. This chapter acts as a prelude, summarizing and projecting the theme of the ensuing book. On this pattern, book 1 occupies a special place, hence it is the first five chapters which serve to introduce not simply the first book but the themes of the entire work. The development of the work may then be elaborated into an introduction and four parts as follows:

Stations on the Journey of Inquiry

Introductory 1.1–1.5

Growing Up:

1. Childhood
2. Youth
3. Adolescence
4. Young Bachelor
5. Transitional

Focusing on Conversion:

6. A Despairing State
7. Intellectual Enlightenment
8. Conversion and Return

From Conversion to Present:

9. Ecstatic Liberty of Spirit
10. Present Posture

Understanding Along the Way:

11. Critical Appraisal of God's Relation to Men
12. Removing Obstacles to Speaking of God
13. Unity of Creation and Redemption

The closest Augustine comes to anything like a theological treatise can be found in the final three chapters of the *Confessions*. It is as though he dare not undertake anything so risky as the interpretation of Scripture until he has brought himself to an awareness of where he stands and whence he has come. Something of the same may be said for us. We can only understand what Augustine is able to write in the measure that we undertake his journey ourselves. And yet we could not be required to have traversed the same distance. We can understand what he is up to, just as he was able to see what he had to do long before he was able to bring himself to do it.

It is perfectly characteristic that his philosophical reflections should be entirely at the service of our reading the Scriptures. The work of the theologian will be to overcome obstacles which may stand in the way of others reading and profiting by the Scriptures. For all understanding is meant to show us a little more of the way, and the Scriptures are the ideal food along the way. Nor can he hope by philosophical analysis to remove those obstacles to reading the Scriptures which we may share with the young Augustine. He can only hope that the earlier part of his own book has prepared us to meet our own obstinacy and pride so that we have done what is possible on our part to remove those obstacles to understanding.

The division which I have presented of the book is an uncomplicated and immediate one, except for the section comprising books 9 and 10. It would seem more natural here to follow Albert Outler's suggestion that book 9 completes Augustine's personal history, placing it all in proper perspective with the death of his mother and the severance of his strongest earthly tie. The rest of the work would then be seen as exploring two closely related problems:

> First, how does the finite self find the infinite God (or, how is it found of him)? And, secondly, how may we interpret God's action in producing this created world in which such personal histories and revelations do occur? Book X, therefore is an explanation of *man's way to God*, a way which begins in sense experience but swiftly passes beyond it, through and beyond the awesome mystery of memory, to the ineffable encounter between God and the soul in man's inmost subject-self. But such a journey is not complete until the process is reversed and man has looked as deeply as may be into the mystery of creation on which all our history and experience depends.[8]

Outler then goes on to show how in book 11 "in the beginning God created the heaven and the earth" is the basic formula of a massive Christian metaphysical world view. Then books 12 and 13 allow Augustine to elaborate the mysteries of creation until he is able to relate the entire round of creation to the point where we can view the drama of God's enterprise in human history on the vast stage of the cosmos itself. In this fashion, Augustine can show how the creator is the Redeemer, and man's end and the beginning meet at a single point.

The division which I have adopted is quite compatible with Outler's, for book 10 is clearly a transitional effort and can be read as part of the more theological writing or (as I have) more closely linked to Augustine's personal history—as he sums up the confessional section: "This, then, is my present state" (10.33). The long section on memory or consciousness then becomes his explicitly reflective glance back over the endeavor he has just completed. Were he not so composed, neither could the work be. I have chosen to link books 9 and 10 together to make evident an epistemological structure which I consider to be one of the most useful, explicitly

---

8. Outler, *Augustine: Confessions and Enchiridion*, 19–20.

philosophical contributions of the *Confessions*. This division also has the advantage of creating a new section precisely at the moment of newness, his baptism. But I have remarked that such a scheme is compatible with Outler's, precisely because a work like the *Confessions* itself is capable of being diversely schematized. It is meant to be put to use in the same manner Augustine puts intellectual schemes to work—to assist human understanding along the way.

UNDERSTANDING AS BECOMING, KNOWING AS KNOWING HOW

It has been remarked that Augustine admirably formulates the crucial dictum of the existentialists—knowing is becoming. I have suggested that the very form of the *Confessions* illustrates this contention, and have tried to show in a schematic manner why the concluding theological sections depend for their efficacy on our participating in Augustine's personal journey. Yet it is possible to come a good deal closer to elaborating Augustine's epistemological position than simply to remark that knowing is becoming.

It will prove fruitful to speak in terms of knowing how to use a particular language, feeling at home in employing it, and realizing the consequences that follow from speaking it. Although Augustine will not put it in these terms, and even though his own remarks about language are rather simplistic and stereotyped (1.8, 11.20), the manner in which he uses prose belies the remarks he may make about using it. The simple fact is that he finds it necessary from his own experience to supplement the Platonist modeling of knowing on a flash of vision or insight. For his experience found him seldom short of insight, yet often unable to respond: "I was astonished that although I loved you and not some phantom in your place, I did not persist in enjoyment of my God" (7.17).

Many have also remarked how Augustine invariably introduces important figures in his life some time before he details their influence upon him. It is as though insight merely introduces us to a new understanding, and that something else must intervene before that understanding becomes our own. What must intervene is on the one hand a gift and on the other hand a struggle. The first we can always count on, the second requires time and effort. Before we can possess what we have glimpsed, we must undertake a style of life which embodies some of the syntax of the new language adumbrated in the original insight.

It is as though Augustine realizes that mere insight must be filled out by expression before we can possess what we have seen. And since expression demands language and language brings with it a structure of consequences, those entailments must reach into the organization of one's life before he can be said to understand in a way that gives him facility with a new language. I have already noted that the couplet books 9 and 10 forms a unit on this interpretation. The ecstatic liberty experienced in book 9 is comparable to a flash of insight, while the probing and confessions of book 10 recount the way of life which must follow upon the experience of liberation in order that one continue to act freely.

Yet perhaps the most pointed illustration of the progressive laying hold of a new language, first by insight and then by grace and discipline, can be found in the couplet of chapters 7 and 8. Chapter 7 recounts Augustine's intellectual enlightenment, and specifically his break-through to a new appropriate language for God, the language of origin or principle: "I entered into the depths of my soul, . . . and with the eye of my soul, such as it was, I saw the Light that never changes casting its rays over the same eye of my soul, over my mind" (7.10). Similarly, for all of creation: "I looked at other things too and say that they owe their being to you. . . . They are in you because you hold all things in your truth as though they were in your hand, and all things are true insofar as they have being" (7.15). Yet the net effect of this new insight was to "realize that I was far away from you" (7.10).

The same pattern is condensed in an account of a dialectical ascent in classical neo-Platonic terms:

> So, step by step, my thoughts moved on from the consideration of material things to the soul, which perceives things through the senses of the body, and then to the soul's inner power. . . . This power of reason, realizing that in me it too was liable to change, led me on to consider the source of its own understanding. . . . And so, in an instant of awe, my mind attained to the sight of the God who *is*. . . . But I had no strength to fix my gaze. In my weakness I recoiled and fell back into my old ways, carrying with me nothing but the memory of something that I loved and longed for, as though I had sensed the fragrance of the fare but was not yet able to eat it. (7.17)

In these highly reflective passages at the end of book 7 Augustine is delineating a twofold intellectual conversion. The first stage recognizes the manner in which "the Platonists" allowed him to find a new direction in his central endeavor of discovering how one might conceive of God. Yet in the very same breath, he notes that the same books which led him to this new understanding failed to enlighten him how to put it into practice—although they were replete with the Word, they could not bring themselves to give it flesh (7.9). At one and the same time, Augustine must acknowledge his debt to the neo-Platonists and seek to enlarge the pattern for understanding which they offered to him. The inspiration for a new pattern is manifestly Christian—the difference between a disembodied word and a word made flesh is precisely the increment which discipline adds to insight. And the inward side of discipline is, of course, a gracious gift of God. So the impetus of the twofold intellectual conversion to Platonism and beyond remains the grace of God, and grace gives this conversion its specific form.

This revolution in models for understanding is carefully catalogued in the following passages collated from the last two chapters of book 7—the chapters which sum up Augustine's intellectual enlightenment and set the stage for the decisive moment of conversion.

> By reading these books of the Platonists I had been prompted to look for truth as something incorporeal, and I caught sight of your invisible nature, as it is known through your creatures. I was certain both that you are and that you are infinite, though without extent in terms of space either limited or unlimited. I was sure that it is you who truly are, since you are always the same, varying in neither part nor motion. I know too that all other things derive their being from you, and the one indisputable proof of this is the fact that they exist at all. I was quite certain of these truths, but I was too weak to enjoy you. (7.20)

> By the gift of grace he is not only shown how to see you, who are always the same, but is also given the strength to hold you. By your grace, too, if he is far from you and cannot see you, he is enabled to walk upon the path that leads him closer to you, so that he may see you and hold you. (7.21)

> It is one thing to descry the land of peace from a wooded hilltop and, unable to find the way to it, struggle on through trackless wastes where traitors and runaways, captained by their prince, who is lion and serpent in one, lie in wait to attack. It is another thing to follow the high road to that land of peace, the way that is defended by the care of the heavenly Commander. Here there are no deserters from heaven's army to prey upon the traveller, because they shun this road as a torment. (7.21)

Language: A Way of Life

It is noteworthy that those chapters of book 8 which express the tension of conflict between what Augustine saw and what he was prepared to do (chaps. 5–10) employ the expressions "intellect" and "will." It seems as if this way of speaking, which opposes the two ingredients of understanding—insight and discipline—is most appropriate to capture the felt hiatus between seeing what must be the case and bringing oneself into line with that train of thought. Yet the language of intellect and will is strictly speaking provisional on Augustine's newfound model for understanding. For the organization of the book and the specific remarks we have collated certainly will not support linking intellect with understanding and will with doing. It is rather that certain things cannot be understood unless we are prepared to incarnate them. The language model allows this point to be made quite precisely: The rules of inference which govern a particular language must become the rules of one's life if he is to use that language with confidence and alacrity. Is this perhaps why, when the tension of opposition between insight and his way of life is released, Augustine quite naturally has recourse to a more primitive mode of expression: "The light of confidence flooded into my heart and all the darkness of doubt was dispelled" (8.12)?

To understand something means to be able not simply to mention it but to go on and speak about it. Hence to understand something is to be able to integrate what we can say about it into a working framework which allows us to say yet other things about what we understand. This, I take it, is at least part of what understanding something amounts to. What Augustine helps us to see is that understanding certain things—things which bear upon our own existence—also means going on to live in a manner every bit as consistent and consequential as is our ability to speak about them. Language is a way of life, and a confident use of language demands a consonant way of living. Furthermore, in the arena of religious discourse, where the things understood challenge our penchant to go on to speak about them in our settled idioms, the way of life becomes decisive. On the model suggested, one can easily satisfy himself that a manner of living consonant with the language he has taken up will feed back on that language to confirm him in its use. The evidence is to be found in the sensitivity with which one detects possible trains of thought and the keenness with which he tracks them down.

Yet in the religious arena, where discourse about God must break through settled habits and rules of inference, a new way of life may need to establish consistencies existentially which will then be embodied in discourse. This, I take it, is the burden of Augustine's complaint that he could not—until book 7, chapter 10—conceive of God as spirit. That is, he had no other language than the ordinary descriptive one, but to use it of God would turn Him into an object in the world. Yet the new language of origin or principle, which is adumbrated in book 7, chapter 15, certainly appears vacuous until one undertakes to live "entirely devoted to the search for truth" (6.11). And this way of living requires a complete turnabout—something which Augustine does not execute until the end of book 8, and whose consequences he continues to plumb in the life which follows that moment of conversion. I am suggesting that Augustine not only improved upon a simple insight model for understanding, but also provided us with a pattern for religious understanding which will be of considerable help in determining precisely how one establishes criteria for religious discourse. If language entails and is entailed by a way of life in the manner in which Augustine demands that it be, then some revolutionary consequences are in store for contemporary analytic philosophy of religion. And the further fact that these consequences can be illustrated on the model of language and language use suggests that this new breakthrough is not a simple evocation of "experience" but rather contains the seeds of a disciplined inquiry into criteria.

UNDERSTANDING OR EXPLANATION?

The observations about a new epistemological model have been gleaned from a critical, reflective reading of Augustine. They are clearly exhibited in the *Confessions*, but nowhere argued to. Their warrant, as the choice of style indicates, is not a further set of statements, but Augustine's own life. Yet that life itself has recently come under a type of scrutiny which challenges the presumed authority of sainthood. In the terms of the challenge, what Augustine hailed as insight simply gives testimony to a conditioned mode of response, for the heart of the matter lies in a struggle between Augustine and Monica.[9] What he reports as a conversion is a surrender, and what looks like discipline following upon insight is rather a behavior pattern confirming his dependency.

Like any explanatory framework, this one pretends to completeness. And Augustine is especially vulnerable. First, because he has made himself so: the warrant for what he says is what he has become, the great deed God has made of him and which he speaks. Beyond this fact, however, he

---

9. The principle references are to a symposium under the direction of Pruyser appearing in the *Journal for the Scientific Study of Religion*, 1965–66, and an earlier article by Kligerman, "Psychoanalytic Study of the *Confessions*."

is simply vulnerable to psychoanalytic probings: There is much evidence to support a "surrender to Monica" reading. The brilliant account of the painful turmoil which issued in the release of his conversion—"it was as though the light of confidence flooded into my heart"—culminates with:

> Then we went in and told my mother, who was overjoyed. And when we went on to describe how it had all happened, she was jubilant with triumph and glorified you, *who are powerful enough, and more than powerful enough, to carry out your purpose beyond all our hopes and dreams.* For she saw that you had granted her far more than she used to ask in her tearful prayers and plaintive lamentations. You converted me to yourself, so that I no longer desired a wife or placed any hope in this world but stood firmly upon the rule of faith, where you had shown me to her in a dream so many years before. And you *turned her sadness into rejoicing*, into joy far fuller than her dearest wish, far sweeter and more chaste than any she had hoped to find in children begotten of my flesh. (7.12)

This passage placed where it is already reveals a great deal. But taken together with the description of the mystical experience he shares with Monica at Ostia (9.10), and reinforced by his own perception of steady indulgence countered by repeated blows for freedom, the possibility that Augustine could have acted other than he did grows more and more remote. He simply lost a long and violent tug of war, falling at last into the arms of Monica and of mother church. Think, for example, how little mention there is of Christ the mediator in the *Confessions*, and how prominent is the church.[10] And it will become even more prominent, as his ill-resolved Oedipal tendencies appear refracted into doctrinal disputes with Donatus and Pelagius. The sufficiency of church and of God's grace is at issue in these instances and Augustine responds by extolling man's dependency. In each case, it is man who depends and whose glory lies in utter surrender.

One seldom knows what to do with "explanations" like these; they prove (or disprove) so much. Yet it would prove perilous to reject them wholesale. Consider by contrast the following explanation offered for Augustine's frequent use of *fovere*:

> God's fostering care is something depicted in the medicinal image of the Omnipresent as "bathing or fomenting" either the wounds of Augustine's sinfulness or the spiritual eyes which need clearing so that he can come to "see." That medicinal care

---

10. Dittes, "Continuities between Life and Thought," 132; Bakan, "Some Thoughts on Reading Augustine," 151.

is often accompanied by therapeutic pain, giving it a paternal character. At other times, it takes a more maternal form. Then God is like the mother-bird already mentioned, beneath whose wings the chick finds both protection and nourishment to fledge it for mature flight, or like a mother or a nurse, feeding the believing "little one" from what Isaias terms the "breasts of His great consolation," or (in another meaning of the term) "caressing" and "fondling" him, patiently teaching him to walk, then run, along the road of the spiritual life.

But before maternal omnipresence can teach the soul to walk, it must bring it back from wandering; before the fallen soul can be strengthened to run and fly, it must be little enough to "confess" that until now it has been fleeing, running away from where it most profoundly wished to go. Augustine's mother for years had to watch her son pursue life's journey with presumptuous, grown-up confidence, his back to the Light, his eyes upon the empty realities that Light enlightened. She had to listen to him as, sick with sinfulness, he blamed his sores upon a primitive catastrophe for which he claimed to bear no guilt; the sufferings of mortal life he never ceased complaining of, not counting them as salutary, therapeutic chastisement for his own primordial sinful choice, but as the doing of a hostile "race of darkness." He was like a child, tired of her maternal attentions, running off impatiently to seek distraction with his playmates. Playmates, alas, can be cruel; their games can end in loss, frustration, scraped knees, and scalding tears. She could have told him that, but children never listen. Headstrong is the word for them.

But mothers know how to wait their moment. Knees scraped, eyes streaming, even the most headstrong child comes back again, wailing that life has cheated, deluded him, failed to live up to its deceptive promise. Back now he comes, content to climb upon her waiting lap; for one last protest he looks back upon the way on which he ventured forth so hopefully in the morning brightness. This is her moment: with tender maternal hand she caresses his fevered head, gently turns his eyes away from what had been the cause of his complaining, places his head against her breast. Calmed, he sleeps, and wakes, and finds that all is well again.[11]

Fortunately, the issues need not be polarized about a rhapsodic outburst or a psychoanalytic reduction. On balance, the psychoanalytic

---

11. O'Connell, *St. Augustine's Confessions*, 35–36.

scheme, no matter how crudely employed, offers a firmer grip for understanding. In fact, the greater one's psychological awareness in approaching the text, the more courageous will he find Augustine. Lesser men would never have attempted the task. The utter candor and relentless analysis with which Augustine executes it should give pause to a latter day analyst, however orthodox his persuasion. For the same candor and analytic power which provides material of fine enough grain and sharp enough focus to tempt reasonable psychologists into proffering a diagnosis, testifies in its own behalf. A man so courageous and so perceptive, we are tempted to say, must do more than instantiate a psychological typology. There is no doubt, as we shall see, that psychological tools can sharpen our image of the man, but it is difficult to suppress the suspicion that working on the image present in the *Confessions* should help hone those very tools as well. An inquiry as reflective as Erikson's into Luther would seem to be called for; one which takes the opportunity to improve one's tools as well as to display them in use.[12] For as one writer remarks: "Augustine, like other men of unusual gifts, *used* his conflicts."[13]

What were those conflicts? How did he use them? How did they handicap him? Can we understand his writings any better if we can answer these questions? Would we be any better equipped to ferret out systematic consequences, recognize them to be distortions, and be able to say why they were? The initial psychological inquiries available allow some tentative responses to each of these questions, suggesting that more reflective and comprehensive investigation would prove immensely illuminating. But before using the investigations we have, and to signal the caution with which I shall employ them, a summary observation is in order. If, as intimated, Augustine's "conversion" is really (i.e., can be satisfactorily explained as) the belated surrender of an indulged child to the indulging and devouring mother, it should spell the end of the line—psychological death. Yet the movement itself is not only experienced as a great release, but also triggers an outburst of theological and cultural explorations of astounding fertility and creativity. (I am thinking not merely of the sheer volume of work but notably of his treatise on the Trinity, his discussions of teaching, or freedom and grace, as well as his monumental essay in sociopolitical criticism, *The City of God*.) The very terms of psychological analysis itself warn against doctrinaire diagnosis in a case as challenging as this.[14]

---

12. Erikson, *Young Man Luther*.
13. Woollcott, "Some Considerations of Creativity," 282.
14. Clark, "Depth and Rationality," 145.

Autonomy versus Dependency

Certainly the most comprehensive of the psychological studies is that of Dittes, who proposes to link Augustine's account of his own life together with his prevailing doctrinal positions.[15] And this is, of course, what Augustine himself invites. Nor is Augustine entitled to take issue with Dittes's summary of his doctrine nor with Dittes's analysis of the manner in which his life contributes to the positions he assumed in matters of doctrine. For Dittes is proposing a depth-analysis, which could well be utterly revelatory to the individual concerned. But we are entitled to take issue, if we can, with the manner in which Dittes employs his analytic tools.

In summary, Dittes finds that Augustine conceives God more as an impersonal force and power from which everything emanates, rather than as a person in his own right. Furthermore, the church rather than Christ is mediator for Augustine. Freedom is characteristically resolved with a firm insistence on the unqualified authority and power of the creating God. A man's role is utterly and absolutely dependent upon the intentions of God. Hence the overall picture which Augustine leaves us of God and the world involves "the utter dependence of man on God, [and] his own virtual impotence and ineffectiveness before God." God, on the other hand, is characterized by "remoteness, aloofness, absoluteness, impersonality, and unapproachability—except in the abject humility of confession [before] this controlling God."[16]

One could certainly contest this summary account of Augustine's thought. It seems especially tied to a literal reading of the *Confessions*, wherein the very literary form of the piece is overlooked and hence undue weight given to the statements made therein. Augustine cannot be blamed for having recourse to the only conceptual framework available to him—Neoplatonism—but it is incumbent on his readers to detect the ways in which he puts this framework to use. Hence, for example, the only manner in which Augustine may have been able to "conceive God" would be in some formula of emanation, but the fact that the entire work is itself a prayer addressed in the first person to God would certainly modify the way in which we receive his explicit emanationist formulas.

What is more important to our considerations, however, is the manner in which Dittes "explains" this particular doctrinal complexion. That it takes the unique shape it does may be traced to a prolonged struggle for autonomy in the face of an overweening mother—a struggle which Augustine finally

---

15. Dittes, "Continuities between Life and Thought."
16. Ibid., 133.

lost as he settled for dependency.[17] There are abundant clues in the *Confessions* which would lead us, as we have seen, to be sympathetic to this explanation. The indulgent mother who has transferred her own sexual longings from husband to favorite son may well so threaten him with her seductive and protective overtures that he will resolve (without evening knowing it) never to let intimacy encroach upon his life. Hence the only plausible figure for God would be an utterly autonomous one. In fact, Augustine's bid for autonomy—a move so violent that it induced a nearly fatal illness (5.9)—was met by Monica's journeying herself to Milan. Hence the only practical solution for Augustine was to give in to that same overweening presence, forsaking autonomy for dependency.

Characteristically, this defeat would be unable to resolve the earlier fears of intimacy, and hence would have to be covered with a celibate life style. Furthermore, in anyone as passionately desirous of unity as Augustine, his own capitulation would inevitably lead him to extirpate striving after autonomy in others. Enter Augustine the champion of mother church against Manichee, Donatist, and Pelagian. Nor did Augustine have many scruples about pursuing a vigorous persecution of heresy and heretic, for the terms of his own capitulation had already led him to subordinate the goodness of God to his power.[18] Such would inevitably be the result of a surrender sacrificing both autonomy and any hope of intimacy.

Dittes's account is at once perceptive and persuasive. Yet it succeeds as well as it does by a customary mirror trick. On the one hand is a summary of Augustine's thought which prepares the way for the analysis, and on the other a disarmingly simplistic use of the categories, "autonomy" and "dependency," as though they were polar opposites. As for the summary of his theology, I have already mentioned the way in which Dittes overlooks how utterly personal are the *Confessions* as a work. With regard to the emphasis on church he sees as against Jesus, one could reasonably argue that Dittes's expectations are themselves peculiarly Protestant. The *Confessions* more plausibly represent an implicit Christology where Jesus's life in His Church was the experienced reality. What distinguished the Christian would not then be his "relation to Jesus" but rather his newfound access to God as father in the community of brothers which is Christ. Certainly Augustine's *Commentary on the Psalms* is replete with this form of implicit Christology.

But more importantly for our purposes is the manner in which Augustine's inner conflict is represented as a tug of war between two opposing forces—autonomy and dependency. On this scheme, the end of the eighth

17. Ibid., 136.
18. Ibid., 138–39.

book would prove decisive: Augustine surrenders to his mother. Yet we have already seen that this simple solution runs counter to the obvious creativity of Augustine's subsequent life. Drawn up short by this fact, we are tempted to ask whether autonomy and dependency are really that simply opposed one to another. Can it not be argued that the genuinely autonomous person is precisely the one who has come to accept the basic parameters of his life? Does not the person who acknowledges his dependency stand more of a chance for genuine autonomy and creativity? In Augustine's own case, must we not modify Dittes's scheme with a time vector, so that Augustine gradually rehearses an unentailed autonomy until he can sustain accepting a deeper dependency, and so find his way through to the autonomy which is his? Would not an interpretation like this be closer to the facts of the case as well as more faithful to the inner dynamics of autonomy and dependency?

Wholeness

Yet if Dittes does not in the end offer an explanation, he does bring a good deal of illumination. His observations about Augustine's childhood correlate carefully with those of Woollcott, Bakan, and Kligerman: Augustine was definitely an indulged child. Here we have a useful clue to his formulation of the freedom question: *Homo non liber est nisi liberatus*. For the indulged child never senses himself to be free; with good reason he is ever worried about indulging himself. One thinks immediately of the latter portion of book 10, where Augustine recounts his present state and reproaches himself for following the inclination of his own appetites. Woollcott calls attention to Augustine's narcissism, and notes his inability to "integrate his own masculine strivings."[19] Bakan, distinctly more critical, takes up the theme of reproach, and links it with an unentailed narcissistic ego which is itself alienated from existence, "and which leads Augustine to build an image of God essentially alienated from existence—a God whose primary activity is reproach."[20] All this leads Augustine to overrate a simple tree-stripping episode, attach himself to the church as mother, live a life compulsively reacting against sexuality, and finally be overtaken by a "Jesus complex."[21] For Bakan, his major sin is to undo the work of God.

What strikes the reader about Bakan's analysis is the utter confidence with which it is uttered. It is quite obvious that Bakan brings to the work a set of definite and differing religious views which make it difficult for him to

---

19. Woollcott, "Some Considerations of Creativity," 276–77.
20. Bakan, "Some Thoughts on Reading Augustine," 149–50.
21. Ibid., 150–52.

enter into Augustine's views with sympathy. The best clue to this insensitivity is the way in which he misses the pear-tree episode, where Augustine is relating a paradigm case of senseless activity. Woollcott, whose reading is far more sensitive, himself completely misreads the crucial passage where Monica (presumably) sends Augustine's mistress home. Woollcott has it that he "sent his mistress packing without remorse."[22] But the text reads,

> The woman with whom I had been living was torn away from my side as an obstacle to my marriage and this was a blow which crushed my heart to bleeding, because I loved her dearly. . . . Furthermore the wound which I had received when my first mistress was wrenched away showed no signs of healing. At first the pain was sharp and searing, but then the wound began to fester, and though the pain was duller there was all the less hope of a cure. (6.15)

In each case there is evidence that those features of the *Confessions* which cater to the respective theories received more attention than less palatable passages.

Augustine's Self-Reproach

Nothing seems more obvious to a modern reader of the *Confessions* than the author's inveterate tendency to reproach himself from infanthood on. Yet, interestingly enough, this observation seems compatible with Pruyser's remarking "the relative absence of self-directed aggression" and "a peculiar absence of true remorse."[23] In fact, these shrewd observations of Pruyser help to explain how Augustine could continue in his attitude of self-reproach in the face of God's affirming mercy toward him. One feels that the grace of God which Augustine celebrates so generously should in ten years have worked a greater self-acceptance than the continued tone of self-accusation betrayed in the *Confessions*. Yet this tone would be more understandable were Augustine constitutionally unable really to accuse himself. And this Pruyser suggests is the case: "Indeed, very little guilt feeling is expressed directly."[24] Is it that Augustine tended to view himself in his past (and present) activities rather than simply acknowledge That was/is *me*? Were he so unable to present himself available for forgiveness, continued self-reproach in the face of forgiveness believed would be that much more understandable.

---

22. Woollcott, "Some Considerations of Creativity," 278.
23. Pruyser, "Psychological Examination: Augustine," 288–89.
24. Ibid., 288.

Pruyser's reading would also account for the emphasis Augustine places on the necessarily complementary prayers: "Master me, God!" and "Thank you for allowing me to live with your life and to love with your love." In response to Dittes's surrender theory, I would insist that Augustine's theology of grace is compatible with either or both of these attitudes, although we find the first more prominent in his writings, especially in the *Confessions*. There is further evidence to show that this incapacity to acknowledge his own sinfulness quite simply and directly is linked with a lingering unwillingness to surrender, still present at the time of writing the *Confessions*. I suggest this interpretation in view of the obvious stoic ideal of self-control operating as he assesses his present state in book 10. Predilection for such an ideal would certainly characterize the indulgent child, precisely because self-control suffered such frequent defeats. To speak in this way, of course, demands a more subtle use of "surrender" than Dittes's simple opposition with "autonomy." Yet the ability to use "surrender" in this fashion is another argument for a more relative employment of that opposition.

BEYOND EXPLANATIONS TO INTERPRETATION

It should be clear by now that a simple application of orthodox psychoanalytic doctrine does not prove very useful in understanding Augustine. However some degree of illumination has certainly been offered by the preliminary attempts available to us. By illuminating the sources and shape of his personal conflicts, this style of investigation allows a sensitive reader to remark how Augustine managed to put those conflicts to use, as well as how they continued to handicap him. A similarly sensitive reader with theological training will be able to recognize in many cases how these conflicts may have introduced specific distortions into the manner of formulating and illustrating major themes in Christian theology. Precisely because the theologian, and above all this theologian, is so intimately involved in his work, studies of this sort seem a hermeneutic necessity.

On the other hand, the main intent of his major theological breakthroughs is hardly deflected. I am thinking particularly of his staunch anti-Pelagian position and its crucial role in the history of doctrine. For one can grasp the heart of this series of affirmations announcing the primacy and sufficiency of God's grace in a form which remains quite neutral to the manner in which we conceive God: that the standards of human excellence no longer conform to a pattern which we might conceive, but rather are themselves transformed to the point where no patterns are left (13.22).

Nor need we be worried that Augustine "describes a mystical ecstatic experience he shares with his mother . . . in rhythm, flow, and imagery [which] strike the reader as passionately orgastic."[25] For what other language can a human being employ? Furthermore, our critical reading of the psychological critics confirms that a religious and psychological viewpoint are hardly incompatible, if such confirmation were necessary. (One would have thought that viewpoint-language offers itself precisely to suggest compatibility, but one of the writers in the symposium finds it "evident that Augustine's life cannot be viewed through both perspectives simultaneously without contradiction."[26] The discussion here is a response in content as well as in form to such a contention.) Yet we were able to acknowledge that the two viewpoints, religious and psychological, were compatible specifically by showing how psychological explanations are most useful when clipped of their endemic pretentions to completeness.

In fact, the central methodological principle of Augustine's *Confessions* has proven useful in assessing assessments of it. That is, if we recall, that we should be misled in our quest for understanding were we simply to rely on our efforts to identify the conceptual frameworks he is employing by tracing down the major influences upon his thought. Beyond this historical sophistication, we are asked to become more and more conscious of the manner in which he put the frameworks which he had to use. The simplest way to awaken this consciousness is to become more responsible in employing the interpretative frameworks which we possess. The inspiration comes from Augustine; we can only hope to bring our human quest for understanding to term by engaging our all-too-human selves upon it. This means trusting the insights we are given and not fearing to take up a form of life consonant with the formulation we give those insights. Living consistently with the consequences of these words made flesh will invite and guide whatever correction becomes necessary.

In matters religious, understanding demands that we attempt to live what we are trying to speak. The demand is a logical one, and is borne in upon anyone the moment he realizes that man has no way of speaking straightforwardly and coherently of God. Augustine's conscious manner of constructing the *Confessions* displays this demand of logic and provides some practical hints how to carry it out. Hence in its role as a work of edification, the *Confessions* succeeds in laying out an epistemology as well. The task of this essay has been to remove some of the obstacles that may have prevented us from laying hold of what Augustine is doing. Some of the

---

25. Kligerman, "Psychoanalytic Study of the *Confessions*," 483.
26. Havens, "Notes on Augustine's *Confessions*," 143.

difficulties arise from ourselves; some reflect flaws in his execution of the project.

And since the project extends through word to flesh, locating certain obstacles to understanding amounts to identifying weaknesses in Augustine himself.[27] Need we remind ourselves that we are in a position to make this identification precisely in the measure that Augustine has proven faithful to his own epistemological demands? Yet whether we are reminded or not, these results in fact enhance the *Confessions* as a hymn of thanksgiving and praise to the Creator who revealed himself in Jesus: "I have cheerfully made up my mind to be proud of my weaknesses, because they mean a deeper experience of the power of Christ" (2 Cor 12:9). Although Augustine does not seem to be able to bring himself to speak these words with the alacrity of a Paul, he acknowledges their force in undertaking the *Confessions* and displays that force in executing them. By a rigorous application of his own epistemology, we should have expected the *Confessions* to show even more than they are able to say.

---

27. Especially relevant here are the latter chapters of Brown's study, *Augustine of Hippo*, as Augustine exercises more and more authority as bishop, against a background of crumbling Roman authority.

Chapter 13

Religious Life and Understanding

ONE OF THE MOST crucial battles of our present and recent past rages about understanding. A rebellious few have been goading college and university for the past few decades, accusing them of replacing understanding with knowledge. When the president of one of our "great universities" announced that the sum total of knowledge had doubled within the past decade, the rebellious few were joined by a rebellious many, who questioned the legitimacy of any educational institution whatsoever. The irony here—the biting if not tragic irony—is that the rebellious many were quite obviously the products of an educational system which had indeed sold out education in favor of accumulating knowledge. Yet beyond the slogans and the instant overexposure of the media, there are some who would renew our faith in understanding, and do so by the witness of their lives and writings. This effort dare not take the form of a campaign, but can make its point only by manifesting an ever more personal dedication and grasp of what it is one is about. So the socio-political situation adds a poignant urgency to a developing realization that understanding is nothing less than a style of life, a surrender to one's personal destiny.

In a further bit of irony, disaffection with higher education has shifted that peculiar mode of understanding that we call *religious* into a rather privileged position. To be sure, many of those people who call themselves religious would not engage in this sort of understanding, but that need not detain us here. The central point of these reflections will be an attempt to display a mode of understanding which one might properly call religious.

I shall undertake this from a frankly philosophical perspective, but one which remains conscious that philosophic reason also stands in need of illumination. My own conviction holds that attempts of men to delineate the mode of understanding called religious have often been most useful in recalling us to that style of living called philosophic. I think this will prove to be more and more true today, as we try to understand what it means to do philosophy after its demise has been announced and celebrated.

The fact that we live in a post-philosophical as well as a post-religious era demands a fresh approach. We have been accustomed, in studies of this sort, to take either philosophy or religion to be something given, and then to seek some rapprochement between the two. Yet neither philosophy nor religion is a thing to be studied—except abstractly and academically as a form of knowledge. But each does aspire to a style of life, and one which traditionally and presently has much to gain from the other.

In fact, as the case has often been before, the sort of reflective awareness about our own understanding and the lack thereof which a conscious study and practice of religion forces upon us, may well provide the necessary catalyst for finding our way to some form of philosophic understanding. For I take Richard Taylor to be correct when he announces in concert with Wittgenstein and others that "the philosopher's claim to philosophical knowledge is a pretense."[1] Taylor catalogues in sufficient detail the various ways in which this pretense can earn a living, but this fact merely testifies once more to the sell-out of college and university to knowledge in favor of understanding.

It is interesting in a corroborative sort of way that a clarion call of some leading German thinkers in religion now centers about understanding, or as they would call it, *hermeneutic*. The appeal is clearly for a mode and style of reflection which can help an inquiring spirit recover that quality of awareness which incorporates a highly personal understanding of where it is that he himself stands. And where he is going. In reflecting on the roles understanding might play in matters of religion, the image of a pilgrimage spontaneously comes to mind. For it is an archetypal religious image of life: a journey with a goal quite out of the ordinary, freighted with expectation, carrying the promise of transformation. Yet the narration concerns itself not with the goal but with the way there. Intelligence, human intelligence, functions along the way and functions best when it eschews the temptation to map out the entire project, and contents itself with plotting how to take the next step. On this view, understanding serves man best when it places itself at the service of life. In its critical and interpretative role, it will

---

1. Taylor, "Dare to Be Wise," 615.

always be at work evaluating overall conceptions of life—directions taken in the journey—but it does not pretend to construct these so much as to understand them: to guide one in the way of living by them, assessing them, critically espousing or rejecting them.

There are other roles, certainly, that have been advanced for reason in human life. In stark contrast to the one I have sketched above, which operates *within* a mythic context, is a more overtly explanatory one which seeks to replace the enchanted journey with one mapped out. It will be my contention that this ingression of scientific reason into the way we live our lives is an inversion of priorities, and gains its plausibility by preempting all critical powers to itself. On the contrary, I shall try to show how reason can be appropriately critical in an ancillary function, and in fact more effectively critical, for it is freed from the business of constructing alternative myths and defending its own constructions. Three of the authors I shall consider illustrate this contention in diverse ways: Johann, Preller, and Fackenheim; and one Neville, demonstrates it eloquently in spite of himself.

JOHANN

The least pretentious of these books best introduces us to a style and use of reason in human affairs that comes closest to what we might wish to call understanding at the service of life. Robert Johann has collected a series of essays on quite occasional topics to illustrate his most basic contention about the role of intelligence in human life.[2] Taking his cues and many of his quotes from Dewey, but employing them in a fashion characteristically his own, he reminds us again and again of the simple yet exigent manner in which we ask intelligence to show the way—even when, and especially when, we no longer demand that it build us a world.

Johann renders the religious dilemma with deftness: to absolutize the particular is superstition and idolatry; to refuse to particularize the Absolute is to deprive it of practical bearing. Religion then is either dehumanizing or without significance, an impediment to human progress or a waste of time. Either way, man is better off without it (181). The irony is that "atheism as a way of life not only is compatible with a theistic interpretation of human creativity but can even be construed as demanded by it. Any effort to move theism from theory to practice seems bound to further estrange us from God's reality" (185).

---

2. Johann, *Building the Human*. [Ed. note: In-text citations in this section are to page numbers in Johann's work.]

Johann exhibits a keen grasp of dialectic as well as a feel for much of the concrete frustration of his fellow men with religion. His own way of meeting the dilemma is twofold. One is to recall what he himself sketches in these pages and elsewhere: that the "inherent ideal of the personal is a universal community of persons which can be conceived and actually intended only as a response to a transcendent initiative. In other words, the common recognition and celebration of God's reality is a prerequisite for the full realization of personal life" (186).

Johann never really *argues* this point, except to propose that some sort of "communal acknowledgement of the Transcendent" is the only thing powerful enough to "keep man from worshipping idols" (186). And perhaps there is no other argument available. Here again Johann exhibits a style of life which is superbly open and free, willing to listen and to find illumination from any quarter, and so demonstrating something of the resilience of the source whence his reflective understanding flows and which it ever seeks to make more available for others.

Something is flawed, however, about Johann's idiom and mode of presentation. He would explain his own manner by stating that "intelligence is our responsive encounter with Being itself" (187). Hence analysis remains at the service of communion. Yet communion is not always possible nor always to be sought. And "being" hardly illuminates what Johann is searching for or responding to. Nowhere does he show us why that name is better than another; seldom does he delineate the dialectical character of *response*, which could help us discriminate one invitation from another.

In short, Johann's movement of thought is always freighted with implicit norms—more weightily, that is, than that of most of the rest of us. His own style and manner cries out that intelligence should help us all carry these burdens more easily and more responsibly. Yet he does not tarry with us long enough to let us see how it is that he lives so easily with them, how it is that norms and the normative provision rather than burden a journey. There are gaps here of which Johann needs to become more aware, for his sake as well as for ours. The clue to my judgment lies in the language: "being" comes in too quickly and too cavalierly to do the job that is asked of it. And my judgment is backed, appropriately enough, by the manner which Johann proposes for understanding. What is demanded is that his manner become more explicitly itself, that he go on to exhibit in a more perspicuous form what he wants to say and already knows cannot be said.

Before going on to assess the other authors, I should give a summary statement of my own norms for rendering the sort of judgment I have of Johann. Perhaps the quickest way of stating them is to acknowledge how much my own understanding of understanding, especially matters religious, has been powerfully informed by Kierkegaard, and given shape by Wittgenstein. Lest some feel this to be a strange combination, let me insist that there is a Kierkegaard which many who think they know him seem quite unaware of. That is the Kierkegaard of powerful philosophic acumen, the man who actually carried out the sort of dialectic which to the end of his life Hegel continued to talk about. This is a Kierkegaard whom those reading him a few decades ago under the shadow of the Barthian *nein!* were neither predisposed nor often equipped to recognize. The leap remains, but is not longer celebrated for its own sake. The focus is rather on a dialectic powerful and sensitive enough to bring one to the point where he can execute the kind of personal maneuver which Kierkegaard finds himself calling a leap. By that time, whoever executes it will also understand why the leap is more efficacious and more radical when one succeeds in landing in the same place whence he leapt.

Bodying forth as he does the inherently paradoxical character of religious understanding, together with its multiple and perspectival exercises, Kierkegaard witnesses more to a supple intellect at the service of faith than to a cavalier despair of understanding. The role of that intellect was many-sided and reflective, and of course humorous. Which is to say that Kierkegaard's intelligence was at the service of something else—a longing, a quest, a love affair.[3] And many of the same things can be said of another judged neurotic, Wittgenstein. Here too intelligence is at the service of something else. For life is not composed of problems, as though we relied on the problem-solvers to build us an environment in which we could live. It is rather problems that block our living and our understanding, and the specialized role of intelligence which undoes its own kinks and makes straight its own path can never represent understanding in its full *élan*. Wittgenstein would probably not have endorsed the image of a leap, but would certainly have understood why, if one felt compelled to adopt it, the most beautiful and transcendent leap of all would be one which landed a person in the very same place. For however wide the arc of understanding may swing, it is always an effort to understand where I stand. The searchings about for an appropriate idiom—call it primal thinking, linguistic phenomenology, or whatever—are guided principally by this requirement: it must render more perspicuous where it is I stand and illuminate the way from here.

---

3. One of the most lucid expositions is Holmer, "Kierkegaard and Philosophy."

PRELLER

In *Divine Science and the Science of God* Victor Preller executes a reformulation of Aquinas in terms of a contemporary linguistic awareness, specifically in terms of Wilfrid Sellars's epistemology.[4] The immediate effect is to pinpoint a line of demarcation between myth and metaphysics, between what can be said and what must be shown, or (in Kierkegaard's terms) between aesthetics and dialectic proper. In this respect, Preller's approach is remarkably contemporary, for he shows how Aquinas can help to clarify by example today's concern with method, hermeneutic, and the decision about an appropriate language. It is significant that Preller locates the line of demarcation between myth and metaphysics in Aquinas by subjecting his work to a quite complete reformulation. Whether or not the result is Aquinas may be endlessly discussed. The linguistic reformulation brings into striking relief this writer's researches into Aquinas on naming God, and there seems no other norm with which to judge an interpretation except the "measure of exactitude, extent and light" which it brings to bear upon the statements of the author being elucidated.[5] Perhaps Preller's work will help some to understand, nonetheless, the appeal which Aquinas has for those who have experienced his logical and semantic tutelage. This is extensively illustrated as Preller brings his writings under the severe scrutiny of reformulation into an idiom of high semantic sophistication, and the joints appear in the statements of Aquinas. His writings not only sustain such an analysis but the reconstruction illuminates his original statements.

Preller's hermeneutical task is to bring Aquinas's numerous assertions about our knowledge of God, namely that we cannot know Him, into harmony with the plethora of assertions which he makes about God. What does he intend by stating, for example, that God exists, is one, eternal, and the rest—and further clarifying that these predicates are here stated of God himself, yet insisting withal that "all of our *affirmations* have the effect of signifying to *us* how God is *not*" (175—*ST* 1.3.intro)? And furthermore, can we *show* what it is which Aquinas intends from the context of the assertions themselves? Do his convictions about not-knowing actually shape his theology, or is there a fatal discrepancy between stated method and the method employed? Is this, as some have argued, an irreconcilable strain in Aquinas—say, between the philosopher and the mystic? Or was he relatively

---

4. Preller, *Divine Science and the Science of God*. [Ed. note: In-text citations in this section are to page numbers in Preller's work. Passages from Aquinas are provided within the text as well.]

5. Cf. my own "Aquinas on Naming God" (no need for pages numbers here) and on interpreting Aquinas: Lonergan, *Verbum*, 181.

all of one piece? And if so, how can he say one thing and then go on to do another—such as compose all those articles in the *Summa* (*ST* 1.3–26) which purport to tell us so much about God, and form the source of what many know as "classical theism"?

The question: what does Aquinas intend by his assertions? it is worth noting, already intimates a distinction between myth and metaphysics, between what is said and what is intended. Otherwise the question could not even arise. That there might be a difference is suggested by Aquinas's explicit statements about what can and cannot be known or said about God. That there *is* a difference is the burden of Preller's study.

The interpretative key is found in what Aquinas does with the "proofs" (*ST* 1.2) as well as the manner in which he speaks so affirmatively about God in the face of his own reflective remarks about our inability to say anything at all about Him. Preller argues that the affirmations in *Summa Theologiae* 1.3–26 are vacuous when regarded as philosophical assertions, yet Aquinas is within his rights to assert them in the *theological* context in which he does. We are misled only when we fail to recognize that Aquinas's project is explicitly theological, and doubly misled if we expect philosophy to do more than he himself demanded of it. Speaking loosely, it can supply the logical form but not the content for theological assertions.

It is question two—the "proof" schemata—which has always suggested that Aquinas expected too much from reason. Preller adopts a strongly contextual reading of this question as a chapter in a theological treatise, and notes in detail how none of the schemata offered will do the job apparently intended. Yet he also notes how Aquinas pushes each schema to point beyond the question at issue to the existential question. Within the context of questions 3–26, Preller has Aquinas saying in question 2: if there were a God (which I believe there is) our way to understanding him would be as the explanation for anything's existing. Yet the fact that something exists is not the sort of fact we can get at directly. Hence all the hints—from motion, contingency, order, and the rest. Furthermore, since "... exists," when used in this radical way, is not a concept within our language but makes reference to the language's being applied or not, whatever explained it would be radically unknown and unknowable to us.

Yet we are able nonetheless to expose the logic of the notion:

> Thus, to say that God "exists" is to say that there is another conceptual system (an ideal language) in terms of which a syntactical move isomorphic in usage with our syntactically significant existential assertion ("—") could be used in conjunction with an entity radically unlike the entities which are existentially

> assertable in our language.... If our analysis of the essentially analogous status of "exists" was correct, we could know that the world could in theory have uses other than those which are significant in terms of our conceptual system. To say that God "exists" in some unknown sense of the word is not necessarily irrational. (173)

The exercise of the "proofs" leads to the plausibility of an enterprise which might otherwise look utterly ridiculous: to outline the syntactical structure of a language which—were anyone able to use it—would explain why there is something rather than nothing.

Questions 3–26, viewed in their character as philosophical exercises, are designed to convince us that we could know something of how such a language functioned even though it is not in our possession. (Try this as a translation of the manner in which metaphysics represents man's aspiration yet always escapes being a human science, how it was said to participate in a higher wisdom, offer glimpses of an order sought after but not accessible to us.) For while

> to say that God "exists" is to say that there *is* a conceptual framework in terms of which the proposition "God exists" would be intelligible, it is nevertheless true that the proposition is *not* intelligible in terms of *our* conceptual framework, and thus, insofar as the word "exists" plays an intrasystematic role in our language, it must be *denied* of God. (174)

This leads Preller to speak of Aquinas's self-conscious statements about God as "hard" paradoxes for

> I can tell you in what sense I am *denying* a word of God, but I cannot tell you in what sense I am *affirming* it. I can only tell you the *reason* that I affirm it, and why the affirmation is not irrational. (174)

Now the reason Aquinas affirms that God "exists" is that the existence of the world would otherwise be radically unintelligible. This is the general thrust of each of the proof schemata. (Preller of course notes that the demand for intelligibility itself outreaches any single formulation, so the "proofs" take hold only at that point where one sees he must make a decision about the horizons of his inquiry [172].) Yet the statement intends to refer to God himself, not the relation of creator to its world. The *way* in which it signifies remains totally opaque (*modus significandi*), but the possibility of applying it remains open. The reason is a logical one:

> Terms such as "good" or "intention" may be given a transcendental use such that they *must* appear in the meta-language of any conceptual system in terms of which reality is rendered intelligible. Nonetheless, when they are hypothetically and analogically applied to *other* conceptual systems, the meaning that they have in *our* conceptual system (where they *also* play an intrasystematic role) must be denied. Thus, while Aquinas denies in article two of question thirteen of the first part of the *Summa* that all of our statements about God are purely negative or used to signify the relation between God and the world, he nevertheless claims that all of our affirmations have the effect of signifying *to us* how God is *not*. (175)

This sophisticated semantic pattern provides Aquinas with a simple schema for the dark knowing of faith. What faith offers is a partial, tenuous hold on this language. Not that a man of faith can use it confidently or even straightforwardly—as preachers soon find out. But the *way* in which he uses it to make within it the assertions he can *displays* something of the hold he has on it—and so suggests that it is not an utterly vacuous language for him. That he finds some application for the language is not demonstrated by his turning up a referent, but in the deftness with which he uses it and in his ability to bring it to bear upon certain dimensions of our experience in a manner which genuinely illuminates.

Although there is much familiar to the student of Aquinas in Preller's rendition, the fact remains that he has laid out the issues surrounding man's knowing and speaking about God with a sophistication only possible after the linguistic turn. In this way, Preller offers us a model for reading classical figures in contemporary terms. For by recasting Aquinas in the linguistic mode, he brings to startling clarity the coherence and semantic genius in Aquinas's God-talk, unseats many a Thomistic accommodation, and displays a coherent and persuasive model for relating reason and faith by displaying the role reason plays in constructing a language which can be used only by one who believes.

I suggested at the outset of this section that Preller succeeded in demarcating a line between myth and metaphysics. Since I regard this as the most significant result of the work, I would like to draw upon the preceding summary to make it a little clearer. In the first place, most of us are probably convinced by now that we shall never free ourselves of myth, and some might even be so converted as to welcome that fact, wondering why anyone ever thought he should be. And what is true of human life itself is *a fortiori* true of that aspect of life—religious life—which also seeks to comprehend it. To think oneself to be freed from myth is to be in bondage to another. The only way "out" is the way of critical awareness: to appreciate myth as myth, by understanding its impulse—that we *have* to try to say what cannot be said—and by assessing its role of providing a form of thought for our epoch. In this sense of the term, the organization plan of the *Summa* itself reflects a myth of all things emanating from God and returning to him through their efficacy. Since this is the overall plan, it determines to some extent which questions will be taken up, and certainly affects the responses given to some of them as well.

By "myth," then, I mean an overall schema of intelligibility, a pattern for explanatory predilections. Like a familiar background, these are hard to heave into view, and usually appear most evidently when an alternative emerges—normally, to a later age. Hence Whitehead's suggestive term of an epochal form of thought. Metaphysics, I should contend, does not conceive of itself as spinning out such schemes, but simply exercises critical watch over them. In this basic sense metaphysics is not a science, for it does not concern itself with objects as the sciences do, but is rather an activity pure and critical. The evidence that it is misleading to class metaphysics with the sciences—even if we make it the most general of them all—emerges from the effort to construe it as one. This would involve listing the principles whereby it criticizes, spelling out its criteria. But the "criteria" of a critical, metaphysical awareness turn out to be paradoxical. For they cannot themselves be *stated* without their own formulation being subject to criticism. This is the point which Wittgenstein saw so clearly and formulated in the *Tractatus*: "My propositions serve as elucidations in the following way: anyone who understands *me* eventually recognizes *them* as nonsensical, *when* he has used them—as steps—to climb up beyond them" (emphasis added.)[6] The constitutive principles of metaphysics must be, if anything, *self-evident*. But not in an ocular Cartesian sense but more after the manner of Hegel: these "principles" are constitutive of the inquirer himself, and the more consciously he becomes just that—an inquirer—the more aware he is of how he is constituted.

The metaphysical point, then, would be the desired fixed point from which relative epochal forms of thought could be assessed. And so "it" is. Not in the desired way however; fixed and attainable; but in an utterly *necessary* way. That is, there must be some point from which these touted forms of thought are seen to be relative and can be recognized in their role of informing an epoch, for something must account for the assessments which we find ourselves rendering. And the structure of a critical assessment shows what I can and cannot mean by a "metaphysical standpoint,"

---

6. Wittgenstein, *Tractatus*, 6.54.

for it allows us to discriminate the mythical from the metaphysical in *that* statement. The reference to a metaphysical standpoint is mythical in so far as it implies a position from which the ensuing judgment need not be an explicitly critical one. For if the position were construed on the simple model of a privileged viewpoint, then the resulting assessment would not be a genuinely critical one, since it would not consciously call in one's own position for self-scrutiny. In other words, what resulted would not be an *assessment* at all, but simply a better look. (One thinks of Kant's privileged access which allowed him to select just the categories he did and no others.) Yet when the statement about a metaphysical standpoint simply implies (in a consciously metaphorical way) the fact that we do make assessments and hence are in possession of critical ways of using our intelligence—ways which bring myself into question as well as the object of my inquiry—then we are making a consciously critical metaphysical statement (in this case about metaphysics itself).

If there are any metaphysical statements, then, they will be at once first and second-level statements, for in *stating* something about something they will also be *showing* why what is said must be said and nothing more. Perhaps it would be more accurate to say that we can recognize a genuinely metaphysical statement only by the manner in which it is used—the context in which it is employed, the things that are said and those that are not said, etc. For these factors are what guide the employment of a proposition, and in the case of a metaphysical statement, would allow it to show—in the way in which something is said about something—what can and cannot be said. These observations simply dramatize the fact that metaphysics is not a science but an activity. For a science can be adequately if not imaginatively characterized by listing its key propositions, as any textbook does.

To document this point: when we do string out the very same statements which might have been employed metaphysically but instead simply state them as though they constituted a scheme of sorts, what results is a myth. The form of the statements will necessarily be quite general, since the key terms will be those which reflect the shape of the conceptual framework itself, so the result of their being taken in a straightforward affirmative manner will be a purported description of the general features of the world. And this, of course, is what myth is and does.

What discriminates myth from metaphysics, then, is not the form of the statements but their use. The metaphysician uses them so as to exploit the fact that they are inherently unstable—that is, can be properly (or metaphysically) used only by someone who is aware of their dual yet integrated role: to state in such a way as to show what cannot be stated. This way of putting the issues might illuminate what Hegel kept insisting about "dialectical understanding" and why it alone is commensurate with doing metaphysics. What is at stake is a consciously critical use of proposition over against a simple asserting of it.

What is so welcome about Preller's Aquinas here is that he lays out a theory of knowing which articulates this understanding of metaphysics in a way which makes it possible to discriminate what is said in God-statements from the intent. For *what is said* yields a picture: e.g., the emanation-return scheme of the *Summa* itself, or the picture of God as one, eternal, simple, and the rest. The intent, however, displays the intellectual exigencies operating in any statement about God. Exigencies like transcendence, for example, which lead Aquinas to say, in the Aristotelian form of thought, that God cannot belong to any category, even that of substance, since he is the source of all things. The "since" here reflects not a yet more general picture of what transcendence is like, but purely and simply the logical demands ingredient in a critical assessment of this sort. And these demands elicit our attention, whatever the fate of the prevailing myth or epochal form of thought.

Let me illustrate this by invoking a myth popular in philosophy of religion. The myth is called "classical theism," and represents a picture consonant with the statements of Aquinas (especially in *ST* 1.3–26) taken as descriptions of the general features of God. Was Aquinas himself a "classical theist"? We have no access to the picture he preferred, but we can be certain, after Preller's analysis, that what is called "classical theism" does not represent Aquinas's "doctrine of God," precisely because he did not present anything purporting to describe the general features of God. Nor can one insist, thanks to Preller's logical clarity, that "classical theism" is a logical consequence (or a concrete understanding) of Aquinas's more austere presentation. For if anything, it represents a misunderstanding of the role of theological statements as he understood and employed them. That many people did this is evident; that Aquinas is responsible runs counter to the evidence here. And what is important about this point is not the assigning of blame, but a greater clarity about the role of philosophical and theological understanding.

In summary, Preller makes clear in an unprecedented way what Aquinas meant when he insisted that "metaphysics transcends imagination." For it consists not of a body of assertions but of attempts to articulate the posture of one engaged in understanding critically and consciously. (Think of Wittgenstein in the *Tractatus* and his degree of awareness of what he is about.) Hence metaphysics does not set out to state anything about anything. But the imagination must be fed. That is the role of myth. Hence one who understands metaphysics as the activity that it is does not depreciate myth. Nor does he pass over another's attempt to do metaphysics by treating his critical assertions as statements about the world, or on the other hand, by trying to pass off myth as metaphysics himself. The distinction is not a formal but a functional one. It can be sustained only by noting the degree of critical self-awareness an author displays. Preller has shown how useful a linguistic reformulation can be in bringing this factor of self-awareness to light. For it seems to be reflected normally in one's logical acumen and feel for the limits of language.

I have often referred to Preller's Aquinas to avoid the question of historical interpretation as well as to circumvent a pervasive prejudice about "classical" authors, namely that they could not possibly evince as much self-awareness as Preller's Aquinas does. Let me say simply that I do feel that one can meet the question of what Aquinas meant, by exposing his writings in a manner which is consistent and illuminating. If what he meant is up for understanding, then the most illuminating understanding of it wins out. There simply is no other way of adjudicating the issue of meaning, though of course one may always feel a need to do some more textual work. The prejudice, however, is more tenacious. To expose it, we must first note that "classical" is a typology of ours, not of the classical authors. Hence it is we—not they—who find it necessary to conceive what we read "classically" when we read them. The pleasure of great books seminars consists largely in people discovering how contemporary classical authors really are. One hoped-for result of so exposing an intellectual prejudice would be the warning: don't feel constrained to conceive classical authors classically. Yet the world is full of warnings. An object lesson would work much better. Fortunately we have one at hand.

NEVILLE

Robert Neville's *God the Creator* is closely packed with fine print and elaborate argument.[7] Perhaps that should be a warning that it is not meant so much to provision a journey as to relieve us of the need to make one. In fact Neville's style and argument do not lead us on to an understanding appropriate to one searching out some light on his God, but rather into a curiosity shop of classical problems. To be sure, it seems to be the house where Neville dwells, and it is elegantly wrought, but the issues about which he discourses seem rather to hang like trophies on a wall than to breathe the air of live adventure. One has the feeling that any issue could be domesticated here, and if there were not space enough, a room could be jiffy-built.

7. Neville, *God the Creator: On the Transcendence and Presence of God*. [Ed. note: In-text citations in this section are to page numbers in Neville's work.]

What grounds these impressions? Certainly nothing lacking in the author's classical knowledge nor his incisive and fine-grained power of argument. In fact, he succeeds in making many a classical point better than the classical authors themselves, and makes not a few of his own. Perhaps the flaw lies here: undertaken in a style grander than the grand masters themselves, this work is more reminiscent of a John of Saint Thomas than of an Aquinas. Neville's presentation shares little of the tentative and probing character of Aristotle's metaphysics, and none of Plato's irony. And in its efforts to reconcile and harmonize the classical patterns of thinking, it proceeds in a magisterial commentary style which appears to be innocent of either the critical turn executed by Kant or the critical-linguistic turn proposed and demonstrated by Wittgenstein.

The style and approach is captured in Neville's explicit aim: to reweave the fabric of thought (306). It is as though philosophy were a toga which houselled one through life, and Neville's arguments could persuade us to indwell there. But perhaps that is what philosophy is. What right have I to represent Neville's effort to weave a covering garment as though the very enterprise were flawed? Am I simply airing my own predilection for a lightly clad, pilgrim life? Let us try to locate the flaw in Neville's approach, and locate it in such a way as to exhibit the superiority of the approach I am proposing.

Neville sets out to establish that being is a common property—although he would not want it put that way. Yet his results amount to the same thing, for he begins his critique of analogy as an inference ticket precisely in order to show that one can only speak responsibly of being when he is speaking univocally (19, 42). His argument for a univocal ground of any analogical predication proceeds as follows: two things cannot differ in the sense in which they are what they are. This is understandable enough, but the *sense* in which Neville wants to establish something's being what it is turns out to be being-itself. He clarifies this usage of "being-itself" as the "ontological one that unifies the many determinations of being" (21). This will allow him to name God as "the univocal being-itself that is common to creatures" (21n12).

However pretentious the language, Neville's intent is quite clear: unless being *is* something, the route to God as final explainer is jeopardized. A theory of analogy is always in danger of evaporating substantive issues into language. And if anything is an issue at all for Neville, it is a substantive issue. So he could not object to my enlisting Aristotle's aid to look a little more closely at the apparent truism: two things cannot differ in the sense in which they are what they are.

Aristotle executed one of his now classic emancipations from Platonic realism by noting that the *sense* in which something is what it is or has what it has cannot itself be said or spelled out in any straightforward way. The only way we can grasp anything so intimate to the whole business of predication as the "sense in which something is what it is" would be to capture it as it is displayed by the form of the predications in question. And this Aristotle set out to do by articulating from the logic of predication, for example, how the formal implications issuing from qualitative predication differ from those attendant on substantial predication. Thus, from "Socrates is a man" and "man is an animal" we may conclude "Socrates is an animal"; whereas "Socrates is white" together with "white is a color" yields nothing.

By this simple yet genial maneuver, Aristotle succeeds in displaying what cannot be said—namely, the *sense* in which something is what it is. This sense can be given a name—substantial or qualitative—only if we have *shown* what those expressions mean by displaying a difference in the formal structure of the statements embodying these diverse ways of being. Ontological issues are rooted in the world, and ontological questions rise from wonder, but most if not all of what can be said in response to them must be displayed by uncovering differences in the logical forms of the typical statements involved. In this sense, *logos* and *eidos* are connected, and mind is at the heart of reality.

What does all this say to Neville? Simply that Aristotle could and did explicate his truism in an extremely illuminating way, and one which allowed him to speak of *being* without requiring that he be talking about *something*—paradoxical though that may sound. For if "being" is shorthand for "the sense in which something is what it is," and if that *sense* cannot be said but can only be grasped by displaying the form of the typical statements involved, then *being* simply does not fit *in* the predication routine. Since the sense in which something is what it is cannot be said of it, a fortiori nothing can be said about that sense. So "being" cannot serve in either a subject or in a predicate position.

This is why, on Aristotle's interpretation, being cannot be a ground, nor can we speak of determinations of being—as we can, for example, determinations of color (24). The best we can do is to display them, as Aristotle discriminated substantial from accidental predication by displaying the differences. Paradoxically, being is not itself anything, for if it cannot be said of anything else—either property-wise or genus-wise—it cannot itself have properties or belong to a genus.

All that we have recalled does not yet make an argument but simply propounds an alternative, albeit paradoxical position. For Neville explicitly takes another route from Aristotle. But since there are so many Aristotles, it is useful to have a clear picture of what I regard as a viable alternative to Neville before showing that his way of speaking about being cannot avoid the pitfalls carefully mapped out by Aristotle. For Neville proposes to skirt what he calls the dilemma of ontology by asserting some things about being itself, specifically that it is necessarily univocal and also indeterminate. The dilemma of ontology is familiar enough:

> On the one hand, being-itself must be ubiquitous; absolutely everything has it in one mode or another, and nothing lacks it.... On the other hand, any positive or determinate characterization of being-itself must have a significant contrast term to be meaningful. This is true *even if the determinate characterization is that being-itself is indeterminate*. (40, emphasis added)

Neville avoids the dilemma only by failing to appreciate the logical sophistication imbedded in it. He continues innocently on the same path which forced him to conclude the univocity of being on the grounds of its being a ground: *the* sense in which everything is what it is. He goes on to conclude that it must be an indeterminate ground. The argument proceeds according to standard onto-logic and is designed of course to avoid the stated dilemma. Yet many of those who locked horns with this dilemma through the ages were quite adept at logic, and perhaps the reason they did not propose Neville's way out was that none of them could bring himself to *state* that being is indeterminate. And since these onto-logicians were certainly not hamstrung by criteria of empirical verification, it must have been that they recognized the proposed statement as a non-statement.

For it follows from Neville's straightforward treatment of determination that to say that something is indeterminate is a way of remarking that we cannot *say* anything about it. For to say that something is determinate only serves to announce that we know something about it, that the expression standing in for it can assume the subject place in a well-formed sentence. So insisting that something is indeterminate denies this possibility, and thereby reveals itself to be a self-defeating statement. For the statement "being is indeterminate" employs the most serviceable form we have for conveying that something is determinate—the subject-predicate form—to deny what the form itself displays.

This contradictory result suggests why the medieval logicians so exercised in onto-logic found it more perspicuous to observe that the predicate form of "to be" is systematically ambiguous: namely, that its subject form can take no classifying predicate. In other words, the expression standing for being cannot properly function as a subject in any sentence. For if being cannot be classified, it certainly cannot be modified adjectivally. The very best we can say is that 'being' is analogous, where the single quotes remind us that we are not talking about an *it* but about a predicate, a use, a linguistic role—and one of a very special sort. Yet if language is a way of life, then we are quite beyond verbal play, or games, in any superficial sense of that word. So this tack does not carry us away from reality, as some still believe, but moves us towards it by calling forth from us an understanding of ourselves—as language users.

By recalling us to reflect on the ways in which we use language and can or cannot shape it to our needs, we can expose the traditional metaphysical questions for what they are: probings into the world as a world for us, as intelligible. Here lie the common roots of Kant's critical revolution, the linguistic turn, and Heidegger's primal thinking—if I might be permitted a seminal phrase. Neville bypasses what looks to him to be a detour through the inquiring subject, a linguistic turn or a reflective reversal, and ends up permanently detoured in a world of non-statements masquerading as affirmations—like "being is indeterminate."

Part two—purportedly critical—in fact yields more of the same, this time under the rubric of explanation. We are offered a "cosmogonic ideal of system" which pretends to "include the explanation of the first principles per se" (151). Neville is perfectly aware that the primary role which first principles play in any explanatory endeavor demands some unusual moves if we wish to explain *them*. In fact, he wants to move to a creator: an indeterminate principle of the primary determinations called unities or harmonies. But since he fails to appreciate the logical differences between asking "why does $x\,y$?" and "why are harmonious patterns harmonious?" the subsequent onto-logical affirmations are rendered suspect. For asking why a unity is a unity is not asking for an explanation so much as it is posing a question for reflection. It is like asking why an explanation explains. Plato succeeded in exhibiting questions like these for what they are—questions for reflection—by actually reflecting the answer to them into the very structure and movement of some of the dialogues. Neville's response overlooks this feel for a reflective question, and proposes a straightforward "cosmogonic explanation . . . that being-itself is the creative ground of all determinations of being" (157).

The rest of the work proceeds in the same relentless fashion, evidencing in spite of itself that the price of overlooking the Kantian critical maneuver and the linguistic turn is excessively high. For there seems no way out. If one cedes to the "temptation to think that calling the reality of God indeterminate is a way of saying something positive or direct about the reality" (166), then he is woven tightly into a seamless robe. Once he realizes, however, that this statement—"God is indeterminate"—*asserts* nothing, he will understandably begin to question a type of inquiry which gives the appearance of achieving its aim but in fact leads nowhere. Metaphysics cannot be served by ignoring its own judgments upon its earlier forms. Yet ironically enough, Neville's greatest service might well be to have demonstrated the futility of classical metaphysics—classically conceived. And most ironically, enterprises classically conceived are always more polished, more secure, and less contemporary than the classical writers themselves.

FACKENHEIM

Emil Fackenheim's presentation of Hegel represents a reformulation in textual and historical understanding every bit as thorough and illuminating as Preller's work with Aquinas.[8] For Fackenheim succeeds in breaking through a stereotype of Hegel already "classical": the mind and soul of an omnivorous rationalism, the thinker of thinkers whose "system" dispenses one from making any journeys at all. By patiently holding him to his words, Fackenheim makes Hegel elucidate the role which religious self-understanding, cult, and practice play in the working out of man's understanding of himself and his world. In this sense, the title chosen for this study, *The Religious Dimension of Hegel's Thought*, is too abstract, too Hegelian, for it fails to convey the direction in which the book moves. The title suggests a discourse on what Hegel thought *about* religion, yet the book concerns itself with thinking or understanding as Hegel articulates it and the role he demands religion play in that process.

Hegel, as we know, was concerned with showing how philosophy is a manner of reflection which allows man to understand himself as understanding his world. The straightforward and accepted reading of the *Phenomenology of Mind* has been a frankly atheistic one: to rise to the level of dialectical self-understanding is to transcend any need for religion. Religious faith is essentially a moment in a dialectic which, if consistently and relentlessly applied, carries man beyond the need for God-as-other to appreciate the manner in which he himself is divine.

Fackenheim does not take direct issue with this interpretation, but rather proceeds to show that "transcending" is not a simply linear process. In doing so, of course, he is eminently faithful to Hegel's insistence that the logic of *Aufhebung* is thoroughly dialectical. Hence Fackenheim will insist that a "moment" cannot simply be compared to a station stop along the route, but remains an essential element in the outcome of dialectical

---

8. Fackenheim, *Religious Dimension in Hegel's Thought*. [Ed. note: In-text citations in this section are to page numbers in Fackenheim's work.]

thinking. Consequently neither the *Phenomenology* nor the *Encyclopedia* can reach their common goal unless the Christian religion intervenes as infinite life to mediate between finite thought and infinite thought (117). To insist on the *reality* of the process and of the transitions is to accent what Hegel always accented but sometimes seemed to forget in his own expositions of dialectical understanding: its concrete intent and character.

If the self-understanding of Spirit is to be in the last moment itself infinite and divine, then the philosophical inquiry—the many-faceted process of interior growth—which leads to that point demands the actual divine/human encounter of religion precisely in order to transfigure what would otherwise remain mere thought (162). Unless something like encounter takes place, the God who is immanent presence would logically amount to nothing more than a construction of the human spirit. Yet Hegel is not Feuerbach. Religious life is indispensable for Hegel, but only if it is something alive and genuine. Yet it must be so, for nothing else could provide the encounter with an event which itself cannot be invented (172). The dialectic cannot assure but must presuppose the genuineness of religious encounter.

In fine, Fackenheim argues from Hegel's own writings that speculative thought can be nothing less than a divine activity in man, but that man would find himself unable to give himself over to that activity had he not undergone the experience of radical receptivity which is religious faith—and notably that bodied forth in Jesus. Without this free reception of the divine as an element integral to it, philosophic thought in its highest instance could not claim what Hegel claims for it, and would lie open to criticism as a vain project (191). Dialectical understanding would remain hopelessly abstract if it pretended to overreach the facticity of man without constantly living with that paradox. What is offered in religious life and cult is a way of living out the paradox through re-enacting it (202, 206).

In this subtle argument, Fackenheim suggests a way of understanding what Johann has called "the religious dilemma." There is no claim that the self-understanding of the man of faith is an adequate one. Clearly it need not be. Yet his very encounter with concrete symbols of cult, which always fall short and often betray the divine they are signs of, nonetheless provides an opportunity for this man to encounter in a dramatic fashion the concreteness of his own existence in the face of the infinite. Without such an encounter, dialectical understanding would cease to be dialectical. By insisting on the essential role of a religious encounter in understanding—lest it lose its dialectical character—Fackenheim has given us a Hegel far closer to his brilliant and critical pupil, Kierkegaard, than most other Hegels. Which is to say that the Hegel we come to appreciate through Fackenheim's exposition is not himself a Hegelian. This is perhaps the strongest reason for inclining one toward Fackenheim's reading of the texts, for it seems that no great thinker could ever have tolerated or been tolerated as a member of his "school."

CONCLUSION

There is something gratuitous about a religious form of life. And that would be true whatever the prevailing cultural or philosophical assessment of it as a form of life. Gratuity is at the heart of religion in the measure that it embodies men's response to their God articulated in cult and life. Religion is neither an enterprise nor a duty, though men and nations may press it into either mold. As a response, it retains a measure of freedom, and remains as free as the invitation is gracious.

In that measure, any attempt to insist that men must be religious to experience their full humanity, or conversely to identify the norm of human fulfillment with being religious, subverts what is most precious: grace. This, I take it, is the anthropological dimension of the medieval distinction between *nature* and *graced-* or *super-nature*, however that conceptual device may have subsequently been employed to subvert this very point. What religion offers to man is gratuitous, then, yet turns out to be utterly central to his understanding of himself. Hence a religious person is likely to consider religion indispensable to anyone's becoming what he is to become, because of the role it plays in his own life. Yet were he to do so, he would betray what makes religion so integral to his experience. That is, of course, its very gratuity, which allows him to understand himself as one responding.

What religion offers to understanding, then, is not primarily data, but rather a new light on oneself as *responsive*. Johann adopts this perspective from the outset; Fackenheim shows how integral a role it plays in Hegel's attempt to unfold the quest for understanding. It could be said, then, that religion offers nothing new in the way of data, yet renews all—by granting fresh illumination. It is as Wittgenstein says of "good or bad acts of will"—not of ethics, let it be noted—"their effect must be that it becomes an altogether different world. It must, so to speak, wax and wane as a whole. The world of the happy man is a different one from that of the unhappy man."[9] Hegel, as Fackenheim presents him to us, tries to capture both contraries at once by insisting that gratuity and response lie at the heart of the Spirit's grasp of itself which pinnacles man's quest for understanding.

Here lies the paradox which religion accentuates yet often in fact betrays: that man is infinitely more than man. Philosophy represents in one

9. Wittgenstein, *Tractatus*, 6.43.

fashion or another men's attempts to articulate their paradoxical selves along the way to becoming one. Religion offers a way of living which embodies an understanding of man and his quest as a response. It is that understanding which philosophy of religion tries to serve by laying bare its roots and its reach. Needless to say, it has often been less than successful. Yet these books—notably Preller and Fackenheim—offer fresh ways of reaching for the quality of understanding required here. If philosophy itself is currently in an epistemological crisis of the profoundest sort—if this be the lasting significance of the linguistic turn, as Rorty for one believes it is—then the work patiently being done in philosophy of religion to break through the prejudices paralyzing inquiry on both sides may well cast some light on issues central to doing philosophy today. For these issues will have to be posed afresh. I would hope that this essay has shown in some instances how that is now taking place.

Bibliography

Abelard, Peter. *Dialectica*. Edited by Lambertus Marie de Rijk. Assen: Van Gorcum, 1956.
Ackrill, J. L., trans. *Aristotle's Categories and De Interpretatione*. Oxford: Clarendon, 1963.
Albertus Magnus. *Commentarium in Priorum Analyticorum*. In *Opera omnia*, edited by A. Borgnet. Paris: Vivès, 1890.
———. *De predicabilibus*. In *Opera omnia*, edited by A. Borgnet. Paris: Vivès, 1890.
Albritton, Rogers. "Present Truth and Future Contingency." *Philosophical Review* 66 (1957) 29–46.
Al-Ghazali. *Faith in Divine Unity and Trust in Divine Providence (Kitāb al-Tawhīd wa'l-Tawakkul)*. Translation of Book XXXV of *The Revival of the Religious Sciences (Ihyā' 'ulūm al-dīn)*. Translated by David B. Burrell. Louisville: Fons Vitae, 2001.
———. *The Ninety-Nine Beautiful Names of God (al-Maqsad al-asnā fī sharh asmā' Allāh al-husnā)*. Translated with notes by David B. Burrell and Nazih Daher. Cambridge: Islamic Texts Society, 1992.
Anderson, Alan Ross. "Completeness Theorems for the System E of Entailment and EQ of Entailment with Quantification." *Zeitschrift für Mathematische Logik* 6 (1959) 201–16. Originally published as Technical Report No. 6, Office of Naval Research Contract no. SAR/Nonr-609 (16). New Haven, CT, 1959.
Anderson, Alan Ross, and Nuel Belnap Jr. "The Pure Calculus of Entailment." *The Journal of Symbolic Logic* 27 (1962) 19–52.
———. "Tautological Entailments." *Philosophical Studies* 13 (1962) 9–24.
Aquinas, Thomas. *Expositio super librum Boethii de Trinitate*. Edited by Bruno Decker. Leiden: E. J. Brill, 1958.
———. *In Aristotelis Libros de Caelo et Mundo, de Generatione et Corruptione, Meteorologicorum Expositio*. Edited by Raimondo Spiazzi. Taurini: Marietti, 1952.
———. *In Aristotelis Libros de Sensu et Sensato, de Memoria et Reminiscentia Commentarium*. Edited by Raimondo Spiazzi. Taurini: Marietti, 1949.
———. *In Aristotelis Libros Peri Hermeneias Expositio et Posteriorum Analyticorum*. Edited by Raimondo Spiazzi. Taurini: Marietti, 1955.
———. *In Aristotelis Librum de Anima Commentarium*. Edited by Angelo M. Pirotta. Taurini: Marietti, 1948.
———. *In decem Libros Ethicorum Aristotelis ad Nicomachum Expositio*. Edited by Raimondo Spiazzi. Taurini: Marietti, 1949.

———. *In duodecim Libros Metaphysicorum Aristotelis Expositio*. Edited by M. R. Cathala and Raimondo Spiazzi. Taurini: Marietti, 1950.

———. *In Librum Beati Dionysii de Divinis Nominibus Expositio*. Edited by Ceslai Pera. Taurini: Marietti, 1950.

———. *In Librum de Causis Expositio*. Edited by Ceslai Pera. Taurini: Marietti, 1955.

———. *In octo Libros Physicorum Aristotelis Expositio*. Edited by Mariani Maggiòlo. Taurini: Marietti, 1954.

———. *On Being and Essence*. Translated by Armand Maurer. 2nd ed. Toronto: Pontifical Institute of Mediaeval Studies, 1949.

———. *Quaestiones Disputatae*. Edited by Raimondo Spiazzi. 2 vols. Taurini: Marietti, 1949.

———. *Quaestiones Quodlibetales*. Edited by Raimondo Spiazzi. Taurini: Marietti, 1956.

———. *Scriptum super Libros Sententiarum magistri Peter Lombardi Episcopi Parisiensis*. Edited by Pierre Mandonnet and Marie Fabien Moos. 4 vols. Paris: Lethielleux, 1929–47.

———. *Summa Contra Gentiles*. Edited by Ceslai Pera. 3 vols. Taurini: Marietti, 1961.

———. *Summa Theologiae*. Blackfriars edition. 61 vols. London: Eyre and Spottiswoode, 1963–81.

———. *Summa Theologiae*. In *Opera omnia*, Leonine edition. Rome: Typographia Vaticana, 1882–.

———. *Tractatus de Substantiis Separatis*. West Hartford, CT: Saint Joseph College Press, 1962.

Aristotle. *Metaphysics*. Translated by Richard Hope. Ann Arbor: University of Michigan Press, 1960.

———. *The Works of Aristotle*. Edited by W. D. Ross and J. A. Smith. Translated by E. M. Edgehill et al. 12 vols. Oxford: Clarendon, 1908–52.

Audet, J. P. "La 'benediction' juive et 'l'eucharistie' chretienne." *Revue Biblique* 65 (1958) 371–99.

Augustine. *Confessions*. Translated by R. S. Pine-Coffin. Baltimore: Penguin, 1961.

Ayer, A. J. *Language, Truth, and Logic*. New York: Dover, 1946.

Bakan, David. "Some Thoughts on Reading Augustine's *Confessions*." *Journal for the Scientific Study of Religion* 5 (1965) 149–52.

Balthasar, Hans Urs von. *Science, Religion, and Christianity*. Translated by Hilda Graef. London: Burns and Oates, 1958.

Barfield, Owen. *Saving the Appearances: A Study in Idolatry*. London: Faber and Faber, 1957.

Bellarmine, Robert. *De gratia et libero arbitrio*. In vol. 4 of *Opera omnia*, edited by J. Giuliano. Napoli: Apud J. Giuliano, 1858.

Bennett, Jonathan. "Meaning and Implication." *Mind* 63 (1954) 451–63.

Black, Max. "Presupposition and Implication." In *Models and Metaphors*, 48–63. Ithaca: Cornell University Press, 1962.

Blanche, F. A. "L'analogie." *Revue de philosophie* 30 (1923) 248–70.

Bochenski, I. M. "De consequentiis scholasticorum earumque origine." *Angelicum* (Rome) 15 (1938) 92–109.

———. *History of Formal Logic*. Edited and translated by Ivo Thomas. Notre Dame: University of Notre Dame Press, 1961.

———. *La Logique de Théophraste*. Fribourg en Suisse: Librarie de l'Université, 1947.

———. "On Analogy." *Thomist* 11 (1948) 424–47.
———. "On the Categorical Syllogism." *Dominican Studies* (Oxford) 1 (1948) 35–57.
Bouillard, Henri. *Conversion et grâce chez saint Thomas d' Aquin: étude historique*. Paris: Aubier, 1944.
Broad, C. D. *Examination of McTaggart's Philosophy*. Vol. 2. Cambridge: Cambridge University Press, 1933.
Broglie, Guy de. *De Gratia: notes prises au cours par les élèves*. Paris: Institut Catholique, 1947.
———. "Sur la place du surnaturel dans la philosophie de S. Thomas." *Recherches des Sciences Religieuses* 15 (1925) 5–53.
Brown, Peter. *Augustine of Hippo*. Berkeley: University of California Press, 1969.
Burrell, David B. *Analogy and Philosophical Language*. New Haven: Yale University Press, 1973.
———. "Aquinas and Islamic and Jewish Thinkers." In *Cambridge Companion to Aquinas*, edited by Norman Kretzmann and Eleonore Stump, 60–84. Cambridge: Cambridge University Press, 1993.
———. *Aquinas: God and Action*. Notre Dame: University of Notre Dame Press, 1979.
———. "Aquinas on Naming God." *Theological Studies* 24 (1963) 183–212.
———. "Autonomous Reason versus Tradition-Directed Inquiry: Mulla Sadra, Lonergan, MacIntyre, and Taylor." *Lonergan Workshop* 21 (2008) 33–42.
———. *Faith and Freedom: An Interfaith Perspective*. Oxford: Blackwell, 2004.
———. *Freedom and Creation in Three Traditions*. Notre Dame: University of Notre Dame Press, 1993.
———. *Friendship and Ways to Truth*. Notre Dame: University of Notre Dame Press, 2000.
———. *Knowing the Unknowable God: Ibn Sina, Maimonides, Aquinas*. Notre Dame: University of Notre Dame Press, 1986.
———. "Mulla Sadra on 'Substantial Motion': A Clarification and a Comparison with Thomas Aquinas." *Journal of Shi'a Islamic Studies* 2 (2009) 369–86.
———. "A Note on Analogy." *The New Scholasticism* 36 (1962) 225–32.
———. "A Postmodern Aquinas: The *oeuvre* of Olivier-Thomas Vénard, O.P." *American Catholic Philosophical Quarterly* 83 (2009) 231–38.
———. *Questing for Understanding: Persons, Places, Passions*. Eugene, OR: Cascade, 2012.
———. *Towards a Jewish-Christian-Muslim Theology*. Malden, MA: Wiley-Blackwell, 2011.
Carnap, Rudolf. *Meaning and Necessity: A Study in Semantics and Modal Logic*. 2nd ed. Chicago: University of Chicago Press, 1956.
Cassirer, Ernst. *Substance and Function and Einstein's Theory of Relativity*. Translated by William Curtis Swabey and Marie Collins Swabey. New York: Dover, 1953.
Cavell, Stanley. *The Claim of Reason: Wittgenstein, Skepticism, Morality, and Tragedy*. Oxford: Oxford University Press, 1979.
———. *Must We Mean What We Say?* Cambridge: Cambridge University Press, 1969.
———. "What's the Use of Calling Emerson a Pragmatist?" In *Emerson's Transcendental Etudes*, edited by David Justin Hodge, 215–23. Stanford: Stanford University Press, 2003.
Clark, Walter Houston. "Depth and Rationality in Augustine's *Confessions*." *Journal for the Scientific Study of Religion* 5 (1965) 144–48.

Copi, Irving. "Objects, Properties, and Relations in the 'Tractatus.'" In *Essays on Wittgenstein's Tractatus*, edited by Irving M. Copi and Robert W. Beard, 167–86. New York: Macmillan, 1966.

Courcelle, Pierre. *Les Confessions de saint Augustin dans la tradition littéraire: Antécédants et posterité*. Paris: Etudes Augustiniennes, 1963.

———. *Recherches sur les Confessions de saint Augustin*. Paris: E. de Boccard, 1950.

Crary, Alice, and Rupert Read, eds. *The New Wittgenstein*. London: Routledge, 2000.

Crowe, Frederick. "St. Thomas and the Isomorphism of Human Knowing and Its Proper Object." *Sciences ecclésiastiques* 13 (1961) 167–90.

D'Ales, Adhémar. "Science divine et décrets divins." *Recherches des Sciences Réligieuses* 7 (1917) 1–35.

Daly, C. B. "The Knowableness of God." *Philosophical Studies* (Maynooth) 9 (1959) 90–137.

Denzinger, Heinrich. *Enchiridion symbolorum, definitionum et declarationum de rebus fidei et morum*. Boniface II 530–32, Confirmation of the Council of Orange II, 25 Jan 531. Friburgi Brisgoviae: B. Herder, 1911.

Dewey, John. *Reconstruction in Philosophy*. New York: Holt, 1920. Reprinted in enlarged edition with new introduction by Dewey. Boston: Beacon, 1948.

Diamond, Cora. *The Realistic Spirit: Wittgenstein, Philosophy, and the Mind*. Cambridge: MIT Press, 1991.

Dittes, James. "Continuities between the Life and Thought of Augustine." *Journal for the Scientific Study of Religion* 5 (1965) 130–40.

Doig, James C. *Aquinas on Metaphysics: A Historico-Doctrinal Study of the Commentary on the Metaphysics*. The Hague: Martinus Nijhoff, 1972.

Ducasse, Curt John. "Truth, Verifiability, and Propositions about the Future." *Philosophy of Science* 8 (1941) 329–37.

Dunne, John S. *City of the Gods: A Study in Myth and Morality*. New York: Macmillan, 1965.

———. *A Search for God in Time and Memory*. New York: Macmillan, 1969.

Emerson, Ralph Waldo. "Self-Reliance." In *Selected Essays*, edited by Larzer Ziff, 175–203. New York: Penguin, 1982.

Erikson, Erik. *Young Man Luther: A Study in Psychoanalysis and History*. New York: Norton, 1956.

Fabro, Cornelio. *Participation et causalité selon S. Thomas d' Aquin*. Louvain: Publications Universitaires de Louvain, 1961.

Fackenheim, Emil. *The Religious Dimension in Hegel's Thought*. Bloomington: Indiana University Press, 1967.

Finance, Joseph de. *Être et Agir dans la philosophie de Saint Thomas*. 2nd ed. Rome: Gregorian University, 1960.

Fitzgerald, John J. "Peirce's Theory of Signs as the Foundation of His Pragmatism." PhD diss., Tulane University, 1962.

Flew, Antony. "Divine Omnipotence and Human Freedom." In *New Essays in Philosophical Theology*, edited by Antony Flew and Alasdair C. MacIntyre, 144–69. London: SCM, 1955.

———. "Theology and Falsification." In *New Essays in Philosophical Theology*, edited by Antony Flew and Alasdair C. MacIntyre, 96–109. London: SCM, 1955.

Gallie, W. B. "The Metaphysics of C. S. Peirce." *Proceedings of the Aristotelian Society* 47 (1946/47) 27–62.

———. *Peirce and Pragmatism*. Harmondsworth: Penguin, 1952.
Garrigou-Lagrange, Reginald. *De Gratia*. Turin: R. Berruti, 1947.
Geach, Peter. "Assertion." *Philosophical Review* 74 (1965) 449–65.
———. "Entailment." *Proceedings of Aristotelian Society*, Supplementary vol. 32 (1958) 157–72.
———. *Mental Acts*. London: Routledge and Kegan Paul, 1957.
———. *Reference and Generality: An Examination of Some Medieval and Modern Theories*. Ithaca: Cornell University Press, 1962.
Geiger, L.-B. "Abstraction et séparation d'après saint Thomas in *de Trinitate*, q. 5, a. 3." *Revue des Sciences Philosophiques et Théologiques* 31 (1947) 3–40.
———. "Synthèse de St. Thomas." In *La participation dans la philosophie de St. Thomas*, 313–63. Paris: J. Vrin, 1942.
Gilby, Thomas. *Between Community and Society: A Philosophy and Theology of the State*. London: Longmans, Green, 1953.
Gilson, Étienne. *Being and Some Philosophers*. Toronto: Pontifical Institute of Mediaeval Studies, 1949.
———. *God and Philosophy*. New Haven: Yale University Press, 1941.
Ginnane, W. G. "Thoughts." *Mind* 69 (1960) 372–90.
Grant, C. K. "Pragmatic Implication." *Philosophy* 33 (1958) 303–24.
Hare, Richard M. "Decisions of Principle." In *The Language of Morals*, 56–78. Oxford: Clarendon, 1952.
Harris, Zellig S. "Distributional Structure." In *The Structure of Language: Readings in the Philosophy of Language*, edited by Jerry Fodor and Jerrold Katz, 33–49. Englewood Cliffs, NJ: Prentice-Hall, 1964.
Hartshorne, Charles. *Man's Vision of God and the Logic of Theism*. New York: Harper, 1941.
Havens, Joseph. "Notes on Augustine's *Confessions*." *Journal for the Scientific Study of Religion* 5 (1965) 141–43.
Hawkins, Canon D. J. B. "Two Conceptions of Freedom in Theology." *Downside Review* 79 (1961) 289–96.
Hens, Nikolaus. *Die Augustinusinterpretation des hl. Robert Bellarmin bezüglich der wirksamen Gnade*. Krefeld: van Acken, 1949.
Holmer, Paul L. "Kierkegaard and Philosophy." In *New Themes in Christian Philosophy*, edited by Ralph M. McInerny, 13–36. Notre Dame: University of Notre Dame Press, 1968.
Ishiguro, Hidé. "Use and Reference of Names." In *Studies in the Philosophy of Wittgenstein*, edited by Peter Guy Winch, 20–50. London: Routledge and Kegan Paul, 1969.
Jaeger, Werner. *Aristotle: Fundamentals of the History of His Development*. Translated by Richard Robinson. 2nd ed. Oxford: Clarendon, 1948.
Johann, Robert O. *Building the Human*. New York: Herder and Herder, 1968.
Jung, Carl Gustav. *Aion: Researches into the Phenomenology of the Self*. Translated by R. F. C. Hull. Collected Works of C. G. Jung 9, pt. 2. Bollingen Series 20. New York: Pantheon, 1959.
Keynes, J. N. *Studies and Exercises in Formal Logic*. 4th ed. London: Macmillan, 1906.
Kligerman, Charles. "A Psychoanalytic Study of the *Confessions* of Saint Augustine." *Journal of the American Psychoanalytic Association* 5 (1957) 469–84.
Kneale, William. *Probability and Induction*. Oxford: Clarendon, 1949.

Koninck, Charles de. "Introduction à l'étude de l'âme." *Laval Théologique et Philosophique* 3 (1947) 9–65.
Körner, Stephan. *The Philosophy of Mathematics: An Introductory Essay*. London: Hutchinson University Library, 1960.
Lash, Nicholas. *Theology for Pilgrims*. Notre Dame: University of Notre Dame Press, 2008.
Lennerz, Heinrich. *De Gratia Redemptoris*. 3rd ed. Rome: Gregorian University, 1949.
Leroy, M. V. "Abstractio et separatio d'aprés un texte controversée de saint Thomas." *Revue Thomiste* 48 (1948) 328–39.
Lewis, Clarence Irving, and Cooper Harold Langford. *Symbolic Logic*. 2nd ed. New York: Dover, 1959.
Lieb, Irwin. Review of *Word and Object*, by Willard Van Orman Quine. *International Philosophical Quarterly* 2 (1962) 92–109.
Lonergan, Bernard J. "Cognitional Structure." In "Spirit as Inquiry," special issue, *Continuum* 2 (1964) 530–42.
———. "The Concept of *Verbum* in the Writings of St. Thomas Aquinas." *Theological Studies* 7 (1946) 349–92; 8 (1947) 35–79, 404–44; 10 (1949) 3–40, 359–93.
———. *Insight: A Study in Human Understanding*. New York: Philosophical Library, 1957.
———. "Saint Thomas' Thought on *Gratia Operans*." *Theological Studies* 2 (1941) 290–324; 3 (1942) 69–88, 375–402, 533–78.
———. "Self-Affirmation of the Knower." In *Insight: A Study in Human Understanding*, 319–47. New York: Philosophical Library, 1957.
———. *Verbum: Word and Idea in Aquinas*. Edited by David B. Burrell. Notre Dame: University of Notre Dame Press, 1967.
Lubac, Henri de. *Surnaturel: Études historiques*. Paris: Aubier, 1946.
Łukasiewicz, Jan. *Aristotle's Syllogistic from the Standpoint of Modern Formal Logic*. 2nd ed. Oxford: Oxford University Press, 1957.
Malcolm, Norman. "Nature of Entailment." *Mind* 49 (1940) 333–47.
Marcel, Gabriel. "Presence as a Mystery." In vol. 1 of *The Mystery of Being*, 244–70. Chicago: Regnery, 1960.
McCool, Gerald A. "The Philosophy of the Human Person in Karl Rahner's Theology." *Theological Studies* 22 (1961) 537–62.
McDermott, Timothy. "Appendix 12: Simplicity and Unity (Ia. 3 & 11)." In *Summa Theologiae*, vol. 2, *Existence and Nature of God (Ia. 2–11)*, translated and edited by Timothy McDermott, 213–17. London: Eyre and Spottiswoode, 1964.
McInerny, Ralph M. *The Logic of Analogy: An Interpretation of St. Thomas*. The Hague: Martinus Nijhoff, 1961.
———. *Studies in Analogy*. The Hague: Martinus Nijhoff, 1968.
McTaggart, John M. E. *The Nature of Existence*. Edited by C. D. Broad. Vol. 2. Cambridge: Cambridge University Press, 1927.
Merlan, Philip. "Abstraction and Metaphysics in St. Thomas' Summa." *Journal of the History of Ideas* 14 (1953) 284–91.
Misch, Georg. *A History of Autobiography in Antiquity*. 2 vols. London: Routledge and Kegan Paul, 1950.
Moody, Ernest A. *Truth and Consequence in Mediaeval Logic*. Amsterdam: North-Holland Publishing, 1953.

Moore, G. E. "External and Internal Relations." In *Philosophical Studies*, 276–309. London: Routledge and Kegan Paul, 1922. Originally published in *Proceedings of the Aristotelian Society* 20 (1919/20) 40–62.
Mullahy, Bernard I. "Thomism and Mathematical Physics." PhD diss., Laval University, 1946.
Murphey, Murray G. *The Development of Peirce's Philosophy*. Cambridge: Harvard University Press, 1961.
Neville, Robert C. *God the Creator: On the Transcendence and Presence of God*. Chicago: University of Chicago Press, 1968.
Newman, John Henry. *An Essay in Aid of a Grammar of Assent*. London: Longmans, Green, 1906.
Nielsen, H. A. "Sampling and the Problem of Induction." *Mind* 68 (1959) 474–81.
Novak, Michael. "A Key to Aristotle's 'Substance.'" In *Substances and Things: Aristotle's Doctrine of Physical Substance in Recent Essays*, edited by M. L. O'Hara, 190–208. Washington, DC: University Press of America, 1982. Originally published in *Philosophy and Phenomenological Research* 24 (1963) 1–19.
Nowell-Smith, P. H. "Contextual Implication and Ethical Theory." *Proceedings of the Aristotelian Society*, Supplementary vol. 36 (1962) 1–18.
O'Connell, Robert J. *St. Augustine's Confessions: The Odyssey of Soul*. Cambridge: Belknap Press of Harvard University Press, 1969.
Ott, Heinrich. *Denken und Sein*. Zürich: Evangelisher Verlag, 1959.
Outler, Albert, ed. *Augustine: Confessions and Enchiridion*. Library of Christian Classics 7. London: SCM, 1955.
Owen, G. E. L. "Logic and Metaphysics in Some Earlier Works of Aristotle." In *Aristotle and Plato in Mid-Fourth Century*, edited by Ingemar Düring and G. E. L. Owen, 163–90. Göteborg: Elanders Boktryckeri Aktiebolag, 1960.
Pascal, Roy. *Design and Truth in Autobiography*. Cambridge: Harvard University Press, 1960.
Peirce, Charles Sanders. *The Collected Papers of Charles Sanders Peirce*. Edited by Charles Hartshorne and Paul Weiss, vols. 1–6; edited by A. W. Burks, vols. 7–8. Cambridge: Harvard University Press, 1931–35, 1958.
———. "Letters to Lady Welby." In *Charles S. Peirce: Selected Writings (Values in a Universe of Chance)*, edited by Philip P. Wiener, 380–432. New York: Dover, 1958.
Pieper, Josef. *The Silence of Saint Thomas: Three Essays*. Translated by John Murray and Daniel O'Connor. New York: Pantheon, 1957.
Plato. *Great Dialogues of Plato*. Translated by W. H. D. Rouse. Edited by Eric H. Warmington and Philip G. Rouse. New York: New American Library of World Literature, 1956.
———. *Platonis opera*. Edited by John Burnet. 5 vols. Oxford Classical Texts. Oxford: Clarendon, 1900–1907.
Preller, Victor. *Divine Science and the Science of God: A Reformulation of Thomas Aquinas*. Princeton: Princeton University Press, 1967.
Prior, A. N. "Facts, Propositions and Entailment." *Mind* 57 (1948) 62–68.
———. *Formal Logic*. Oxford: Clarendon, 1955.
Pruyser, Paul. "Psychological Examination: Augustine." *Journal for the Scientific Study of Religion* 5 (1966) 284–89.
Regis, L. M. "La philosophie de la nature, quelques 'apories.'" *Etudes et Recherches Philosophie* (Ottawa: Collège dominicain) 1 (1936) 127–56.

Robert, J. D. "La métaphysique, science distincte de toute autre discipline philosophique selon saint Thomas d'Aquin." *Divus Thomas* (Piacenza) 50 (1947) 206–22.

Robinson, J. M., and J. B. Cobb Jr., eds. *The Later Heidegger and Theology*. New York: Harper and Row, 1963.

Ross, James F. "Analogy as a Rule of Meaning for Religious Language." *International Philosophical Quarterly* 1 (1961) 468–502.

———. "A New Theory of Analogy." *Proceedings of the American Catholic Philosophical Association* 44 (1970) 70–85.

Ryle, Gilbert. *Dilemmas*. Cambridge: Cambridge University Press, 1954.

Salamucha, Jan. "The Proof 'Ex Motu' for the Existence of God: Logical Analysis of St. Thomas' Arguments." Translated by Boleslaw Sobocinski. *The New Scholasticism* 32 (1958) 327–72.

Sayre, Kenneth M. *Plato's Analytic Method*. Chicago: University of Chicago Press, 1969.

Searle, John. *Speech Acts: An Essay in the Philosophy of Language*. Cambridge: Cambridge University Press, 1970.

Sellars, Wilfrid. "Counterfactuals, Dispositions, and the Causal Modalities." In *Concepts, Theories and the Mind-Body Problem*, edited by Herbert Feigl et al., 225–309. Minnesota Studies in the Philosophy of Science 2. Minneapolis: University of Minnesota Press, 1958.

———. "Empiricism and the Philosophy of Mind." In *The Foundations of Science and the Concepts of Psychology and Psychoanalysis*, edited by Herbert Feigl and Michael Scriven, 253–329. Minnesota Studies in the Philosophy of Science 1. Minneapolis: University of Minnesota Press, 1956.

———. "Grammar and Existence: A Preface to Ontology." *Mind* 69 (1960) 499–533.

———. "Time and World Order." In *Scientific Explanation, Space, and Time*, edited by Herbert Feigl and Grover Maxwell, 527–616. Minnesota Studies in the Philosophy of Science 3. Minneapolis: University of Minnesota Press, 1962.

Sertillanges, Antonin-Gilbert. *Saint Thomas d'Aquin*. 4th ed. Vol. 1. Paris: Alcan, 1925.

Simmons, Edward D. "The Thomistic Doctrine of Three Degrees of Formal Abstraction." *The Thomist* 22 (1959) 37–67.

Simon, Yves R. "On Order in Analogical Sets." *The New Scholasticism* 34 (1960) 1–42.

Smart, J. J. C. "Theory Construction." In *Logic and Language* (second series), edited by Antony Flew, 222–42. Oxford: Blackwell, 1953.

Smiley, T. J. "Entailment and Deducibility." *Proceedings of Aristotelian Society* 59 (1958/59) 233–54.

Strawson, P. F. *Individuals: An Essay in Descriptive Metaphysics*. London: Methuen, 1959.

———. *Introduction to Logical Theory*. London: Methuen, 1952.

———. "Necessary Propositions and Entailment-Statements." *Mind* 57 (1948) 184–200.

———. "On Referring." In *Essays on Conceptual Analysis*, edited by Antony Flew, 21–52. London: Macmillan, 1952. Originally published in *Mind* 59 (1950) 320–44.

———. "A Reply to Mr. Sellars." *Philosophical Review* 63 (1954) 216–31.

Taylor, Richard. "Dare to Be Wise." *Review of Metaphysics* 21 (1968) 615–29.

———. "The Problem of Future Contingencies." *Philosophical Review* 66 (1957) 1–28.

Von Wright, G. H. "Concept of Entailment." In *Logical Studies*, 166–91. London: Routledge and Kegan Paul, 1957.

———. *Logical Studies*. London: Routledge and Kegan Paul, 1957.

———. "A New System of Modal Logic." *Proceedings of Eleventh International Congress of Philosophy* 5 (Brussels, 1953) 59–63.
Weil, Simone. "The *Iliad*, Poem of Might." In *Intimations of Christianity among the Ancient Greeks*, edited and translated by Elisabeth Chase Geissbuhler, 24–55. London: Routledge and Kegan Paul, 1957.
Weiss, Paul. "Entailment and the Future of Logic." *Proceedings of Seventh International Congress of Philosophy* (Oxford, 1930) 143–50.
———. *Nature and Man*. New York: H. Holt, 1947.
Weyl, Hermann. *Das Kontinuum*. Leipzig: Veit, 1918.
Whitehead, Alfred North. *Science and the Modern World: Lowell Lectures, 1925*. New York: New American Library, 1956.
Wicker, Brian. *Theology and Culture*. London: Sheed and Ward, 1966.
———. *Toward a Contemporary Christianity*. Notre Dame: University of Notre Dame Press, 1967.
Will, Frederick L. "Justification and Induction." *Philosophical Review* 68 (1959) 359–72.
Williams, Donald. "The Sea Fight Tomorrow." In *Structure, Method and Meaning*, edited by Paul Henle et al., 282–306. New York: Liberal Arts Press, 1951.
Wisdom, John. *Paradox and Discovery*. Oxford: Blackwell, 1965.
Wittgenstein, Ludwig. *Philosophical Investigations*. Translated by G. E. M. Anscombe. New York: Macmillan, 1953.
———. *Tractatus Logico-Philosophicus*. Translated by D. F. Pears and B. F. McGuinness. Introduction by Bertrand Russell. London: Routledge and Kegan Paul, 1961.
Woollcott, Philip, Jr. "Some Considerations of Creativity and Religious Experience in St. Augustine of Hippo." *Journal for the Scientific Study of Religion* 5 (1966) 273–83.
Zemach, Eddy. "Wittgenstein's Philosophy of the Mystical." In *Essays on Wittgenstein's Tractatus*, edited by Irving M. Copi and Robert W. Beard, 359–76. New York: Macmillan, 1966. Originally published in *Review of Metaphysics* 18 (1964) 38–57.

Index

abduction, 96, 99
analogical,
  act, 66
  attribute, 155
  causality, 156
  concept, 159, 160
  discourse, 157
  extensions, 119, 165
  God and creation, 156
  and hypothetical, 56, 211
  metalinguistic, 160
  model, xl
  predication, 157, 159, 160, 216
  terms, 155, 158, 160, 162, 163, 165
  transcendental structure, xxxviii
  usage, xxi, xxxvii, 155, 156, 172, 173
analogous,
  being, 160, 161, 219
  concept, xxxix, 131, 159, 160
  content, xxxix
  criteria, xliv, 144, 150
  elements, 161
  form, xxxix
  meaning, 156, 168
  notion, 42, 44, 72n40
  order of knowing, xx
  predication, 47, 159, 160
  proportionality, xxxi, 159
  resources, 177, 178
  terms, xxxvi, xxxviii, xxxix, 16, 155, 162, 163, 170–73
  transcendental affirmation, 161
  transcendentals, 2
  universality, 58
  usage, xxxix, 155, 170–73, 177
analogy,
  of apprehension and judgment, 158, 163
  for Aquinas, 154–69, 170
  of articulation and assertion, 25
  of artisan, 65–68
  assertion, 97, 160–61, 162–68
  of attribution, xxi, 155
  of being, xvii, 160, 161, 216
  of "being," 161
  for Cajetan, 155, 157, 159, 165
  and causality, 70n33
  cognitive continuity, 170
  common notion, 156, 165, 166
  of community and individual, 102
  and creation, 65–68, 72n40
  diverse contexts, 177
  and divine names, 157–62
  and divine perfections, 161, 162, 165–66
  equivocation, 64n13
  esse, role of, 176–78
  existence, 173–74, 175n9, 176
  extended use, 167–68
  focal meaning, 156
  for Frege, 138
  as functioning framework, 144, 147, 148, 150
  implication scheme, 170
  and judgment, xx, 97, 108, 153, 161, 162
  knowledge of the divine, 167
  language, role in, 147, 174–77
  logic of, 154–69

analogy, *(continued)*
   as logical doctrine, 131n6, 155, 160
   for Lonergan, 111
   for McInerny, 154–62
   of meaning, 156, 158, 160–64, 168
   metalinguistic, 160
   as metaphor, 155, 172
   as metaphysical doctrine, 155, 160
   as model, 39
   modus significandi, 164–65
   of names and terms, 157, 170
   negative judgment, 160, 168
   part/whole, 87
   performance, xxxi
   of potency and act, 64
   primary usage, 155–56, 158, 159, 160, 165
   of proportionality, 155–59, 159n14, 163n28, 168
   relation between Creator and created, xxxi, 158, 159, 165–67, 173–74
   in religious discourse, 154–69, 159, 170
   res significata, 163–65, 166–67
   resemblance, 175–76
   of responsibility, 102
   for Ross, 157, 162–69, 170–72
   for Scotus, 162, 168
   semantic doctrine, 155n1, 157, 160
   structure of language, 174–76
   talk of God, xxxi
   theory of, xxxi, 157, 160, 165n35, 170–78, 216
   of thought and assertion, 102
   transcendent knowing, 166–68
   transcendental discourse, 160, 161–62
   of understanding and judgment, 111
analytic, xv, xix, xxi, xli, 20, 79, 103, 128, 161n24, 174, 183, 192, 195, 196, 200
assertion,
   as action, 98–100, 110
   and analogy, 162–68
   Aquinas's usage, 208, 209, 211
   and articulation, xxxix, xl, xli, xliii, xlvi, 4, 21–22, 25
   and assertible, 98, 99, 101, 102
   assertory element, 98–101, 104, 110, 112–13
   awareness and self-involvement, 25
   about being, 218
   and belief, 101, 109–10
   within community 102
   as compulsion, 110
   as conceptual sign, 98
   criteria for, xliv
   decision, 150
   and deduction, 47
   and definition, xix
   displays something, 211, 214
   distinguished from comprehension, 160
   and existence, 126
   existential, 210
   and feeling, 110, 112
   about future contingencies, 29, 32
   about God, 161, 173, 208, 209
   intelligibility, 137
   interiority, 25
   judgment, xix, xl, 97, 99, 100, 109, 161, 168
   judgment:understanding:: articulation:assertion, 111
   and making statements, xxxvii, 5, 6, 9, 14, 22–25, 215
   matter:form::subject:predicate, 50
   and meaning, 98, 98n3, 102
   metaphysical, 214, 220
   names and verbs, 6
   negative theology, 208, 214
   philosophical, 209
   and predication, 49, 51
   and premise, 47, 49
   and propositions, 45, 98, 101, 103, 110, 111
   purpose, 103, 104
   as a relation, 50, 51, 86
   response to individual, 24, 25
   responsibility, 101–2
   secondness, 99
   self-assertion, 102
   subject-predicate form, 47, 98, 110

Index   237

and substance, xviii, xxxvi, 2, 19
thought:assertion::
   community:person, 102
transcendental, 161, 168
and truth, 29, 32, 98
volitional character, 99, 101
what is the case, xxvi, 9

being, xxxix, 38, 40, 68, 128, 129n54, 130, 162, 189, 206, 217
analogous, xx, xxi, 160, 161, 219
analogy of, 161
answer to questions of inquiry, xxxvii, 132
for Aristotle, xvi, xvii, 217–18
basic constituents of, 132
as being, 129n54
being-itself, 216–19
categorial, xviii
categories of intelligibility, 111
common causes of, 129n54
common property, 216
corporeal motion, 65–67
created, 65, 66
derived, 190
exists in another, 174
exists in itself, 174
God's manner of, 173
heuristic character of, 137, 139
identify with complete intelligibility, 137–40
identify with the real, 137, 138, 140
indeterminate, 218, 219
and judgment, xx, 140
manners of, 174, 175
metaphysical object, 134
modes of, 73
notion of, 137, 139, 160
objective of unrestricted desire to understand, 137–39
order of, xvii, xx
per essentiam, 160, 161
per participationem, 160, 161
primary, 14, 15
proportionate, 62, 140
secondary agents, 74
spiritual, 125n41
structures of understanding, 132

subject-object, 131
that-being, xxxix, xliv
transcendent, 140
transcendental terms, xviii, xxxvi, xxxviii, xlv
univocity of, 218
what-being, xxxix, xliv

categorial, xviii, 21n7, 100, 112, 113
categorical,
appraisal, modes of, xxxviii
categoricals, 30
contexts, xxxvi
differences, 174
division, 2, 178
explanation, 99
syllogism, 54, 55
transcategorical, xxxviii
cause, 61n2, 62, 67, 69, 69n30, 70, 72, 72n40, 73, 88, 91, 146, 166
causes, 31, 74n44, 129n54
first, 173, 175
classification, 87, 116–17, 121, 122, 171
context, 2, 6, 7, 8, 11, 16, 22, 27, 51, 68n29
of analogous terms, 156, 156n4
of Aquinas, 63
Aristotelian, 8
of assertion, 208
as background, 8n10
context-invariant descriptions, 16
discursive, xxxvi, xli
of expressions, 12, 177
factor of judgment, 108
history of human subjectivity, 184
of inquiry, xli, 17
linguistic, 7, 9, 26
of *manuductio*, 125n41
of metaphors, 172
of metaphysical statements, 213
method of verification, xxxvii
mythic, 205
of naming God, 168
of a question, 174, 209
reflective, xxxiv, xxxv, xxxvii, xxxviii, xliv
said of God, 174

context, *(continued)*
  of self-asserting, 22
  sensitive, xxxvi, xxxix
  of a statement, 3, 12
  theological, 209
  and transcategorical structures, xxxviii
criteria, xliii, xliv, xlvi, 94, 104, 137, 143–44, 147, 149, 183, 192, 212, 218

deduction, xvii, 45–50, 57, 96, 99
definition,
  as assertion, xix, 22
  first feature of substance, 18
  and formal features, 20n15
  in inquiry, 16, 17, 18
  intelligible-unity, 17, 18
  and judgments, 181n2
  and modality, 34
  proper principles, 99
  role of, 15–18
  as statement-making sentence, 10, 11, 13, 15, 24
demonstration, 47, 52, 54, 82n1, 118n12, 120, 131, 140, 141
dialectic, 82, 84, 89, 100, 101, 107, 130, 132, 184, 206, 207, 208, 220, 221
  transcendental, 130n55
dialectical, xxiv, 17, 72n40, 82, 93, 180, 181, 206, 214, 220, 221
dialectician, 4, 77, 130
discourse,
  analogical, 157, 158, 170, 171
  for Aquinas, 125n42
  for Aristotle, xvii, 11
  "categorical" differences in, 174
  category specific, xxxviii
  common opinion, 80
  descriptive, 177
  elements of, 4–12
  facts and, 151, 151n4
  fact-stating, xl
  formal features of, 177
  framework of, 81
  about the future, 40
  about God, 165n35, 168, 176, 191

  inquiry as, xxxvi, 153
  intersubjective, 101
  limiting statements and, 145
  in metaphysics, 124, 125, 175
  names as basic unit of, 3, 6
  about "now," 39
  ordinary, 168
  in philosophy, 76, 114
  propositions as, 22n19
  religious, 157, 159, 168, 191, 192
  responsible, 78
  sentence as basic unit of, 3, 9, 11
  statement-making function of, 11
  structures of language-world, 174
  subject-predicate form, 4
  temporal, 28, 37, 40
  tensed, 28, 32, 42
  theological, 158
  within time and space, 164
  transcendental, 160
  universe of, 24, 27
  verbs as basic unit of, 6
  world-referring, xxxvii

element, 1–2, 122, 148, 166
  of action/reaction, 100
  affective, 161n24
  analogous, 161
  assertory, 98–102, 104, 110, 112, 113
  context of, 2
  contingent events, 71
  in *de Interpretatione*, 4–5
  of discourse, 4–12
  distinct from principle, 3
  esthetic, 110
  formal, 121, 123
  functional in Peirce, 96
  indexical, 99
  intellectual, 161n24
  in language, 2, 3, 132
  material, 163
  order of, 5–9
  personal, 102
  as a premise, 47
  in a sentence, 5, 9
  of speech, 5, 6, 12
  of the state, 93

and syllogism, 44n3
of transcendental assertion, 161, 168
of unit, 2
volitional, 101
what we talk about, 14
elucidation, 5, 84
entailment, 43–59
  analogous notion, 44
  for Aristotle, 46, 48, 49
  Barbara, 52, 53, 56, 57
  connection of meanings, 45, 52
  demonstrability, 46n9, 47
  distinguished from implication, 44, 45
  extensional, 45
  intensional, 45–46
  for Moore, 43, 44, 48
  predication, 49
  structure of consequences, 43–44, 189
  tautological, 45, 59
epistemological, xvii, xx, xxi, xxviii, 97, 111, 113, 148, 150, 185, 187, 188, 192, 202, 223
equivocal, xxxvi, 64, 125n40, 156n4, 169, 171
esse, 62n7, 67, 67n27, 159n15
  role of, xix, 176–78
essence, xvii, xviii, xix, xxxv, xxxvii, xxxix, 18, 74, 111, 159n15

formal features, 20n15, 84, 151n4, 175
formal properties, 163, 163n28, 164

God,
  absolutely unconditioned, 73
  achieves His ends, 60–74
  act of existence, 65, 68
  analogy of attribution, 155–56, 161, 163
  analogy of proportionality, 155–56, 158–61
  assertions made of, 162, 208
  conceive of, 189, 192, 200
  and contingent events, 37–39, 41, 70, 72
  creates, 66–74, 187, 196
  creative love, xlv
  deeds of, 183
  discourse about, 191
  divine action, 61, 187
  divine attributes, 127, 157, 163, 165, 209
  divine intention, 73
  "doctrine" of, 214
  emanation, 212
  esse ipsum, xx
  existence of, xxi, 136, 139, 140, 174, 208–10
  features of, 214
  formal properties, 162–65, 178
  genus, (not) within a, 129, 162, 163, 174, 214
  grace of, 61, 190, 193, 199, 200
  God-as-other, 220
  God-statements, 214
  God-talk, xxxi, 211
  guided by, xx
  and human freedom, 26, 42, 61, 66, 69
  and human history, 187
  image of, 74, 198
  immanent presence, 221
  instrument of, 68, 71
  intentions of, 196
  knowing, mode of, 38–41, 40n28, 70n35, 74, 125
  knowledge of, xxxi, 208
  language for, xxv, 173, 178, 179n11, 189, 192, 208–10
  modus significandi, 164
  moves the will, 61–64, 68, 70n33, 73
  mystery of, 61
  naming, 157, 159n16, 168, 208, 216
  nature of, 176
  negative theology, 175n9
  omniscience, 26, 37, 39, 40, 42, 62, 68, 69
  people of, xxxii, 183
  possession, mode of, 166
  praise of, 183
  predication, 208–9
  primary agent, 73
  proofs for, 208–10

God, *(continued)*
  reality of, 136, 139–41, 174, 208–10
  relation of God and creation, 68–70, 72n40, 73, 158, 159, 163–68, 173–78, 184, 187, 196, 197, 209, 211, 212
  res significata, 163–65
  simple, xviii
  speak of, xvi, 155–57, 166, 169n47, 183, 210, 211
  statements about, 166, 173, 176, 178, 208–11, 214, 220
  and time, 38–41
  transcendence, 63, 64
  understanding of, xxxi, 184
  unknown, 163
  willing, mode of, 40n27, 72, 73
grammar,
  logical, 4, 12, 171
  and ontology, 7
  predication, 171

hermeneutic, xliv, 12, 179, 180n1, 182, 183, 200, 204, 208
  circle, 17, 148
heuristic, 100, 104, 130, 137, 139
hypothetical, 17, 30, 182
  applied terms, 211
  framework, 81, 82
  inquiry, 16, 22, 25, 88, 100
  propositions, 30n9
  scheme, 184, 185
  scientific knowing, 122, 129
  stage, 24
  state, 21
  syllogism, 54
  use of statement-making sentences, 24

individual, xxxvii, xxxix, xl, xli, xliii, 12, 13, 13n12, 19–25, 27, 49, 71, 73, 167
  living, growing thing, 13, 19, 23, 25
  paradigm for substance, xl, 19, 25, 159n15
individuality, xxxiv, xxxix, xl, 19, 23, 24, 25, 159n15
  of substance, 4, 19, 20

and unity, xl, xliii, xliv, 20
induction, 96, 99, 167
inquirer, xxx, xxxv, xl, xli, 61, 84, 101, 105, 109, 110, 113, 118n8, 136, 171, 177, 212
inquiry,
  appeal to authority in, 81
  for Aquinas, 114–35, 154–69, 178, 208–15
  arguments, role of, 90
  for Aristotle, 1–25, 47–58
  Aristotle's *aporia*, 24
  articulating and asserting in, 22, 23–25
  for Augustine, 179–202
  categorial, 100
  and certitude, 79
  cognitive, 104
  communal, xxxv
  community and tradition, role of, xii, 104
  consummated in action, 100, 104
  context of, xli
  definitions, role of, 16, 17, 18
  dialectic, 82, 85
  dialogical, xl
  dialogue form, 84
  direction of, 5, 99, 100, 104, 106
  as a discipline, 77
  and the divided line, 84
  and explanations, 86
  features of, xxxvi, 77, 83
  feel for the subject, 93, 109, 112
  first steps of, 79, 80
  formal objects of, xlii
  further questions, 82, 104
  general outline of, 106
  goal of, 5, 99, 100, 106, 109, 113
  and the good, 93
  as a habit, 109
  for Hegel, 100
  heuristic scheme, 104
  hypothesis, role of, 18, 22, 82
  hypothetical, 16, 25, 100
  and the inquirer, xl, xli, 83, 109
  intuition, 143
  judgment, xxxix, 97, 103–6, 111, 113

Index   241

language and, 152, 192, 223
logic, role of, 91
for Lonergan, 112, 136–40
mathematical, 105
metaphysical, 177, 178, 213, 220
negative judgment (*separatio*), 115, 116, 123, 124, 124n38, 126, 127, 129n54, 131, 134, 135
object of, xxxiv, 14, 17, 23, 24, 25
pattern for, 153
for Peirce, 96–113
phenomenological categories, 99
philosophical, xliv, 77, 94, 221
in Plato's *Dialogues*, 75–95
in *Posterior Analytics*, 17, 22, 128n50
pragmatism and, 106
premises, role of, 22
process of, 18, 80, 85, 87, 106
as quest for understanding, 83
question, role of, 17, 22
into questioning itself, 78
reason as tool of, 46
reflective, xvi, xxxiv–xxxvii, xxxix, xlii, xlvi, 75, 76, 84, 89, 152, 192
resolution of, 18, 24, 25, 94, 97, 138
"sense-data," role of, 79
schema for, 77–78, 85, 88, 89
scientific, 16, 25, 82n1, 99, 116, 129, 148
self-understanding, 84, 185, 221
speech and, xli
stages of, 85, 89, 91–93
statement-making sentence, role of, 5, 10, 22, 24
styles of, 106
substance and, xxxvi, 20, 22
theory of, 4, 16
transcendental, xv, xvi
truth as regulative ideal, 104, 106
as a way of living, 92, 152–53
way of proceeding, 75
intelligibility, xxi, 15, 17, 69, 69n30, 72n40, 111, 129, 130n54, 134, 136–41, 159n15, 166, 210, 212
interiority,
for Aquinas, 178
and growth, 83, 221

language of, 25
of logic, 150
intersubjective,
dimension of thought, 102
discourse, 101

judgment,
abduction, 99
and action, xliii, 185
analogy and, xx, 161, 173
apprehension and, xx, 158, 158n9, 162, 163, 165, 168
approximating, 106, 111
for Aquinas, xvii, 111, 123, 124, 126n43, 128, 129n54, 159n15
assertion, 100, 110
assertory element, xix, 101, 104
and being, xx, 137–40
and belief, 109
certitude and, 142–53
conceptual signs, 98
criterion-based, xliv
decision, 97, 153
deduction, 45
dialectical reasoning, xxiv
discriminating, 137
ethics, 108
explanatory accounts and, xxxiv
finality of the intellect, 161
function of, 125, 182
generality, 106, 112, 130
grammatical investigations, xliv
habit of thought, 103
heuristic method, 130
humility, 94
in inquiry, 22, 97, 103, 104, 106
intelligibility, 139
intelligibility of being, 137–40
intersubjective discourse, 101
"intuition," 106
language and, xxix, 181, 181n2
for Lonergan, 111–13
in mathematics, 105
metaphysics and, xvii, 124, 133–34, 161, 213, 220
mystical, xlv

judgment, *(continued)*
  negative, 115, 116, 123, 124, 124n38, 126, 127, 129n54, 131, 134, 135, 158, 160, 168, 175
  pragmatism, 97, 113
  and propositions, 99
  reasoning, 103
  recurrent patterns, 125
  reflective, xx, 94, 97, 108, 113, 138, 184
  responsibility, xliv, 102, 138
  role of self-consciousness, 134n73
  role of inquirer, xxxv, xliii, xliv, 109
  self-awareness, 94
  self-correcting, 97, 113, 138
  sentential, xvii
  sign and meaning, 96
  Socrates, 91, 93, 94
  subjective, xix, xxi, 149
  sufficient evidence for, 112n21
  theoretical, xviii
  theory of judgment, 96–113
  thirdness, 112, 113
  thought, 97
  transcendental predication, 167
  transcendentals and, xxxvii, xxxviii, xxxix
  to truth, xxiv, 104
  and understanding, xxxi, 97, 111, 112, 138, 139, 159, 159n15, 161n23, 185, 206
  unrestricted desire to know, 138, 140
  virtually unconditioned, 112, 137, 169
  volitional character, 99

language,
  act of assent, xix
  analogous use, 160, 161, 165n35, 172, 173, 177, 178, 216
  to articulate insight, 188–89, 191
  "categorical" differences imbedded in, 174
  of choice, 150
  confident use of, 191
  context of, 9
  of decision, 150
  descriptive, 146, 172, 192
  of dialectician, 77
  epistemology, xviii
  factual, 6
  of faith, 211
  forms of, 91, 132
  function of, xxxvii
  functioning, 146–49, 171
  for God, xxv, 173–76, 189, 209, 210
  grammar, 176, 177
  idle use of, 140, 184
  of interiority, 25
  judgment, xxix, 181, 181n2
  language-game, xliii
  language-making, 178
  language-world, 174
  limits of, 215
  logic of, 87, 152
  material features of, xli
  meta-language, 211
  new, 145, 189
  ontological, 28
  ordinary use of, 164, 167, 171
  of origin, 189
  of principle, 91
  propositional, 27
  reaching for God, 173
  reference through use, 138
  reflects ontological structure, 176
  reflexive, 191
  relates to the world, 1, 142, 143, 145, 177
  religious, 154–69, 201
  resources of, 176, 177
  responsibility, 149
  rules, 163
  rules of inference, 191
  significant tool, 11
  speaking, 4, 188
  structure of, xviii, 79, 86, 91, 125, 166, 175
  structure of consequences, 189
  syntactical structure, 210
  task of, 142
  temporal, 28, 41, 42
  and understanding, 189, 191
  of unities, 21

user of, 4, 12, 24, 78, 108, 172, 177, 178, 219
as a way of life, 147, 152, 188, 191–92, 219
linguistic,
  analysis, xii
  awareness, 208
  axioms, 163
  clues, 22
  context, 7
  convention, 155
  fact, 13, 127
  form, 9, 22
  framework, 144, 147, 151, 152
  inquiry, xxxvi
  metalinguistic, 131, 160, 160n21, 165, 168
  metaphysics, 127
  mode, 211
  phenomenology, 207
  reference, 126n43
  reformulation, 208, 215
  role of subject, 13n12
  structures, 132, 173
  terms, xxiii
  "transcendental Thomism," xvi, xviii
  turn, 211, 216, 219, 223
  unit, 11
  usage, xv, 27, 219
logic,
  abduction, 96, 99
  of analogy, 131n61, 154–69
  Aquinas's approach, 208–15
  Aquinas's use of Aristotle, 38–41, 120
  Aristotelian, 8, 22, 26–42, 43–59
  of assertory element, 113
  Barbara, 48, 52, 55, 58
  for Bochenski, 54–56
  conditional statements, 43
  consequence, 43, 55, 59
  contradictories, 27
  contraries, 27
  deduction, xvii, 45–48, 50, 57, 96, 99
  deducibility, 43
  definition, 17
  of dialectic, 221
  for dialectician, 77
  entailment, 43–59
  and ethics, xxviii, 102, 103
  extensional, 51, 58–59
  of first operations, 160
  formal, 78, 105, 218
  formal features of, 84
  of future contingencies, 26–42
  of God's knowledge, 38, 40–41
  induction, 96, 99, 213
  of inquiry, 152
  intensional, 33, 44, 58–59
  of interiority, 25, 150
  of judgment, 96, 97, 99, 124
  for Keynes, 58
  of language, 87, 152, 215
  logica utens, 102, 103
  logica docens, 102, 103
  for Lukasiewicz, 43–44, 54–56, 58
  of mathematics, 105, 118–20
  medieval usage of, 48, 55, 218
  meta-logic, 55
  metaphysical, 129n54, 131, 133n67, 155
  modality, 33, 34, 36
  negation of, 72
  of negative judgment, 129n54
  positivistic, 124
  predication, 48, 126, 171, 217
  of proposition, 54, 56, 58, 102, 103
  propositional calculus, 105
  propositional language, 27, 45
  pseudo-traditional, 117
  question of truth, 26, 27
  of relations, 120
  role in inquiry, 91
  as science of argumentation, xxxi
  semantics, 131, 155n1, 157, 208
  and social principle, 103
  for Socrates, 77, 87
  of speaking of God, 201, 208, 209, 211, 214
  of substance, 20
  syllogism, 48, 52–58
  of terms, 27, 47, 57
  of "this-here-now," 20
  of time as B-series, 38

logic, *(continued)*
  trivalent, 26
  truth-assessment, 150
  universal laws of, 24, 54
  for Wittgenstein, 181n2
logical,
  assertion, 98, 99
  content, 43
  discourse, 81
  distinct from ontological, 12
  explanation, 72, 73, 81
  following, 57, 58, 170
  framework, 81, 82, 145, 150
  grammar, xxi, 3, 4, 12, 131, 171, 177
  interpretant, 107, 109
  observations, 153
  reasoning, 46, 102, 108
  reduction, 54
  rules of inference, 16, 51, 54, 55n27
  space, 152
  statements, 102, 217
  structure of language, 79
  structure of a work, 182
logician, 26, 27, 53, 77, 99, 108

mathematics, 52n3, 62, 84, 100, 105, 105n9, 107n10, 115, 118–20
  Aquinas's notion of, 121
  Aristotelian ideal of knowing, 118
  certitude, 118n8
  constructivity, 119
  formal abstraction, 116, 117
  hypothetical character of, 122
  and imagination, 119–21, 119n18
  intellectual freedom, 119
  model of scientific method, 118, 119
  organizing power of, 121, 122
  philosophy of, 123n30
  principles of, 121
  and physics, 115, 116n3
meaning,
  analogous, xxxvi, 159, 159n14, 161, 162, 168, 170, 211
  apprehension and judgment, 158, 167, 168
  and assertion, 98, 101, 102, 110
  common core of, 164, 165
  common notion, 130, 164, 165, 166, 168
  connection of meanings, 45, 52
  definitions, 34
  determining, 98
  first-level, 130
  and formal properties, 163, 164
  inner core of, 128
  and material element, 163
  ordinary, 155, 156, 163, 168
  pragmatic maxim, 98
  primary, 130, 131, 160n21, 155, 156, 168
  proportioned, 131, 155, 160n21
  reduce to denoting, 106
  and reference, 1, 9, 10, 12
  semantic theorem of analogy, 160
  sentence as minimal context for, 11, 12, 156
  shifting, 78
  sign and, 96, 113
  single, 127
  usage related to one, 130, 156, 159
  viable theory of, 158
metalinguistic, 131, 160
metaphysical,
  anti-metaphysical, xlv, 124
  considerations, 115
  discourse, 177
  dogmatism, xxi
  fact, 184
  ideas, 184n7
  inquiry, 116, 150, 177, 214
  issues, 177n14
  mind, xxviii
  notion, 126, 128, 131
  perspective, 62
  question, 219
  reasons, 46
  reversal, 69
  scheme, 184
  situation, 118, 120, 123
  speculation, xx, xxi
  statement, 212, 215
  theories, 177n14
  tradition, xlv
  truths, xli, 117n7

Index 245

world view, 187
metaphysician, 4, 26, 130, 213
metaphysics, xviii, xxix, xlii, 4, 7n8,
    26, 67, 69n30, 72, 114–35,
    129n54, 185, 210, 213, 214, 220
  and analogy, 155, 160, 161
  for Avicenna, xxv
  bare particulars, 3
  critical activity of, 212–15
  constitutive principles of, 212
  descriptive, 132
  formal features, 175
  and inquirer, 212
  and judgment, xvii, 133–34, 213
  and mathematics, 118
  and myth, 208, 209, 211, 213
  negative judgment, role of, 114–35
  object of, 116, 118, 123–25,
      125n42, 127
  possibles, 38
  primary and secondary agents, 64
  (not) a science, 212
  and subject, 131

negative judgment, 115, 116, 123, 124,
    124n38, 126, 127, 129n54, 131,
    134, 135, 158, 160, 168, 175

objective, xvi, xix, 25, 131, 149, 151
  content, 159, 163n28, 165
  modality, 28
  norms, 149
  of unrestricted desire to understand, 138, 139
objectivity, 127, 131, 133, 149
one, 129n54
  analogous term, 2
  individual, 23, 25
  intelligible unity, 19
  principles, 19
  substance as, 10, 13, 14, 19
  and "this-something," 20, 24
  unit, 1–2
  usage, 1–2
ontological,
  affirmations, xlv
  categories, 6
  composite structure, 176

  distinguish logical from, 12
  hierarchy, 111
  language, xviii, 28
  ontologically first, 7
  order, 166n39
  questions, xxxiv, 39, 42, 116, 217
  univocal being-itself, 216
ontology, xx, 3, 6, 117, 132, 218
  grammar and, xxi, 7

phenomenology, xxi, 62n9, 66n25, 96,
    99, 128, 207
predication,
  accidental, 217
  analogical, 157, 159, 160, 168, 216
  in Aquinas, 132
  Aristotle's syllogism, 47, 48
  Barbara, 48–49
  declarative sentence, 49
  and entailment, 47, 49–50
  formal implications of, 217
  fundamental logical relation, 48,
      86, 171
  and judgment, xliii
  logic of, 126, 217
  order of enveloping generality, 48
  principles of, 129n54
  qualitative, 217
  responsibility, 101
  and substance, 13
  substantial, 217
  transcendental, 158n9, 167
  universal affirmation, 49, 57
principles,
  "common causes of being," 129n54
  constitutive of inquirer, 212
  of deduction, 16
  or definition, 99
  of demonstration, 82n1
  ethical, 125n41
  of explanation, 72
  first, 134, 219
  formal, 120n19
  of judgment, 93
  mathematical, 121, 122
  matter-form, 3, 19, 24

principles, *(continued)*
   of metaphysics, 117n7, 124, 129n54, 212
   name-verb, 3
   potency-act, 19, 64–67, 111, 111n18
   regulative principles of reason, 46
   role of, 19

reason, 69, 79, 115, 119n18, 127, 189, 209
   beyond, 116, 117
   desire of, 122
   faith and, xxv, 211
   non-secular, xx
   principle of sufficient, 67, 166
   pure, xvii
   reasons, 81, 86, 89, 104, 107, 127
   role of, 85, 88, 89, 91, 108, 205, 211
   scientific, 52, 205
   self-critical, xxxiv 108, 109, 205
   tool of inquiry, 46
reasoning, xxiv, xxv, xxxi, 33, 46, 47, 52, 102, 103, 104, 107, 125
reflective, 24, 66, 75, 92, 93, 152, 177
   analogous terms, xxxix, 172
   awareness, xxxviii, 148–49, 151, 204
   context, xxxiv, xxxvii, xliv
   critical consciousness, 77, 107, 138
   critical reading, 192
   dialogical form, xxxv
   discipline, 76
   inquiry, xxxiv–xlii, xlvii, 82, 85, 89, 187, 195
   insight, 184
   judgment, 108, 112, 147
   linguistic turn, 219
   negative judgment, 175, 209
   non-reflective, xxxiv–xxxviii
   performative, xliii
   pre-reflective, xxxiv
   question, 84, 85, 92, 145, 181, 219
   response, 83–84
   self-correcting, 107, 113
   subjectivity and objectivity, 149–51
   understanding, xxxv, xxxvii, 75, 85, 179, 181, 206, 207

sense and reference, xviii, xix, 1, 132
sentence,
   assertion, 9, 22–23
   basic unit of discourse, 3, 4, 9, 11
   in *Categories*, 12–14
   as context, 8, 9, 11
   in *de Interpretatione*, 5, 9–10, 22, 49
   declarative, 49
   definition as, 15–18, 24
   distinction of articulation and assertion, 21–24
   distinguish from name, 10
   entertain possibilities, 22, 24
   form of, 5, 9, 18, 174
   inquiry, role in, 24
   in *Metaphysics*, 14–15
   parts of, 3, 7, 9–12
   part/whole scheme, 9–11
   performatory, 1–25
   predication, 49
   as premise, 49
   primary element of signification, 9
   referring, 9, 12
   role of, 5, 6, 11
   signifies substance, 12–14, 18
   to speak about individuals, 49
   speech-act, 4, 7, 11
   statement-making, 3, 5–12, 15, 22, 23
   structure of the subject, 174
   subject-predicate form, 4
   "this-something," 18–21, 23
   unity, 21–22, 23
   we talk in sentences, 14
   what is the case, 8
   what is it, 18, 24, 25
speech,
   and assertible, 101
   and assertion, 101
   for Aristotle, 5, 12, 49
   elements of, 5, 6, 12
   fact-stating, xxxvi
   inquiry and, xli
   and judgment, xlv
   and metaphor, 147
   ordinary, 49, 50, 102
   parts of, 11

performatory, 1–25
  and the sentence, 11
  significant sound, 5
  signifying, 167
  speech-act, xliii, 4, 7n8
  statement-making, xlv, 5, 11
  transcendental structure of, xxxviii
  what it does, 5
  for Wittgenstein, xliv, xliv
subjective, xvi, xxi, 25, 131, 150, 151
  judgment, xix, 149
subjectivity, 74, 149, 150, 151, 184
substance, 1–25
  for Aquinas, 37, 64, 214
  for Aristotle, 3–4, 12
  asserting, 22–25
  in *Categories*, 12–14, 19
  created agent and, 74
  definition, role of, 15–18
  facts, 18
  as first principle, 129
  formal feature of, 20, 21
  individuality of, 4, 19, 20
  inquiry, role in, 18, 22
  intelligible unity, 15, 18, 20, 23, 24
  logic of, 133
  "meaning" of, 101
  in *Meno*, 104
  metaphysics, 4
  in *Metaphysics*, 12, 14–15
  modification of verb, 6, 7, 18
  name, 7, 12
  noun-subject, 6, 7
  as an object, 20
  one, 19, 20
  ontologically first, 7
  paradigm for, 19, 131, 159
  for Peirce, 109
  performatory, 1–25
  principles, role of, 19
  pseudo-Scholastic notion of, 167
  role of, 3–4, 7
  separated substances, 125, 129
  statement-making sentence, 2–4, 15, 18, 22–24
  subject-predicate form of a sentence, 4
  "this-here-now" feature, 19, 20
  "this-something," 18–19, 20
  unity and individuality, 20, 21
  what is it, 7, 18, 22

tautological
  entailments, 45, 59
  sense, 27
tautology, 35, 36, 82n1
theological, xvi, xxi, 26, 41, 42
  affirmation, 133
  context, 209
  discourse, 158
  perspective, xxiii
  reflection, xxvii
  statements, 39, 187, 209, 214
  training, 200
  understanding, 66, 179–202, 214
  use, 36, 116n3, 209
transcendence, 62, 63, 133, 214
  divine, 63, 64, 66, 66n25, 70n33, 71, 72n30, 214
transcendent, 41, 62, 68, 70, 72, 135, 206, 207
  agent, 74
  first cause, 173
  knowing, 136, 140
transcendental,
  affirmation, 161, 169
  assertion, 161, 168
  deduction, xvii
  dialectic, 130n55, 220
  discourse, 160
  inquiry, modes of, xv, xvi, xvii
  order, 72n40, 74n44
  philosophy, xxi
  predication, 167
  role, 146
  situation, 73n41
  structure, xxxviii
  terms, xxxvi, xxxvii, xxxix, xlv, 55n28, 211
  Thomism, xvi, xviii
truth, 45, 59, 77, 93, 98, 104, 151, 152, 189
  approximation to, 104, 109, 111
  concept of, 112
  correspondence theory of, 27
  criteria for, 143, 147

truth, *(continued)*
  and desire for understanding, xxiv
  empirical, 27
  or falsity, 22, 26, 27, 150
  function, xix, 44, 45, 46, 51
  and functioning frameworks, 145, 147
  and the good, 133
  and historicity, 142–53
  inquiry, role in, 107, 109
  intuition of, 106
  and judgment, xxiv, 106, 142–53
  metaphysical, xli, 117n6
  notion of, 97
  proclaiming the, xxiv, xxv
  reflective understanding, xxxviii
  regulative ideal, 104
  and responsible action, 100, 101
  search for, 144, 190, 192
  semantic definition of, 27, 28, 31, 33, 36
  shared concern, 143
  of a statement, 166
  theories of, 142, 153
  transcendental term, xviii, xxxviii, xlv
  truth-question, 147, 148, 151, 152
  truth-seeking, xxxiv, xxxix

understanding, xxxii, xxxiv, xxxv, 23, 41n29, 62, 64, 118, 134, 186, 188, 206–7
  act of, 112, 132, 137, 139, 140, 160
  for Aquinas, xvii, 117n7, 159, 214, 215
  for Aristotle, xxxvi, 14, 16
  for Augustine, 179–202
  critical, 181, 182, 186, 214
  desire for, xxxvi, 138–41
  dialectical, 214, 220, 221
  and discipline, 190
  discursive, xxxviii
  distinct from knowledge, 203
  drive of, 132
  experience of, 139
  faith and, 203, 207
  of God, 64–66, 74, 167, 178, 184
  and hermeneutics, 179, 204
  historical, 181, 182, 220
  and insight, 190
  and intelligibility, 136, 138
  on journey of inquiry, 78, 79, 186
  and judgment, 21, 22, 45, 97, 111, 112, 130, 138, 139, 153, 159, 159n15, 161n23, 185
  and language, 1, 87, 164, 191
  and mathematics, 120
  metaphysical, 134, 214
  model for, 190, 192
  negative judgment, 129n54, 134
  new, 189, 190
  non-reflective, xxxvii, xxxviii
  obstacles to, 202
  philosophical, xvi, 204, 214
  for Plato, 81, 83, 84, 87
  as a quest, 152, 201, 222, 223
  reflective, xxxiv, xxxv, xxxvii, 75, 85, 181, 204, 206
  religious discourse, 192
  religious life and, 203–24
  self-understanding, xxxv, xxxix, 84, 180, 185, 219–22
  structures of, xvii, 132
  of substance, 16, 22
  theological, xxxvii, 64–66, 179–202
  transcendent, xvi, 72n40, 75
  unrestricted act of, 139, 140
  and way of life, xxxv, 191, 201, 203, 204, 205
  where one stands, 152, 153, 184, 185, 204, 207
  the world, 1, 220
unity, 197, 219
  accidental, 23
  being, 134
  diversity in, xxxviii, xxxix
  of existing thing, 68
  formal, xxxvi
  formal feature, 20, 21
  and individuality, xxxvii, xxxix, xl, xliii, 20, 24
  or intelligibility, 15
  intelligible, xl, 14, 18, 19, 20, 23, 24
  of object, xxxvi
  society, 93
  and the soul, 90

statement, xxxvi, 18, 23, 24
of substance, xxxvi, xxxix
and "this-something," 21, 23, 25

transcendental category, xxxviii, xlv
univocal, 73, 130, 162, 169, 171, 216, 218

www.ingramcontent.com/pod-product-compliance
Lightning Source LLC
Chambersburg PA
CBHW021654230426
43668CB00008B/618